SURVIVING AGAINST ODDS

SURVIVING AGAINST ODDS

The Marginalized in a Globalizing World

Edited by
DEBAL K. SINGHAROY

MANOHAR
2010

First published 2010

ISBN 978-81-7304-877-7 (Hb)
ISBN 978-81-7304-878-4 (Pb)

Published by

Ajay Kumar Jain *for*
Manohar Publishers & Distributors
4753/23 Ansari Road, Daryaganj
New Delhi 110 002

Typeset at

Digigrafics
New Delhi 110 049

Printed at

Salasar Imaging Systems
Delhi 110 035

To
My friend James Goodman
for all his inspiration
and support

Contents

Preface

Researching on the area of marginalization encounters a host of challenges. The foremost challenges arise out of the intricacies of this subject, its overt and covert manifestations, interlinkages with the dynamics of inequality and social stratification, social exclusion and economic exploitation, new identity politics, social protest and social movements. This area of study thus not only needs an empirical depth and perceptive understanding of the issues of poverty, livelihood insecurity, illiteracy, social denial and deprivations but also on their intertwining with the wider social, political and economic processes. Moreover this area of study also needs a sound balance between social empathy and sensitivity of the researcher on the sufferings of the marginalized people on the one hand, and his/her simultaneous objective reflexivity in dealing with these issues academically on the other. In the wake of globalization these challenges have been multiplied and have become complicated. However, notwithstanding these challenges, a section of socially sensitive and intellectually articulate researchers and academics have undertaken serious studies on the theme of the marginalized all over the world. This collection endeavours to collate some of these efforts. Several institutions and individuals have contributed in this endeavour.

At the very outset I am thankful to the contributors of this volume who have always stimulated me by providing new ideas and thoughts in due course of finalization of this collection. Hence my thanks are due to James M. Jasper, the City University of New York, New York; Vibha Arora, Indian Institute of Technology, New Delhi; Satish Deshpande, University of Delhi, Delhi; Ashish Saxena, University of Jammu, Jammu; Kristin Heffernan, College at Brockport, New York; Atluri Satyanarayana, Allahabad University, Allahabad; Subhash Sharma, Boarder Road Development Board, New Delhi; Jose Kalapura, St. Xavier's College, Patna; P.S. Vivek, University of Mumbai, Mumbai; Kamlesh Mohan, Panjab University, Chandigarh; D.C. Sah, Madhya Pradesh Institute of Social Science Research, Ujjain; Nandini Sahu, Mokbul Ali Laskar, A. Malathy and Ajay Mahurkar, Indira Gandhi National Open University (IGNOU), New Delhi.

Most of the papers in this colleation was presented in the international conference in Social Development, Social Movements and the Marginalized held in New Delhi in Febuary 2008 under the auspieces of Indira Gandhi National Open University (IGNOU), New Delhi with the co-sponsharship of the Research Committee 48: Social Movements and Collective Action, International Sociological Association (ISA), Madrid; Indian Council of Social Sciences Research (ICSSR), New Delhi; United Nations Development Programme (UNDP), Country Office, New Delhi and CASA, New Delhi. I am grateful to IGNOU, ISA, UNDP, ICSSR and CASA for their support. This conference was organized under the chairpersonship of Prof. V.N. Rajasekharan Pillai, Vice-Chancellor, IGNOU. I am highly thankful to Prof. Pillai, for his encouragement and support to organize this conference and thereafter to this new academic initiative.

My sincere thanks are to Prof. Omprakash Mishra, Pro-Vice-Chancellor, IGNOU and Prof. Maitrayee Chaudhuri, Professor of Sociology for their valued contribution in shaping this volume. I am also thankful to Prof. Parvin Sinclair, Pro-Vice-Chancellor and Prof. Uma Kanjilal, Director, School of Social Science for their timely support. I am thankful to Prof. T.K. Oommen, Jawaharlal Nehru University, New Delhi, Prof. Sharit Bhowmik, Tata Institute of Social Sciences for their constant encouragement and support.

I am also grateful to by friends and colleague from IGNOU, especially to Prof. S.C. Garg, Prof. Pandav Nayak, Prof. Kapil Kumar, Prof. A.S. Narang, Prof. D. Gopal, Prof. Pardeep Sahni for their valued suggestions and supports. I am thankful to my departmental colleagues Prof. Tribhuwan Kapur, Dr. B. Kiranmayi, Dr. Nita Mathur, Dr. R. Vashum. Dr. Archana Singh and Dr. Rabindra Kumar for their cooperation.

I am especially thankful to my wife Dr. Prava Debal for her in-depth observations, comments and valued support and for taking keen interest in my academic pursuits. I am deeply indebted to by daughter Purbali and son Anirudha for allowing me their time for this work.

My office staff Sri Shailendra Kumar Singh and Sonia have taken the pain in finalizing the manuscript of this collection with all sincerity and commitment. Indeed it would have been impossible for me to organize this work without their support and help.

I am thankful to Mr. Ramesh Jain of Manohar Publishers & Distributors, New Delhi for accepting the manuscript and bringing out this collection with utmost efficiency and in time. My thanks are also due to Mr. Siddharth Chowdhury for comments and help.

DEBAL K. SINGHAROY

Introduction

DEBAL K. SINGHAROY

The issue of marginalization has emerged to be an area of critical concern in contemporary social research, social policy analysis and in the developmental initiatives. In the wake of economic globalization, increasing local–global inter-connectivity, social decontextualization of pre-existing forms of collective living, changing nature of the state and the civil society interaction, the process of marginalization has also acquired several new dimensions, while many of the continuing processes have got reinforced. It has been widely used by the academics, planners, researchers, political leaders to interchangebly mean either processes of seclusion and relegation of a section of population or identified social groups at the margin of the society or pushing them outside the mainstream of the society. Though the dimensions of social exclusion (Luhmann, 1982), non-participation (Germani, 1980), non-integration, non-involvement in societal affairs (Hammer, 2003), lack of freedom in social, economic and political expressions and capacity deprivation (Sen, 2000) have been delineated as the key elements of marginalization, in essence it has emerged to be a far broader and interrelated concept, than ever before, in the contemporary world. As a social process, besides having interrelations among these dimensions, marginalization has also acquired multiplicity in its contents as it is reflected in many areas of lives—economic, social, cultural, political and special—locally and globally. Though at times marginalization manifests itself in a single dimension of life, while its interrelations with the other dimensions of collective live may remain mostly covert and latent. Marginalization indeed, is a composite and cumulative process and thus has a plural component of 'multiple marginality', which may be shaping its course either vertically or horizontally or in combination of the both. Though marginalization is circumscribed by the time and space consideration, it has a continuity with the past and relation with the surroundings.

Within the interactive social processes it is historically rooted, culturally legitimized and politically conditioned. In the functioning of the society, marginality has remained ideologically linked to the institution of caste, race, class, ethnicity and patriarchy; and substantially coupled with the arrangements of social segregation, labour market discrimination, economic exploitation and political subordination. These are manifested through the casualization of workforce, rampant poverty, illiteracy, livelihood insecurity, unemployment, ill-health, forced migration and displacement, lack of choices, sustained subordination and increasing dependency which are linked to social alienation, dejection, isolation, non-integration, non-participation and capacity deprivation of significant sections of population. Significantly marginalization exists as a function to a social order wherein a limited few are in the healm of social, economic amd political command and domination, and the majority contributes towards the sustenance of such command and domination by remaining at the margin. Thus marginalization is a product of certain political practices, and becomes a function of several political arrangements like colonialization, capitalism, imperialism (Perlman, 1976: 91) and globalization.

Marginalization, however, meets with protests, resistance and revolt. Higher the extent of marginalization, higher becomes the intensity of such protests, resistance and revolt. Marginalization as a social process has now got globally inter-connected not only through their manifestations but also through interrelated protests and articulation of new identities. Thus besides primordial forms of marginal identity as reflected in the practices of caste, gender, ethnicity, racial, minority religious and linguistic arrangements, it also becomes discernible through living in the backward, rural, hilly, desert and slum areas, living as migrants or immigrants, practising socially stigmatized profession, having physical disabilities, becoming asylum seekers or refugees due to hostile political regimes, becoming development or disaster induced displaced, and so on. Even though remain institutionalized within the wider social order, many of these identities get transformed into communities for protest and resistance cutting across localized predefined boundaries due to sustained marginalization.

Marginalization takes place in a given cultural, economic and political context. In the Western context the cultural dimensions of marginalized are predominantly delineated and they have been specifically known as uprooted people to the cities with a large body of stigma and negative attributes attached to them as 'dangerous classes' or 'never do well communities'. Culturally they are also conceived as the marginal man 'whom fate has condemned to live in two societies, and in two, not merely different but antagonistic cultures . . . his mind is the crucible in which two different and refractory cultures may be said to melt and, either wholly or in part, fuse' (Park, 1937). The recent usage of 'visible minority' to denote the non-whites in the culturally and numerically dominant white societies widely depicts the predominance of cultural dimensions marginalization in these societies. There is no denying to the fact that economic and political dimensions have remained intertwined to this cultural dimension of marginality.

In India marginalization has widely been depicted through the practice of the caste system whereby the lower caste people have been relegated to the margin of society, running through the practice of ritual hierarchy, purity and pollution, occupational segregation and endogamous marriage. The *antyaja*, lower caste living outside the fourfold (*chaturvarnashrama*—Brahmin, Kshatriya, Vaishya and Shudra) division of the Hindu social order, has always formed the core of the marginalized groups of people in India being deprived of the access to livelihood security, educational opportunities, formal political power structure and avenues for social recognition.The Brahminical philosophy and the practice of *chaturvarnashrama* has created a vast category of ritually described *avarna*, i.e. the untouchables. They lived outside the village. They were frequently referred to as *antyaja*, *antiya, antyavasin*, *bahriya*. To Ambedkar, they were the 'broken man', aliens and who lived outside the village and emerged out of defeated nomadic tribes. Herein marginalization is also understood as the manifestation of Dalit (ground down) realities of lives which are conditioned by regular social exclusion, economic exploitation and political domination within the caste order (Ambedkar, 1937). They have remained at *antya* (edge of the society), being victims of the inhuman practice of untouchability.

The practice of untouchability was a sort of violence against the lower castes. As these sections of the population were traditionally denied of the opportunity to have access over knowledge and other resources for social mobility, they were engaged in the activities which were considered unclean and impure. They were forbidden to enter temples, not allowed to go to schools and other learning centres, and many other public places, were not supposed to come in front of the members of the higher castes in many parts of the country. Mahatma Gandhi called them 'Harijans' (God's men) and initiated a social movement to redress this social imbalance and stop these inhuman practice by inculcating and practising new social values and morality in Indian society. The marginalized sections have also resisted and revolted against untouchability and social discrimination all through the history. Marginalization is thus linked explicitly not only to the social and cultural values in Indian social order but also with its culture of resistance and revolt.

In the context of advanced capitalist society marginalization has been understood in economic terms by the Marxists. It has been linked to alienation and explained as the historical outcome of proletarianization of labour force. The capitalist mode of production contributes to the exclusion of the labour force from the possession of the productive resources paving the way for their miseries and subhuman existence in the capitalist society. To Marx and Engels

> The present-day capitalist mode of production presupposes the existence of two classes on the one hand, that of the capitalists, who are in possession of the means of production and subsistence; and on the other hand that of the proletarians, who being excluded from this possession have only single commodity to sell, the labour power of theirs in order to obtain possession of the means of subsistence, and who therefore have to sell their labour power of theirs in order to obtain possessions of means of subsistence (Marx and Engels, vol. III, 1970: 86).

This process of exclusion expands alienation of the working class from his or her 'species essence' as a human, from the work and the production process, from the society and from themselves (ibid., vol. I, 1970).

The emergence of new political economy in the wake of globalization and introduction of structural adjustment programme which have introduced new forms of marginalization has also reinforced many of its the pre-existing ones. Many facets of marginalization have emerged to be a function of global economic order. The poverty stricken, illiterate, unskilled and semi-skilled labourer functions as the cheap pool of the labour force of the global market. Many of the old practices (e.g. caste, race and gender hierarchy) of marginalization rather than getting weakened and eradicated are getting reinforced to provide legitimacy to pre-existing social and economic segregation. Even within the developing country itself social segregation, political disempowerment and economic exclusion remains to be a function to the emerging social and the political order of the society. Hence despite all odds the marginalized survive in contemporary world. In recent decades several questions are raised as to what have been the changing form and dimensions of marginalization in a globalized world? What have been the nature of intertwinings of caste inequality with marginalization? What have been the nature and forms of marginalization of the tribes, dalits, religious minorities, peasants, farmers and children in the contemporary society? How do the marginalized people articulate their protest? This collectcion aims to address some of these issues. There are altogether four themes covered in this collection dealing with the concepts and perspectives on marginalization, focusing on the core issues of inequality, injustice, denial, deprivation, exclusion, domination, etc., that form the foundation of marginalization; emerging facets of marginalization of the tribes, dalits, religious minorities, and children; land, labour and marginalization and the issues of marginalization of consumers amd service users in contemporary world.

The first section deals with the conceptual issues and some of their manifestations as seen through race and caste inequalities in contemporary world. Important political and collective emotional issues and identities are inbuilt in it. James M. Jasper in his paper 'Strategic Marginalizations and Emotional Marginalities: The Dilemma of Stigmatized Identities' underlines that marginalization is a central political strategy, and at the centre of marginalization is an effort to create a damaged or stigmatized identity for a group, as a way to disadvantage them strategically. To him, these in many ways are the assaults on basic human dignity of the marginalized which matters more than the material deprivations that usually result from it. He examplifies marginalization as an opportunity to suggest the possibilities of a strategic and emotional vision of protest. Here he explains the dilemma of stigmatized identities whereby the marginalized desires to mobilize to change or eliminate the identity, but they use that same identity to mobilize people. Hence they run the risk of strengthening the label they are essestially opposed to. This is a dilemma both at the level of means, of how to get what you want, and at the level of ends, since moral dignity arises both from abolishing the stigma and from organizing politically. He brings forth these dilemmas and emotions and links them with the strategy of protest of the marginalized focusing on the cases of African–Americans in the United States and Dalits in India.

Debal K. SinghaRoy in his paper 'Marginalization and the Marginalized: Some Reflections on the Relational-Cumulative Dynamics' examines the concept of marginalization and various dimensions of this process. He points out that, in the context of globalization, fast transition of society and emergence of new conditions of sustenance of social injustice and exclusion, the process of marginalization has acquired several new dimensions besides getting the old ones redefined in the emerging contexts. Herein efforts of circumscribing marginalities in terms of singularity of criterion and describing it to specific locale are gradually losing their hold. He suggests a relational-cumulative perspective to describe the process of marginalization in transitional societies by delineating the intertwining among the social, economic and political denials and deprivations, legitimization and reproduction, domination and hierarchy, mobility and protests on the one hand and their cumulative imports on the marginalized on the other. He examines the phenomena of marginalization within the broad processes of transformation of contemporary society in India, focusing on rural West Bengal, with a 'relational-cumulative' perspective.

Marginalization is depicted through poverty and social injustice. In the contemporary world the issues of poverty and social injustice have acquired global connotations. Marek Hrubec in his paper 'The Global Poor and Social Justice' analyses several dimensions of global social injustice in relation to the social rights of the global poor as the marginalized. He explains the process of an extra-territorial recognition of right-holders through the development of a concept of social recognition at the supranational level. He differentiates between a traditional subject of social misrecognition and the global poor and suggests that everyday struggles of the global poor are ought to be recognized. To him the nation states perceive limits of their capacity for extra-territorial social recognition of the persons in other countries *vis-à-vis* the rising power of transnational economic and financial agents. The increase of influence of economic and financial agents in the wake of globalization creates misrecognition of demand of global poor and establishment of new supranational and global arrangements. In the background, there are discontents of those who suffer from hunger and severe poverty in the contemporary order even if their dissent has not received enough public articulation.

One of the most efficient ways to understand the dynamics of marginalization in India is through the study of caste-based social inequalities. Satish Deshpande brings forth emerging patterns of caste-based social inequalities in India in his paper 'Recent Trends in Caste Inequalities: Comparison of NSSO Consumption Expenditure Data of 2000 and 2005'. He delineates the caste-based social inequality based on consumption patterns. Here he makes a comparative caste-disaggregated analysis of monthly per capita consumption expenditure data from the last two quinquennial (big sample) surveys of the NSSO conducted in 1999-2000 and 2004-5 respectively. It effectively shows the preliminary indications of trends in inter-caste inequality, for an overall sense of the ways in which caste continues to be a salient aspect of economic status, and for the emerging patterns of social mobility (or immobility) in contemporary society. By comparing average consumption expenditure levels across castes; different internal segments of the consumption expenditure distribution of each caste; and the relative 'caste gap' separating the so-called 'upper' castes from the other caste and tribe groups he demonstrates that caste continues to be an important dimension of economic inequalities in Indian society. He delineates the trends that urban inequalities are worsening, that rural STs and urban SCs are the worst off groups in contemporary Indian society and that the 'upper' castes remain distinctly privileged relative to other castes despite six decades of a modern constitution that outlaws caste privilege.

The second section of this collection deals with the emerging facets of marginalization surrounding the use, control, ownership and management of land. Land relates itself to the collective identity and culture of the people, who use those land. In the wake of globalization the introduction of big development projects and new market driven culture of consumption have not only brought changes in the use, control, ownership and management of land, these have also contributed to the loss of identity and culture and marginalization of a large section of the population. The paper on Walking the 'Shangri-La' Sikkim Trail by Vibha Arora, explains the complex interplay between new usage of land for the development of hydroelectric projects in Sikkim in north-east India and the perceived threat against the loss of cultural identity of the indigenous tribal people therein. She has developed a critical understanding of this phenomena by underscoring the universal occurrence of description of utopia and dystopia and situate their role in the social construction and representations of the self in relation to others. She also explains that the former Buddhist kingdom of Sikkim have get transformed into a 'Shangri-La' (stimulacra) for global consumption. Based on in-depth empirical data she develops a critique of development and the process of marginalization of indigenous people in the land of Sikkim.

Throughout the world, the cultural practices, livelihoods and knowledge systems of indigenous peoples have been threatened and have been marginalized by the colonialist forces and more recently, by the globalization ethic. Indigenous people have been uprooted and displaced from their traditional habitats, leading to severance of traditional community bonds, destruction of age-old lifestyles and a general loss of cultural identity. Malathy A. in her paper 'We are the Land; The Land is Us: Land and Identity in Australian Aboriginal Culture' discusses the significance of land in constructing identity in Australian aboriginal culture. She points out that land and the human relationship have always figured conspicuously in the Australian aboriginal consciousness. However, making historical reference, she points out that the advent of colonialism has disrupted this sense of aboriginal interconnectedness with the land. Against the background of the debates regarding traditional rights of aboriginals to land and native rights, this paper explores Australian literary texts that document the traumatic consequences in aboriginal life, and their alienation from the land.

There are over 28,000 small farmers in sugar cane plantation in Mauritius. They are mainly of Indian origin. They have relentlessly toiled over three generation for making the island nation worthy of human existence for more than one and a half century. The hardships meted out to the Indian indentured labour in Mauritius (since the second half of nineteenth century) forced them to inculcate tenacity and resilience for their own survival. Though the erstwhile Indian indentured labour has been incorporated as integral part of the Mauritian society now, these planters, even after the country's independence from British rule in March 1968, have been systematically neglected by the planners, policy makers and political elites in the country. In this backdrop P.S. Vivek in his paper 'Mauritian Sugar Cane Planters Struggle for Survival' highlights the present plight of the small planters in Mauritius. It takes a closer look at their struggles and collective protests in a historical perspective to comprehend their trials and tribulations for rightful citizenship of that country. The paper also offers some alternatives as corrective measures to overcome the calamities on these people being unleashed by the high and mighty in the island nation of the Republic of Mauritius.

Social uncertainty, unemployment, ill-health, public humiliation and state apathy and tortures were some of the crucial aspect of the life of immigrant workers in Mauritius. These are related to the themes of governence. Ajay Mahurkar in his paper 'Flogging and Marginalization of Plantation Workers in Mauritius: A Case Study' seeks to explore some aspects of such issues. Researching on this theme with the help of Mauririus Governor's Correspondence, Mauritian local newspapers and official reports in the archives of Mauririus it is pointed out that by ordering an investigation into the death of an indentured immigrant prisoner in Port-Louis prison the governor opened up the entire context in which the indentured immigrant from India lived and functioned. He presents a case study of a plantation worker's death to highlight reasons about the debate on Seechurn's death in the local newspaper and official reports. His paper seeks to make a link between the conditions of Indians working and settling in the Mauritian context and to the questions of the changing paradigm of governance in Manritius.

A. Satyanarayana in his paper 'Agrarian Development, Marginalization and Unionization of Peasants in Meerut' examines the nature of agrarian development, everyday interactions of cultivators with proliferated middlemen and interpretations of such interactions prior to the emergence of collective actions in Meerut commissary. Analysis of agrarian development in the commissary reveals that although agriculture has become capital intensive with mechanization and commercialization, familial form of organization of production is predominantly retained. In the context of such agrarian development the 'moral density' of cultivators with urban capitalism magnified and the credit institutions, electricity board, industry, state, proliferated middlemen have imposed unilateral contracts on the cultivators. Not only the terms of trade went against agriculture in terms of prices but also the everyday interactions with proliferated middlemen reveal underdog political position, status degrading and socially humiliating interactions with the cultivators. The cultivators compare their position with that of proliferated middlemen, landless labourers, artisans and service castes and experience deprivations of egoistic nature that are shared in various meetings organized by the BKU leaders in the commissary where the 'private worries are converted into public concerns'. It promoted their consciousness to reason out their problems as structurally determined. In order to renegotiate the terms of contracts with the proliferated middlemen and the state, unified action was perceived as indispensable by the marginalized farmers.

Subhash Sharma in his paper 'Why the Marginalized Protest: Environment Movements as a Critique of Dominant Development Discourse' discusses some of the facets of protests of the marginalized people who have been the victims of displacement from land in the wake of initiation of new development projects, deforestations and globalization. Focusing on the issues of construction of mega dams on rivers, taking over of the common property resources by the state, he delineates the reasons of the marginalized peoples' protest. He has presented a view that the marginalized people's environmental movements not only question the dominant development discourse but also provide a time-tested vision of alternative development paradigm.

In the third section of this collection issues of the dalits, tribals, minorities, and children are discussed with specific focus. Jose Kalapura in his paper 'Globalization and Livelihood: Increasing Marginalization of Dalits and Tribals in India' attempts to show with relevant data that while there have been benefits of globalization in many aspects of life, the economic globalization without a touch of humanism has deepened the rich–poor divide, and has further marginalized the dalits and tribals. It shows that since over 81 per cent of the dalits live in rural areas, a combination of feudalism, capitalism and globalization work in their disfavour because of which the dalits are badly affected, their rights as human beings are violated, their standard of living has gone down, and their right to health and education are not honoured. Similarly the tribals, who enjoyed rich natural habitat, are increasingly being alienated and displaced from their own land due to deforestation and industrial activities such as mining, manufacture, and production by MNCs and TNCs which work in collusion with the governments. He concludes that dalits and tribals, comprising the largest segment of India's poor, are increasingly being marginalized within this emerging arrangement to encounter in their daily lives the problems of unemployment, loss livelihood, worsening food security, destruction of environment, growing inequality, suppression of democratic rights and de-culturation.

Ashish Saxena in his paper 'Locating Prospects of Dalits in the Era of Globalization' discusses with reference to the dalits the social implication of globalization, changing position of the nation state to tackle the 'social concern' (welfare goals) and the possible ways to protect and promote their human rights in India. To him economic liberation may be observed as the manifest consequences but it may lead to several latent consequences like decline of nation state, threat to cultural identity, and uniqueness of society. With reference to dalit however it has shown a differential impact. While on the one hand it has produced local and regional entities with a new orientation, it has also enhanced their consciousness at global level. It has oriented a section of them to the forces of market and finance on one hand, and on the other increased their access to revolutionary means of communication and media. Thus instead of being a threat to such identities, it has become a means for their identity construction. To him, by appropriating strategies of representation, organizations and social mobilization the marginal interest groups now simultaneously empower themselves and influence that global system.

D.C. Sah in his paper 'Social Exclusion and Marginalization: Poor among Tribals in Village Democracy', based on data from three predominantly tribal villages in Madhya Pradesh, examines the form and extent of tribal marginalization, process of creation of social capital in this tribal belt as well as the role played by social capital in tribal development. It is argued that the lack of formal institutional structures, lack of development and social exclusion have been the traditional hindrance for the formation of social capital in this tribal regions. However, the recently acquired awareness about marginalization and exclusion has strengthened the associational activities and trust among the social groups and individuals, and collective actions for shared goals. The study demonstrates that social capital in south-western tribal belt of Madhya Pradesh manifests itself through social hierarchy and moves to political domain, though with varying intensity. Significantly the bridging social capital between community and outsiders have brought economic opportunities in remote tribal areas. He significantly brings out the class dimension of this social capital as the well-to-do are able to develop these bridges and control development decision made at the grassroot level.

Marginalization is also reflected in the minority status in the society. Makbul Ali Laskar in his paper 'Group Rights of Minorities: A Critical Reflection in the Indian Context' examines the concept of minority and analyses whether minority as a group can claim group-specific rights, and, if so, what are the group rights of minorities. He also analyses the history and dynamics of the group rights of minorities in India and examines the impact of the federal political process on the group rights of minorities, problems being faced by minority groups in liberal democracies; including those faced by disadvantaged minorities, minorities within minorities, and searches alternative options in order to address the rights of various minority groups. Making a historical analysis the author points out that inequalities existing between majority and minority groups can also be tackled politically by giving more individual rights to the members of the minority groups; and, not necessarily to the group as a whole.

Children constitute an important segment of the marginalized people. According to UNICEF and ILO, around the world today, some 250 million boys and girls between the ages of five and fourteen are exploited in perilous labour conditions. It is estimated that about 5.5 crore (55 million) children in India between the ages of 5 and 14 are labourers. One in every four working children in the world is an Indian. Indian literature has widely reflected on the plight of child labour. Nandini Sahu in her paper 'Double Colonization for the Marginalized Children: A Literary Delineation' makes a situational analysis of the marginalized status of the childern in India and examines the structurally defined roles of the marginalized children since time immemorial by making a literary analysis of two most famous novels by Mulk Raj Anand. She underlines through these writings the forces of the conventional society which colonized the poor and the untouchables with a religio-social-superstitious attitude and further dehumanized the condition of the child labour who are predominantly from these economic and social categories.

The last section of this collection deals with the issues of service user and the consumer who are the most visible community in the global consumerist world. Here the issues of service user and the consumer are discussed in the contexts of a developed and the developing societies respectively. 'Service user' advisory representation is required by law and regulation in social, health and educational programmes in the developed countries. Much good can come from introducing social policies that require service providers to involve those who use health and social care services in the development and evaluation of these services. However, there remains uncertainty about how best to identify and empower such individuals to participate in 'service user involvement' without their continued marginalization due to the effects of labelling, which often creates an 'us' and 'them' context. Kristin Heffernan in her paper 'Are We Meeting the Needs of the Most Marginalized with Service Users Involvement?' presents findings from a focused group study on the 'service user' in British social and health care services delivery. It examines the meaning of 'service user' and 'service user involvement' from the point of view of persons often categorized as 'service users', by social policy, health and social care providers and academics, but who do not take part in self-organized 'service user groups'.

Globalization has brought a good variety of challenges for the middle class in a fast transitional country like India. The emerging consumerist culture has created a tension in the society and the Indian middle class is yet to cope with such tensions. In this backdrop Kamlesh Mohan in her paper 'Learning Consumerist Culture: The Indian Middle Class's Experience in the Periphery' explicates the extent and nature of changes in material culture of the Indian middle class, their interface with satellite television and cable network which has become a potential source and instrument of value-formation for global entrepreneurs in finance/business, entertainment industry, health and religious faith, etc., organizations. She argues that the persistent exposure of the middle class to colourful and seductive images of consumerist products and life styles through transnational flows of information and programming has brought drastic changes not only in cultural environment but also in the ways of seeing and thinking of the consumers. To her, though there have emerged strategic partnership between global entrepreneurs in economy and media, there have been an inverse relationship between conspicuous consumption and social development, and the Indian consumerist middle class is yet to get fully integrated with the emerging economic and cultural order of the globalizing world.

This collection is not self-contained. Many of the related issues of the marginalized people, especially their protests and discontents, livelihood and development are discussed in the collections on *Dissenting Voices and Transformative Actions: Social Movements in a Globalizing World*, and *Interrogating Social Development: Global Perspectives and Local Initiatives* brought out simultaneously along with this collection.

REFERENCES

Ambedkar, B.R. (1937), *Annihilation of Caste*, Bombay: Thacker & Co. Ltd.

Gist, N.P. and R.D. Wright (1973), *Marginality and Identity: Anglo Indians as a Racially Mixed Minority in India*, Leiden: EJ. Brill.

Germani, G. (1980), *Marginality*, New Jersey: Transaction Books.

Gordon, M.M. (1964), *Assimilation in American Life: The Role of Race, Religion, and National Origins*, New York: Oxford University Press.

http://www.world-affairs.org/globalc 'Gandhi—Savior of Harijans'.

Hammer, T. (2003), 'Youth Unemployed of Social Exclusion in Europe: A Comparative Study', *Journal of Sociology*, 33, no. 6 (1928), pp. 881-93.

Luhmann, N. (1982), *Differentiation of Society*, New York: University of Columbia Press.

Moller, I.H. (1998), 'On the Spoor of Conceptual Clarification', Paper prepared to the INPART study.

Park, L.E. (1937), *Human Migration and the Marginal Man*, Chicago: Bobbs-Merrill.

Marx, K. and F. Engels (1970) (rpt), *Selected Works*, vol. I, Moscow: Progress Publisher.

——— (1970), (rpt), 'Economic & Philosophical Manuscripts of 1844', *Selected Works*, vol. III, Moscow: Progress Publisher.

Prakash, P. (1993), *Ambedkar: Politics and Scheduled Castes*, New Delhi: Ashis Publishing House.

I. GLOBALIZATION AND MARGINALIZATION: CHANGING DIMENSIONS AND EMERGING PERSPECTIVES

CHAPTER 1

Strategic Marginalizations and Emotional Marginalities: The Dilemma of Stigmatized Identities

JAMES M. JASPER

As befits this volume, and the conference on which it is based, let me start with the root metaphor of a margin, a seemingly spatial and hence structural image. But I would like to point out the active work behind it, which is not really structural at all. 'Margin' is a complex word, taken almost straight from Latin, and no doubt derived from Indo-European before that.

First of all, a margin is a border, and especially what is just inside that border: on the edge, peripheral, superfluous, not fully fitting in. But at the same time, when it comes to the printed page, it is a place for notes and commentary—marginalia—that can be extensive and important. In the case of sacred scripture, for instance, it is often the marginalia that explain it, and which do the real work of telling believers what to do. These interpretations are often more elaborate than the scriptures themselves. And this in turn shades into a third meaning, of margins as a kind of buffer that protects the core, as in a margin of error or a margin of profit. So we run the gamut from rather negative to quite positive meanings of the word.

This range of meanings suggests that, despite the idea of a distinct place, a part of a structured whole, margins are, like everything else, culturally constructed. Hence the term 'marginalization', which is a process rather than a state of being. To marginalize someone is an active strategy, although it need not be an intentional one; it could be a byproduct of something else. And yet, because it *is* such a powerful strategy—in that it excludes a player, typically a group, from an arena—I suspect that it is usually quite intentional.

But it is also quite an emotional strategy. All strategies involve emotions, of course, but with some, emotional effects are the main intent. With marginalization, there is not just formal exclusion, but the creation of a *feeling* of exclusion, of being an outsider, of being, well, marginal. It strips human dignity from someone, as well as stripping them of the confidence needed to act politically, to be a player. (That confidence is hugely important for successful strategic engagement.)

I should add that the original meaning of the English verb 'marginalize', in the nineteenth century, was to write margin notes on a text, in other words to cast light on the centre, to interrogate it, rather than to push something from the centre into the margins. And so this conference and volume are meant to examine the margins in order for us to understand the whole of society.

Marginalization is a central political strategy, and at the centre of marginalization is an effort to create a damaged or stigmatized identity for a group, as a way to disadvantage it strategically. And in many ways, that assault on basic human dignity matters more than the material deprivations that usually result from it.

I would like to use the example of marginalization as an opportunity to suggest the possibilities of a strategic and emotional vision of protest (drawing on Jasper, 2006). I will proceed by talking about one strategic dilemma, what I call the *Dilemma of Stigmatized Identities*, and show how it's related to several other dilemmas.

Now, thinking in terms of strategic dilemmas and trade-offs is already a fairly new approach to the study of protest (Jasper, 2004). But I want to challenge you even more by bringing in emotions and linking them with strategy. This is also a fairly new—or at least revived—topic in the study of protest (Jasper, 1997, 1998; Goodwin et al., 2000, 2001; Goodwin and Jasper, 2006; Clarke et al., 2006), and one which at first seems very distant from strategy. In fact, the classic opposition in research and theory has been to contrast expressive movements with more purposive, rational, strategic movements—a deeply mistaken approach, I believe, which distorts every kind of movement.

Although this is a theoretical argument, I shall illustrate it with two cases, African–Americans in the United States and dalits in India. I employ only secondary sources for each. My knowledge of the dalit case is especially scanty.

The *Dilemma of Stigmatized Identities* is as follows: You want to mobilize to change or eliminate the identity, but you need to use that same identity to mobilize people. So you run the risk of strengthening the label you're opposed to. This is a dilemma both at the level of means, of how to get what you want, and at the level of ends, since moral dignity arises *both* from abolishing the stigma *and* from organizing politically.

One sign of this kind of struggle is cycling through different names for a group, in efforts to soften the stigma for certain audiences. For American blacks, one hundred years ago, 'coloured people' was the accepted term (as in the National Association for the Advancement of Coloured People (NAACP), founded in 1910), then for much of the twentieth century it was 'Negroes'. 'Blacks' became popular in the 1960s, linked to the black power movement. There was Afro–American, people of colour, and more recently African–American, although the term Black remains popular as well. My impression is that there has been a similar series among India's Scheduled Castes, untouchables, exterior castes, depressed classes, Harijan, dalits, and so on. In addition to implying slightly different groupings with different boundaries, behind each term there's a political agenda, aimed at having an effect on a certain audience. Sometimes the audience is within the group, other times it is outsiders.

This agenda links the stigmatized identity dilemma to another common strategic dilemma, the *Janus Dilemma*, over how much attention and effort to put into your own membership *versus* how much to put into outsiders: reaching in *versus* reaching out (Mansbridge, 1986; Jasper, 2006: 125). The ways that you take pride in your own identity are rarely the same ways that you appeal to others (but make no mistake: both are strategic acts: Bernstein, 1997). Separatism is always appealing. I gather that for dalits, there has been a tension between placing one's caste in the ancient Hindu texts, for example finding a heroic ancestor, and converting altogether to another religion—Ambedkar's famous approach towards the end of his life (Ambedkar, 1948/1990).

It is not only the groups themselves that must grapple with the Dilemma of Stigmatized Identities. Authorities and supporters often do as well. For instance the Nehruvian state refused to collect data on caste, and none were collected until the end of the 1990s (Deshpande, this volume). The Government of India was grappling with the Dilemma of Stigmatized Identities: would it reinforce caste to collect these data? How could this be balanced with potential benefits? At the same time as the state created reservations to help the oppressed castes, reinforcing the identity and igniting resentment on the part of others, it hesitated to collect the data that would help it judge whether it was succeeding. (An aside: from a purely strategic perspective, this is reasonable: a player tries to avoid setting up clear criteria of success unless it is pretty sure it can meet them.)

The Dilemma of Stigmatized Identities also links up with what I call the *Extension Dilemma*: how large, how extensive, a team do you try to build? How inclusive are you? A stigmatized population may consist of many sub-units that feel no solidarity with each other, and instead often feel mutual hostility. This seems especially the case of lower castes, who can always find someone even lower to hate.

So a stigmatized caste may be able to go back in history or in classical texts, and find a hero that it can link to its caste, in an effort to arouse pride, but the very specificity of that effort is going to emphasize the one caste, not link it to other stigmatized castes in any broader solidarity. On the other hand, the Bahujan Samaj Party (BSP), say, can compose songs that praise the strength and history of dalits generally, but they will lack the particular resonance of symbolic individuals, who are mostly going to be from a single caste (Narayan, 2006: 79).

Among African–Americans, too, there was always some tension between those with lighter skin and those with darker skin (Landry, 1987), but nothing like the caste tensions in India. A better US parallel might be the tensions between poor whites and poor blacks, which has rarely worked out well. One source of the tension is privileges granted strategically by those in power: many black Americans worked for schools and the government, and risked losing their jobs if they fought for civil rights. Just as castes like the Pasis often worked as henchmen for landlords, imposing their discipline upon other, even lower castes (Narayan, 2006: 89-90).

The rhetorical use of history raises another dilemma closely related to the Stigmatized Identity Dilemma: between emphasizing the atrocities perpetrated against a group, which plays up oppressors as villains but at the same time reinforces the group's victimhood *versus* emphasizing a group's heroic actions, which gives it confidence for further action and mobilization (van Deburg, 1992: 272-80). The two approaches can coexist: African–Americans told the legends of Shine and Stagolee, of John Henry, as well as the histories of Harriet

Tubman and Nat Turner. But the two can be combined only in the heroism of endurance, strength in the ability to survive, which is morally impressive but not always the best basis for new mobilization. It provides dignity but not the confidence for strategic engagement. Although Martin Luther King Jr. exhorted his followers, 'Don't get weary. We will wear them down with our capacity to suffer', the setting, in Albany, Georgia, represented one of King's few failures.

Affirmative action programmes obviously get entangled in the Dilemma of Stigmatized Identities: there are real benefits to gain from these programmes, but those same programmes highlight and make permanent the categories you are fighting against. In the United States, many blacks and especially Hispanics do *not* want to be hired with the help of affirmative action, although even when the special help becomes informal, they often can't avoid some suspicions (on the part of others, usually) that there was some ascription rather than merit involved. Just as some castes in India in the 1930s debated whether or not to get on to the Schedule. At least one refused to be counted an exterior caste in the 1931 census, but did go for the Schedule in 1936 (Mendelsohn and Vicziany, 1998: 39).

In both the cases, affirmative action has spawned a backlash. Many working-class white Americans flocked to Reagan and the Republican Party in the 1970s and 1980s because they saw the federal government as favouring blacks (Edsall and Edsall, 1991), just as today many members of Hindu castes see their own government as pampering dalits, providing more reservations than is deserved (Gadekar, this volume).

Stigmatized groups often advance by finding new audiences with whom they are not stigmatized. They manage to gain new pride through these new interactions, as well as resources in some cases. International arenas benefited American blacks as well as Indian dalits. In the 1950s, politicians at the federal level in the United States were concerned with the nation's reputation abroad, as the Soviet Union used race to portray the United States as hypocritical. How could this government talk about democracy and liberty for other nations, when it denied basic political rights to so many of its own citizens (Skrentny, 2002)? Similarly dalits, in the 1990s, were able to attract considerable attention and some mobilizing resources from sympathetic international NGOs (Bob, 2007). In trying to assess the benefits and costs of globalization to dalits it is found that the harm is mostly because they are poor, while many of the benefits come from international audiences with whom the dalits are not stigmatized (my interpretation, not theirs).

For both these stigmatized groups, large-scale migration to emerging industrial cities was also a boon, breaking the back of more traditional forms of subordination. Dalits have been able to simply ignore or disguise their backgrounds. Urban black Americans in the middle of the twentieth century were able to develop institutions outside the watchful eyes of whites, as well as to accumulate some resources that could be channelled through black churches to the southern civil rights movement (Morris, 1984). Cities offered refuge from the direct, personal subordination and humiliation that was especially devastating to both dignity and confidence.

One final issue also shows the common strategic situation of groups with stigmatized identities. For both African–Americans and dalits there are ongoing debates over average IQ scores—reflecting efforts to pseudo-speciate the group as part of its stigma and to undermine support for affirmative action programmes.

I don't want to give the impression that a strategic approach is a matter of cold calculation, of maximization, or hyper-rationality, as economists and rational-choice theorists might have it. So I want to mention briefly some of the emotions that are a central part of the dilemmas around stigmatized identities.

First, there are the emotions of potential recruits, who almost by definition harbour shame from the stigma (Gould, 2001). Recruiters have to transform shame into pride, although how they do this will depend on the substance of the stigma and shame: What exactly are they based on? If they are based on *weakness*, recruiters presumably have to arouse a sense of power, which at any rate is crucial to mobilization in general. If they are based on some sense of inherent *pollution*, organizers must presumably craft a way out of the cultural codes that define pollution, such as by converting to a new religion. If the stigma is based on *pseudo-speciation*, on seeing and treating the group as though they were animals and not fully human, then the effort goes into finding heroes who embody human dignity, who have intellectual accomplishments, or are religious virtues, and so on. The propensity to call the leaders of these two movements *Doctor* King and *Doctor* Ambedkar is presumably an effort of this kind.

None of this is easy work, because stigmatized groups are caught in a vicious circle. No matter how large they are, they lack a sense of agency, of confidence in their own ability to act, and yet it is mobilization that best gives them that confidence.

Of course, there are complicating emotions, such as outrage over atrocities, and hatred and hostility for the oppressors, which a focus on past oppression can stoke up. Shame and rage can combine in a vicious way that I think helps us understand the motivations of suicide bombers in many nations, for whom destruction of the enemy has become an end in itself.

Then there are the emotions of other players. They may feel disgust for the stigmatized group, or they may feel fear of it. At least fear recognizes it as dangerous, powerful, and threatening, a characterization that might help the group attain some pride on that basis. Many white Americans have been afraid of black men, but that very recognition of the latter's power has been a source of pride, of organizing, and eventually of more positive tropes, such as sports heroes, action heroes in movies, or even armed guerilla heroes like the Black Panthers.

Disgust is a tougher emotion to work with, since it operates at such a gut level: it is one of a small number of reflex emotions, which have a kind of automatic quality to them. In its most primitive form, sheer physical contact can trigger disgust, making alliances difficult.

I have only suggested some of these pathways for research that could help us understand the dynamics of stigmatized, marginalized groups, and the potential ways they have out of their status. The world of strategic engagement is complex, with few easy choices. Instead, it is full of dilemmas—choices among several alternatives, each of which comes with a long list of costs, benefits, and risks, each a combination of predictable and unpredictable outcomes.

Let me sum up by pointing out a central advantage of a strategic approach—its concreteness. There have been lots of essentialist debates about marginal groups: Is caste in India similar to racism in the United States? Is racism an essential part of American culture? Is caste a central part of Hinduism, or a perversion of it? It seems to me that questions like these are unanswerable, because they are about what root metaphors we should use, and about what mysterious underlying structures there are at work in a society. They portray as timeless truths what are in fact the outcomes of constant struggle over meanings and practices.

In contrast there is nothing mysterious about strategic choices.

They are easily observed. You can see groups making them. It doesn't matter how race and caste are different or similar: You see concrete groups, real people, facing similar decisions. You can compare their choices, you can compare their effects, you can work with variables rather than essences. (Emotions are also eminently observable, or at least more observable than our cognitions.)

Essences may be all right for philosophy or religion, but they disrupt social science, they prevent us from understanding what is going on right in front of us. In general, I think we need to pay attention to the little things, rather than starting with the big ones. We need to build from the bottom up, not start at the top and deduce from abstractions and essences what we should find at the bottom.

REFERENCES

Ambedkar, B.R. (1948/1990), 'The Untouchables' in Vasant Moon (ed.), *Dr. Babasaheb Ambedkar: Writings and Speeches*, VII, Bombay: Government of Maharashtra.

Bernstein, M. (1997), 'Celebration and Suppression: The Strategic Uses of Identity by the Lesbian and Gay Movement', *American Journal of Sociology*, 103, pp. 531-65.

Bob, C. (2007), '"Dalit Rights are Human Rights": Caste Discrimination, International Activism, and the Construction of a New Human Rights Issue', *Human Rights Quarterly*, 29, pp. 167-93.

Clarke, S., P. Hoggett and S. Thompson (eds.) (2006), *Emotion, Politics, and Society*, London: Palgrave-Macmillan.

Edsall, T.B. and M.D. Edsall (1991), *Chain Reaction: The Impact of Race, Rights, and Taxes on American Politics*, New York: W.W. Norton.

Goodwin, J. and J.M. Jasper (2006), 'Emotions and Social Movements', in J. Stets and J. Turner (eds.), *Handbook of the Sociology of Emotions*, New York: Springer.

Goodwin, J., J.M. Jasper, and F. Polletta (2000), 'The Return of the Repressed: The Fall and Rise of Emotions in Social Movement Theory', *Mobilization* 5, pp. 65-84.

Goodwin, J., J.M. Jasper, and F. Polletta (eds.) (2001), *Passionate Politics: Emotions and Social Movements*, Chicago: University of Chicago Press.

Gould, D. (2001), 'Rock the Boat, Don't Rock the Boat, Baby: Ambivalence and the Emergence of Militant AIDS Activism', in J. Goodwin, J.M. Jasper, and F. Polletta (eds.), *Passionate Politics: Emotions and Social Movements*, Chicago: University of Chicago Press.

Guru, G., and A. Chakravarty (2005), 'Who Are the Country's Poor?', in Raka Ray and Mary Fainsod Katzenstein (eds.), *Social Movements in India*, Lanham, Md.: Rowman and Littlefield.

Jasper, J. M. (1997), *The Art of Moral Protest*, Chicago: University of Chicago Press.

——— (1998), 'The Emotions of Protest: Affective and Reactive Emotions in and Around Social Movements', *Sociological Forum* 13, pp. 397-424.

——— (2004), 'A Strategic Approach to Collective Action', *Mobilization*, 9, pp. 1-16.

——— (2006), *Getting Your Way: Strategic Dilemmas in Real Life*, Chicago: University of Chicago Press.

Joshi, B. (ed.) (1986), *Untouchable!*, London: Minority Rights Group.

Landry, B. (1987), *The New Black Middle Class*, Berkeley: University of California Press.

Mansbridge, J.J. (1986), *Why We Lost the ERA*, Chicago: University of Chicago Press.

Mendelsohn, O. and M. Vicziany (1998), *The Untouchables*, Cambridge: Cambridge University Press.

Morris, A. (1984), *The Origins of the Civil Rights Movement*, New York: Free Press.

Murugkar, L. (1991), *Dalit Panther Movement in Maharashtra*, London: Sangam Books.

Narayan, B. (2006), *Women Heroes and Dalit Assertion in North India*, New Delhi: Sage Publications.

Pai, S. (2002), *Dalit Assertion and the Unfinished Democratic Revolution*, New Delhi: Sage.

Rajshekar, V.T. (1987), *Dalit: The Black Untouchables of India*, 3rd edn., Atlanta, Ga.: Clarity Press.

Sachchidananda (2001), 'Voluntary Action for Social Development and Empowering the Marginalised in Bihar', in Debal K. SinghaRoy (ed.), *Social Development and the Empowerment of Marginalised Groups*, New Delhi: Sage.

Skrentny, J.D. (2002), *The Minority Rights Revolution*, Cambridge: Harvard University Press.

Van Deburg, W.L. (1992), *New Day in Babylon*, Chicago: University of Chicago Press.

Zelliot, E. (2001), *From Untouchable to Dalit: Essays on the Ambedkar Movement*, 3rd edn., New Delhi: Manohar.

CHAPTER 2

Marginalization and the Marginalized: Reflections on the Relational–Cumulative Dynamics

DEBAL K. SINGHAROY

In social science vocabulary though the usage of the notion of marginalization is not new, in recent years it has acquired a place of significance in the context of globalization, adoption of new perspectives of social development, transition of society and emergence of new conditions of sustenance of social injustice and exclusion. Marginalization has been conventionally understood in a specific societal context and with distinctive connotation to delineate social groups living in peripheral and adverse situations and at times with alleged negative attributes. However, in the contemporary world, the process of marginalization has acquired several new dimensions besides getting the old ones redefined in the emerging contexts. Consequently the efforts of circumscribing marginalities in terms of singularity of criterion and limiting it to specific locale are gradually losing their hold in the wake of fast transition of society. Marginalization indeed, has remained to be a persistent phenomenon in one form or the other for a vast section of the population despite fast social and economic transition in the society.

The social, economic and political dynamics of marginalization have remained interlinked to make a vast sections of population victims of several forms of denials and deprivation, inequality and injustice, domination and hierarchy. These elements of marginalization have also been simultaneously cumulatively reproduced over a long period of time to keep these people in the margin of the society. Against this backdrop the present paper aims to scrutinize the concept of marginalization and its changing dynamics in the globalizing society. Besides explicating the intertwining of marginalization with ongoing multiple social processes, it elucidates marginalization of vast sections of population with in-depth information as persistent historical reality and analyses the socio-political implications of such marginalization for India. It suggests a relational–cumulative perspective to study marginalization by integrating the interrelated social, economic and political dimensions of marginalization with their historically cumulatively acquired dynamics. Focusing on rural West Bengal it examines the emerging facets of marginalization within the broad processes of transformation of contemporary society with this 'relational–cumulative' perspective.

CONCEPTUALIZING MARGINALIZATION

Marginalization, as a complex process of relegating specific group(s) of people to the lower or the outer edge of the society, operates as function, as cause and also as a social product. It has been delineated in many intellectual and development discourses as a social process that operates and promotes through the practice of discrimination, oppression, subjugation, and domination which gets legitimized and reproduced through the normative and institutional arrangements of society. Significantly, marginalization as a dynamic process has got socially reformulated and reshaped and intellectually redefined with the impact and expansion of capitalism, imperialism, modernization, industrialization, globalization and related processes of social transition. Several ideological inter-pinnings have also got associated with the explanation of this process. Consequently 'marginality has been used in many debates as a smokescreen behind which several ideological battles—such as the nature of the social system, the processes of modernization, or the implications of capitalism and imperialism—continue to be fought' (Perlman, 1976: 91). However, as a socio-historical reality, marginalization has been also understood with specific social, historical, cultural and intellectual traditions.

In conventional Spanish and Portuguese usages 'marginal' as social collectivities are usually understood as 'shiftless, dangerous, never do well communities who are associated with the underworld of crime, violence, drugs and prostitution'. Similarly in the European and American traditions, these poor, in one sense or the other, are described as the 'dangerous classes', or persons living in 'regions of squatter and woe' and also as the 'communities of blight' (ibid.: 92).

In the Indian subcontinent and especially within the broad fold of Hindu social orders, the marginalized are designated to be the out-castes represented by the *antyajas* and the *shudras* belonging to the social categories of untouchables and others practising unclean ascribed occupations and extra-mural manual activities of various sorts. Within the conventional cultural framework of the *varna* system they are provided with stigmatized existence and are considered to be impure and are kept away from varieties of social and cultural interactions with the higher *varnas*, i.e the brahmins, kshatriyas and vaishyas. They are designated as 'broken men' by Ambedkar and Harijan by Gandhi. They are conditioned to survive at the margin of Hindu society—socially, culturally, politically, economically and even geographically. Caste system in India has given the lower caste people not only lower ritual and social status, they have also been cumulatively denied access to the opportunities for education, wide social interaction, information networks and participation in formal decision-making processes. Traditionally they have remained associated to ascribed occupations compelling them to concentrate on low-paying jobs, to accept exploitative terms and conditions of work and to remain insecure socially and politically. Many of these social and cultural stigmas are also extended to women, tribal and religious minority groups.

In social science the notion of the marginalized has been extensively used to denote overlapping groups of the poor, jobless, migrants, members of sub-cultures, racial and ethnic minorities, slum dwellers, aged, physically challenged, drug addicts and deviants of many sorts and so on. In recent decades however, the scope of usage of this term has been wide open. In the context of globalization, it has been widely used to describe the social categories which have remained only partly integrated or remained excluded from the 'mainstream' of society (see UNDP, Human Development Summit 1995; Human Development Report 1996). Within these wide spectrum sociologically marginality is understood in a societal context in terms of 'non-participation', 'non-integration' and also in 'reference to exclusion' of groups or sections of population from several of the key activities of society.

The phenomena of *non-participation* may arise under several conditions and get operationalized through several processes. The dynamics of non-participation debars selected groups of people from full participation in the societal activities through normative or traditional practices to retain over them the primordial hegemony of the dominant group. The dominated groups may not be provided with adequate social, economic and political opportunities in acquiring the desired potential for full participation in decision-making, having access to the sources of power, and in sharing of societal, economic and other resources. Hence, the marginalized may have the desire for full participation but lack the opportunities for the same (Germani, 1980).

Integration entails full involvement in several parts/sub-systems, institutional arrangements and processes, and sustained interaction with several cultural and the symbolic meanings of the society. As a corollary, *non-integration* amounts to non-involvement in one or more related areas of society, which can be examined in reference to one's role and status (both ascribed and achieved) that largely determine the form and extent of one's interaction with the rest. Marginalization examined with reference to *non-integration* amounts to non-involvement in one or more related areas of society (Hammer, 2003). As there are diverse forms and extent of non-integration there are varying degrees of marginalization.

Marginalization is again examined in reference to a continuum in society running through inclusion, marginality and exclusion (Luhmann, 1982). Exactly where on the continuum (inclusion, marginality and exclusion) an individual is situated depends to a large extent on his or her overall possession of and capacity to mobilize not only economic resources, but also social, cultural and symbolic resources (Moller, 1998). Considering the possibility of differentiating the society and its sub-systems in diverse ways and with diverse combinations one can formulate varying degrees of inclusions, marginalization and exclusion. This may again lead to many competing and even contradictory analyses of inclusion and exclusion in modern societies. According to Luhmann (1982) exclusion and marginality are characterized by vicious circles while inclusion is not, as inclusion into one sub-system is seldom linked to inclusion into other systems, while exclusion from one sub-system probably involves exclusion from other systems too. Here marginalization is used to characterize an intermediate position somewhere between full integration and social exclusion (Luhmann, 1982).

Marginalization moreover has a composite bearing on *social exclusion*. Social exclusion has been extensively examined conceptually in relation to capacity deprivation. Sen (2000) extends the formulation of Adam Smith that social exclusion is directly a part of capacity deprivation and that 'not being able to appear in public without shame' or inability to act freely with others are important deprivations. 'Being excluded from social relations can lead to other deprivations as well thereby further limiting living opportunities'. The social capability deprivation is by implication related to the experience of poverty and lack of freedom. Social exclusion can thus be *constitutively* a part of capacity deprivation as well as *instrumentally* a cause of diverse capacity failure (Sen, 2000: 5). Social exclusion as the extreme phenomena is the resultant consequence of sustained capacity deprivation in the social, economic and political areas of lives which is promoted both by the circumstantial and inherited inequality and poverty; labour and credit market segregation; gender, caste, race, ethnic discrimination; health care, food security, educational opportunity, etc., deprivation and persistent political domination.

Social exclusion indeed, is a product of add on process of marginalization in several domains of lives. The Irish Partnership 2000 Agreement (1996) defined social exclusion in terms of 'cumulative marginalization: from production (employment), consumption (income poverty), social networks (community, family and neighbours), decision-making and from a decent quality of life (Irish National Organisation of the Unemployed, Partnership for Inclusion, Employment and Competitiveness 2000). There are a variety of groups that for a several of reasons find themselves on the margins of society. The process of cumulative marginalization is a spatialized one with specific marginal area becoming associated with marginal groups over time. As a related phenomenon there are the possibilities of multiplicity of marginality.

The marginalized are poised on the edge of several groups but fully accepted by none of them (Merton, 1957). Multiple non-integrations thus amount to 'multiple marginality'. The different dimensions of marginalization are separate but related phenomena. For example, the practice of *cultural marginality* (language, behaviour, manner, diet, rituals, attire) and s*ocial marginality* (formalized aspects of the intergroup or inter-personal relations) function to reinforce, pattern and govern marginality protocol or set of taboos prohibiting designated forms of interaction (Dickie-Clark, 1966; Gist, and Wright 1973). Again, the placement of the marginal group in such environmentally degraded and poverty stricken area serves to enhance the powerlessness of this group (Hoggart, 2005: 191).

The practice of discriminatory social protocol and norms helps to evolve the ideology of marginality in diverse ways. As marginality operates as functions of an ideology, the ideology of marginality is reflected in different dimensions of social structure, the occupational, the spatial, the stratification system, the consumption patterns, income distribution, the culture, the psychosocial system of individual behaviour and in the power structure. Thereby 'marginality as a phenomenon is not a political determinant but a political outcome' (Castells, 1983).

Marginalization thus is not an isolated, but a rather relational, cumulative, socially reproduced and legitimized phenomenon. Indeed marginality is spatially and *horizontally relational* with reference to the economic, social, cultural and political undercurrents of society. It is *vertically cumulative* over time with add-on impacts of these related denials, deprivations, insecurity, domination, segregation; and legitimization and reproduction of marginality. The relational and cumulative dimensions of marginality in fact are circumscribed by the consideration of time and space. Notwithstanding the profound processes of sociocultural disembeddedness across the globe (Gidden, 1991) marginalization of the marginalized continues, in a different shape though, integrating the relational and cumulative dynamics to it. Sustained marginality generates new varieties of collective identity and urge for protest. These protests may be directed in the relational and cumulative dynamics of marginalization in society depending on the subjective awareness on their margination, availability of immediate local organizational resources and linkages with the wider society. This is because 'actors in subordinate positions are never wholly dependent and are often very adept at converting whatsoever resources they possess into some degree of control over the conditions of reproduction of the system' (Giddens, 1982b: 32). They may not immediately resist domination, rather they may comply. However, 'compliance of the subordinate within the power relations should be explained not by lack of resistance, but by the absence of the means to implement such resistance'. Thus there have been resistance and struggle of various forms against this domination (Mann, 1985). These struggles reflected in the articulation and recognition of new forms of identity (Stewart, 2001). The process of articulation of new identities and protest of the marginalized are in essence shaped by the relational and cumulative dynamics of their marginalization.

As against these back drops in order to develop a comprehensive understanding of marginalization process, it is rather imperative that we use the 'relational–cumulative framework' of marginality analysis that integrates both the horizontal and vertical dynamics of marginalization in a given context with historical reference. The foundation of this framework is laid on the analysis of following dimensions of marginality: denials and deprivations, insecurities and uncertainties hierarchy and domination, legitimacy and reproduction, mobility and protest which are interrelated and mutually exclusive in nature.

Dimensions of Denial and Deprivation

The process of marginalization economically:

- Denies a large section of the society to have equal access to *productive resources*, avenues for the realization of their productive human potential, and opportunities of their full capacity utilization; and relegates them to the margin of the economic arrangement with a sub-human existence to live with rampant poverty and livelihood insecurity.
- Pushes them to concentrate on the underclass occupational activities, to unstable low paying jobs which are not part of mainstream economy (Perlman, 1976: 95), to fall in the regime of wage discrimination and casualization in the workforce.
- Subjects them to labour market segregation by moving them away the kernel of the market to the end where the individual is finally excluded via more and more precarious labour market positions (Johannessen, 1997).
- Makes them victim of underemployment, seasonal employment and prolonged unemployment, migration and economic disintegration from the preexisting network (Paugamn, 1992).
- Disintegrates them through industrialization, urbanization and construction of large development projets, like dam, road, railways, etc., by making them the providers of cheap labour through uprooting, transition and migration (Perlman, 1976: 114) and downward mobility.
- Promotes sustained non-integration by denying new body of technological innovations, knowledge, opportunities and choices.

Socially marginalization:

- Deprives them of effective social capital, space for their social mobility, new avenues for social and human development.
- Relegates them to get lower social status, designating them to belong to lower caste, inferior race, gender and ethnicity.
- Constructs negative social images and stereotyping by designating them as rustic, uncivilized, dull, lazy, criminal, and excriminal and deprives them of social sympathy.

Politically this process:

- Denies these people to have access to the formal power structure and participation in the decision-making processes.
- Leads to their subordination to and dependency on the economically and politically dominant groups of the society.
- Subjects them to political apathy.
- Subordinates them to the hegemony and coercion of dominant sections and pushes them ultimately to become the underdogs, un/underrepresented and disempowered in society.

Culturally this process:

- Relegates them to the periphery of the society to become the 'part society with part culture' (Redfield 1959), 'outsider from within', alienated and disintegrated. They are pushed to be aliens in their own land, in the process of historical contacts and colonization (Stavenhagen, 1970; Casanova, 1970), and to remain socially and culturally embedded with such alienation even in the post-colonial period.
- Pushes them to be migrants and to enter into the domain of 'marginal man' who remains in the margin of two cultures and societies and is never completely interpenetrated and fused. He becomes a distinctive personality type ('marginal man') 'as the stranger who enter a society from the outside and remain on the periphery of it'. The fate that condemns him to live, at the same time, in two worlds is the same which compels him to assume, in relation to the worlds in which he lives, the role of a cosmopolitan and a stranger (Park, 1928).
- Relegates them to become members of different sub-cultures and at times counter-cultures. They live in a 'culture of poverty', lacking effective participation and integration with the major institutions of the larger society, living in suspicion, and apathy.

They are non-integrated in the larger national culture and become a sub-culture of their own' (Oscar Lewis, 1966).

- Reinforces their non-integration in the cultural life through the practice of cultural segregation, differentiation, purity–pollution and hierarchy, ascribed superior–inferior status differential leading to the formation of a sub-society composed precisely of racial or ethnic marginal man (Gordon, 1964).
- Inculcates the sociocultural barriers to limit and obstruct social interaction and cultural interchange between members of groups in order to reinforce social distance between individuals and the collectives. Such cultural barriers construct a stigmatized cultural existence, an ascribed low social status and endure cultural segregation of the marginalized. They also impose restrictions on integration into another group based on the differences of their cultural or racial heritage; and limited cultural interchange or social interaction (Gist and Wright, 1973). The strict sense of barriers again involves 'rank order discrimination' in preventing or reducing cultural interactions in many of the core areas of society, for example, imposing strict restriction on intermarriage among different racial groups (Myrdal, 1944).
- Deprives people from getting access to the opportunities of education, training and other capacity building facilities through linguistic, dress, and other cultural barriers.

Dimensions of Insecurities and Uncertainties

The process of marginalization sets in motion several varieties of *insecurities* by:

- Dislodging a large segment of the population from habitats for the initiation of large developmental projects (big dams, industrial townships, Special Economic Zones).
- Pushing them to work in insecure and hazardous working condition to earn a livelihood.
- Constraining them to accept job insecurity, lack of social security and legal protection by compulsion and not by choice.
- Making them vulnerable to accidents in highrisk factories, underground mines, chemical and pesticide industries, sewage repairing, high-rise construction sites, and so on.
- Conditioning them to suffer basic health security (by living without basic facilities like safe water, electricity, proper housing and road, clean toilets) and to live with disease and illness.

- Exposing them to all varieties of man-made and natural calamities like cloud blast, flood, drought and other human miseries.
- Compelling them to bear the burden of pollution and over-consumption of natural resources by the affluent sections of the society worldwide. They are also the early victims of 'risk society'. The Human Development Report 2007 writes:

> In today's world, it is the poor who are bearing the brunt of climate change. Across the developing world millions of the poorest people are already being forced to cope with the impact of climate change. Increasing impacts of drought, intense storm, flood, environmental stress, etc., holding back the world's poor to build a better life for themselves and their children. 'While the world's poor walk the earth with a light carbon footprint they are bearing the brunt of unsustainable management of our ecological interdependence. . . . Climate change is retching up the risks and vulnerabilities facing the poor. (UNDP, 2007: 1-9)

Dimensions of Hierarchy and Domination

Marginalization is a man-made and socially constructed process, which is permuted and continuously reproduced through unequal structure of hierarchy. It

- Produces artificial structures of hierarchy by converting even the natural differentiation into an order of hierarchy to sustain the systemic principle of domination and subordination. Construction of gender, caste, and race, ethnic, etc., hierarchies are the outcomes of this artificial structure.
- Articulates hierarchical ordering of the group in terms of differential access to prestige, privilege and power (Gist and Wright, 1973: 21).
- Shapes the process of stigmatization, devaluation and derecognition of the contribution made by these people in society. For example, women's household and reproductive activities have remained non-recognized as work for long in society, manual activities of agricultural labourers, construction workers, cleaners, sweepers, and all categories of service providers have been constructed to be stigmatized and demeaning culturally.
- Discourages the dominant group (if they want to stay dominant) from sharing their powers and opportunities with the subordinate

strata, even though they may apparently encourage subordinate groups to adopt some of their attitudes (Dickie-Clark, 1966).

Dimensions of Legitimacy and Reproduction

Marginality gets legitimized and reproduced through the strong institutional and normative arrangements of society. This process:

- Legitimizes primordial and historically inherited forms of caste, race, ethnic and gender-based exploitation, social segregation, inequality and disempowerment through the normative and ideological arrangements of society.
- Reproduces hierarchy to sustain the hegemony of the dominant group.
- Provides legitimacy to exploitation and inequality through the ideology of class, caste, patriarchy, race and ethnicity.
- Endures and reproduces their exploitation, social segregation, inequality, disempowerment, domination, and discrimination through the processes of socialization, education, politicization, and enculturation. Thus over a period of time the socially constructed marginalized categories tend to appear to be the empirical categories.

Dimensions of Mobility, Identity and Protest

Sustained marginality:

- Promotes deviant, non-conformist social behaviour of the deprived, denied and the insecure groups and gradually converts them into passive drop-outs or active critics of the society.
- Contributes to develop awareness in the 'groups-in-itself' and to assume an assessment of their differences with others, construct a moral judgement of their strengths and weaknesses, virtues or vices *vis-à-vis* other groups.
- Constructs marginal identity by way of narrowing social distances 'within the group' and intensifying a consciousness of identity, generating community solidarity based on the experiences of deprivation, discrimination, exploitation (Gist and Wright, 1973).
- Promotes the phenomenon of ethnocentrism 'influenced by other directed attitude of hostility or friendliness, of prejudice

or preference, of the need or desire to identify with another group and be accepted by it, or the desire to avoid such an identity (Gist and Wright, 1973: 30).

- It breeds radicalism, violence, social disruption and provides a firm foundation for radical political views (Germani, 1980) and helps to construct strong resistant identity of the marginalized. Thus the marginalized hold the potentials of revolutionaries. They behave in violent and socially disruptive ways and hold political beliefs of a radical nature (Perlman, 1976).

There are several intertwining among the latent and manifest dimensions of marginalization. Manifested marginalization in the economic front may be related to deprivations in the political, social and cultural fronts of the society and the vice versa. These facets of marginalization may be related to the issues of increased insecurity, lack of political and legal protections, and victimization in the developmental processes and so on. Marginalization again may be related to wider economic, social, cultural and political arrangements and may get institutionalized as a process through the well-knit sociocultural and normative arrangements and interactive social processes. It may be simultaneously cumulative as marginalization is widely shaped within the historically inherited social processes. Thus the relational–cumulative perspective is to take cognizance both the latent and manifest dynamics of the contemporary and historically arranged social processes and institutions, and their sustained interlinkages that shape and reproduce marginalization of vast segment of population in every society.

As against these analysis marginalization as a process is conceptualized as cumulatively acquired and spatially related phenomena of social, economic, cultural and political denials and deprivations, in-securities and uncertainty, hierarchy and domination which get legitimized and reproduces by the functioning of several normative and societal arrangements to relegate several sections of the population at the social margin despite their protests and resistance. As the marginalized people have little resources to alter the normative and societal arrangements through legitimized means, they remain as function of the unequal arrangement of the society; and cause of many of the social unrest, protests and movements. The broad process of socio-economic transition and routinized state action only strengthen the process of marginalization of the marginalized as these actions are executed through the pre-existing societal and insti-tutionalized arrangements. These fomulations will be examined in the context of socio-economic transformation in India, focusing on contemporary West Bengal.

SOCIO-ECONOMIC TRANSITIONS AND THE MARGINALIZED IN INDIA

India stands at the threshold of a buoyant knowledge economy. Sharp increase in the use of ICTs in daily life, exponential growth of knowledge industries, and proliferation of technical and professional manpower, high rate of economic growth and fast occupational diversification now characterize India's economic transition in contemporary world. India has also seen the real growth of national income by 125 per cent in the post-reform period. The annual economic growth rate had shot up to 9.4 per cent in 2007. Amidst all the success, however, there has been quantum increase in the volume of social and economic inequality, hunger, poverty, landlessness, livelihood insecurity, casualization in the workforce, illiteracy, displacement, migration, social instability and vehement social protests, especially of the marginalized segment of the population.

In India 28 per cent of the population lives *below the poverty* line (NSS, 2004-5). In terms of income 34.3 per cent of the population lives *below earning poverty line* earning less than $1 per day while cumulatively 84.4 per cent of the population earn less than $2 per day (UNDP, 2008). More than 92 per cent of the Indian workforce is employed in the unorganized sector of the economy and 77 per cent of the workers in the unorganized sectors do not have even Rs. 20 per day for consumption (National Commission for Enterprises in the Unorganised Sector, Government of India, 2008; NSS, 2004-5). In the rural areas 14.4 per cent households are landless, and 62.5 per cent are either sub-marginal or marginal households (NSS, 2004-5). There are 42.6 million slum dwellers constituting 22.6 per cent of the urban population of the states and union territories reporting slums. More than 91 per cent of the slum population belongs to the 'other' category of workers who mostly work in the unorganized sector. There are 12 million unemployed, 13 million child labour (Census, 2001) (NGO estimate 75 million child labourers), 2 million sex workers (CNN, 2008) in the country. Besides there are more than 360 million illiterates (constituting 35 per cent of the population), more than 60 million primary and middle level school drop-outs (constituting 26.45 per cent of the drop-outs at the primary level, and 49.95 per cent at the middle level) (MHRD, Government of India 2008), 21.9 millions physically handicapped (constituting 2.13 per cent of the population), 77 million aged population (constituting around 8 per cent of the total population). All these categories of population suffer from several immediate economic, social and political deprivations and are either denied or deprived of economic, social and political opportunities of mobility in society.

Significantly all these categories have explicit intertwining with caste, ethnic and gender divisions of society. Scheduled Tribes (ST), Scheduled Castes (SC) and Other Backward Classes (OBC) who form 8.2, 16.2 and 27 per cent respectively of the total population of the country represent not only the lower rung of the Hindu caste order but also concentrate on the low-paying economic activities in the unorganized sectors. Significantly, of all the agricultural labour households, 14.1 per cent are represented by the STs, 34.1 per cent by the SCs and 36.4 per cent by the OBCs (Census, 2001). Around 88 per cent of the STs and SCs, 79.9 per cent of OBCs and 84.5 per cent of the Muslim workers working in the unorganized sector are economically poor and vulnerable (National Commission for Enterprises in the Unorganised Sector, Government of India, 2008). School drop-out rates at the primary and the high school levels among the STs are still 41 and 77 per cent, respectively; and those for the SCs are 37 and 71 per cent respectively. Social and cultural deprivations of the STs, SCs, OBCs and religious minorities have widely remained integrated with the prevailing economic and political opportunity deprivation. The predominant section of these groups experience extreme form of downward social mobility, extra economic coercion, seasonal migration, livelihood insecurity, poverty, unemployment, illiteracy, low wage, resourcelessness, starvation death, social discrimination and ultimately marginalization and social exclusion.

Rural India is in the process of rapid social transformation and getting integrated with the wider world in the wake of globalization. In this context West Bengal has got a special place of prominence as this state has distinguished itself with three uninterrupted decades of communist rule and has been following the reformative Marxist path of social transformation. It has a sizeable proportion of STs, SCs, OBCs and Muslim minority population and has initiated distinctive reformative actions to espouse the cause of the marginized and has a long history of grassroot mobilization by the state, political parties and the civil society organization. These broad processes have affected the existing patterns of marginalization in several ways and it would be worthwhile to examine the emerging dimensions of marginalization of the marginalized within the broad processes of social transformation in rural West Bengal.

DEVELOPMENTAL INITIATIVES AND EMERGING FACETS OF MARGINALIZATION IN CONTEMPORARY A RURAL SOCIETY OF WEST BENGAL

In recent years West Bengal has emerged to be one of the fastest growing states of India with over 8 per cent growth rate of economy. More than 59 per cent of state GDP comes from the service sector of the economy. Industrial growth rate is about 12 per cent. Investment in the IT sector is growing at the rate of 48 per cent. It is a known hub of the trained human resources; and a favourable destination for investment both by the national and multi-national companies. However, a vast segment of West Bengal society is far away from getting integrated with these developmental processes. In a caste-based stratified society in West Bengal, with persisting economic backwardness and social inequality, marginalization of a vast section of population has remained attached to its social structure. Herein the interrelated dynamics of denial, deprivation, insecurities, social hierarchies and political dominations have generated rampant poverty, unemployment, illiteracy, ill-health, and downward mobility of vast section of population. The government of West Bengal with broad guidance from the central government have introduced several legislative and administrative measures since Independence for the removal of these problems that hold the foundation of marginality. These measures envisaged far-reaching structural reforms in the society through rural development and land reform programmes. However, due to the lack of political will and popular initiative from the grassroots for the effective implementation of the measures the pre-existing forms of marginalization persisted in rural West Bengal. The mass movements at the grassroots, like the Tebhaga (1946-7) and the Naxalite (1969-71) movements, though have questioned the processes of persistent marginalization, in effective term have neither been able to remove this process nor alter the systemic arrangements immediately that promote and perpetuate the same. However, a new phase has started since late 1970s to question and demolish the processes of marginalization by implementing the administrative and legislative measures through grassroots mobilization and institutionalized political means.

Since 1977 the United Left Front Government (an alliance of 14 left wing political parties) in West Bengal has been introducing several initiatives to set in motion new processes of social transformation with a view to smoothen economic and social well-being of the rural marginalized; to reverse the process of *proletariatization* of the lower strata of the society and to bring a holt to the process of marginalization of the marginalized. Some of the important initiatives are rigorous implementation of land reforms (especially to acquire and distribute surplus vested lands among the rural poor, provide tenurial security to the tenants through *Operation Barga* Programme), rejuvenation of the Panchayati Raj institutions (to institutionalize collective mobilization of the rural poor at the grassroots), instituting several employment generation programmes like Food For Work (to provide rice, etc., as wage for daily employment in the lean seasons of agricultural operation), West Bengal Rural Employment Guarantee Scheme (to provide at least 100 days of assured employment to every rural household with preference given to the poorest of the poor, SCs, STs, and parents of child labour withdrawn from hazardous occupation), Swarnjayanti Gram Swarozgar Yojana (SGSY) (to provide employment to the families living below the poverty line), Pradhan Mantri Gram Sadak Yojana (PMGSY) (to provide connectivity to the unconnected habitations in the rural areas), Indira Awaas Yojana (IAY) (to help construction of dwelling units for SCs, STs and people living below the poverty line), Provident Funds for Agricultural Labourers (to promote social security for the agricultural labourers), Sishu Siksha Kendras and Anganwadi Centres (to promote educational well-being for the children for the marginalized sections and the poor and workers parents), Self Help Groups programme (to promote the movement of micro credits among women and the other members of marginalized groups), Community Health Care Management Initiative (CHCMI) (to promote health care facilities for the community), Integrated Wastelands Development Programme (IWDP) (to promote the use of wasteland for agricultural use), Comprehensive Area Development Programmes (to promote the process of integrated development for the backward areas of the state), and also a host of other development programmes for the welfare of small cultivators, backward and tribal villages.

The agrarian reform programmes have brought significant changes in the rural society of West Bengal. Over the decades there has been a phenomenal decline in the large, medium and small landholding in the state. Through land reform the United Left Front government of West Bengal has distributed 1.04 million acres of surplus vested land (covering 7.8 per cent of the arable land of the state) among 2.54 million (34 per cent) of the agricultural households. Again 1.1 million acres (covering 8.2 per cent of the arable lands of the state) are brought under the tenancy reform. It has provided occupancy rights to 1.5 million tenants under the Operation Barga programme who altogether constitute 20.2 per cent of the agricultural households (Government of West Bengal, 2002). There has been again a substantial decline in the landless households in the state from 10 per cent in 1961-2 to 6.2 per cent in 2003 (NSSO, 2005).

Land reforms have brought phenomenal change in the agrarian social structure of West Bengal by way of declining the large size and increasing marginal size landholding in the state. Table 2.1 shows

TABLE 2.1: CHANGING PATTERN OF LANDOWNERSHIP IN WB BY CATEGORIES OF LANDHOLDING (IN HECTARE)

Categories of landholding	1961-2	1971-2	1982	1992	2003
Marginal (0-1.00)	 (17.45)	77.62 (27.28)	81.6 (30.33)	85.88 (41.29)	92.06 (58.23)
Small (1.01-2.00)	 (25.97)	12.64 (25.69)	11.5 (28.77)	9.48 (28.11)	5.70 (25.71)
Semi-Medium (2.01-4.00)	 (28.81)	7.30 (27.72)	5.54 (27.23)	3.94 (22.98)	1.40 (11.88)
Medium (4.01-10.00)	 (24.30)	2.39 (18.61)	1.28 (12.12)	0.71 (7.62)	0.20 (4.02)
Large (10.00+)	 (3.38)	0.05 (0.70)	0.08 (1.54)	0.00 (0.00)	0.00 (0.00)
Total	100 (100)	100 (100)	100 (100)	100 (100)	100 (100)

Source: NSS, 1961-2, 1971-2, 1982, 1992 and 2003.

Note: Figures in parentheses are the percentages of the area owned by each category.

that the semi-medium, medium and the large cultivators who altogether comprised more than 9.75 per cent of the rural households and occupied more than 47 per cent of the rural agricultural lands in 1971-2 now comprise only 1.6 per cent of the rural households possessing only 15.9 per cent of the lands (in 2003). As a corollary the proportion of the categories of marginal cultivators has increased from around 78 per cent to 92 per cent and the areas covered under such holding increased from 27.28 to 58.2 per cent during the same period.

Indeed, the success in land reform is to be seen not as an administrative initiative but as an outcome of long drawn political mobilization of the peasantry that has generated a pressure from below for the implementation of the land reform laws and securing political stability to the United Left Front government in the state. Because of sustained political stability the 'government has been motivated by a vision of political, economic and social change. (West Bengal Development Report, 2004). Herein in recent decades the ULF has initiated several administrative and political measures for more private investment in the state for integration of the state economy with the global economic processes. Significantly it has emerged to be a favourable destination of MNCs for investment in industry and Information Technology. Have the new vision for change, new initiative been able to eradicate the economic and social vulnerability of the marginalized section of rural population?.

EMERGING SOCIAL PROCESSES AND THE MARGINALIZED IN WEST BENGAL

Though land reforms and political decentralization through the Panchayati Raj Institutions have helped ensure political stability in the state, and increase in private investment has added to occupational diversification, in all these have not been able to end the process of marginalization of the marginalized. The National Commission of Rural Labour mentions:

> The reforms have been supported by adequate political pressure from below exerted by the articulate and well-organized groups of rural poor. However the other and the less happy side of the picture is that the reforms have hardly helped the rural poor to become economically viable and to overcome the socio-economic barriers keeping them on the periphery of the society, polity and the economy. (NCRL, 1990: 9)

The West Bengal Development Report writes: "Despite some apparent successes in certain sectors, on the whole the process of global integration has not seen any dramatic improvement in the material conditions of most of the population and generally has added to their greater vulnerability and insecurity" (West Bengal Development Report, 2004).

Indeed, the increasing quantum of their vulnerability, insecurity and the processes of keeping them on the periphery of the society, polity and the economy have got rooted in the following interrelated dimensions of rural society of West Bengal.

Increasing Vulnerability of Rural Poor: In West Bengal more than 72 per cent of the population lives in the rural areas. Around 32 per cent of the state's population lives below the poverty line. The successful implementation of land reform programme has been accompanied by the dimension of increasing vulnerability of the marginalized sections of rural population. There has been a sharp decline in the per household landownership from over 1.00 hectare in 1962 to 0.29 hectare in 2003 as against the national average of 0.79 hectare per household in 2003. The decline in the land–man ratio has been accompanied by a phenomenal increase in the category of semi-landless (possessing less than 0.040 hectare of lands) forming 37.4 per cent of the rural households. The NSSO report shows that 98 per cent of these semi-landless households possess only homestead land. The semi-marginal landowning households (possessing 0.041 to 0.50 hectare sizes of land) from another 36.7 per cent of the rural households and the marginal landowning households with 0.51 to 1.00 hectare sizes of land form another 12.41 per cent of the households there. Cumulatively the landless, semi-landless, semi-marginal and marginal cultivators altogether form 92.7 per cent of the rural households there in West Bengal. These households are highly valuable economically though with a different intensity. Table 2.2 shows the emerging patterns of landholding at the bottom of the agrarian hierarchy and the nature of their economic vulnerability in agriculture.

Food Insecurity and Poverty: These households are again highly unsecured so far even as their minimum food requirement is concerned. The average productivity of land has increased in West Bengal. It however, has not altered the state of food insecurity of the

TABLE 2.2: PROPORTIONS OF ECONOMICALLY VULNERABLE HOUSEHOLDS OF WEST BENGAL 2003

Categories of Economically Vulnerable Agrarian Households	Proportion of Rural Households (%)	Extent of Economic Vulnerability Within Agriculture
Landless	6.2	Extremely high
Semi-landless .002-.040 (hectare)	37.4	Extremely high
Semi-marginal 0.041-0.50 (hectare)	36.7	Very high
Marginal 0.51-1.00 (hectare)	12.4	High
Total	92.7	

Source: Compiled from NSSO, 2003.

landless and semi-landless who form 43.6 per cent of rural households. The fact that even with higher agricultural yield of around 22 quintals (the average per hectare rice productivity in West Bengal) per hectare, 49 per cent of the rural households (having lands between 0.041 to 1.00 hectare with less than 0.40 hectare average sizes of holding) gets in an average 5.5 quintals of crops. The average size of the rural household in West Bengal is 5.6 persons. This production is indeed insufficient even to meet the basic food requirement of the household even if all these households have got the highest average yield from their tiny plot of land.

According to the 61st round NSS Report (2004-5) the percentage of rural households not getting enough food in some months of the year is highest in West Bengal (10.6 per cent) among all states and union territories in India. And the percentage of the households that do not get sufficient food everyday in any month of the year is second highest in West Bengal. Though over the years there has been progressive decline in the proportion of population living below the poverty line in West Bengal in rural areas, a vast section of the population still lives in abject poverty. It is reported that more than 35 per cent of the rural population lives below the poverty line there (NSS, 2005).

Declining Work Participation and Downward Mobility in Agriculture: According to the census data in 1971 in the whole of West Bengal

58.43 per cent of the total workers were employed in agriculture (both as cultivators and agricultural labourers); while in 2001 it declined to 44.15 per cent. In rural West Bengal this decline has been from 78 to 58.6 per cent during the same period. Significantly, work participation as cultivators has reduced to half among the rural workers, i.e. from more than 51 per cent in 1961 to 25.52 per cent in 2001, while work participation as agricultural labourers has increased from 19.59 per cent to 31.12 per cent during the same period. These show an increase in the livelihood insecurity of the peasantry. Data shows that the extent of work participation as agricultural labours has been higher among the SCs, STs and OBCs and among the women of these categories. For example, in West Bengal 31 per cent of the tribals work as cultivators while 49 per cent are agricultural labourers; again 61 per cent of the tribal women workforce work as agricultural labourers. This phenomenon is liked more to their resourcelessness, lack of education and capacity building, than to culture alone. Indeed work participation as agricultural labour is conditioned by economic compulsion and not by choice. In Indian society these work is still culturally stigmatized and economically exploitative.

Preponderance of Casual Work Participation: The process of casualization of the workforce has conspicuously marked the process of work participation in rural West Bengal. According to the NSS report (2007), as many as 39.5 per cent of the working population of West Bengal are wage/casual labourers in terms of their engagement with the principal economic activities. Casualization is higher among the rural male with 40.4 per cent than among rural female with 34 per cent. Higher the extent of casualization in workforce, the higher in degree of economic uncertainty and deprivation in society (see Table 2.3).

Increase in Marginal Workers: Besides the preponderance of casual work participation there has been a phenomenal increase in work participation as marginal workers (who get less than 183 days of employment in a year). In 1981 only 2.2 per cent of the total population of the state was marginal workers; in 2001 this is reported to have increased to more than 10 per cent. Over last 20 years there has been fourfold increase of the marginal workers. They altogether form 34 per cent of the total workforce in West Bengal.

TABLE 2.3: DISTRIBUTION OF WORKING POPULATION BY PRINCIPLE ACTIVITY IN WEST BENGAL IN 2006

Categories	Self-Employed	Regular Wage/ Salaried	Wage/Casual Labour	Total Employed
Total	48.3	17.0	34.5	100
Total male	48.2	15.9	35.7	(100)
Total female	47.1	23.6	28.3	(100)
Rural male	50.4	9.1	40.4	(100)
Rural female	50.5	15.5	34.0	(100)
Total rural	50.6	9.9	39.5	(100)

Source: Compiled form NSS, 2007.

Increasing Job Insecurity, Low Wage and Gender Disparity: Work situation of the agricultural labourers in West Bengal, as in most parts of the country, is widely characterized by lack of employment security, seasonal nature of employment, low wages, seasonal and gender-based wage variations, unspecified time schedule of work and lack of social security, primordiality and lack of legal and organizational protection. Despite rigorous grassroots mobilizations, gender-based wage variations continue unabated in West Bengal. According to the latest NSS report the average daily wage for a casual male labourer is Rs. 49.96 and Rs. 40.36 for a female labourer (NSS, 2003). In many parts of the state women labourers still get half the wage of their male counterparts (SinghaRoy, 2004). As the scope for upward mobility has been limited among them due to lack of literacy, training and other resources, they continue to slog for a livelihood.

Increasing Rate of Unemployment: In the period between 1987-8 and 1999-2000 West Bengal witnessed a decrease in the growth of employment in agriculture by 9.48 per cent in spite of growth of income in agriculture. It is to mention here that West Bengal has the second highest rate of rural unemployment in the country with 17 per cent as against the national average of 7.20 per cent. The current status of unemployment among the rural youth (15-29 years) is as high as 26.60 per cent (Planning Commission, 2004).

Increasing Incidences of Migration: The quantum of migration has increased in West Bengal in recent years. Rural migration is now to the extent of 23 per cent and rural male migration is 28.5 per cent. More than 36 per cent of the migrants of the state migrate to the urban areas of other states, and 21 per cent to the urban areas of the same state. The economic cause of migration dominates over other causes (NSS, 2000). As there has been increasing pressure of population in agriculture, a section of the poor peasantry is pushed to seasonally migrate from agriculturally backward areas not only in the developed parts within West Bengal but also outside the state. *Namal* (seasonal migration of the agricultural labourers) in Bankura, Purulia and Midnapur are on the increase. One can easily find migrant Bengali labourers working in large numbers as construction labour, rag pickers, vendors, and maid-servants in Delhi, Punjab, Haryana, Gujarat, Goa, Mumbai and other places of the country; most of these workers have peasant backgrounds and are pushed to migrate out of the state due to declining land–man ratio and increasing unemployment.

Lack of Retention in the School System Among the Youth: In West Bengal majority of the children and the youth in the age group (5-29 years) are in the schooling system. However, a 37.7 per cent high of this population has discontinued studies and another 16 per cent has never attended the school. This phenomenon is more conspicuous among the rural female than rural male (see Table 2.4).

Women do not attend school either because of livelihood insecurity or gender role expectation. Poverty pushes a vast section of the youth to drop-out from the schooling system. Learning deprivation at the early age contributes to capacity deprivation and limited options for vertical social mobility in future.

Horizontal Mobility and Occupational Diversification: Because of increasing unemployment in agriculture a vast section of rural

TABLE 2.4: PERCENTAGE DISTRIBUTION OF PERSONS IN THE AGE GROUP OF 5-29 YEARS NOT ATTENDING SCHOOL IN WEST BENGAL (2006)

Persons	Never-attended	Discontinued/ Drop-out	Total Not Attended	Currently Attending
Persons	15.9	37.7	53.6	46.3
Total male	13.7	38.8	52.5	46.7
Total female	18.3	36.5	54.8	43.9
Rural male	15.4	37.5	52.9	46.3
Rural female	19.6	45.2	54.9	43.5
Total rural	17.4	36.4	53.9	45.0

Source: NSS, 2007.

population has opted for non-agricultural activities in the ruaral areas. According to the NSS report 2005, 34.7 per cent of the rural households with 41.2 per cent of the working population of West Bengal are reported to have non-agricultural activities as primary occupation. Studies conducted at the village level show that in the rural areas though non-agricultural activities have emerged as alternative avenues of employment, and have widened the scope of horizontal social mobility all of these activities are not potentially rewarding to ensure livelihood security (SinghaRoy, 2004). As indicated earlier, this has pushed to migrate a section of the rural workforce in the prosperous parts of the country.

Vulnerability of the SC and ST Population: Of the total rural population of West Bengal 28, 6 and 29 per cent are represented by the SCs, STs and Muslims respectively. The situation of the ST and SC in the agrarian economy of the state is very precarious. Around 94 per cent of the rural households of these social categories belong to the categories of landless/semi-landless/marginal cultivators. A glimpse of the status of the SCs, STs, OBCs in the state and others is given in Table 2.5.

The STs at 14 per cent have the highest extent of landlessness followed by the SCs at around 6 per cent. This phenomenon is lowest among the OBCs with only 1.5 per cent landless households. More than 45 per cent of the STs, 51 per cent of the SCs and 28 per cent of the OBCs belong to the category of landless and semi-landless rural households. Though all these social categories have the

TABLE 2.5: EMERGING PATTERNS OF LANDHOLDINGS AMONG VARIOUS SOCIAL CATEGORIES IN WEST BENGAL IN 2003

Sizes of Landholding in Hectares	Scheduled Tribes	Scheduled Castes	Other Backward Classes	Other	All Categories
Landless	14.0	5.9	1.5	5.8	6.1
0.002 to 0.040	31.2	44.7	26.6	35.6	37.4
0.041 to 0.50	31.3	33.6	39.5	38.7	36.7
0.51 to 1.00	16.1	9.3	20.6	12.6	12.4
1.01 to 2.00	5.8	5.3	9.8	5.4	5.7
2.01 to 4.00	1.7	1.1	1.9	1.5	1.4
4.01+	0.0	0.1	0.2	0.3	0.2
All Sizes	100.0	100.0	100.0	100.0	100.0

Source: NSSO, 2003.

households with high concentration in the semi-landless and semi-marginal landowning households, the OBCs have a relatively better representation so far as the marginal and above categories of landholdings are concerned. However, notwithstanding these variations the fact remains that agricultural and other labourers are predominantly drawn from these sections of the society who are pushed to work there for a subsistence living out of economic compulsion. It is again that the extent of unemployment and poverty is high among these sections of the population.

There has been high concentration of the non-literate population among the SCs, STs. According to 2001 census more than 41 per cent of the SCs and 57 per cent of the SC females; 57 per cent of the total STs and 61 per cent of the ST female population are non-literates. Due to the preponderance of illiteracy, there have been high concentration of agricultural labourers and marginal workers among them. According to 2001 census more than 26 per cent of the SC workers are marginal workers, while 32 per cent of the main workers are agricultural labourers and 20 per cent are cultivators. As high as 34.5 per cent of the ST workers are marginal workers, while 24 per cent of the main workers are cultivators and 45 per cent are agricultural labourers. There is a positive co-relationship between the high concentration of work participation as agricultural labourers with high incidences of poverty, illiteracy, livelihood insecurity and unemployment among these groups. Representation of SCs and the STs in the government jobs is to the extent of 13.2 and 3.3 per cent respectively and their participation in political decision-making bodies never crosses the prescribed levels of reservation.

Gender Disparity and low Status of Women: West Bengal shows high intensity of gender disparity in all areas, i.e. literacy, sex ratio, work participation, and participation in the decision-making processes. According to the National Human Development Report 2001, the Gender Disparity Index (1991) for West Bengal was 0.63, compared to an all-India average of 0.67. This places West Bengal at a rank of 28 out of 32 states (NHDP, 2001). Because of persisting gender disparity in human development, vast section of women in West Bengal have remained to be socially insecured, economically exploited and politically disempowered. This has been highly obvious for the women from the SC, ST, OBC and religious minority communities.

Vulnerability of the Minorities: Deprivation of the Muslim religious minorities in West Bengal has worsened in recent years. They have not only low level of literacy and low level of political participation, but also high concentration in the unorganized sector for the work participation. The Sachar Committee Report has highlighted the most glaring cases of Muslims' deprivation in government jobs in the state of West Bengal 'where, according to common perception, egalitarianism has been the cherished norm in all walks of life. In West Bengal where almost 25 per cent population practices the Muslim faith, their share in government jobs is a paltry 4.2 per cent (Sachar Committee, 2007).

Sustained Social Hierarchy and Cultural Domination

As socially these people belong to the low castes, tribes, women and other vulnerable sections of the society they are subjected to the social hierarchy and cultural domination as articulated by the traditional values of caste, gender and ethnicity. They are frequently made victims of stereotypical social image of ***chasa*** (rustic), ***abhadra*** (uncivilized), ***bhoranga*** (dull), and so on in the rural areas. These domination and discrimination are maintained through the construction and reproduction of Bhadralok domination in Bengali society. The Left politics has cultivated a space for the dominance of Left supporting Bhardralok leadership in rural areas who provid leadership for political mobilization at all levels (SinghaRoy, 2004). Much of the political influence within the CPIM is also wielded by the middle class and these Bhadraloks (Kohli, 1983). Vast sections of the marginalized have remained to be tied within the ***abhadra*** domain of culture. Hence notwithstanding the representations of a limited few of the marginalized in the local decision-making bodies, majority of them remain politically dominated and disempowered.

Insecurities and Uncertainties

Contemporary West Bengal stands at the threshold of a fast transition of economy, phenomenal occupational diversification and expansion of the services sector of the economy. However, a vast chunk of the marginalized people has been unable to get integrated with the emerging transition of the society and the economy. The persisting problems of landlessness, sub-marginal landholding, unemployment, low wage, gender-based wage variation, downward mobility in agriculture, seasonal migration, poverty, casualization and increasingly 'marginal status' as worker have widely added to the persistent social and economic uncertainties of the marginalized people. The quantum of such uncertainties has been high for ST, SC, OBC and the religious minority groups.

Developmental initiatives as initiated by the ULF government have not been able to eradicate such uncertainties. Significantly this uncertainty has increased for a section of the rural people who possess little education, skill, training, social networking abilities, potential for alternative options of employment and livelihood security to get integrated with the changing economy. They have been only partly integrated into the emerging economy by becoming casual, migrant, marginal, low-paid workforce. Herein as the economic initiatives have largely failed to bring a halt to their marginality, a vast section of the rural poor follow the political path of collective mobilization, under different political pursuits, to widen the options to get rid of these uncertainties.

Political Mobilization, Dependency Relations and Resistance

West Bengal has long been the site of organized social protests of the marginalized, manifested in different issues over a long historical period of time. The Rajbanshi movement (1938-47) took place to consolidate the caste idendity of the Rajbanshi caste people and a claim for their khastriya status in society. The Tebhaga movement (1946-7) took place based on the slogan 'land to the tiller' and a demand for 66 per cent of the produce of land, instead of 50 per cent, by the sharecroppers. The Naxalite movement (1967-71) again demanded the implementation of the 'land to the tiller' philosophy through seizure of state power by radical means. The Gurkha Land movement (1980-6) and its recent resurgence demands for separate statehood for the hill tribes in the Darjeeling district of the state. Similarly the Kamtapuri movement of the Rajbanshi started in the late 1970s demands for separate statehood of the Rajbanshi people in the northern part of Bengal based on their distinctive culture, language, history and ethnic identity. The very recent (2009-10) resurgent Naxalite/Maoist movement in the southern part of Bengal highlights, through violent means, issues of economic backwardness, poverty, cultural segregation, political disempowerment of the rural poor. The movements of the Krishi Jami Suraksha Committee (Committee to Protect Agricultural Land and the Bhumi Ucced Pratorodh Committee (Committee to Resist Eviction from Land) in Singur and Nandigram respectively in the southern part of the state in 2007-8 by the poor agriculturalists against the initiatives of the state government for acquisition of cultivable lands for industrial purpose have added several new dimensions to the culture of protest and collective mobilizations of the marginalized.

As indicated earlier the ULF government of West Bengal has used grassroots mobilization as the key vehicle for the implementation of the rural development and land reform programmes. These mobilizations are also used as the instruments to keep the marginalized attached to the political party and to the strategy of popular governance. However, institutionalization of mobilization of the marginalized has reinforced their marginalization in rural West Bengal. Political mobilizations of the 1970s strongly impeded the primordial forms of domination of the marginalized. However, grassroots mobilizations of the 1980s and thereafter have introduced tacitly large-scale domination of political party activists over the marginalized people by converting the political capacity to distribute into a tool for domination by the political party in power.

Due to persisting un/under-employment, poverty and livelihood insecurity vast sections of the rural population long to be beneficiaries of development programmes and schemes. Benefits are distributed through the gram panchayats; and the panchayat members many a time distribute these as personalized benefits. As power has become personalized, malpractices have also become rampant in the panchayat functioning (Williams, 1999: 235). Besides, benefits are distributed among the party affiliates as normal practice (Ruud, 1999: 262-3). Indeed the capacity to provide benefits has not only helped the communist parties to attract more and more participation for grassroots mobilization, but has also kept the vulnerable section dependant on them for their economic and social security (SinghaRoy 2001: 204). In the last few decades there have been unprecedented growth of Communist party workers in West Bengal. It is widely due to the fact that it has the power to distribute patronage among the followers (Chatterjee, 1998: 132). The politics of distribution has been deep rooted with the inculcation of a culture of dependency of the marginalized on the political party in power and on a regular basis on their workers.

Efforts are made in contemporary West Bengal to integrate vast areas of the life and consciousness of the marginalized people into the hegemony of the state through various means. Co-option of civil society activism has been an effective tool towards this endeavour. At the local level most of the civil society institutions have been subject to politicization and co-option by the state. They have emerged to be 'the state in disguise' as leaders of the political parties in power play a key role in the functioning of these institutions.

Civil society always plays crucial roles in developing organized contestations against the hegemony of the state, making public criticisms of power, suggesting several viable alternatives to the on-going arrangements of domination, and in generating awareness among the marginalized sections of the society about their rights and entitlements. However, in the well-knit nexus between the state, political party and grassroots mobilization, most of the organs of civil society have been co-opted in the political fold of the state. In the management of the local civil society organization (viz., school, clubs, committees for cultural activities like youth and local festivals, etc.) the party workers and political representatives dominate to smoothen and regularize co-option. This co-option is both ideological and tactical and helps retain domination of the political party in power in the society at time through coercive means. As the beneficiary driven economic options are limited in their potential to break the barriers of marginality, and the political options are also coersive, the marginalized suffer the brunt of marginalization cumulatively. Within these processes the further marginalization of the marginalized has not only got legitimized but also reproduced.

In the wake of globalization and introduction of new and liberal economic order the marginalized people have also emerged to be paradoxically posited. Under the given scenario the state has emerged to express more commitment to the global market forces than to the cause of the marginalized people. The state government has of late accepted rapid industrialization as the panacea for all economic ills in society. Accordingly it has offered concessions to the magnates of the private sector and multinationals to set-up industries in the state. But in the process the government has ended up robbing Peter to pay Paul, grabbing agricultural land (without paying adequate compensation to the farmers) and subsidizing the investor industrialists by huge tax reliefs and other concessions that eat into the state exchequer. The dissenting voices were initially ignored; and then vehemently crushed. In this process the state government has borrowed from its old Stalinist basket, all the methods of institutional coercion, and physical intimidation to suppress dissent and keep civil society under its control (Banerjee, 2008).

In the emergins world order the contemporary state has emerged to be stronger then ever. While at the grassroots the state has been successful in co-opting the selected collective initiatives with the state, at a wider level it has got all the support from multinational companies and global forces to condition and contain the movements of the marginalized. However, the dissenting voices and organized resistance of the marginalized have surfaced in several juncture of transition of the society notwithstanding its hagemonic and coersive character.

Sustained Marginality and Construction of Resistant Identities

Social identities of are never permanently fixed. Rather these get constructed and deformulated both in terms of the situational interactions with the surroundings and the socio-historical experiences of the individuals. As the individual experiences becomes the reflections of collective selves ('we'), many of pre-existing identities either get reformulated or reinforced to response to the collective need of the respective group.

In the context of sustained marginalization and increasing socio-cultural disorientations and uncertarities caused by penetration of new economic and social forces on the one hand and lack of knowledge and skill to get integrated with these forces on the other, the marginalized fall back on the traditional economic and primordial social resources to construct alternative political view and reinforce pre-existing cultural identities. The Gurkha and Rajbanshi identity movements have largely been shaped by the socio-economic denials, deprivations and dominations and reinforcing of the pre-existing cultural identities of these population. Contemporary West Bengal has also witnessed the resurgence of minority identity of the marginalized Muslim population. Though their political and ideological positions have not remained fixed, religions ethnic identity has come to play an important role in recent years. The Ulema-e-Hind is engaged in articulating the issues of social, economic and political deprivation of the Muslim minority population of West Bengal.

In the wake of increasing threat of the dispossession of land caused by the state's attempt to establish TATA Nano motor factory in

Singur and SEZ in Nandigram marginalized construct a protest identity to develop resistance against such dispossession. It is reflected in this collective mobilization to protect the dignity of '*Ma, Mati or Manush*' (mother, land and agriculturalists). Significantly the collective resistance of the marginalized against the forceful acquistion of land is not apolitical. Rather they develop political affiliation with ideologies of diverse pursuits to develop interconnected resistence against domination. Hence they question: 'Shaner Nano Dhaner Khete Keno?' (Why the Nano motor of the city on the agricultural field?). Indeed they tried to reconstruct the agriculturalist identity against the domination of the state.

The process of mobilization of the marginalized and manifestations of their protests through organized movements have remained rooted and interlinked both with the local and wider social, economic and political processes of the society. At times the dissenting voices of the marginalized are manifested following the caste and ethnic routes. While in many other cases these protests are articulated to espouse the economic cause of the rural poor. Significantly, the overwhelming participation in these protests and resistance has been from the ST, SC, OBC and ethnic marginalized communities. The mobilizations initiated by Maoists in Lalgarh have raised the issues of social, economic and political deprivations of the tribal and other marginalized groups. Persisting economic, social and cultural denials and deprivations, insecurities, and uncertainties, domination and subjugation and reproduction and legitimization of these processes by state and the society have given birth to the protests and movements of the marginalized. At time these protests and movements based on caste or ethnic identity have remained localized as the resistant identity movement exclusively, while in many juncture of the transition of society the marginalized have been part of larger social protests and social movement that addressed the issues of oppression, domination and exploitation. As the developmental initiatives, reformation state actions and strategies of co-options of grassroot initiative have not been able to redress the process of marginalization, the protest and resistance of the marginalized continue in one form or the other against the dominant societal arrangements which are intertwined socially, culturally, economically and politically.

Marginalized communities however are not a homogeneous one, so are the reasons behind the construction and reconstruction of their identities. With the penetration of new social and economic forces they are emerging to be socially, culturally and economically de-contextualized, and are also in the process of reconstruction of multiple identities criss-crossing the boundaries of pre-existing social collectivities. These are also fluid and diversified; getting fragmented at one end and unified at another. As the secular economic and political bases of marginality are not eradicated, many of the non-secular bases of marginal identity have now come into play to hegemonize over the other bases. The issues of marginality are now in the process of getting co-opted into religious, ethnic and other forms of collective identities. These identities also have emerged to be potential political resource to organize protest by becoming effective means to attain political end.

Sustained marginalization and mobilization of the marginalized very often lead to the formation of resistant identities against the emerging forms of domination. These are generated by those actors that are in positions/conditions devaluated and/or stigmatized by the logic of domination, thus building trenches of resistance and survival on the basis of principles different from or opposed to those permeating the institutions of society. The identity for resistance leads to the formation of communes or communities. It constructs new forms of collective resistance against unbearable oppression, usually on the basis of the identities that were apparently defined by history, geography or biology making it easier to essentialize the boundaries of resistance (Castells, 1997).

CONCLUSION

Historically vast sections of Indian population, like those of West Bengal, have experienced all varieties of denials and deprivations, insecurities and uncertainties, social hierarchies and dominations. The core elements of marginalization are transmitted from one generation to another despite periodic resistance. The contemporary social process and institutional arrangements, that have emerged to be highly interrelated in the wake of globalization, have reinforced the historically accumulated elements of marginalization making it situationally relational and historically cumulative. Marginalization continues progress in its own course both through the relational and cumulative dynamics. The realities of contemporary social, economic, cultural and political marginality are posited to have strong positive correlationship with low access to education, illiteracy and training opportunities, low levels of capacity building and social and human development. These deprivations in turn have not only contributed to low levels of access to the channels of upward social mobility, lack of access to new livelihood options, lack of effective political participation, but also to the sustenance of poverty, unemployment, ill-health and perpetuation of domination and hegemony on them by the dominant sections of the society. Significantly the marginalized have neither been excluded totally from the labour force nor from the social, economic and political intercourse. They continue to survive within these arrangements as subservient to dominant order with the syndroms of multiple marginality that have remained historically rooted and get culturally legitimized and reproduced in their specific areas through the functioning of the caste, tribal, gender ethnic arrangements on the one hand and the dominant state order on the other.

In recent years the quantum of such marginalization has got accentuated with the emergence of added economic uncertainties, loss of traditional sources of livelihood, and devaluation of their cultural identities, increasing political apathy on their drudgery of lives and social dislocations. The state failure to stop the processes of relational and cumulative marginalization, on the one hand and increasing state patronage to industrialization and economic liberalization at the neglect of the marginalized on the other has helped to rejuvenate varieties of collective identities with new language of protest and violence in recent years. The social history of India is replete with the repeated resistance and protests of the marginalized that have questioned the bases of their marginalization. Significantly these protests against sustained marginalization have produced varieties of protests with consolidation of resistant identities. The process of proliferation of resistant identities emerging out of prolonged process of marginalization now have posed severe threats to the secular and democratic foundations of the country resorting to religious and ethnic fundamentalism and collective extremism, and becoming the expression of the exclusion of the excluded by the excluders (Castells 1997). This potential threat indeed can only be encountered by developing positive correlationship between inclusive development, equity and peace; economic development of the country and social development of the marginalized; good governance and social sensitivity of the state and proactive civil society activism.

REFERENCES

Banerjee, S. (2008), 'A Political Cul-de-sac: CPI (M)'s Tragic Denouement', *Economic and Political Weekly*, vol. XLIII, no. 42, pp. 12-15.

Castells, M. (1997), *The Rise of the Network of Society*, Blackwell: Oxford University Press.

———. (1983), *The City and the Grass Roots: A Cross-Cultural Theory on Urban Social Movements*, Berkeley: University of California Press.

Chatterjee, P. (1998), *The Present History of West Bengal: Essays in Political Criticism*, New Delhi: Oxford University Press.

Dickie-Clark, H.F. (1996), 'The Theory of the Marginal Man and its Critics' in H.F. Dickie-Clark (ed.), *The Marginal Situation*, London: Routledge and Kegan Paul.

Ferguson, M. (1992), 'The Mythology About Globalization', *European Journal of Communication*, vol. 7, no. I: 69-93.

Germani, G. (1980), *Marginality*, New Jersey: Transaction Books.

Giddens, A. (1982), 'Power, the Dialectics of Control and Class Structuration', in A. Giddens (ed.), *Social Class and Division of Labour*, Cambridge: Cambridge University Press.

———. (1991), *Modernity and Self-identity*, Cambridge: Polity Press.

Gist, N.P. and R.D. Wright (1973), *Marginality and Identity: Anglo-Indians as a Racially Mixed Minority in India*, Leiden: E.J.Brill.

Gordon, M.M. (1964), *Assimilation in American Life: The Role of Race, Religion, and National Origins*, New York: Oxford University Press.

Government of West Bengal (2004), West Bengal Human Development Report 2004, Kolkata: Development and Planning Department.

Government of India (1971, 1981, 1991, 2001), *Census of India*, New Delhi: Ministry of Information and Broadcasting.

Government of India (2007), *Sachar Committee Report*, New Delhi: Ministry of Minority Affairs.

Germani, Gino (1972), 'Aspectos Teoricos de la Marginalidad', *Revista Paraguaya de Sociologia*, 9, no. 30 (op. cit. Parlmen, 1976).

Hammer, T. (2003), 'Youth Unemployed of Social Exclusion in Europe: A Comparative Study', *Journal of Sociology*, 33, no. 6 (1928), pp. 881-93.

Hoggart, K. (2005), 'Inequalities at the Core: A Discussion of Regionality in the EU and UK' in M. Phillips (ed.), *Contested Worlds: Introduction to Human Geography*, Aldersort: Ashgate Publishing Ltd.

Johannessen, A. (1997), 'Marginalitet som Socialpolitisk utfordring', paper presented at the 9th Nordic Society Research Seminar, cf. Moller (2002), 'Understanding Integration and Differentiation: Inclusion, Marginalization and Exclusion', www.eurozine.comurozine.

Kohli, A. (1987), *The State and Poverty in India: The Politics of Reform*, Cambridge: Cambridge University Press.

Kolaja, J. and S.J. Kaplan (1960), 'Case Study in Multiple Marginality', *Phylon*, 21, p. 338.

Lewis, Oscar (1996), 'The Culture of Poverty', *Scientific American*, 215, no. 4, pp. 19-25.

Lind, J. and I.H. Moller (1999), 'The Labour Market in the Process of Change? Some Critical Comments', CID Studies, no. 22.

Luhmann, N. (1982), *Differentiation of Society*, New York: University of Columbia Press.

Mann, H. (1985), *The Sources of Social Power*, vol. 1, Cambridge: Cambridge University Press.

Marx, K. (1852) (rpt. 1974), Excerpts from 'The Class Struggle in France 1848–1850', and 'The Eighteenth Brumaire of Louis Bonaparte', in K. Marx, and F. Engels, *Selected Works*.

Merton, Robert (1957) (ed.), *Social Theory and Social Structure*, New York: The Free Press.

Ministry of Human Resources Development (2008), *Annual Report 2008*, New Delhi: Government of India.

Moller, I.H. (1998), Understanding Integration and Differentiation: Inclusion, Marginalisation and Exclusion. http:/www.eurozine.com/articles/2002-6-21-moller-en.html

Mullaly, B. (2007), 'Oppression: The Focus of Structural Social Work' in B. Mullay (ed.), *The New Structural Social Work*, Don Mills Ontario: Oxford University Press; pp. 252-86.

Myrdal, G. (1944), *An American Dilemma*, New York: Harper and Brothers.

NSSO (1961-62, 1971-72, 1982, 199, 2003, 2005, 2007), Report of National Sample Survey, Ministry of Statistics and Programme Implementation, New Delhi: Government of India.

National Commission on Rural Labour (1990), *Report of the National Commission on Rural Labour*, New Delhi: Government of India.

National Commission for Enterprises in the Unorganised Sector (2008), Report of the National Commission for Enterprises in the Unorganised Sector, New Delhi: Government of India.

Park, R.E. (1982), 'Human Migration and the Marginal Man', *American Journal of Sociology*, 33.

Park, Robert E. (1928), 'Human Migration and the Marginal Man', *American Journal of Sociology*, vol. 33: 881-93.

Parleman, J.E. (1976), *The Myth of Marginality: Urban Poverty and Politics in Rio de Janeiro*, London: University of California Press.

Planning Commission (2001), *Tenth Five Year Plan 2002-2007*, New Delhi: Planning Commission, GOI.

Redfield, Robert (1959), *The Folk Culture of Yucatan*, Chicago: University of Chicago Press.

Rudd, A.E. (1999), 'From Untouchable to Communist: Wealth, Power and

Status among the Supporters CPM in Rural Bengal', in B. Rogaly et al. (eds.), *Sonar Bangla, Agricultural Growth and Agrarian Change in West Bengal and Bangladesh*, New Delhi: Sage.

Sen, A. (2000), 'Social Exclusion: A Critical Assessment of the Concept and Its Relevance', A paper prepared to the Asian Development Bank.

SinghaRoy, D.K. (2004), *Peasant Movements in Post Colonial India: Dynamics of Mobilisation and Identity*, New Delhi: Sage.

———. (2005), 'Peasant Movements in Contemporary India', *Economic and Political Weekly*, 24 December.

Stavenhagen, Rudolfo (1970), 'Marginality, Participation, and Agrarian Structure in Latin America', Bulletin 7.

Stewart, A. (2001), *Theories of Power and Domination*, London: Sage.

Tonnies, F. (1957), *Community and Society*, East Lansing: Michigan State University Press.

UNDP (1995), 'Declaration of the Social Development Summit', Copenhagen, New York: UN.

——— (1993), *UNDP and Civil Society*, New York: UNDP.

——— (1996), *Human Development Report 1996,* New Delhi: Oxford University Press.

——— (2007), *Human Development Report 2007,* New Delhi: Oxford University Press.

——— (2008), *Human Development Report 2008,* New Delhi: Oxford University Press.

Wieviorka (2005), 'After New Social Movements', *Social Movements Studies*, vol. 4, no. 1, pp. 1-19.

Williams, G. (1999), 'Panchayati Raj and the changing Micro Politics in West Bengal', in B. Rogaly et al. (eds), *Sonar Bangla? Agricultural Growth and Agrarian Change in West Bengal and Bangladesh*, New Delhi: Sage.

World Bank (1997), *World Development Report 2007*, New Delhi: Oxford University Press.

CHAPTER 3

The Global Poor and Social Justice

MAREK HRUBEC

INTRODUCTION

Pursuing social justice in the contemporary global context has to deal with an issue of *un*recognized rights-agents and *mis*recognized rights-holders. One of the reasons why the global poor as the marginalized are misrecognized is that rights-agents are not specified precisely in relation to their obligations in the new global economic and legal arrangements. If we want to help solve the problem of global social justice and develop an alternative to the contemporary order, we have to define properly whose obligations have to be prescriptive, be it nation states, transnational corporations or international financial institutions.

This paper analyses global social injustice and a potential for social development in relation to the social rights of the global poor as the marginalized. It articulates of an extra-territorial recognition at right-holders by means of the development of a theory of social recognition at the supranational level. Part two of the paper differentiates between a traditional subject of misrecognition and the marginalized global poor. I stress that we have to respect a specific kind of struggle for recognition of the global poor. In part three, I articulate contemporary legal possibilities of extra-territorial recognition that are bound to the nation states hitherto. These possibilities are spread in the international legal treaties, e.g. the International Covenant of Economic, Social and Cultural Rights. Part four concentrate on an extension of extra-territorial recognition in terms of the regulation of transnational capital, especially of corporations and financial institutions. Part five, shows the insufficient possibilities of extra-territorial recognition and a need of supranational recognition.

I take note that the nation states as fading rights-agents perceive limits of their extra-territorial recognition of the persons in other countries *vis-à-vis* the rising power of a transnational capital. Transnational corporations (TNC) and international financial institutions (IFI) have gained control over many aspects of economic and financial spheres during the last decades, and their impact has created problems for many people, especially in the Third World.

The analysis of the current international legal structures can clarify the limits of the expected legal influence of the nation states. The weakness of the individual states to apply extra-territorial recognition and control activities of TNCs and IFIs need not be only the bad news. It could also provide motivation for creating transnational and global regulative mechanisms in favour of social justice. It seems to be a dynamics of the historical development from misrecognition unsolved at the national and international levels to a transnational and global level of recognition. Social agents dissatisfied by contemporary international solutions could be transformed into subjects of societal change who would require new global institutional structures of social justice.

Therefore, the increase of influence of TNCs and IFIs in these decades and their inadequate national and international regulation creates misrecognition as a motivational condition of demand and establishment of new supranational and global arrangements. In the background, there are discontents and objectives of those who suffer from hunger and severe poverty in the contemporary order even if their dissent has not received enough public articulation yet as traditional subjects of moral and political protest have.

AN IDENTIFICATION OF THE MISRECOGNIZED SUBJECTS

An elimination of social injustice is determined from below if it stems from the requirements of the damaged people. The sources of their resistance are articulated in the framework of experiences concerning a violation of expected recognition. In his theory of social conflicts, Axel Honneth states the 'processes of societal change are to be explained with reference to the normative claims that are structurally inherent in relations of mutual recognition'.[1] Misrecognition can be transformed into the motivational basis for resistance. In order to identify motivations for change, we have to realize that experiences of disrespect play a role of the catalyst of hurt feelings that can be generalized and transformed into a grammar of social conflicts. In this way, we can indicate the logic of social conflicts that explains the dynamic of misrecognition and recognition of the people.

Such an explanation requires an intersubjective articulation of misrecognition within a community. The shared ideas of violated expectations make possible an identification of the social causes of injuries and their use in collective protests: 'as soon as ideas of this sort have gained influence within a society, they generate a subcultural horizon of interpretation within which experiences of disrespect . . . can then become the moral motives for a collective "struggle for recognition".'[2]

Social agents affected and dissatisfied by the contemporary solutions of global social injustice are in the process of becoming the subjects of societal change who can ask not only for the development of contemporary national and international legal instruments but also the creation of new supranational and global institutional legal structures. The current empowering of TNCs and IFIs is followed by reactions of the misrecognized people, i.e. by the protests of unemployed and exploited people, social movements such as social forums at various levels from local to global ones, and also the discontent of the masses of dying and poor people, especially in the South.

In spite of the fact that the mass media and the majority of population of the Western countries almost ignore millions of people who suffer from hunger and severe poverty everyday, it does not mean that they do not exist. We have to regard and respect those people as a specific kind of protesters against the contemporary global regime. Of course, a successful protest requires the articulation and means of its demonstration that must be strong enough to be influential. That is the reason why a potential subject of societal change living under the worst living conditions mostly in the South is almost invisible. But those people call for a change by means of their own medium of expression. They articulate claims by means of their *everyday* struggles for solving problems connected to satisfying elementary conditions of their survival in severe poverty. Drawing a parallel to slaves who were not considered human beings by many people before the abolition of slavery, today those suffering from hunger and extreme poverty have not really been recognized as a protesting subject by the majority of the people yet.[3]

However, global poverty claims attention. The Annual Report 2007 of the United Nations Development Program states that the gap between the poor and the rich is growing. Two per cent of the richest adults own more than 50 per cent of 'the global household wealth' and 50 per cent of the poorest adults own less than 1 per cent of that wealth.[4] In this social order, social injustice pushes millions of people into various forms of poverty. Forty-five per cent of humankind is living under the poverty line, defined by the World Bank by means of $2/day; 18 per cent of people are reported to be living under the $1/day. About 18 million people die every year, i.e. about 50,000 everyday, because of problems related to poverty.[5] Over 10 million of them are children under age five especially from developing countries.[6] It means that the annual poverty-related deaths are higher than the annual deaths during World War II. From this point of view, we experience the deadliest epoch in human history.

The Millennium Declaration that was adopted in the Millennium Summit in 2000 formulates core goals focused on poverty, gender equality, international trade, etc. These targets, developed as the Millennium Development Goals, are to be achieved by 2015. States have planned 'to halve by the year 2015, the proportion of the world's people whose income is less than $1 a day and the proportion of people who suffer from hunger'; and 'by the same date, to have reduced maternal mortality by three quarters, and under-five child mortality by two-thirds, of their current rates'.[7] If the child death rate of 1990 has to be diminished, as it is required, it 'would mean *just* 4 million child deaths in year 2015' (emphasis added).[8] The question could be raised if we really want to only decrease these deaths by 2015? Do we really mean only to halve the number of people suffering from hunger?[9]

However, humanitarian aid in practice is even worse than the modest proposals of the Millennium Development Goals. According to the UN Human Development Report, if the contemporary 'trend continues . . . from 2003 to 2015 the accumulated human cost of missing the target (i.e. the Millennium Development Goals) will be 41 million dead children' (as is given in Figure 3.1).[10]

It is a fact that dying people suffering from hunger and severe poverty are not too visible to most people. Their discontent and objectives are not formed into pictures that are apparent in every respect today. In this sense, there is no alternative strong enough to compete with the contemporary order. But as soon as we try to identify normative claims of the global poor who experience social misrecognition, we should not be fixed only on the normative

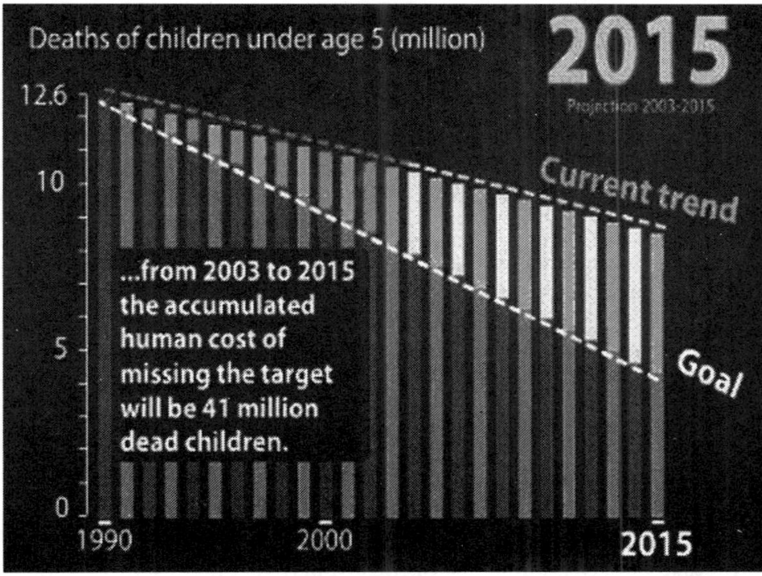

Source: UNDP, *Human Development Report 2005*, Human Development Trends, 2005.

FIGURE 3.1: CHILD DEATHS—THE CUMULATIVE HUMAN COST OF MISSED TARGET

objectives that have already received public articulation.[11] The people get accustomed to expect a form of discontent which is typical of the traditional subject of moral and political protest, i.e. labour movements, the proletariat and new social movements that reflect various kinds of activist movements oriented to peace, ecology, gender, multi-culturalism, etc. Incidentally, already the term social movement invites us to implicate a move. However, the masses of people suffering from hunger and severe poverty are tightly bound to the places of their everyday life and, metaphorically taken, almost cannot 'move' in order to protest while globalization winners can 'fly' easily. The global poor represent a different kind of movement. It is a movement based especially on everyday local struggles for survival that are not too visible.

Of course, focusing on the classical and the new social movements is relevant. However, in this manner spread in the public sphere within the contemporary mass media, social suffering can be inadvertently diminished to the publicly visible discontent of the activist movements. Such an approach to social suffering could ignore the marginalized everyday forms of feelings of social injury that have not been publicly noticed yet or received only a little or temporal attention. However, the social experience of injustice that has been deprived publicity could be the most pressing one, as the example of the global poor suffering from hunger and severe poverty shows.

Although a publicly articulated experience of social injustice plays an important role in struggles for justice, it could not be a criterion of relevance.[12] An application of this affirmative criterion would reproduce the dominant kinds of discontent and could not come down with other forms of social suffering which should also be a legitimate source of our attention. It would maintain restriction on the current level of articulation of misrecognition.

In the debate with Nancy Fraser, Axel Honneth is right, on the one side, when he argues that Fraser underestimates social movements other than those that received public recognition.[13] Thereupon she reduces her analysis and aims for the publicly visible present-day social movements. However, on the other side, Honneth does not reflect that Fraser studies important global issues, requisitioning their incorporation into the theory, particularly the changing role of the nation states in the global context.[14] From this point of view, Honneth underestimates a global scope of analysis. In the same way as his research takes into account the relevant movements of the past, it should not ignore the contemporary significant changes. On the one hand, the theory needs responsiveness in respect of the fact that the dissent of the global poor has not evolved into the manifest powerful and sometimes militant forms that working class movements and the new social movements have demonstrated. On the other hand, an understanding of the discontent of the marginalized global poor and their normative claims necessitates a study of the contemporary international and transnational arrangements in order to address the needs of the global poor as well as limits that block them.

My argument is that it is requisite to examine also everyday struggles of social recognition even if they have not received much public attention and, at the same time, develop a social research of the global constellations, especially in the light of the global poor. And if we accept the premises that there is the fact of millions of people dying of hunger- and poverty-related causes, especially in the

South, and that there could be serious protests in the form of the social experience of misrecognition that has not been in the centre of public attention, we should admit that we have to do with the biggest protest movement in human history. Then, the theoretical articulation has to be sensitive enough to realize the human catastrophe that calls for a transnational and supranational solution.

Seeing that some kinds of recognition are already embedded in the international legal documents, let us see what contemporary legal obligations that could help eliminate such a catastrophe are there because it would make no sense to invent something that was already at least formally guaranteed. We will find out whether the discontent of the global poor could find at least some legal grounds there. At any rate, their discontent and normative objectives can be revealed and articulated against a background of the normative legal constraints.

EXTRA-TERRITORIAL RECOGNITION

'Poverty is a violation of basic human rights', argues the United Nations High Commissioner for Human Rights.[15] The Universal Declaration of Human Rights pronounces various rights, together with 'the right to a standard of living adequate for the health and well being . . . including food, clothing, housing and medical care,'[16] and, in relation to a cross-border reach, it states that '[e]veryone is entitled to a social and international order in which rights and freedoms . . . can be fully realized'.[17] Basic social and economic rights are legally specified in the International Covenant on Economic, Social and Cultural Rights (ICESCR). The Covenant contains a state-centric approach,[18] and it has international validity. Originally it was adopted unanimously by the General Assembly of the United Nations,[19] and now it is ratified by more than 150 states of the various cultural, economic and political regimes.[20] The Covenant states that 'in no case may a people be deprived of its own means of subsistence',[21] and it recognizes 'the right of everyone to an adequate standard of living for himself and his family, including adequate food, clothing and housing, and to the continuous improvement of living conditions'.[22] The Covenant sets out the obligation:

> Each State Party to the present Covenant undertakes to take steps, individually and through international assistance and co-operation, especially economic and technical, to the maximum of its available resources, with a view to

achieving progressively the full realization of the rights recognized in the present Covenant by all appropriate means, including particularly the adoption of legislative measures.[23]

The specification 'by all appropriate means, including particularly the adoption of legislative measures', is explained by the UN Committee on Economic, Social and Cultural Right in its comment. The comment notes explicitly that it is politically and economically neutral in the sense that it does not require any particular kind of political or economic system: 'a socialist or a capitalist system, or a mixed, centrally planned, or laissez-faire economy, or . . . any other particular approach'.[24] Therefore, it depends on every state how it defines appropriate means and legislative measures.

It is useful to compare this Covenant with the International Covenant on Civil and Political Rights (ICCPR)[25] because the nation states have to implement the obligations of the latter but they are obliged to pursue only progressive implementation of the former. However, some obligations of the ICESCR have to be realized not only progressively but uniformly in all the states now. The states must not discriminate, for example, for reasons of race, sex, language or other status.[26]

The legal obligations of the nation states are focused especially on agents in their territory and under their jurisdiction. However, in an age of globalization, both state and non-state actors heavily influence the people also beyond their territories in other countries. Particularly the Third World countries are almost powerless in this context. The Western states have bigger—even if only limited—extra-territorial power and possibilities.

Duties of the nation states that ratified the ICCPR seem to be focused on human beings who are in their territory or under their jurisdiction. Nevertheless, concerning the ICESCR, it is possible to require also an extra-territorial recognition because a scope of action of the ICESCR is not limited in the treaty.[27] Thus, an application of the Covenant's social right can go beyond a territory of the state.[28]

The ICESCR notes that states should fulfil the rights 'individually and through international assistance and cooperation' through 'international contacts and cooperation' and 'international action'.[29] Such notes open two interpretations. Firstly, a realization of rights *individually* demands more state responsibility. Second, *international* assistance, contacts, action and cooperation allow a less ambitious approach of the state that would only share responsibility with other states. Moreover, a notion of international assistance seems to refer either to offering merely humanitarian aid of the state or to taking part in international humanitarian aid. Nevertheless, even if this general specification of a scope of application is not too precise, I will show later that the Covenant is specific enough to help more here.

The statement is worked out when a territorial scope of the ICESCR is specified by its substantive scope falling within the terms of the right to water, the right to food, the right to adequate housing, etc. Concerning the right to water,[30] for example, the Committee on Economic, Social and Economic Rights stresses that the states should not impose embargoes that prevent the distribution of water and activities necessary for realizing the right to water.[31]

There are three levels of obligations that are imposed on the states: (1) to respect, (2) to protect, (3) to fulfil (in an original proposition also to assist) which contains obligations to facilitate and to provide.[32] As for the third parties, in case of the right to food, the states have obligations to *respect* and *protect* what advocates of the rights and other members of civil society do when they *assist* in the realization of the right to food.[33] The states themselves have an international obligation to:

> recognize the essential role of international cooperation and comply with their commitment to take joint and separate action to achieve the full realization of the right to adequate food. In implementing this commitment, States parties should take steps to respect the enjoyment of the right to food in other countries, to protect that right, to facilitate access to food and to provide the necessary aid when required.[34]

Therefore, the states are expected to satisfy all three levels of the obligation, at least the minimum level that is necessary for a human being to be free from hunger. While the importance of the World Food Program, UNICEF, the Food and Agriculture Organization, and UNHCR is recognized by the United Nations, the states are responsible in the individual and joint way to cooperate in order to provide humanitarian assistance. In these cases, 'the most vulnerable populations' have a priority over the others. It should be applied to assistance to refugees as well.[35]

I would also like to pay attention to the fact that social rights under the Covenant could contradict some obligations under various legal regimes that the states also ratified. Moreover, the ICESCR may come into conflict with economic sanctions imposed upon some states internationally and unilaterally, and also by the UN Security Council.[36] While only the sanctions authorized under the UN Charter by the Security Council could prevail because the UN Charter has priority in cases of conflict, states still keep a responsibility for possible negative consequences of their decision to impose sanctions and they have to respect that the parts of the Charter that have a relation to human rights have to be applicable also in these cases. The UN Committee on Economic, Social and Cultural Rights recalls that various economic sanctions had a negative effect on the population of the target country. The comments on the right to food and the right to water mention that the states should not at all times impose any embargoes that endanger the supply of water and access to food, including services for securing the water and conditions for food production.

> Water should never be used as an instrument of political and economic pressure.[37]
> Food should never be used as an instrument of political and economic pressure.[38]

These statements are fully explicit and show that political and economic reasons do not have priority over the rights to food and water.

The Committee adopted a special comment on the relationship between economic sanctions and respect for economic, social and cultural rights. It says, on the one side, that it does not cast doubt upon the necessity of sanctions in appropriate cases but, on the other, that sanctions almost at all times 'have a dramatic impact' on social and other rights, often cause the maldistribution of food, clean drinking water, pharmaceuticals, the malfunctions of education and health systems, can reinforce the oppressive elites, etc. The comment emphasizes:

> whatever the circumstances, such sanctions should always take full account of the provisions of the International Covenant on Economic, Social and Cultural Rights.[39]

As an explanation, the comment states that 'lawlessness of one kind should not be met by lawlessness of another kind'.[40]

REGULATION OF TRANSNATIONAL CAPITAL

We cannot think that especially weaker states would be able to exercise full juridical effective control in their territories and apply the rights in the face of the powerful capital of transnational corporations, international financial organizations and strong states via an unequal cooperation. As is well known, the corporations, the World Trade Organization (WTO), the International Monetary Fund (IMF) and the World Bank (WB) have pursued their interests and policies that brought on losses among the most disadvantaged and poorest populations. The contributions of adjustment measures and other activities have initiated popular protests both in the North and the South. The people protested against the negative impact of various kinds of liberalization mandated via structural adjustment and other programmes on inequality and poverty in many countries. It is precisely the negative impact on the most vulnerable parts of the populations what is the core of this kind of argument that is discussed in relation to a regulation of TNCs and IFIs.

I do not want to claim that TNCs and IFIs are fully responsible for the severe poverty of the global poor and for millions of deaths. My argument is that in a world where nation states are losing their power and TNCs and IFIs are the empowering, we have to specify the problem of hunger and severe poverty in relation to the responsibility of TNCs and IFIs.

As for a general responsibility, I claim that any influential actor in the global context, including TNCs and IFIs, should share of the liability for the global arrangement and its negative consequences. Concerning the concrete suffering and responsibility, at first sight it seems to be reasonable that TNCs and IFIs should have a full responsibility for their actions; in other cases, if they have only an indirect influence, they should have only a partial responsibility; and in still others, if they have no influence, then also no responsibility. However, the structure of responsibility has to be more complex because it is hard to say that powerful agents have no influence in the interdependent world. There is a distinction between what the agent brings about and what it merely allowed to happen but it does not bring about.[41] The rationale of the argument is that agents, including institutional orders, are more responsible for their own actions than for actions that they only let happen.

Let us see what are the contemporary legal obligations concerning these problems.[42] TNCs are, at least partly, legally limited by powerful states on a domestic level. However, on a supranational level, they are directly regulated by various norms that are mostly non-binding and offer only guidelines that they may voluntarily follow if they want. The Declaration on the Rights and Responsibilities of Individuals,

Groups and Organs of Society is such an example.[43] The Norms on the Responsibilities of Transnational Corporations and Other Business Enterprises with Regard to Human Rights are also non-binding, they express only voluntary obligations of TNCs to respect restrictions defined by the national and international laws.[44] In the contemporary situation, the only relatively effective accountability and regulation of transnational organizations can be realized via the strong states' extra-territorial recognition.

It is possible to use an extra-territorial regulation of TNCs and IFIs via states that may and should legally exercise their influence over the activities of transnational organizations in other states. The transnational activities of economic and financial institutions should be accountable through their legal relationship to their home states which are bound by terms of international and global legal contracts, i.e. there is a possibility of the development of an extra-territorial application of the international and global norms of social justice. In a host country, particularly in the Third World, where IFIs and TNCs operate, they should be accountable through states where they are incorporated, mainly in the West. This approach helps create a global network of distributive regulation eradicating poverty. It points out the promising fragments of the emerging global legal order of distributive regulation, specifically an extra-territorial recognition of individuals and social groups in foreign countries damaged by the transnational economic and financial organizations. However, now these positive fragments are only part of a limited national/international framework with some transnational overlaps.

It is relevant to mention that while TNCs are non-state agents, IFIs such as the IMF and the WB are in fact multinational or international agents because they are established and organized by individual member nation states. Their actions are mostly transnational. On the one hand, even if TNCs and the IFIs are subjects at least under customary international law and, therefore, have some obligations, nevertheless, they are not legal identities under of the International Covenant on Economic, Social and Cultural Rights and other similar social rights treaties. On the other hand, in the thick version of the treaties' scope of action, we can indirectly impose obligations on them and regulate IFIs and TNCs via the states that signed and ratified the ICESCR and other social rights treaties and are consequently responsible for extra-territorial application of those treaties. Thus, responsibilities of a state beyond its territory should be realized also in case of a regulation of IFIs and TNCs.

The right to water is a good example. In its comment, the UN Committee on Economic, Social and Cultural Rights notes agreements on trade liberalization, for instance, and requires that it should not curtail the capacity of any country to realize fully the right to water.[45] More generally taken, the states as members of international organizations are responsible for their actions concerning the right to water in countries where those IFIs actions take place. This thesis is specified in the comment that says that

> States parties that are members of international financial institutions, notably the International Monetary Fund, the World Bank, and regional development banks, should take steps to ensure that the right to water is taken into account in their lending policies, credit agreements and other international measures.[46]

Any activity of citizens, companies and other agents which is taken within the jurisdiction of state parties should not cause a deprivation of any other state to be able to satisfy the right to water for the people who are under its jurisdiction.

> Steps should be taken by States parties to prevent their own citizens and companies from violating the right to water of individuals and communities in other countries.[47]

A similar case is the right to adequate food. IFIs, particularly IMF and WB are mentioned, should focus on the right to food and its protection when they decide about lending policies, measures regarding the debt crisis, etc. Any structural adjustment must be realized in such a way that a protection of the right to food is satisfied.[48] Also the right to adequate housing cannot be compromised by any policies of IFIs.[49] At a more general level, this is formulated in the comment on international technical assistance measures which are expected to require that 'protecting the rights of the poor and vulnerable'—in a form of major debt relief—should be a basic aim of the possible economic adjustment programme.[50]

Not only the IMF and the WB but also the WTO should contribute to the rule that 'the enjoyment of the right to water is promoted' by their cooperation with the states because the Committee on ESCR takes into account the assistance carried out by 'all other actors'.[51] They should incorporate the right to water, the right to food, the right to adequate housing and other rights in their policies. Dealing with the obligations of agents other than states, also the role of WHO, UNICEF, UNEP, UNDP, FAO, ILO, IFAD, UNHCR, the Red Cross and non-governmental organizations is recognized as important here.

LIMITS OF EXTRA-TERRITORIAL RECOGNITION

An attempt to support contemporary legal mechanisms of extra-territorial recognition and create a regulation on the new (supranational) level is being developed. The protests against the transnational capital, e.g. the Multilateral Agreement on Investment (MAI) negotiation, and other acts of discontent with various kinds of misrecognition show that the globalizing tendencies of the economic system contain also their reverse face in form of an involvement of local and national social forces in the transnational changes. We witness an establishment of transnational economic and financial structures, on the one hand, and the beginning of a formation of transnational social forces, on the other, which create strong contradictions. William Robinson hits off it then he argues that 'by reducing or eliminating the ability of individual states to regulate capital accumulation and capture surpluses, globalization is now bringing—at a worldwide level—precisely the polarization between a rich minority and a poor majority'.[52]

The polarization seems to be a kind of 'the new global social apartheid' which requires a separation of space that enables a social control in order to guarantee the small elite the both the life essential and a consumption of expansive goods. 'The race to the bottom' creates appropriate conditions for the protest that is in the process of formation now. An alternative to the transnational concentration of capital could be a popular project that would also have a transnational character. The grassroots kind of transnational dissent could form a counter-hegemonic bloc.[53]

However, as I mentioned above, we have to bear in mind that millions of people suffering from hunger and severe poverty express their discontent by their own means of protest. They articulate it by the medium of their everyday struggles for water, food, shelter, and other elementary means of survival because their miserable living conditions do not allow them to express their dissent via traditional ways of public protest in the streets, etc. On this account their protest is not visible on the part of the majority of the population in the Western countries as much as traditional protests of the labour movement and the new social movements. Therefore, we may say that the global poor who express this kind of popular disapproval to misrecognition suffer twofold: firstly, because of their poverty; secondly, because of the marginalization of their protest. In spite of this injustice, discontents that articulate the everyday feelings of social injury but have not crossed the boundaries of public attention or have received only a little attention are in case of the global poor the most pressing ones. As soon as we count them together with the more traditional kinds of protest, we can see the possibilities of the development of transnational social forces that could lead to social action.

An explanation of the insufficiency of the contemporary international legal mechanisms and emerging attempts of the new supranational and global legal instruments should reflect a transnational potential of social forces in order to avoid a territorial reification, mainly a reification of the nation state and its regulative national and international mechanisms. The transnationalization of the contemporary economic and financial institutions strengthens the process of creating motivational conditions of a constitution of the supranational and global legal apparatus. The exhaustion of possibilities to solve a problem of misrecognition on the national level could lead the social forces to claims on a higher, supranational level of recognition.

In other words, before moving to a new, supranational stage of regulation, admittedly, people try to use the possibilities of regulation in the contemporary stage of development and, at the same time, realize its limits in this way. An attempt to use regulations and obligations connected with the individual nation states requires, firstly, the identification of recent transnational regulative mechanisms that were not in the centre of attention in the past but could now play an important role in the new constellations of global interdependences. Secondly, it is important to reinterpret and develop these mechanisms in their new empowered role. Thirdly, following limited possibilities of the development of the recent mechanisms, it would probably be necessary to create new supranational mechanisms. To the extent that transnational corporations, international financial and other institutions are transnationalizing and globalizing, the critical analysis should offer an explanation of the historically evolving distributive regulations from the national to the supranational level and herewith help offer an articulation of claims of the global poor.

Strictly speaking, the current struggles for recognition try to empower an extra-territorial application of the contemporary legal norms of economic and social rights, and thereby disclose both a limited power and a weakness of the application. The claims on extra-territorial recognition show as inadequate demands on a nation state's solution of the problem but their formulation is important for an explication of the grammar of social conflicts aiming for a solution in terms of a new supranational stage of legal recognition.

CONCLUSION

The global poor express their dissent by means of their everyday struggles for recognition linked to guaranteeing basic conditions for their survival. An articulation and development of extra-territorial recognition of the global poor as the marginalized seem to be an attempt to make the nation states useful, on the one side, and an exemplary model that identifies a weak role of the nation states in the process of empowering transnational economic and international financial institutions, on the other. It shows that it will probably not be possible to solve the problems only through globalization with a human face in the form of an extra-territorial 'patch'.

Therefore, it is not enough to explain the extra-territorial possibilities of an application of economic and social rights in relation to the nation states. It is also necessary to see that contemporary international legal structures are not designed to respond to the IFIs and TNCs forces, to eradicate world poverty and to develop social justice, and that new emerging regulative legal structures could be articulated in the supranational space, including not only a responsibility of the nation states but also a direct responsibility of TNCs, IFIs and other agents.

In the end, we may raise a question: what is the criterion for the creation of the new supranational and global legal arrangements? Generally speaking, the criterion could be an ineffectiveness of the nation states' influence on the TNCs and IFIs via extra-territorial recognition because the ineffectiveness could motivate the people to struggle for new global arrangements. And concerning instruments of the struggle for recognition, the question remains open whether they will concentrate on a more or less active or passive, partisan or communicative, hidden or public, easy or complicated approach to formulate an opposition against experienced misrecognition. However, the issue of extra-territorial recognition has to be worked out further in order to articulate a dynamic of the protest against social injustice under globalization in relation to unrecognized rights-agents and misrecognized rights-holders.

NOTES

1. A. Honneth (1995), *The Struggle for Recognition: The Moral Grammar of Social Conflicts*, Cambridge: Polity Press, p. 2, See also N. Fraser, and A. Honneth (2003), *Redistribution or Recognition? A Political-Philosophical Exchange*, London, New York: Verso.
2. Ibid., p. 164.
3. In fact, they have been identified only during temporary limited mass media campaigns (e.g. Make Poverty History), the cases of natural disasters or before parliamentary elections. Nevertheless, that kind of identification does not have any significant impact on the real recognition of the global poor and the satisfaction of their needs. Also the EU policies and other similar activities have not made a significant change.
4. UNDP (United Nations Development Program), *Annual Report 2007*, p. 2.
5. T. Pogge (2002), *World Poverty and Human Rights*, Cambridge: Polity, pp. 2, 98, 231. Annex Table 2, 'Deaths by Cause, Sex and Mortality Stratum in WHO Regions', in World Health Organization, *The World Health Report 2004*, pp. 120-5. See also results of the research supported by the World Health Organization: C.D. Mathers and D. Loncar (2006), 'Projections of Global Mortality and Burden of Disease from 2002 to 2030', *PloS Medicine*, vol. 3, issue 11, e 442, pp. 2011-30. The paper is specified by Dataset S1: Deaths by Causes, Scenario, Sex and Age for 2002, 2015, and 2030.
6. UNESCO (United Nations Educational, Scientific and Cultural Organization) Reports; see also, e.g. in relation to energy: Women and Children Overlooked in World Health Organization (2006), *Fuel for Life: Household Energy and Health*, p. 20.
7. *Millennium Declaration*, para 19. http://www.un.org/millennium/declaration/ares552e.pdf
8. UNDP, *Human Development Report 2005*, Human Development Trends 2005, Part 9 (5). Child mortality is closely associated with GDP per capita. As for child mortality, gaps between the rich and poor are widening. UNDP, *Human Development Report 2005*, Figure 1.11, p. 28.

9. In this connection, see T. Pogge (2007), 'Reframing Global Economic Security and Justice', in D. Held and A. McGrew (eds.), *Globalization Theory: Approaches and Controversies*, Cambridge: Polity, pp. 211-12. See also Pogge, 2002.
10. UNDP (2005), *Human Development Report 2005*, Human Development Trends 2005, Part 9 (10); also Figure 1.18, p. 43 (text in brackets added).
11. A. Honneth (2003), 'Redistribution as Recognition', in N. Fraser, and A. Honneth, pp. 114 ff.
12. Theoretically taken, while focusing on a present-day empirical social research, an analysis should always keep in mind also normative theoretical concepts that can help bring into the open a critique of new forms of social suffering.
13. A. Honneth (2003), 'Redistribution as Recognition', in N. Fraser and A. Honneth, pp. 113-14.
14. N. Fraser (2007), 'Social Justice in the Age of Identity Politics', in ibid., pp. 88 ff. See also N. Fraser, 'Reframing Justice in a Globalized World', in D. Held and A. Kaya (eds.), *Global Inequality: Patterns and Explanations*, Cambridge: Polity, pp. 252-72.
15. 'Poverty is a violation of basic human rights, which is very often forgotten. We must count it among the serious gross violations of human rights. People who live in poverty strive for dignity as much as anyone else. . . .' United Nations High Commissioner for Human Rights, *Respect for Human Rights Essential for the Eradication of Poverty*. http://www.unhchr.ch/huricane/huricane.nsf/view01/10F59F4258CBC22CC1256DC20049B1DF?opendocument
16. *The Universal Declaration of Human Rights*, Art. 25(1).
17. Ibid., Art. 28.
18. The Universal Declaration of Human Rights and the UN Covenants focus primariiy on states. However, there are more kinds of agents in the global community that should to be involved in a realization of justice. We have to make clear what we mean by those kinds of agents. There are (A) state actors: nation states, (B) trans-state actors: transnational or multinational corporations, international financial institutions such as the WB and the IMF, human rights UN agencies, international non-governmental organizations, etc., (C) under-state actors: especially peoples, firms and individuals. There is also limited coordination of activities of all the mentioned actors in the global community. And of course, a responsibility structure within this coordination requires a specification of rights.
19. The International Covenant on Economic, Social and Cultural Rights was adopted by all 105 present members of the United Nations General Assembly in 1966, after almost twenty years of the drafting process which was based on the work of the UN commissions and agencies. The

Covenant entered into force 10 years later (1976), after the necessary steps of ratification. For a discussion of various aspects of the economic and social rights, see M. Craven (1995), *The International Covenant on Economic, Social and Cultural Rights: A Perspective on its Development*, Oxford: Clarendon Press.

20. Concerning the Western states, while the EU countries and Japan ratified the Covenant, USA did not do it. Nevertheless, the USA signed it; therefore, they cannot act against the purpose of the Covenant. See Ratifications and Reservations of the International Covenant on Economic, Social and Cultural Rights, http://www.ohchr.org/english/countries/ratification/3.htm#reservations.
21. *ICESCR* (International Covenant on Economic, Social and Cultural Rights), Part I, Art. 1, para. 2.
22. Ibid., Part III, Art. 11, para. 1. See also the comments on its application: CESCR (Committee on Economic, Social and Cultural Rights), *General Comment* 4, 13/12/91, the right to adequate housing (Art. 11 (1)); CESCR, *General Comment* 7, 20/05/97, The right to adequate housing.
23. *ICESCR*, Part II, Art. 2, para 1.
24. CESCR, *General Comment 3*, The nature of states parties obligations (Art. 2, para 1), 14/12/90, para 8. It is neutral provided that human rights are respected.
25. *International Covenant on Civil and Political Rights.* Adopted on 16 December 1966, entry into force 23 March 1976.
26. CESCR, *General Comment 3*, The nature of states parties obligations (Art. 2, para 1), 14/12/90, para 1, 3, 5. Sex discrimination is a good example. It is understandable that poor families in many countries of the Third World invest money into education of sons rather than daughters because it is more complicated to get a job for educated girls than educated boys. The investment that makes less profit would even worsen the situation of poor families. However, if the state eliminates gender discrimination, also poor families can change their investment strategy in favour of girls. In this way, we can avoid punishing the victim.
27. Compare the ICCPR and the ICESCR treaties. It is important to specify that while a theory of recognition deals with a direct recognition of persons, the legal discourse focuses, precisely taken, on the recognition of rights and obligations that, in turn, recognize people. I try to incorporate a legal discourse into a theory of recognition.
28. See also A.P.M. Coomans (2005), 'Progressive Development of International Human Rights Law: The Extraterritorial Application of the International Covenant on Economic, Social and Cultural Rights', in M. Windfuhr (ed.), *Beyond the Nation State: Human Rights in Times of Globalisation*, Uppsala: Global Publications Foundation, pp. 33-50.

M. Craven (2007), 'Violence of Dispossession: Extra-Territoriality and Economic, Social, and Cultural Rights', in M.A. Baderin, and R. McCorquodale (eds.) (2007), *Economic, Social and Cultural Rights in Action*, Oxford: Oxford University Press, pp. 71-88.

29. *ICESCR*, Art. 2, para 1; Art. 11, para 1 and 2; Art. 15, para 4; Art. 23.
30. Ibid., Arts. 11 and 12.
31. CESCR, *General Comment 15*, E/C.12/2002/11. The right to water, para 32.
32. Ibid., *General Comment 12*, E/C. E/C.12/1999/5. The right to adequate food (Art. 11), Art. 15, and note no. 1. See also: *Right to Adequate Food as a Human Right*, Study Series No. 1, New York, 1989, United Nations Publication, No. E.89.XIV.2
33. CESCR, *General Comment 12*, E/C. E/C.12/1999/5. The right to adequate food (Art. 11), para 35. See also S. Narula (2006), 'The Right to Food: Holding Global Actors Accountable Under International Law', *Center for Human Rights and Global Justice*, Working Paper No. 7.
34. It is defined in the spirit of the Charter of the United Nations (Art. 56), *ICESCR* (Arts. 11, 2.1, 23), and the Rome Declaration of the World Food Summit. CESCR, *General Comment 12*, E/C. E/C.12/1999/5. The right to adequate food (Art. 11), para 36.
35. CESCR, *General Comment 12*, E/C. E/C.12/1999/5. The right to adequate food (Art. 11), para 38.
36. See also N.D. White (2007), 'The Applicability of Economic and Social Rights to the UN Security Council', in M.A. Baderin and R. McCorquodale (eds.), pp. 89-107.
37. CESCR, *General Comment 15*, E/C.12/2002/11. The right to water, para 32.
38. CESCR, *General Comment 12*, E/C. E/C.12/1999/5. The right to adequate food (Art. 11), para 37.
39. CESCR, *General Comment 8*, The relationship between economic sanctions and respect for economic, social and cultural rights, U.N. Doc. E/C.12/1997/8 (1997), para 1. In para 2, the comment mentions sanction imposed upon following countries: South Africa, Iraq/Kuwait, the former Yugoslavia, Somalia, the Libyan Arab Jamahiriya, Liberia, Haiti, Angola, Rwanda and Sudan.
40. Ibid., para 16.
41. See, e.g. B. Hayden (2005), 'Extreme Poverty and Global Responsibility', in C. Barry, and T.W. Pogge, *Global Institutions and Responsibilities*, Oxford: Blackwell, pp. 312-13. See also T. Pogge (2002), pp. 41-3.
42. See Kamminga M.T. and Saman Zia-Zarifi (eds.) (2000), *Liability of Multinational Corporations under International Law*, The Hague/London/Boston: Kluwer Law International.
43. *Déclaration sur le droit et la responsabilité des individus, groupes et organs de la société de promouvoir et protéger les droits de l'homme et les libertés*

fondamentales universellement reconnus (Declaration on the Rights and Responsibilities of Individuals, Groups and Organs of Society to Promote and Protect Universally Recognized Human Rights and Fundamental Freedoms). Assemblée générale des Nations unies, A/RES/53/144, 8 March 1999.

44. Norms on the Responsibilities of Transnational Corporations and Other Business Enterprises with Regard to Human Rights, U.N. Doc. E/CN.4/Sub.2/2003/12/Rev.2.
45. CESCR (2003), *General Comment* 15, The right to water (Arts. 11 and 12 of the International Covenant on Economic, Social and Cultural Rights) U.N. Doc. E/C.12/2002/11, para 35.
46. Ibid., para 36. An issue of agreements on trade liberalization is mentioned in para 35.
47. Ibid., para 33; see also para 31.
48. CESCR, *General Comment 12*, E/C. E/C.12/1999/5, The right to adequate food (Art. 11), para 41; CESCR, *General Comment 2*, 02/02/90, International technical assistance measures (Art. 22), para 9.
49. CESCR, *General Comment 4*, 13/12/91, The right to adequate housing (Art.11 (1)), para 19.
50. CESCR, *General Comment 2*, 02/02/90, International technical assistance measures (Art. 22). See also: The Declaration on Social Progress and Development, Convention on the Elimination of All Forms of Discrimination against Women, the Convention on the Rights of the Child, and other treaties.
51. CESCR, *General Comment 15*, E/C.12/2002/11 The right to water, para 60.
52. W. Robinson (1996), 'Globalization: Nine Theses on Our Epoch', *Race & Class*, 38, 13, p. 25 ff. Cf. J. Harris, (2006), *The Dialectics of Globalization: Economic and Political Conflict in a Transnational World*, Cambridge: Cambridge Scholars Press. W. Robinson (2004), *A Theory of Global Capitalism*, Baltimore: John Hopkins University Press.
53. See, for instance, the annual Global Civil Society Yearbooks. H. Anheier, M. Kaldor, and M. Glasius (eds.) (2006), *Global Civil Society 2006/7*, London: Sage.

REFERENCES

Anheier, H., M. Kaldor and M. Glasius (eds.) (2006), *Global Civil Society 2006/7*, London: Sage.

CESCR (Committee on Economic, Social and Cultural Rights), *General Comments* 3, 4, 7, 8, 12, 15. U.N. Doc.

Chase-Dunn, C. and T.D. Hall (1997), *Rise and Demise: Comparing World Systems*, Boulder: Westview.

Chase-Dunn, C. and E.N. Anderson (eds.) (2005), *Historical Evolution of World Systems*, New York: Palgrave Macmillan.

Coomans, A.P.M. (2005), 'Progressive Development of International Human Rights Law: The Extraterritorial Application of the International Covenant on Economic, Social and Cultural Rights', in M. Windfuhr (ed.), *Beyond the Nation State: Human Rights in Times of Globalisation*, Uppsala: Global Publications Foundation.

Craven, M. (2007), 'Violence of Dispossession: Extra-Territoriality and Economic, Social, and Cultural Rights', in M.A. Baderin and R. McCorquodale (eds.), *Economic, Social and Cultural Rights in Action.* Oxford: Oxford University Press.

Craven, M. (1995), *The International Covenant on Economic, Social and Cultural Rights: A Perspective on its Development*, Oxford: Clarendon Press.

Déclaration sur le droit et la responsabilité des individus, groupes et organs de la société de promouvoir et protéger les droits de l'homme et les libertés fondamentales universellement reconnus, Assemblée générale des Nations unies, A/RES/53/144, 1999.

Fraser, N. (2007), 'Reframing Justice in a Globalized World', in D. Held, and A. Kaya (eds.), *Global Inequality: Patterns and Explanations*, Cambridge: Polity.

Fraser, N. and A. Honneth (2003), *Redistribution or Recognition? A Political-Philosophical Exchange*, London, New York: Verso.

Harris, J. (2006), *The Dialectics of Globalization: Economic and Political Conflict in a Transnational World*, Cambridge: Cambridge Scholars Press.

Hayden, B. (2005), 'Extreme Poverty and Global Responsibility', in C. Barry and T.W. Pogge, *Global Institutions and Responsibilities*, Oxford: Blackwell.

Honneth, A. (1995), *The Struggle for Recognition: The Moral Grammar of Social Conflicts*, Cambridge: Polity Press.

International Covenant on Economic, Social and Cultural Rights, 1966.

International Covenant on Civil and Political Rights, 1966.

Kamminga, M.T. and Saman Zia-Zarifi (eds.) (2000), *Liability of Multinational Corporations under International Law*, The Hague/London/Boston: Kluwer Law International.

Mathers, C.D. and D. Loncar (2006), 'Projections of Global Mortality and Burden of Disease from 2002 to 2030', *PloS Medicine*, vol. 3, issue 11, e 442.

Millennium Declaration, http://www.un.org/millennium/declaration/ares552e.pdf

Narula, S. (2006), 'The Right to Food: Holding Global Actors Accountable Under International Law', *Center for Human Rights and Global Justice* Working Paper no. 7.

Norms on the Responsibilities of Transnational Corporations and Other Business Enterprises with Regard to Human Rights, U.N. Doc. E/CN.4/ Sub.2/2003/12/Rev.2.

Pogge, T. (2002), *World Poverty and Human Rights*, Cambridge: Polity.

———. (2007), Reframing Global Economic Security and Justice, in D. Held and A. McGrew (eds.), *Globalization Theory: Approaches and Controversies*, Cambridge: Polity.

Ratifications and Reservations of the International Covenant on Economic, Social and Cultural Rights, http://www.ohchr.org/english/countries/ ratification/3.htm#reservations.

Robinson, W. and J. Harris (2000), 'Towards a Global Ruling Class: Globalization and the Transnational Capitalist Class', *Science & Society*, 64, 1.

Robinson, W. (2001), 'Social Theory and Globalization: The Rise of a Transnational State', *Theory and Society*, vol. 30, no. 2.

Robinson, W. (2004), *A Theory of Global Capitalism*, Baltimore: John Hopkins University Press.

Robinson, W. (1996), 'Globalization: Nine Theses on Our Epoch', *Race & Class*, 38, 13.

Sklair, L. (1995), *Sociology of the Global System*, Baltimore: John Hopkins University Press.

Sklair, L. (2001), *The Transnational Capitalist Class*, Oxford: Blackwell.

Structural Adjustment Participatory Review International Network (2002), *The Policy Roots of Economic Crisis and Poverty: A Multi-Country Participatory Assessment of Structural Adjustment*, Washington.

UNCTAD (United Nations Conference on Trade and Development) (2006), *World Investment Report 2006*, New York and Geneva: United Nations.

UNDP (United Nations Development Program) (2005), *Human Development Report 2005*, New York.

——— (2007), *Annual Report 2007: Making Globalization Work for All*, New York: Office of Communications, UNDP.

United Nations (1948), *Universal Declaration of Human Rights*, New York: United Nations.

United Nations (1998), *Right to Adequate Food as a Human Right*, Study Series No. 1, New York, United Nations Publication, No. E.89. XIV.2.

United Nations High Commissioner for Human Rights, *Respect for Human Rights Essential for the Eradication of Poverty*. http://www.unhchr.ch/ huricane/huricane.nsf/view01/10F59F4258CBC22CC1256DC2004 9B1DF?opendocument

Walden, B. and J. Harris (2002), 'Notes for a New Economy: An Interview with Walden Bello', *Race & Class*, 43, 34.

Wallerstein, I. (1974), *The Modern World System*, New York: Academic Press.

Weber, H. (2006), 'A Political Analysis of the PRSP Initiative: Social Struggles and the Organization of Persistent Relations of Inequality', *Globalizations*, vol. 3, no. 2.

World Health Organization (2006), *Fuel for Life: Household Energy and Health*, Geneva: WHO.

——— (2004), *The World Health Report*, Geneva: WHO.

CHAPTER 4

Recent Trends in Caste Inequalities: Comparison of NSSO Consumption Expenditure Data of 2000 and 2005

SATISH DESHPANDE

INTRODUCTION

This paper has the limited objective of making a comparative caste-disaggregated analysis of monthly per capita consumption expenditure data from the last two quinquennial (big sample) surveys of the National Sample Survey Organisation (NSSO) conducted in 1999-2000 and 2004-5, respectively. Only two time points separated by five years are not sufficient to establish long-term trends; moreover, consumption expenditure data—as different from measures of income and wealth—tends to understate economic inequalities. However, the 55th and 61st rounds are the first two of the new generation of surveys that allow for a reasonably comprehensive caste profiling of Indian society. As such, they are worth analysing for preliminary indications of trends in inter-caste inequality, for an overall sense of the ways in which caste continues to be a salient aspect of economic status, and for the emerging patterns of social mobility (or immobility) in contemporary society.

Three kinds of comparisons are made here: average consumption expenditure levels across castes; comparison of the different internal segments of the consumption expenditure distribution of each caste; and comparison of the relative 'caste gap' separating the so-called 'upper' castes from the other caste and tribe groups. It is found that after adjusting for inflation, average consumption levels have increased slightly for all castes in the rural sector, whereas they have stayed the same or declined slightly in the urban sector, specially for the Scheduled Castes (SC) and the Other Backward Classes (OBC). The 'Upper' Castes (UC) are the only ones to have registered an unequivocal increase in average consumption by all measures in both sectors, while urban Scheduled Tribes (ST) seem to have witnessed a minor spurt in consumption levels.

Coming to a disaggregated analysis of segments of the class spectrum (taking the 5th, 25th, 50th, 75th, and 95th percentiles of consumption expenditure), it is found that for all castes and in both sectors, gains in consumption levels are most at the top quarter of the distribution, though there are anomalies and exceptions. It is noteworthy that the bottom quarter of all castes in the urban sector registers a small decline in consumption levels—in urban India, the poorest sections seem to have become slightly worse off in the first five years of this century. In terms of the 'caste gap'—or the gap between respective percentiles of consumption expenditure for the UC compared to the three other caste groups—the gap generally increases as we go up the distribution. In other words, the gap in consumption expenditure between UCs and other castes increases as we go from the 5th to the 95th percentile. In the rural sector, there has been no significant change in the caste gaps between 2000 and 2005, but in the urban sector the gaps seem to have increased slightly, except for the STs who display a peculiar pattern of caste inequality relative to the UCs.

These are preliminary findings, to be confirmed or refuted once data from the next big sample survey become available. Nevertheless, they establish beyond doubt the strong correlation between caste and economic status in contemporary India, and thus the urgent need for caste-sensitive analyses of economic inequality.

DATA ISSUES

It is only relatively recently that social scientists have begun to pay attention to the social patterning of economic inequality. Traditionally, research interest in poverty and inequality-related issues has been channelled strictly along class lines with some heed paid to regional distribution. Caste in particular was for a long time a 'politically incorrect' variable for the analysis of inequality. This attitude was also reflected in the official statistics, which made it impossible to distinguish any castes other than the STs and SCs. Barring partial exceptions, cross-tabulations of religion and caste were also not available.

The political mobilization around caste and the renewed salience of religious identities has changed this decisively over the last decade. The Mandal reforms extended interest in caste beyond the scheduled categories, and also highlighted the fact that the so-called 'UCs' have been, statistically speaking, the most elusive social group in modern India. More recently, the Sachar Committee made a pioneering attempt to produce a detailed socio-economic profile of the Muslim community. Even the World Bank now devotes considerable effort to analysing the social composition of the poor. All these initiatives have depended heavily on data from the NSSO.

The key innovation was effected in the NSSO's 55th round survey conducted in 1999-2000. Beginning with this round, the NSSO began to report data separately for the OBCs. Given that it had also begun to provide unit-level data to users, it became possible, for the first time in independent India, to construct a fairly comprehensive cross-classification of religious and caste groups. Since OBC data was now available, the residual category of 'Others'—those not belonging to the ST, SC or OBC categories—could legitimately be treated as being roughly equivalent to the 'UCs'.[1] Moreover, cross-tabulation with religion data allowed for the identification and analysis of caste-based differences within religious groups and religion-based differences within caste groups. Although not taken up in this paper, intra-caste and intra-religion differences allow us to take advantage of macro indicators of economic status when examining the claims of different interest groups.

As with all large data sets, specially those based on sample surveys, the NSSO data are not without problems. One issue that is often raised is that in the NSSO surveys, both caste and religion data are self-reported and are not subjected to any further checking or verification by investigators, as is done in the Census. While it needs monitoring, this is not as yet an insurmountable obstacle. On the whole, estimates of ST and SC population shares as per the NSSO have been slightly higher but have remained within acceptable distance of the Census shares extrapolated for the survey years.[2] A second problem is that disaggregated analyses are often ruled out due to inadequate sample size in the relevant sub-categories. Thus, what is a perfectly acceptable sample size for rural or urban India as a whole quickly shrinks to statistically unacceptable levels as disaggregation across caste, religion or region is introduced. This is a well-known issue with sample surveys, and has to be met with judicious strategies of analysis. A much more serious issue that has come to light with the 61st round survey of 2004-5 is that of the significant increase in the sample proportion, and hence the estimated population share of the OBC category compared to the 55th round survey of 1999-2000.

Table 4.1 shows the weighted sample sizes, by caste and by sector, for the two relevant surveys of the NSSO, namely the quinquennial 55th and 61st rounds conducted in 1999-2000 and 2004-5 respectively. It has to be emphasized that the complex sampling design followed by the NSSO does not take account of any social identities, specially not caste or religion. The design does consider size of settlements (villages or urban blocks), and it also tries to oversample affluent households, who would otherwise be very scarce in a national sample. But there is no attempt to create strata based on caste or religion, and their incidence in the sample is supposed to be a by-product of the representativeness achieved through rigorous sampling techniques.

As can be seen from Table 4.1, the estimated share of the rural

TABLE 4.1: WEIGHTED SAMPLE SIZES IN THE 55TH AND 61ST ROUND SURVEYS OF THE NSSO

(1999-2000 and 2004-5, by Caste, by Sector)

	Rural India				Urban India			
Caste Groups	Weighted SS	Estimated % of Popn		Weighted SS	Weighted SS	Estimated % of Popn		Weighted SS
	55R	55R	61R	61R	55R	55R	61R	61R
ST	47,113	10.5	10.3	46,051	5,121	3.4	3.0	4,665
SC	91,732	20.4	21.3	95,709	21,656	14.4	15.0	23,053
OBC	168,525	*37.5*	*42.9*	192,702	45,839	*30.4*	*36.0*	55,288
UC	141,061	*31.4*	*25.5*	114,450	78,003	*51.7*	*45.9*	70,500
Missing	708	0.2	0.1	373	256	0.2	0.0	41
Total	449,140	100.0	100.0	449,286	150,876	100.0	100.0	153,547

Notes: Weights used are the multipliers supplied with NSSO unit level data on disk; sample sizes show number of persons rounded to nearest integer. 'Missing' refers to records with no data in the caste field. All caste groups include members of all religions. UC = 'Upper' Caste, i.e. those not belonging to ST, SC or OBC.

and urban population belonging to the STs and SCs does not vary greatly across the two rounds. The significant changes are for the OBC and for the residual UC group (figures in italics type), and these changes seem to be mutually compensatory. It would seem that between the 55th and 61st rounds, the rural OBC population share increased by roughly 5.5 percentage points (from 37.5 to 42.9 per cent), while the UC population share declined by almost 6 per cent (from 31.4 to 25.5 per cent). In the urban sector, both the magnitude and the direction of change in population shares for these two caste groups is almost exactly the same as that in the rural sector. The urban OBC share has risen by 5.4 per cent (from 30.4 to 36.0) while the UC share has declined by 5.8 per cent (from 51.7 to 45.9). Since the OBC category is a relatively new one with many regional variations, it is possible that the increase over five years reflects better awareness and administrative clarity about the category, so that people who were not sure of their status before are now able to return themselves as OBCs. However, we will have to wait until the next quinquennial round of the NSSO before the matter can be settled. If the population share of the OBCs continues to be unstable in three consecutive big sample rounds, then there is surely cause for worry. If this share settles down around the levels shown in the 61st round—which, by the way, remains quite plausible—then this issue can be laid to rest.

Yet another issue unrelated to the caste question is that of 'contamination' caused by the canvassing of two different reference periods in the 55th round survey of 1999-2000. As is now well known, the simultaneous use (on adjoining pages of the survey instrument) of the traditional thirty-day reference period as well as a newly introduced seven-day reference period for most items of everyday consumption raised the strong possibility that respondents and investigators would have tended to use a single reference period and simply convert it to the other by either dividing or multiplying by four to move from month to week or vice versa. Since the seven-day reference period tended to produce consistently higher estimates of consumption, and since earlier surveys had used the month as the reference period, there was bound to be some 'contamination' of data. Although many attempts were subsequently made to minimize the impact of such contamination, the authoritative view, as expressed by the Planning Commission, is that the 'Mixed Recall Period' (MRP) consumption estimates of the 61st round are the ones that are roughly (but not exactly) comparable to the 55th round estimates.[3] The MRP involves the use of 365-day recall (or reference) period for 'five infrequently purchased non-food items, namely, clothing, footwear, durable goods, education and medical expenses', and 30-day recall period for all other items. Accordingly, this paper relies exclusively on the MRP estimates of consumption for the 61st round. However, this caveat regarding comparisons between the 55th and 61st rounds should also be kept in mind—even with the use of the MRP, the 55th round date remain aberrant and are not strictly comparable with the 61st round. This is another reason why comparative exercises must await the next big sample survey before they can draw any firm conclusions.

One final reminder: this paper discusses economic inequality, but it does so based on consumption expenditure data. In the Indian context, consumption expenditure data has been preferred to income data because of the greater accuracy and reliability of such estimates, and because of the special usefulness of such data in analysis of extreme poverty. However, it has long been recognized that consumption expenditure data tends to significantly understate inequality because it does not take account of savings, investments and stocks of wealth. Given that the share of these non-consumption components of income tends to increase with income levels, it is obvious that looking at consumption expenditure alone will heavily underestimate real differences in economic status. In keeping with general (Indian) practice, and given the absence of reliable macro data on incomes, consumption data provides a fairly good sense of economic inequality in a poor country like India.

COMPARISON OF AVERAGE LEVELS OF CONSUMPTION EXPENDITURE

The first set of comparisons considered are those of average levels of consumption expenditure. Two dimensions are taken up, first the comparisons across caste groups and second, comparisons across the 55th and 61st rounds, or 1999-2000 and 2004-5, respectively. As already indicated, the 'MRP' estimates of consumption expenditure are used for the 61st round. The consumption expenditure data from the 55th round is adjusted to 61st round price levels by using the Labour Bureau price indices as per the Planning Commission Expert Group practice. The price indices in question are, for the rural sector, the Consumer Price Index for Agricultural Labourers (CPIAL) with base year 1986-7=100, and the Consumer Price Index for Industrial Workers (CPIIW) with base year 1982=100. Since both the NSSO surveys considered here were conducted from July to June, the midpoint of this period, or January, is taken as the reference point, and the respective price indices for January 2000 and January 2005 are used to derive the price deflator to be used on the 55th round consumption expenditure estimates.[4]

The simplest comparison is that of median consumption expenditure levels for the different caste groups in the two years, at constant 2004-5 prices. As a positional average immune to the distorting effect of extreme values, the median is an appropriate average to use for skewed distributions. Table 4.2 shows the results of this comparison, which need to be considered across two dimensions, inter-caste and inter-year.

Comparing median Monthly Per Capita Consumption Expenditure (MPCE) gives us an initial perspective on economic hierarchies across caste. In rural India the order from bottom to top is: ST, SC, OBC and UC, giving us the expected caste hierarchy. This holds for both the years. It is noteworthy that only the UC in rural India is above the overall (all castes) average level of MPCE in both years, with the OBC just making it in 2004-5. Comparison across the two years shows that average consumption levels have hardly changed in rural India, with the all India average increasing by less than 1 per cent.

TABLE 4.2: MEDIAN MONTHLY PER CAPITA CONSUMPTION EXPENDITURE

by Caste, by Sector (MPCE in constant 2004-5 Rupees)

	RURAL INDIA			URBAN INDIA		
Caste Groups	1999-2000	2004-5	% Change	1999-2000	2004-5	% Change
ST	378.8	391.4	+3.3	676.1	713.6	+5.5
SC	413.2	421.5	+2.0	624.9	612.8	-1.9
OBC	459.9	472.4	+2.7	715.2	679.0	-5.1
UC	545.4	553.0	+1.4	975.1	983.2	+0.8
ALL	465.4	469.4	+0.9	814.0	776.3	-4.6

Notes: Price deflators used: Rural India, CPI for Agricultural Labour; Urban India: CPI for Industrial Workers. All computations use NSSO supplied multipliers. UC = 'Upper' caste, i.e. those not belonging to ST, SC or OBC.

All castes have positive changes, though these are small. Although they start with the lowest absolute level, the rate of increase is highest for STs at 3.3 per cent, and it is the lowest for the UC, who have by far the highest absolute levels of average MPCE.

Caste hierarchies in urban India seem to be somewhat different and also more complex. It is the SCs rather than the STs who are at the bottom here, followed by the STs, OBCs and the UCs. Here, all castes other than UCs are well below the national average of MPCE for all castes. Comparing across the two years, urban India seems to have fared badly, with average MPCE actually declining by 4.6 per cent. The median MPCE for both SCs and OBCs has declined, with the latter in particular registering a significant fall of 5.1 per cent. On the other hand, urban STs seem to have registered significant increases in average consumption levels of 5.5 per cent, and they have also moved up one rank in the caste hierarchy, being in second place after the UCs in terms of median MPCE. This is a significant finding and needs to be investigated further. What are the factors responsible for the improvement in ST median MPCE? Why are they absent in the case of the SCs and specially the OBCs? These are questions that can only be answered through detailed empirical research.

Although it is a robust and useful average, the median is not amenable to further statistical analysis. In particular, where sample survey results are concerned, estimates of sampling error are not available for the median. In order to address this issue, Table 4.3 reports on the mean MPCE, along with the standard errors of the mean for each caste group. The last column of this table shows the percentage change in the mean MPCE between 1999 and 2005.

For rural India, Table 4.3 confirms the impressions conveyed by Table 4.2: like the medians, the means of MPCE for all caste groups, as well as for rural India as a whole show a positive change, although the magnitude of this change is rather small. The UCs have registered the largest increase in mean MPCE at 4.3 per cent, while the SCs have the smallest at 1.4 per cent. However, for both years, the caste hierarchy retains the same order by mean as by median MPCE—the STs are at the bottom, followed by the SCs, and OBCs, with the UCs on top.

For urban India, the picture presented by Table 4.3 is once again very close to that in Table 4.2. It is clear that urban India has not done very well across these five years, with mean consumption levels

TABLE 4.3: MEAN MONTHLY PER CAPITA CONSUMPTION EXPENDITURES, BY CASTE GROUP

1999-2000 and 2004-5, by Sector, with Standard Errors of Mean

		1999-2000			2004-5			
Sector	Caste Group	Observations	Mean MPCE	SE of Mean	Observations	Mean MPCE	SE of Mean	% Change
Rural India	ST	51,977	430.52	0.97	62,548	439.12	0.93	+2.00
	SC	63,212	464.86	1.23	67,559	471.32	0.91	+1.39
	OBC	131,629	526.11	0.91	153,423	544.98	0.86	+3.59
	UC	127,393	641.14	1.11	114,147	668.86	1.52	+4.32
	ALL	374,853	539.69	0.57	398,024	549.96	0.59	+1.90
Urban India	ST	14,916	842.15	5.25	16,220	869.74	6.67	+3.28
	SC	28,235	742.97	2.64	29,373	731.96	2.72	-1.48
	OBC	63,660	871.13	3.22	74,623	850.45	2.18	-2.37
	UC	117,905	1225.17	3.15	84,479	1282.20	3.78	+4.66
	ALL	225,143	1034.76	1.99	204,789	1031.53	1.96	-0.31

Note: The MPCE distribution has been slightly trimmed by dropping top 10 and bottom 10 values. MPCE is in Rupees at constant 2004-5 prices; price deflators used: Rural India, CPI for Agricultural Labour; Urban India: CPI for Industrial Workers. All computations use NSSO supplied multipliers. UC = 'Upper' Caste, i.e. those not belonging to ST, SC or OBC.

showing a small decline for the sector as a whole. The OBC and SC mean MPCE has declined, but the UC mean shows a significant gain of almost 4.7 per cent while the STs too have gained by about 3.3 per cent. Table 4.3 also confirms the extraordinary showing of the ST category, which is ranked second in terms of mean MPCE in 2005, having moved one rank up from the 1999 level.

Table 4.4 summarizes the implications of the standard errors; it allows to see at a glance which caste groups have registered a statistically significant increase or decrease in mean MPCE across the two surveys. As expected, almost all caste groups, as well as the all-castes grouping register an increase. The only exception are the SCs whose mean MPCE for 2004-5 is *not* significantly higher than the 1999-2000 figure at the 99.9 per cent level of confidence.

Urban India presents a sharp contrast: only the UC group has statistically significant increases in mean MPCE, and it is joined at the 95 per cent confidence level by the STs. The OBCs have significantly lower mean MPCE in 2004-5 at all confidence levels,

TABLE 4.4: CHANGE IN MEAN MPCE BETWEEN 1999-2000 AND 2004-5

Sector	Levels of Confidence (%)	Mean MPCE 2004-5 is Significantly Higher than Mean MPCE 1999-2000	Mean MPCE 2004-5 is Significantly Lower than Mean MPCE 1999-2000
Rural	99.9	ST OBC UC ALL	
	99.0	ST SC OBC UC ALL	
	95.0	ST SC OBC UC ALL	
Urban	99.9	UC	OBC
	99.0	UC	OBC
	95.0	ST UC	SC OBC

but are joined by the SCs at the 95 per cent level. It is noteworthy that the all-castes mean MPCE for 2004-5 is neither significantly lower nor higher than the 1999-2000 figure at all confidence levels.

Though they are indispensable as readily understood summary measures, averages also suppress a lot of information by making a single number represent an entire distribution. The representative claims of the mean or even the median are greatly weakened when the distribution in question is a skewed one, as is the case with consumption expenditure. Therefore it is necessary to go beyond averages to look at the 'shape' of the distribution itself, to see how different sections of it have been affected during the period in question. This is attempted in the next section.

COMPARISON OF PERCENTILES OF CONSUMPTION EXPENDITURE

This section takes a disaggregated look at the MPCE distribution for each caste group by looking at five percentiles—the 5th, 25th, 50th (the median), 75th and the 95th. Thus, instead of a single value in the middle of the distribution (like the median or mean), we are now looking at five values spread along its full range. Table 4.5 shows the five different percentiles for each caste group and for rural India as a whole for the two surveys.

Except for the STs and SCs, other caste groups as well as rural India as a whole show the greatest gains in the highest percentile, i.e. the 95th percentile. The same percentile shows small declines for both STs and SCs, implying that the top of the distribution has remained stagnant across these five years for these castes.

TABLE 4.5: PERCENTILES OF MONTHLY PER CAPITA CONSUMPTION EXPENDITURE DISTRIBUTION

by Caste Groups, 1999-2000 to 2004-5, Rural India

Percentiles of MPCE	Year of Survey	MPCE (in 2004-5 Rupees) of Different Caste Groups				Rural India (All Castes)
		ST	SC	OBC	UC	
p. 5	1999-2000	204	230	257	288	249
	2004-5	199	243	267	289	253
	% Change	–2.70	5.38	3.90	0.46	1.66
p. 25	1999-2000	293	324	357	419	355
	2004-5	299	334	366	417	360
	% Change	1.93	2.89	2.58	–0.42	1.27
p. 50	1999-2000	379	413	460	545	465
	2004-5	391	422	472	553	469
	% Change	3.13	2.09	2.57	1.38	0.77
p. 75	1999-2000	509	542	610	753	628
	2004-5	520	546	623	763	630
	% Change	2.17	0.72	2.12	1.30	0.39
p. 95	1999-2000	814	844	987	1283	1057
	2004-5	803	844	1038	1361	1084
	% Change	–1.39	–0.02	4.87	5.74	2.45

Notes: Percentage change is calculated with 2004-5 as base; MPCE data for 2004-5 (61st round) as per 'MRP' of Planning Commission Expert Committee, which is roughly comparable to 1999-2000 (55th Round). UC=Upper Caste, i.e. all those who are not included in ST, SC or OBC groups. Percentile values shown in cells are rounded to the nearest integer, but percentage change is computed on the accurate unrounded values.

The large amount of information contained in Table 4.5 is better assimilated through a graphical presentation. Figure 4.1 shows the percentiles of MPCE for different caste groups for each of the two surveys. Because they are drawn to the same scale, it is possible to get a sense of both inter-year features as well as inter-caste features of the MPCE distribution. The placement of the caste curves of percentiles remains the same across the two surveys, showing that the UCs are clearly the best off, with the OBCs next, followed by the closely bunched curves for the SCs and STs. The gap between the UC and OBC curves is bigger than the gap between the OBC curve and those for the SCs and STs. Generally, the inter-caste difference at each percentile tends to increase as we move from the lowest (5th) to the highest (95th) percentile. The curve of each slope increases (i.e. it becomes more steep) as we move to higher levels of MPCE, with the segment connecting the 75th to the 95th percentile being the steepest.

The situation in urban India is very different from the rural scene, as Table 4.6 demonstrates. It is immediately striking that so many of the percentiles for so many caste groups as well as for urban India as a whole show a decline between 1999 and 2005. For the poorest of the poor at the 5th percentile, these five years have led to lower levels

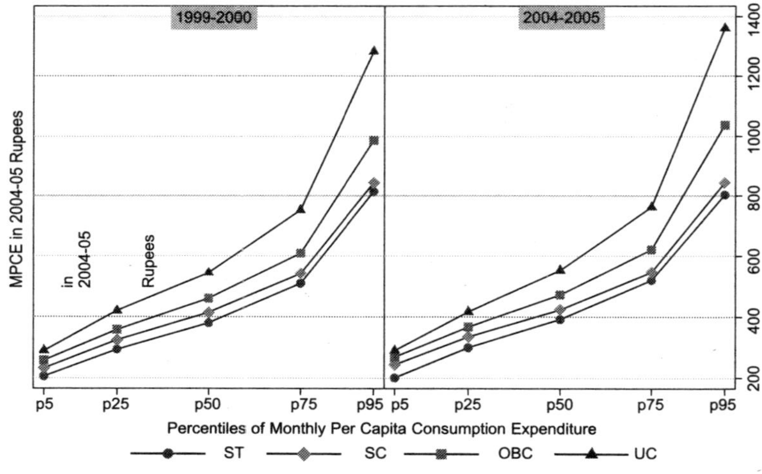

Source: Computed from NSSO 55th and 61st Round Data.

FIGURE 4.1: CASTE AND CONSUMPTION LEVELS, RURAL INDIA 2000–5

of consumption in *all* caste groups. In fact, for the SC and OBC, all percentiles except the 95th register a decline in consumption levels; the same is true of overall urban India.

Figure 6.2 highlights the implications of Table 4.6. The placement of the caste curves shows the UC far above all other castes, with the ST and OBC curves being almost indistinguishable from each other, with the SC curve at the bottom. The ST and the OBC have slightly higher consumption levels than the SC throughout the distribution. However, it is clear that the ST and OBC are much closer to the SC than to the UC curve. It is also striking that the caste gap at each percentile rises sharply as we move up the distribution, with the upper half showing much more divergence after nearly identical starting points for the 5th percentile. The steep upward slopes in all curves between the 75th and 95th percentiles is notable, the most prominent being that for the UCs, whose curve distances itself more and more from all other curves as we go up the distribution. In fact, Table 4.6 tells us that the 95th percentile consumption expenditure level for the UCs is *more than double* that for the 75th percentile in 2004-5! Figure 4.2 also underlines a fact presented in Table 4.6, namely that the only really significant gain in consumption levels across the two surveys is for the 95th percentile of the UC group—the respective

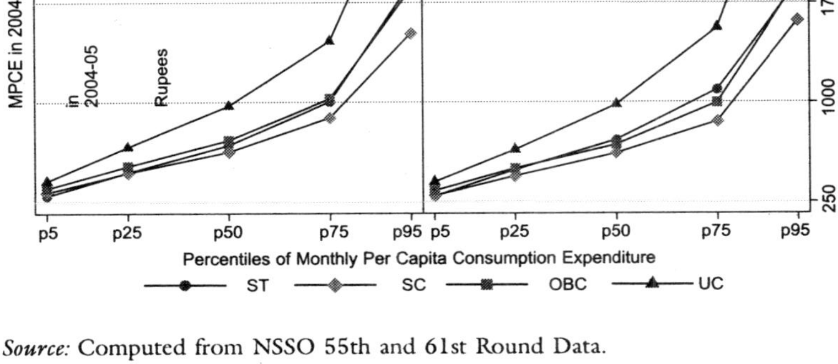

Source: Computed from NSSO 55th and 61st Round Data.

FIGURE 4.2: CASTE AND CONSUMPTION LEVELS, URBAN INDIA 2000-5

TABLE 4.6: PERCENTILES OF MONTHLY PER CAPITA CONSUMPTION EXPENDITURE DISTRIBUTION by Caste Groups, 1999-2000 to 2004-5, Urban India

Percentiles of MPCE	Year of Survey	MPCE (in 2004-5 Rupees) of Different Caste Groups				Urban India (All Castes)
		ST	SC	OBC	UC	
p. 5	1999-2000	297	323	356	410	366
	2004-5	294	297	337	403	346
	% Change	–0.9	–8.9	–5.8	–1.8	–5.8
p. 25	1999-2000	477	470	521	664	567
	2004-5	490	446	504	643	540
	% Change	2.6	–5.4	–3.4	–3.3	–5.1
p. 50	1999-2000	676	625	715	975	814
	2004-5	714	613	679	983	777
	% Change	5.3	–1.9	–5.3	0.8	–4.8
p. 75	1999-2000	1004	887	1028	1463	1230
	2004-5	1094	856	997	1560	1227
	% Change	8.2	–3.7	–3.1	6.2	–0.3
p. 95	1999-2000	1890	1521	1850	2798	2351
	2004-5	1892	1615	1910	3171	2511
	% Change	0.1	5.8	3.1	11.8	6.4

Notes: Per cent change is calculated with 2004-5 as base; MPCE data for 2004-5 (61st round) as per 'MRP' of Planning Commission Expert Committee, which is roughly comparable to 1999-2000 (55th round). UC=Upper Caste, i.e. all those who are not included in ST, SC or OBC groups.

percentile markers for all other castes being more or less at the same level in the two years.

COMPARISON OF 'CASTE GAP' RELATIVE TO THE 'UPPER' CASTES

Although Tables 4.5 and 4.6 in combination with Figures 4.1 and 4.2 do give us some sense of the relative standing of different castes *vis-à-vis* each other, it is necessary to directly examine the extent of caste inequality and its trend over the period covered by the two surveys. In order to do this, a Caste-Gap Index (CGI) is computed, which is simply the difference between the rupee values of consumption expenditure of UCs and the other castes expressed as a percentage of the UC consumption expenditure level for that percentile. Thus, for each percentile p,

$$CGI = \left(\frac{UC_p - (ST, SC, OBC)_p}{UC_p} \right) \times 100$$

The CGI allows us to directly measure caste inequality in a simple and readily interpretable manner. Computing such an index for different percentiles along the distribution allows us a disaggregated view of caste inequality in different class segments.

Table 4.7 (on rural India) presents the rupee values (rounded to the nearest integer) of the five percentiles of MPCE for each caste in the first four rows for ease of reference, followed by the CGI in the last three rows. There is no index for the UCs since they form the reference group. The CGI rows show that for all three castes, the index rises steadily as you read from left to right, i.e. as we move from the bottom to the top of the MPCE distribution. (The only exception to this is for the move from the 5th to the 25th percentile for the STs in the 61st round.) This serves to underline the unsurprising fact that caste inequality increases with levels of affluence and tends to be highest at the top of the class pyramid. It is noteworthy that the OBCs are generally not very far from the UCs, while the STs are generally far below the UCs, with differentials of 30 per cent or more all along the spectrum.

Figure 4.3 presents the CGI data from Table 4.7 in graphical form, where it can be more easily grasped. First, the upward slope of all three curves (the ST curve being a partial exception) shows that inequality rises with consumption expenditure levels. Secondly, the positioning of the curves for each of the three caste groups shows

TABLE 4.7: CGI OF MONTHLY PER CAPITA CONSUMPTION EXPENDITURE, RURAL INDIA

Row Description	Caste	NSSO 55th Round, 1999-2000					NSSO 61st Round, 2004-5				
		p. 5	p. 25	p. 50	p. 75	p. 95	p. 5	p. 25	p. 50	p. 75	p. 95
Percentiles of MPCE	ST	204	293	379	509	814	199	299	391	520	803
in Rupees	SC	230	324	413	542	844	243	334	422	546	844
at 2004-5 prices	OBC	257	357	460	610	987	267	366	472	623	1038
	UC	288	419	545	753	1283	289	417	553	763	1361
CGI:	ST	29.2	30.1	30.5	32.4	36.6	31.1	28.3	29.3	31.8	41.0
UC*p* minus	SC	20.1	22.7	24.2	28.0	34.2	15.9	19.9	23.7	28.4	38.0
(ST, SC, OBC)*p*	OBC	10.8	14.8	15.6	19.0	23.1	7.6	12.2	14.6	18.3	23.7
divided by UC*p*											
and multiplied by 100											

Notes: Computed from NSSO unit level data. *p* = percentile. CGI is expressed in percentage points.

the degree to which they are behind or below the UC consumption levels. Thus the OBC curves are the lowest, with the poorer end of the distribution showing differences that are in single digits, and the upper end peaking under 25 per cent. The STs have the highest curves, showing that even at the bottom end of the consumption spectrum, they are very far behind the UCs. It is noteworthy that the ST curves are above the OBC curves and do not overlap at all, highlighting the fact that the minimum CGI of the STs is above the maximum for the OBCs. One peculiar aspect of the ST curve is the apparent decrease in levels of inequality in the middle of the distribution, particularly for the 2004-5 curve. A third notable feature brought out by Figure 4.3 is that by and large the 2004-5 curves tend to be below the 1999-2000 curves except in the top quarter of the distribution. (The STs are once again a partial exception here.) This indicates that inter-caste inequalities may have declined slightly between the 55th and 61st rounds, though this must be treated as a tentative conclusion given the problems of comparability between these rounds. However, inequality increases sharply from the 75th to the 95th percentile, specially for the STs and SCs.

Table 4.8 presents the CGI data for urban India. It is immediately obvious that inequality levels are higher compared to the rural sector.

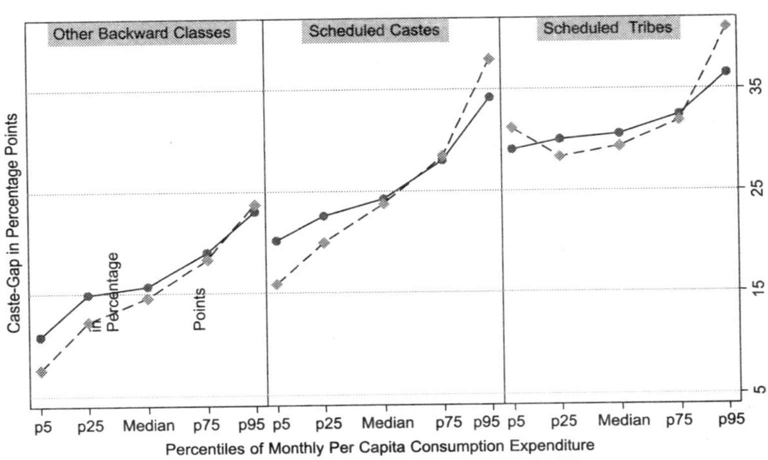

Source: Computed from NSSO 55th and 61st Round Data.

FIGURE 4.3: CASTE-GAP RELATIVE TO UPPER CASTES, RURAL INDIA 2000–5

TABLE 4.8: CGI OF MONTHLY PER CAPITA CONSUMPTION EXPENDITURE, URBAN INDIA

Row Description	Caste	NSSO 55th Round, 1999-2000					NSSO 61st Round, 2004-5				
		p. 5	p. 25	p. 50	p. 75	p. 95	p. 5	p. 25	p. 50	p. 75	p. 95
Percentiles of MPCE	ST	297	477	676	1004	1890	294	490	714	1094	1892
in Rupees	SC	323	470	625	887	1521	297	446	613	856	1615
at 2004-5 prices	OBC	356	521	715	1028	1850	337	504	679	997	1910
	UC	410	664	975	1463	2798	403	643	983	1560	3171
CGI:	ST	27.6	28.2	30.7	31.4	32.5	27.0	23.8	27.4	29.9	40.3
UC*p* minus	SC	21.2	29.2	35.9	39.4	45.6	26.3	30.6	37.6	45.1	49.1
(ST, SC, OBC)*p* divided by UC*p* and multiplied by 100	OBC	13.2	21.5	26.7	29.7	33.9	16.4	21.6	30.9	36.1	39.8

Notes: Computed from NSSO unit level data. *p* = percentile. CGI is expressed in percentage points.

Moreover, unlike in rural India where the OBCs were beginning to catch up with the UCs, or seem to be heading in that direction, there is not much to choose between the three caste groups in urban India. Although the SCs are clearly the worst off, none of the three is dramatically different from the others.

Table 4.8 also shows that, on the whole, urban caste inequalities seem to have worsened between 1999 and 2005. This is immediately confirmed by Figure 4.4, which shows that (despite the usual anomalies associated with the ST group) the curves for 2004-5 are clearly above the curves for 1999-2000. Once again the ST curves are distinctive, showing a significant decline in inequality in the bottom three-quarters of the MPCE distribution; it is only with the 95th percentile that the 2004-5 curve rises above the 1999-2000 curve. For both the SCs and the OBCs, the curves for the two surveys diverge significantly in the top half of the distribution. As the worst off group in urban India, the SCs show the greatest range of inequality, the curves stretching from around 20 per cent at the bottom of the distribution to almost 50 per cent at the top. It is sobering to realize that in 2005, the consumption levels of even the richest (95th percentile) among the urban 'lower' castes are 40-50 per cent lower than that of their UC counterparts.

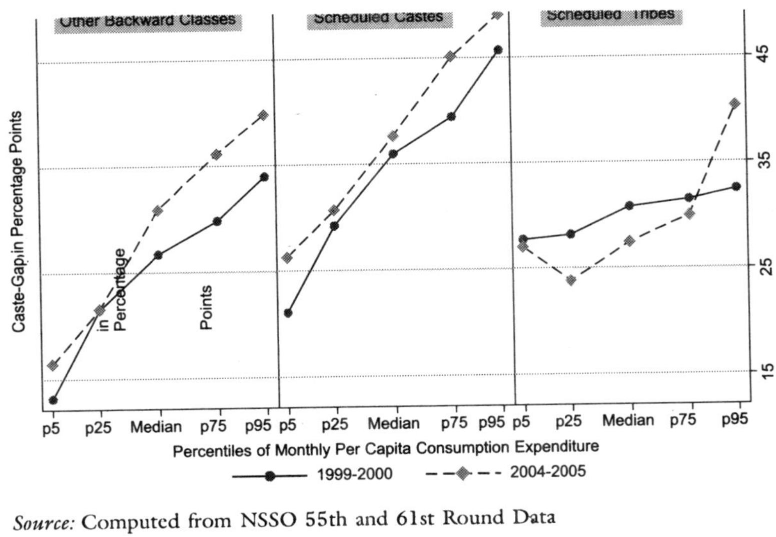

Source: Computed from NSSO 55th and 61st Round Data

FIGURE 4.4: CASTE-GAP RELATIVE TO UPPER CASTES, URBAN INDIA (2000–5)

CONCLUSION

Despite the limitations of such an exercise—pointed out in the beginning of this paper in first section on data issues—it is clear that macro data provide a useful, even indispensable vantage point from which to study caste inequalities. In keeping with the trend towards sociocultural contextualization of economic institutions and processes, it is necessary to consider the social identities of the poor or the disadvantaged as much as the privileged sections of our society. Such an exercise offers useful prophylaxis against the dominant ideologies of caste which tend to treat it as problem located within the 'lower' castes.

As the data in this paper amply demonstrate, caste continues to be an important dimension of economic inequalities. Although we have as yet only two data points, preliminary trends suggest that urban inequalities are worsening, though there may be a slight improvement in the rural situation, particularly at the lower levels of the MPCE distribution. Rural OBCs and urban STs are well worth studying further, particularly because they seem to be following a distinctive trajectory. However, rural STs and urban SCs are the worst off groups in contemporary Indian society and they too must be studied further. It is remarkable that the 'upper' castes remain so distinctly privileged relative to other castes despite six decades of a modern constitution that outlaws caste privilege. Rather than remaining trapped within a perspective that treats the upper castes as being 'caste-less', we need to understand the ways in which caste privilege has secularized and modernized itself so that it can be nurtured by other means.

Acknowledgements: Earlier versions of this paper were presented at seminars at the Centre for Social Development and the Indira Gandhi National Open University, New Delhi. I am especially grateful to Debal SinghaRoy and Prashant Trivedi, as well as members of the audience at both venues. The statistical analysis for this paper was partly facilitated by a Faculty Development Grant from the University of Delhi, which is also gratefully acknowledged.

NOTES

1. Despite the complications that beset all aggregative caste groupings, the term 'upper caste' is in my opinion a better one than the vaguer term

'other castes'. The latter is a product of the dominant (i.e. upper caste oriented) ideology that treats the upper castes as 'caste-less' while highlighting the caste identities of the so-called lower castes.

2. Comparison of the 2001 Census figures for population share of STs and SCs with the 61st Round of the NSSO for 2004-5 shows the following: NSSO estimates of ST population are very accurate, with the rural figures being 0.16 percentage points less and the urban ones being 0.6 percentage points more than the Census. However, NSSO SC population share estimates exceed Census figures by more than 3 per cent (rural=3.41, urban=3.27). See S. Deshpande (2008), 'Dalits in the Muslim and Christian Communities: A Status Report on Current Social Scientific Knowledge', National Commission of Minorities, January, p. 21, Table 3 for details.
3. See the press release of the Planning Commission entitled 'Poverty Lines for 2004-5' of March 2007.
4. Price indices are taken from the Labour Bureau, Shimla website at http://labourbureau.nic.in. The CPIAL price deflator for January 2000–January 2005 is 341/307, while the corresponding CPIIW deflator is 526/431.

II. LAND, LABOUR AND MARGINALIZATION

CHAPTER 5

Walking the 'Shangri-La' Sikkim Trail

VIBHA ARORA

'Shangri-La' Sikkim epitomizes the idea of the simulacra. The efflorescence of Buddhism and poetic representations of a 'Shangri-La' are gaining ground in discourse and in Sikkim's utopian self-presentation to a post-modern world of global capital. Baudrillard candidly said 'history is our lost referential, that is to say our myth' and 'illusion is no longer possible because the real is no longer possible' (1994: 19, 43). Is there a *real* Shangri-La Sikkim? A sceptical reader may indeed doubt my correlating the utopian Shangri-La with the Baudrillard's theory of simulation.

I begin this paper by underscoring the near universal occurrence of descriptions of utopia and dystopia to nuance my reading of such tropes and situate their role in the social construction and representations of the self in relation to others. The next section discusses the context of the emergence of Shangri-La Tibet as a utopia of Western modernist imperialist discourse and its appropriation by Tibetans living in exile. These preceding two sections ground my analytical frame to explain the transformation of the former Buddhist kingdom of Sikkim into a 'Shangri-La' Sikkim for global consumption in the twenty-first century. The Shangri-La Tibet image had powerfully disseminated the imperial myth of an independent Tibet. Does the trope of 'Shangri-La' Sikkim carry any political message? Is it merely a trope for a consuming tourist? As I walk the Shangri-La trail in the third section of this paper, I discover its hidden meaning as a satire about a society experiencing heightened cultural revival yet enduring alienation and disruption to the extent that many indigenous argue that Sikkim has been lost and become meaningless for those who belong to it. The Shangri-La trope slides in this matrix to simulate a Shangri-La Sikkim for the self and the wider world thereby attempting to efface any critique of development.

UTOPIA, DYSTOPIA, HETEROTOPIAS: LOCATING MEANING AND CONSTRUCTIONS

Is utopia merely a spatially located, wish-fantasy? Nearly all societies have visions of utopia, as places of harmony, peace, and everlasting contentment, places that are fecund with everything desirable and free of disease, poverty, and death. Images of dystopia, the source and stuff of nightmares are similarly generated nearly in all cultures and social groups. The anti-utopia or dystopia expresses the fears of those for whom the very things that were regarded promising in utopia became the source of threat to human values. Both utopia and its negation in the dystopia are extra-terrestrial fictions located beyond the here and now of this everyday life (Silverman, 1980: 173).

If utopia and dystopia represent the two vertical poles of an axis, their meeting point on the horizontal axis is the 'here and the now', the heterotopias. Heterotopias require utopias and dystopias to meaningfully understand themselves. The heterotopias indicate a plurality of possibilities in the here and now, including a degenerate utopia (hypertopian) that is desirable or a degenerate dystopia (hypotopian) that is less undesirable (ibid.: 171-3). 'Heterotopias are the places and discourses of spaces, which we occupy, the architecture of our knowledge, and the frames of our interaction' (ibid.: 175). In her article on utopia, Ruth Levitas argues that the content, form, and social role of utopias vary with the material conditions in which these utopias exist. 'When people feel able to influence society, this will be reflected in their utopias; when they do not, this will be reflected too' (Levitas, 1979: 31). In the former, utopias may catalyse action while in the latter case, action directed towards transforming society are going to be unlikely. The features of utopia and the image of the society on which these depend are symptoms of the way people feel about the present (ibid.). Focusing exclusively on Western utopias, Krishna Kumar (2003) argues that while they liberate the imagination they also set their own limits in the given conditions of morality, technology, and society. One society's utopia can be another society's dystopia. These *topoi* about utopia and dystopia are essential discourses which we employ to make sense of our contemporary location, our experiences, and the condition of our social life.

As I argue in the next section, Shangri-La itself was the product of the colonial encounter between Western and non-Western cultures after the First World War. It came to symbolize the quest for a place of universal wisdom and ineffable peace, despite being known by various names in different religious traditions of Buddhism, Jainism, Shamanism in Asia and other Northern areas (Lepage, 1996: 4-7). Shangri-La was a Western utopia that became synonymous with Tibet. Is 'Shangri-La' Sikkim also a Western creation or generated self-reflexively for representing itself to the world? If 'Shangri-La' Sikkim is a utopia then what is the dsytopia here? Are there other discourses that counter Sikkim's definition as a utopia? What is the context of its emergence and circulation in discourse? Does this image have any roots in history or does it have a timeless frame? If yes, then which sections posit and present it to the wider world? Does this 'Shangri-La' image have any connection with the former Buddhist kingdom that became a part of secular democratic India in 1975?

It is in the critical interface of the desirable and the undesirable that we need to locate the meaning and structure of a social formation. Between these two discursive extremes of a ***utopic Sikkim*** and the ***dystopic Sikkim*** are located multiple heterotopias of Sikkim that are in turn generated by referential groups situationally and discursively to make sense of their diverse experiences.

LOCATING SHANGRI-LA AND SHANGRI-LA TIBET

As the world becomes a homogeneous global village breaking barriers of time and spatial distance, the proponents of cultural tourism advertise themselves as vestiges of authentic cultural forms. The technologies and practices of tourism have converted the world into an exhibition and places packaged as postcard images. Any Google search of Shangri-La immediately yields the scenic locations and memorable experiences that are currently being marketed by Shangri-La, the internationally acclaimed chain of luxury hotels. Appadurai's (1986) explanation of 'aesthetics of decontextualization' does explain the process by which Shangri-La can be replicated anywhere and everywhere. The enduring product of a Western paradigm of an Eastern paradise, Shangri-La is resurfacing in Shangri-La Sikkim and in China. In December 2001, an obscure Zhongdian county (*Rgyal thing* in the Tibetan language) in China's Yunan province renamed itself as Shangri-La.

Chronologically, the term Shangri-La was born in the West as a fictional hidden paradise in an English novel *Lost Horizon* published by James Hilton in 1933. The commercially successful cinematic production of this novel by Frank Capra in 1937 impregnated it in the Western imaginary. Over time it has come to signify the idea of an imaginary idyllic utopia or a hidden paradise. Anthropologically, the term alludes to the Eastern utopia of an Orientalist mystique that has engaged the Occidental imagination in the last three hundred years. In the contemporary period, it's become a convenient label for the idealized, idolized Tibet, the country isolated and located on the roof of the world.[1] In a singular analysis of the novel *Lost Horizon*, Masuzawa (1999) suggests that Shangri-La's transformation into a generic utopia and synonym for Tibet today indicates historical amnesia and the obliteration of the colonial markings in the encounter of the West with the non-West.

Before critically analysing the historical underpinning of an essentializing Western utopic vision in Shangri-La and the associated imagery of Shangri-La Tibet, I need to underscore its philosophical roots. The idea of Shangri-La is derived from a religious conception of Shambhala enshrined in the Hindu and the Mahayana Buddhist traditions.[2] *Shambhala* (*bde 'byun* in the Tibetan language) is a Sanskrit term referring to a place of peace or tranquillity and happiness. It is considered a mystical city ruled by a divine king with Mt. Meru at its centre which is inhabited by people of great spiritual accomplishments and described extensively in the sacred texts on *Kalachakra*.[3] For Mahayana Buddhists, Shambhala is the centre of their religious life, the source of spiritual energies, not a myth but an ultimate reality. It is the eminent wisdom centre eluding normal mortals and hidden from the outside world. Closely associated with the kingdom of Shambhala as a paradise is the tradition of establishing *sbas-yul*[4] as places safeguarding *gter-ma*[5] to be revealed by a chosen *gter-ston*[6] at the appropriate time to disseminate wisdom. The *sbas-yul* were founded as places of refuge for select chosen Buddhist followers and spiritually accomplished Buddhist practitioners during times of crises (Reinhard, 1978: 5-6). With sacred treasures such as objects and texts hidden in their landscape, a number of such isolated hidden valleys congenial to human settlement were designated as sanctuaries by the Buddhist patron saint Padmasambhava who propagated Buddhism in Tibet and Sikkim.[7]

The exact geographical location of this celestial eastern Himalayan paradise Shambhala has been intensely debated but eluded any fixity. This has recontextualized and simultaneously made its ideological and geographical appropriation possible. Although several scriptures and some guide-books written in the Tibetan language describe the route to this sacred celestial paradise, nonetheless the factual descriptions of the topography and geographical descriptions become increasingly obscurantist and metaphorical as the narrative unfolds and pilgrims supposedly near their final destination. Such that only the spiritually accomplished recognize the inner and outer doors that lead them into Shambhala and its associative tributaries, the *sbas-yul*. The journey to Shambhala and to these *sbas-yul* is twofold for any pilgrim or Buddhist follower, involving an inner spiritual journey and an outer physical one consisting of the overcoming of immense physical hardship. Sikkim persisting as the heartland of Nyingamapa and Kargyu practices, therefore draws upon its assignation as Padmasambhava's *sbas-yul* to represent itself as a Shangri-La. It is also believed to be the sacred landscape into which the next Buddha will be reborn.[8]

Historically, the idea of Shambala was promoted in Western occult circles by none other than Madame Helena Blavatsky, who founded the Theosophical Society in 1879.[9] Nevertheless, Shambhala remained on the outermost fringe of credibility until the Central Asian expedition of the poet, artist, and Russian theosophist N. Roerich in 1923-6. Thereafter the hidden valleys of the legendary Kun Lun mountains of Tibet are particularly regarded to be its location. Roerich's admirer, Andre Tomas published a book *Shambhala: Oasis of Light* in 1976 (cf. Lepage, 1996: 9-11) to promote this concept. The Western discovery of the *gter*, *Bardo-Thodol* or the *Tibetan Book of the Dead*—published in 1974 after being translated by Evans-Wentz in collaboration with the Sikkimese Kazi lama Dawa Samdup, distilled the transformation of Tibet into the Shangri-La (Bishop, 1989; Lepage, 1996). The idea of Shambhala has been given further impetus by the proponents of Tibetan Buddhism graphically and persuasively representing it in the sacred *mandala*, extensively discussing it during the *Kalachakra* initiations and explaining *Bardo Thodol* (Bishop, 1993: 77; Lepage, 1996).

In current parlance, Shangri-La is used romantically and poetically to refer to Tibet, an idealized religious kingdom of Tibet ruled by the temporal-religious leader Dalai Lama until the Chinese annexed it in 1951. The Western preoccupation with Shangri-La and Shambhala is indicated in the voluminous literature on Tibetan history, culture, esoteric philosophy and more recently films and websites.[10] Tibet was never as isolated as it's imagined to be (van Spengen, 1995), so how could it become the Shangri-La candidate? Shangri has no meaning in the Tibetan language while *la* refers to a mountain pass. So how has Shangri-La become a synonym of the idea of a mythic Tibetan paradise? An object of nineteenth-century imperial desire, the fantasy of Tibet was grounded in the European desire to dominate it politically (Lopez, 1998: 5-6). Bishop (1989) candidly argues in his book *The Myth of Shangri-La: Tibet, Travel Writing and the Western Creation of Sacred Landscape* that Shangri-La was essentially an invention of the British Raj, although it became the dominant mode of depicting Tibetan culture to the Western imagination.[11] The continued threat of globalization and a homogenization of cultures into a uniform dreary materialistic world after the First World War gave an imaginative context for the mythic Shangri-La to be crystallized and geographically located in Tibet (Bishop, 1993: 57). In a subsequent book *Dreams of Power: Tibetan Buddhism and the Western Imagination*, published in 1993, Bishop compellingly argues that 'Tibet has been described with all the qualities of a dream, a collective hallucination' (1993: 16) and considered by the West as its museum of a fantasizing past (1993: 41).

The Western yearning to experience the Shangri-La has not dissipated but intensified after the annexation of Tibet and the resettlement of His Holiness the Dalai Lama and Tibet's government in exile, the gratuitous destruction of Tibet's cultural heritage and religious treasures, and the rapacious exploitation of its beautiful landscape by the People's Republic of China.[12] The need to escape such a regimented imagination of Tibet is appropriately encapsulated by the title of an influential book *Prisoners of Shangri-La* (1998) wherein Donald Lopez analyses the romance of Tibet, ensconced as it is in the Western search for a utopia. 'Tibet was never valued for the people who lived there, but for its treasures' (Lopez, 1998: 5). He argues that 'the language of Tibet not only creates knowledge about Tibet, but Tibet itself, a Tibet which the Tibetan people have appropriated in exile and deployed to gain a standing in the world' (ibid.: 10). Klieger similarly explains this process as 'the collision of an Occidental paradigm of an eastern paradise, Shangri-La, and an indigenous utopia which constructs a distanced, sacred, Tibetan homeland upon the established ideas of Shambhala, Mt. Meru, Mt.

Potala and the divine rule mythology' (1997: 61). For Klieger, the recent post-modern invention of a hyperreal Shangri-La is not of Western origin, but an indigenous self-reflexive representation by Tibetans forced to live in exile. Tibet is being *museumized* by the West by ignoring the modernization of Tibet and the presence of a living secular culture.[13] The notion of Shangri-La should have become extinct after the annexation of Tibet but not Tibetan civilization (Harris, 1999: 13), which is being perceived as an endangered culture. The deconstruction and the torching of Shangri-La imagery in recent Tibetological scholarship conclusively establishes the difficulties of defining Tibet, the identity of Tibetans living in Tibet and as the diaspora (cf. Klieger, 2002: 1). Many Tibetan youth and Tibetans living in Tibet do not subscribe to this Shangri-La Tibet (ibid.; Korom, 1997). These recent critiques influence my ethnographic quest to 'Shangri-La' Sikkim.

WALKING THE SHANGRI-LA SIKKIM TRAIL

The greatest material production of our contemporary world is of cultural form, production of hyperreal images where the real is displaced and lost in mirrors simulating images endlessly for our consumptive world. Advances in technologies of communication and consumer culture collude to frame the social world on the TV screen while advances in transportation egg us to leave the couch and the TV and travel into other time-zones and spaces. Consumer choice becomes the central axis on which our production system revolves, hence the marketing of cultural diversity and heterogeneity become critical for its continued success. Where nothing is sacred, inaccessible, and out-of-bound, where even the celestial paradise is available for our sampling, money becomes the paramount passport of any travel, while the tourism industry emerge the authors and gatekeepers of all utopias and dystopias. This explains how mass culture and tourism imaginatively foreground the Buddhist culture of Sikkim with its scenic rice-terraces, uplifting Himalayan mountain peaks and the forested river valleys, meandering waterscapes, gushing waterfalls, and crystal deep lakes as an out-of-the world celestial paradise. Tourist brochures and picture postcards incisively frame Sikkim as a Buddhist landscape by selectively framing Buddhist *mantras*, sacred texts, figures, murals, religious sites, and rituals. Exhibited by Bhutan, Ladakh and Tibet, albeit these packaged features are not unique to

Sikkim. Nonetheless, they have been restrictively used to describe a Shangri-La Sikkim to a global political economy.

Sikkim is framed as the land of abundant bounty, peaceful, fecund, harmonious, and globally integrated into the world economy. The picture and the word fuse to give an interpretative frame to its image and its imagination:

> Sikkim, the land of mystic splendour
> Sikkim, the land of Kanchenjunga
> Sikkim, the land of the Padmasambhava
> Sikkim, the Buddhist Kingdom of Sikkim
> Sikkim, the Himalayan Shangri-La
> Sikkim, the hidden paradise
> Sikkim, the land of peace and tranquillity
> Sikkim, the ultimate eco-tourism destination

One of the first tourist handbooks on Sikkim written by Rajeev Verma, who is employed in Sikkim's Department of Police, was first published in 1990. In the preface to its ninth edition printed in 1999, I found this description, 'The pristine and unspoilt natural beauty [of Sikkim] includes alpine landscapes and thick luxuriant tropical forests, rivers in torrents, and peaceful lakes—a true Shangri-La . . . in Sikkim there are hardly any beggars, people are well-dressed and crime is negligible' (Verma, 1999: 5). While admitting that the traces of Sikkim's violent and invasive past had faded away, Verma (1999: 6) warns the reader about a quieter invasion that is taking place due to contact with 'cultures from outside'. Despite everything Sikkim continues to maintain a character of its own, because it's free of casteism, child labour, illiteracy, discrimination and poverty that is endemic to other parts of India. Hence, 'it continues to be a Shangri-La beyond the far horizon' (ibid.: 100). Sikkim is perceived to be utopian because it does not exhibit the vices of and many of India-like features. In 2001, I was given a booklet entitled, *Sikkim: Ultimate Eco-tourism Destination* by an official of the Tourist Department of Sikkim. It begins with this description, 'Nestled in the lap of the Himalayas, bounded by some of the highest mountain peaks, amidst spectacular terrain, pristine lakes, luxuriant forests, roaring rivers and gentle streams, Sikkim is a venerable paradise and a destination for all seasons' (n.d.: 1). Recently, I purchased a slick, glossy handbook entitled *Sikkim: The Land of Mystique* comprising ten chapters enticing and beckoning tourists to this Himalayan amphitheatre. This visually rich guidebook carries a seductive narrative about Sikkim's ecology and natural beauty, its ethnic diversity, history and culture, along with practical information for all visitors.[14] Here Sikkim is transformed into a jewel of India (2002: 35). None of these tourist brochures ever suggests Sikkim as a place for us to settle in permanently. Utopias are not places of mortal human settlement and must remain out-of-bound.

Sikkim's 'Shangri-La' image has no author-claimant but historical roots and mythological references in the Buddhist and Lepcha imaginary. Shambhala had its Mt. Meru while reverence for Mt. Kanchenjunga permeates Lepcha and Bhutia mythoscape. Living in the shadow of Mt. Kanchenjunga, the Lepchas regard Sikkim to be an altar for worshipping it. They regard it as the source of grain, rain, medicines, riches, and sacred knowledge. Their mythology sources the creation by Itbu Mu of the first Lepcha couple—Tukbothing and Nazong Nyu—from its untrodden snows. They trace their descent lines to the sacred peaks and lakes of this landscape (Foning, 1987; Gorer, 1938; Morris, 1938; Siiger and Rischel, 1967). In Lepcha folklore, the place below their sacred mountain Kanchenjunga is identified as a celestial paradise, the land of the *máyel* (the land of Eden in the Lepcha language). This *máyel-lyang* is inhabited by seven brothers, who are regarded to be semi-divine beings and considered the progenitors and guardians of the Lepchas. They are responsible for ensuring agricultural fertility in Lepcha-land. The Lepchas worship these *máyel* beings in agricultural festivals of sowing, harvest, and first fruit offerings (Foning, 1987: 50-4). The route towards this *máyel-lyang* follows from the restricted access areas of Dzongu in north Sikkim, which nearly for the past two hundred years has been inhabited by the Lepchas[15] and constitutes *their heartland*. It is in this landscape that the government of Sikkim intends constructing the 280 MW Panan Hydel Project over river Talung, a tributary of the sacred river Teesta.

Tibetan Buddhism regards Mt. Kanchenjunga (its Tibetan name is *Gangs chen mdzod lnga*) to be the guardian deity of Sikkim.[16] According to learned lamas, the area below Mt. Kanchenjunga, which lies in west Sikkim and is identified to be Yoksum, is the heart of *sbas-yul 'Bras-mo-ljongs*.[17] In Mahayana Buddhist literature, Sikkim enjoys special status not merely as a paradise consecrated by the Lotus Born Buddhist saint Padmasambhava (eighth century), but it is also the designated hidden valley where persecuted Buddhists would seek refuge during crises. After Tibet's annexation in 1951, a number of refugees settled in Sikkim. The pilgrimage guide to Sikkim[18] describes it as a place of bliss, abundance, peace and all those born here can achieve great spiritual accomplishment. According to the prophecy outlined in this text, it is *the designated sacred place* where the next Buddha would take rebirth, in the sacred lake Guru Dongmar in north Sikkim (see Acharya, 1998). It is believed that Buddhist saints such as Padmasambhava hid sacred treasures and magical objects (*gter* in the Tibetan language) here that would be revealed by designated personages (*gter-ton* in the Tibetan language) for the earth's well-being.

Since the seventeenth-century Sikkim was ruled by a *Chos-rgyal*[19] belonging to the Namgyal dynasty. This Buddhist kingdom of Sikkim was incorporated into India in 1975. The threat of Sikkim being swallowed by communist China after the latter had annexed Tibet, Sikkim's transformation into a battleground in the 1960s, ethnic unrest within Sikkim against the feudal theocracy, its critical geopolitical location near Siliguri in North Bengal and the chicken-neck 22-km corridor connecting Indian mainland with the north-eastern states prompted the Indian takeover.

The transition into a democratic state should have effaced Sikkim's *sbas-yul* mythoscape and decimated its status as a sacred landscape.[20] However, the global efflorescence of Buddhism in the late 1980s and its importance in attracting international and global tourism, a recognition of this phenomenon as a revenue-earning potential for Sikkim, prompted the national government of India and the state government to build the necessary infrastructure and relax the visitation rules that had kept Sikkim out-of-bound for most tourists and pilgrims. Until the mid-1990s Sikkim was hidden from the gazing global tourist. In contrast, from 2000 onwards, Sikkim has constantly been in the news with the chief minister himself travelling to US and Europe to promote tourism.

After years of conducting research here, I elected to ask the multi-ethnic residents of Sikkim if they believed in 'Shangri-La' Sikkim. Do they believe that they are the chosen people selected to inhabit the blessed Sikkim? Some indigenous Lepchas–Bhutias parroted that only the very learned lamas could comprehend the meaning of *sbas-yul* Sikkim, while others remarked that it was a marketing strategy of the tourism department to promote national and international tourism. To many Lepchas–Bhutias the logic of maximizing revenue justified the marketing of such imaginations and even the construction of the 135-feet tall statue of Padmasambhava at Samdruptse in south Sikkim. Contradicting these views, many Nepali residents sarcastically remarked that they could not imagine Sikkim to be a paradise.

The local Sikkimese[21] may or may not subscribe to the idea of Sikkim being a Shangri-La but some sections of Sikkim *do* make an effort to cater to this tourist imagination *by* appropriating Sikkim's Tibetan Buddhist heritage and cultural history. Sections with vested commercial interests imagine Sikkim in a particular manner. This is strongly indicated in the naming of numerous hotels and tourist lodges such as Hotel Tashi Delek, Hotel Tibet, Norbu Ghang, Chumbi Residency, Hotel Bayul, Hotel Meylong, Denzong Shangri-La and names of tourist agencies such as Namgyal Treks and Tours, Snow Lion Tours, Yak and Yeti Tours, Denzong Adventures and Potala Treks, such names cash on the Shangri-La image and expectation. Very few of the listed and existing hotels and tour operators have culturally ambiguous names (e.g. Hotel Hill Top, Central Hotel, and Blue Sky Tours). Many Tibetan refugees settled in Sikkim (and also Darjeeling) are now economically dependent on this imagined Tibetanized Sikkim. As hotel-owners and tour-operators these Tibetan refugees have actively contributed to marketing Sikkim's Buddhist heritage, Sikkimese and Tibetan cuisine, and serene splendour.[22]

Having documented the Rathongchu movement,[23] I decided to approach its leaders and activists for an explanation. At the height of their protests against the Rathongchu hydroelectric project, the lamas had threatened to burn their sacred scriptures if the government did not stop desecrating the centre of the hidden valley of Sikkim. Is the Shangri-La image a metaphorical extension of the sacred landscape that those activists had wanted to be protected at any cost from all developmental activities? Was the popularization of 'Shangri-La' Sikkim imagery in tourism a victory for their cause? I hoped they would provide me with a convincing explanation. Sitting in the monastic echelon of the Deorali temple, turning his rosary an anguished Sonam Paljor Denjongpa[24] impressed on me

> Sikkim does not exist anymore. Your search for Sikkim is useless. If you want to understand our *real* culture then go to Bhutan. It is only a mythology of Sikkim that we try to hang on to today. We are losing the only history we had with these numerous hydroelectric projects that deface our landscape and desecrate our sacred landscape. We don't have a real Sikkim, because Sikkim has ceased to become the *sbas-yul 'Bras- mo-ljongs* after the massive

influx and settlement of first the Nepali and later all these Indians. Submerged among these faces in the streets and villages, where do I find the Denjongpa [indigenous Sikkimese]?

Sonam Paljor had undertaken a twenty-nine day fast and spearheaded opposition against the government planned Rathongchu project. Faced with ethnic turmoil, the government's timely decision to shelve the project in 1997 had solaced many such cultural and religious custodians of Sikkim. A distressed Sonam Paljor said, 'the proposed twenty-seven hydropower projects on Teesta will uproot the Denjongpa and root Indians in our Sikkim'.

How could this happen? Most monasteries in Sikkim are dependent on revenue from their monastic estates, donations, and government grants while other larger monasteries such as Rumtek, Tsuglakhang, Deorali, additionally have recourse to substantial financial resources and international donations. All around, I documented an explosion of Sikkim in visual culture, in the reconstruction and restoration of Buddhist monasteries, reinstatement of forgotten rituals, in residents selling a Buddhist Shangri-La and tourists purchasing its rich experience and simulating it to others through travel-blogs and pictures ad finitum. A simulation which Sonam Paljor Denjongpa has actively and knowingly contributed to when he undertook the responsibility of supervising the construction and sanctification of the 108-feet tall statue of Padmasambhava in Samdruptse near Namchi in south Sikkim. The fourteenth Dalai Lama laid the statue's foundation stone in October 1997. Constructed at the cost of an estimated Rs. 4.55 crore and made of cement and copper, this statue was religiously sanctified with prayers for weeks before being publicly inaugurated by the Dalai Lama in February 2004. Funded by the governments of India and Sikkim, its construction was managed by a team selected by the Reverend Dodrupchen Rinpoche, who is currently heading the Nyingmapa order of Mahayana Buddhism. The government tourist brochure emphasizes that the current Chief Minister Pawan Chamling was the guiding force in conceptualizing it. The state government of Sikkim appears to be aggressively engaged in preserving the culture and heritage of Sikkim while simultaneously constructing, and implementing manifold development projects. Development of Sikkim is the *mantra* buzzing in the corridors in the Tashiling complex at Gangtok, which is the hub of state administration. As a state, Sikkim is totally dependent on the central government for begetting grants to meet all the necessary administrative and development expenses. Largely an agriculturally backward state, the economic integration of Sikkim into the global economy is exclusively dependent on the government channel. Growth exigencies permit joint investment from Indian and transnational capital in infrastructural development including power generation and telecommunications, education (e.g. the Manipal Engineering and Medical Colleges at Rangpo in east Sikkim), health (Manipal Hospital at Tadong), etc. With the ministry of power's special thrust on hydropower, Sikkim has been aggressively promoting its potential over the past few years and encouraging private companies to bid for these projects.

Not very far from the monastic quarters of Sonam Paljor and below the Sikkim Institute of Higher Nyingma Studies lies the famous Namgyal Institute of Tibetology established in 1958 by the then Sikkim *Chos-rgyal* Tashi Namgyal.[25] This institute contains a library and provides a home to the scholarly collections of Buddhist philosophy and treatises of Buddhist teachers, and serves as a museum preserving historical artefacts and sacred statues of Buddhist saints. The top floor of the institute's main building is a visual exhibition about historic Sikkim comprising a photographic history of the Namgyal dynasty sourced from visual collections in museums and private collections. The institute is fast emerging as the academic locus documenting Sikkim's history and unique culture and the Government of India has funded many of its projects. Just below this institute is lodged the newly constructed ropeway connecting Deorali with the Sikkim Secretariat that provides a panoramic view of Sikkim's capital Gangtok and its surrounding landscape. Bypassing this shorter and quicker aerial route, I chose to slowly walk up to the bazaars of Gangtok. Traffic snarls and road congestion not merely generate intolerable noise and air pollution, but transform this meandering mountainous road into a walker's nightmare. Numerous tourist lodges and hotels line this road connecting Deorali with the bazaars of Gangtok whose shops are flooded by Chinese goods, which have come via the Nathula Pass reopened in June 2006.

In June 2007 walking on the historic Tibet Road of Gangtok, I met Dawa Lepcha, Tenzing Lepcha, Athup Lepcha, Tseten Lepcha, and other Lepcha leaders and numerous Lepcha youth supporting and participating in an indefinite hunger strike outside the Bhutia–Lepcha house at Gangtok. It was not coincidental that I chose to walk this route since it's the path which the thirty-five year old Lepcha film-maker Dawa Lepcha had traversed from the Namgyal Institute of Tibetology that employed him on a visual anthropology project documenting the fast disappearing Lepcha culture and religion. Sitting under the inspiring image of a *khada*[26] covered Gandhi, Dawa Lepcha and Tenzing Lepcha explained to me that they were on an indefinite fast and fighting particularly but not exclusively to save the holy land of Dzongu from being desecrated by the proposed seven hydroelectric projects including the 280 MW Panan Hydel Project. Unanimously they enunciated their position: 'We are not against development, but will fight against development that will extinguish our culture.' Arbitrarily imposed on the Lepchas, 'without taking us into confidence or informing us about the details of this project, this Panan Hydel project violates our basic human rights as the indigenous people of Sikkim, of India and the world'. As the other participating Lepcha youth stressed, 'we are not powerful and organized to counter the government which provides us with employment and other essentials'. The Coordinator of Affected Citizens of Teesta (ACT),[27] Tseten Lepcha pointed out 'these hydro projects are being touted as harbingers of immense money and prosperity but it has also made us a minority in our own homeland'. Twenty-one year old Tenzing Lepcha and thirty-five year old Dawa Lepcha who are general secretaries of Concerned Lepchas of Sikkim (CLOS),[28] and ACT have vowed to even sacrifice their life for this cause. Dawa Lepcha, stressed, 'the double standards of the State Government is revealed in the fact that while on one hand, it has accorded primitive tribes status to the Lepchas of the State, on the other hand, it has plans to take away the very land and indigenous culture of the people is claims it is protecting'.

Religiously inspired, strongly motivated, staunch in their commitment to preserve Lepcha culture, possessing strong leadership and enjoying a high moral standing within the Lepcha community, Dawa and Tenzing's fast began on 20 June 2007 and lasted until 21 August for 63 days. It was ended after being assured that the government would stop construction activities and a climate of negotiation would be created to address their demands. Opposition to the government is being led by a Joint Action Committee of the Lepchas of Sikkim organizationally composed of the ACT, CLOS, the Sangha of Dzongu,[29] organizations of Lepchas based at Kalimpong and Darjeeling in North Bengal[30] while being supported by other civil society organizations such as Kalpavriksh, Delhi, Forum, Intercultural

Resources, River Basin Friends, Legal Initiative for Forests and Environment (LIFE), Centre for Organisation, Research and Education (CORE), Manipur, who are engaged in opposing the implementation of ecologically questionable development projects, especially hydroelectric projects in India and South Asia.

Athup Lepcha had forewarned me about the impending battle during my fieldwork in Dzongu in 2006. Other Lepchas had similarly communicated that they would not give a No Objection Certificate unless their minimum conditions of higher compensation rates for all those families displaced and affected by construction activities were met. In Athup Lepcha's words,

> The [hydel] project has rudely irresolutely shaken us from our indolent idyllic complacency. How will you study Lepcha culture if we the Lepchas themselves are displaced from our homeland? If this Panan project is permitted to be constructed here in Dzongu then our future and our culture will be irretrievably lost. Dzongu is the only place we the Lepchas feel secure and at home, it is the last bastion where our culture and practices are being followed. If we don't speak now against these development projects now, then our future generations will question us the meaning of being a Lepcha. Our living culture will be forced to being ossified in museums and history books, if this project invades our homeland.

According to Dawa Lepcha, although only nine Lepcha families are being displaced, 1,500 Lepchas are indirectly affected. The concerned Lepchas have demanded written assurances from the government that no outsiders would be settled in Dzongu that is inhabited exclusively by 7,000 Lepchas. Nevertheless their fears of settlement of technically qualified and skilled migrants required for construction and efficient running of the project are neither unfounded nor baseless.

Undoubtedly, the projects are located in ecologically sensitive regions that are rich in biodiversity. The government claims that the number of families who will be displaced by these hydropower projects is not large. On its part, the government stresses that hydropower will generate immense revenue, provide employment, and facilitate infrastructural development of transport and communication links in the state. Recently, M.K. Pandit, the director of the Centre for Interdisciplinary Studies of Mountain and Hill Environment (CISMHE), under whose supervision a carrying capacity study of the Teesta basin was conducted over nearly six years has admitted that Stage I-III of the Teesta project are neither environmentally advisable nor feasible.[31] Some of the larger Teesta projects require the construction of large dams diverting the river waters through long head race or underground tunnels (HRTs) before the water is dropped back into the river at a downstream location after passing through a powerhouse.[32] It is widely acknowledged by many including bureaucrats preferring anonymity that the projects would cause immense destruction of existing flora and fauna, degrade forests, disrupt the hydrological cycle, while blasting activities will trigger numerous landslides.

Pressurized by these activists the government constituted a review committee in September 2007 but its composition has been unacceptable. Athup Lepcha who was the sole activist nominated for inclusion in it, has declined to participate. Determined to agitate against the arbitrariness of the government, these activists have sent numerous delegations to Delhi to appraise ministers in the central government. A thirty-member delegation successfully staged a *dharna* on 5-6 December at Jantar Mantar in Delhi in collaboration with other human rights activists. Emotionally charged and saddened Lepchas voiced out during this *dharna*:

> Villages are divided, clans are divided, friends and well wishers are divided and worst of all families are divided. Dzongu has become like the India before the East India Company came to India. We are divided for the interest of outsiders who promise prosperity while taking away our land, our culture, the environment, and our very identity.

'Dams over Dzongu will be built over our dead bodies' proclaimed the banner on 6 January 2008 that marked the 200th day of their relay hunger strike and public opposition. Releasing the ACT flag, the activists asserted:

> We are happy with what we have and what we have survived thus far. We know development is necessary, but not at the cost of obliterating the very identity of the Lepchas, the original inhabitants of Sikkim. Eco tourism can do what hydel can and can be a better and right approach. When we the people are not happy with the project, the why is the government forcibly imposing this on us?

To break the impasse with the government, the activists are aggressively joining hands with other civil society organizations, gathering forceful support from the Akhil Bharatiya Adivasi Parishad, approaching political parties such as the Communists for legislative support while awakening ethnic sentiments in Sikkim and the neighbouring Darjeeling Hills.

SIMULATIONS AND 'SHANGRI-LA' SIKKIM

> Simulation is no longer that of a territory, a referential being, or a substance. It is the generation by models of a real without origin or reality: a hyperreal. The territory no longer precedes the map nor does it survive it. It is nevertheless the map that precedes the territory—precession of simulacra—that engenders the territory, and if one returns to the [Borges] fable, today it is the territory whose shreds slowly rot across the extent of the map. It is the real, and not the map, whose vestiges persist here and there in the deserts that are no longer those of the Empire, but ours. *The desert of the real itself.*
>
> (Baudrillard, 1994: 1, emphasis original)

Baudrillard begins his influential essay 'The Precession of Simulacra' by citing the famous Borges fable about the cartographer's detailed map ending up covering the territory itself. For Baudrillard representation and simulation are opposed. Representation stems from the principle of the equivalence of the sign and the real. However, simulation stems from the principle of equivalence since an image has no reality whatsoever (1994: 6). The simulacrum as theorized by Baudrillard (1994) is the copy without an original, stimulating what never existed in the first place. Disneyland is regarded the perfect simulacra. 'Disneyland is presented as an imaginary for us to believe in the fiction of a real America, when none exists. Disneyland exists in order to hide that it is the real country, all of real America that is Disneyland' (Baudrillard, 1994: 12-14). The simulacrum becomes true when the imaginary of representation disappears. Simulation is not pretending as it collapses the boundary between true and false, real and the imaginary. It is no longer a question of distinguishing between real and imitations since 'it is a question of substituting the signs of the real for the real' (Baudrillard, 1994: 2-3). Hyperreality emerges when cultural representations no longer have a social or human reality against which to verify themselves, but become autonomous and free of all reference.[33] The hyperreal cannot combine with the real, so the society experiences a double kind of closure. There is no other alternative but to play with the pieces in this situation.

Are we simply left with images having no referents? Questions of authenticity are not outmoded as post-modernists such as Baudrillard theorize in ideas of simulacra and the hyperreal. Baudrillard advanced an extreme version of the loss-of-meaning thesis. The status of 'reality' and 'meaning' are questions of radical importance today. Critiquing the nihilism of hyperreality, king suggests we should analyse how a culture constructs a reality for itself through its discourses and the way in which these discourses are historically located (1998: 59). The simulacra had no political function in Baudrillard's argument, but in the post-colonial development context of Sikkim, the simulacra can become a symbolic tool to deflect and efface all political dissent. Stereotypes are powerful referents simulating typical images effacing all traces of any imagination. Hyperrealism derails time and space and denies agency and power.

Reading Baudrillard's *Simulacra and Simulations*, I suddenly comprehend the eruption of the contemporary 'Shangri-La' Sikkim on the world-stage. The deserts of the real are fascinating because they have no depth and reference points. 'Shangri-La' Sikkim emerges as a post-modern utopia of global capital marketed by the tourism industry and actively promoted by the state government of Sikkim. Government representatives and bureaucrats repeatedly state that Sikkim is the model democratic state free of social conflict endemic to neighbouring Nepal, Bhutan, and other north-eastern states of India. In the government posturing, these numerous voices protesting and opposing developmental hydroelectric projects do not belong to 'Shangri-La' Sikkim, which is the perfect shining example of a consensual democratic polity. They claim these voices are politically misguided by outside interests wanting to destabilize all development in Sikkim. As they opine, public affirmation and public consensus with the government plans and policies is evident in the assent of the thirty-one democratically elected representatives actively participating in the deliberations of the Sikkim Legislative Assembly. They argue that if there are some protesting voices, pleading voices of *some* Lepcha youth sitting on indefinite hunger strike, then they are marginal, anti-national and simplistically by any interpretation profusely anti-Sikkimese. This is precisely how the chief minister of Sikkim, Pawan Chamling framed the Affected Citizens of the Teesta and their leaders during his public speech on the occasion of the Indian Independence Day celebrations on 15 August 2007 at Gangtok in Sikkim.

I had not grasped the deeper meaning of Sonam Paljor's statements and had displayed my puzzlement to him in my meeting. He had uncannily been very Baudrillardian in his analysis. America needed Disneyland while Sikkim needs 'Shangri-La' Sikkim. Sonam Paljor, Dawa Lepcha, Tenzing Lepcha and other activists protesting against the numerous hydroelectric projects on the river Teesta picture Sikkim as a desecrated, threatened and sacred landscape. Sonam Paljor Denjongpa was not being hyperbolic about drastic changes in Sikkim's ethnic profile, the decline of Buddhist values in a transnational materialist world, and the ecological costs borne by its landscape in the name of development. Lamenting about a *dystopic Sikkim*, Denjongpa's trope had compared it with social life in the former kingdom of Sikkim and also in the neighbouring Bhutanese kingdom. In the moments when the Sikkim of Sonam Paljor Denjongpa's vision disappeared from the here and now, a Shangri-La Sikkim erupted on the global surface to remove all traces of Sikkim by becoming its own self-referent.

Images and imaginations of Shangri-La simulate each other in a Sikkim which is not real anymore for many who belong and are rooted in its landscape. Like the cartographer's map in the Borges fable, the ethnic landscape owned by those indigenous to Sikkim has withered away and is now recoverable only in its vestiges, albeit models continued to be generated about the government protecting the indigenous in Sikkim. Tibet had been museumized by a modern Western imagination, while social constructions of 'Shangri-La' Sikkim are busy museumizing the indigenous in Sikkim. The former was generated in a specifically colonial encounter to imagine an independent Tibet while the latter belongs to the post-colonial world reconciling Sikkim with development and statehood.

Acknowledgements: I thank Mike Tomlan and V. Sanil for comments and encouraging me to write this paper. A section of this paper was presented at the International Seminar of Young Tibetologists, SOAS London, 9-13 August 2007. On 16 February 2008 this paper was presented at the International Conference on 'Social Development, Social Movements and the Marginalized: Perspectives and Concerns' at IGNOU, Delhi. I thank the participants for their valuable comments. I am grateful to the Commonwealth Scholarship Commission (2000-4), the Beit Fund for Commonwealth History (2001-3), and the Indian Institute of Technology, Delhi for funding support. The usual disclaimers apply.

NOTES

1. Historically, Tibet has been romanticized as either a fabled Shangri-La or pejoratively as a superstitious, backward, despotic nation (Korom, 1997a: 1). Waddell's book *The Buddhism of Tibet or Lamaism* was one of the first extensive accounts of Tibetan Buddhism, published in 1895. This book bolstered the negative images of Tibet being a superstitious and backward culture. It is interesting to note how the educated elite of Sikkim referred to it constantly to represent themselves to others. This book is extensively cited by many tourist guidebooks and travel guides as an authoritative book about Buddhism in Sikkim.
2. The first information that reached Western civilization about Shambhala came in the seventeenth century form two Jesuit missionaries, Stephen Cacella and John Cabral who were stationed at Shigatse.
3. *Kalachakra* belongs to the highest class of tantric teachings, the Anuttara Yoga. It means the doctrine of the wheel of time.
4. A word in the Tibetan language meaning hidden valleys.
5. A word in the Tibetan language meaning concealed treasures, which can be in the form of texts, objects, places, features of the landscape and in persons. These mystical *gter* (treasure) texts comprise an important source of teachings and ritual practices of the Nyingmapa sect of Buddhism.
6. A word in the Tibetan language meaning treasure-revealer.
7. The number of these *sbas-yul* is uncertain since the possibility exists of their being revealed by discoveries of new treasures. Khumbu, Helambu, Khembalung, Sikkim, Nubri, Dolpo, Rongshar, and Lapchi are recognized as being *sbas-yul*. Bhutan is believed to contain some more (Reinhard, 1978: 6).
8. Reiterated by several highly learned Nyingmapa lamas and tantric practitioners of Sikkim during my interviews with them between 2001-7.
9. For details of the Theosophical Society and Madame Blavatsky's spiritual philosophy refer to http://www.ts-adyar.org/history.html. Accessed on 20 May 2007.
10. Prominent among a long list of books on this subject are those by Bishop (1989, 1993), Allen (1999), Lopez (1998), Lepage (1996), Westwood (1987), Korom (1997), Dodin and Heinz (2001).
11. McKay (1997: 83) furthers the political underpinning of this mystical image of Tibet by arguing that it was critical for promoting Tibet's separate identity as a nation.
12. The period of the Cultural Revolution (1966-76) is associated with the mindless destruction of Buddhist monasteries that preserved religious artefacts and priceless treasures, and the concurrent ethnocide of Tibetan monks and nuns.

13. Museums expressively frame public conceptions of cultures while archiving memory and cultural objects. This process of preserving culture or 'mummifying cultural essence' in museums is not innocent but long been recognized to be an instrument of cultural domination and essentialism, which denies agency to living cultures. In the context of Tibet, the museumization of Tibet was epitomized in a 1990s' travelling exhibition entitled, *Wisdom and Compassion: The Sacred Art of Tibet* designed initially for the Asian Art Museum of San Francisco (Harris, 1999: 13, 37-8).
14. Its back cover advertises that this is the 'first comprehensive guidebook' and is illustrated with 120 stunning pictures. Priced at Rs. 600, it is produced by the Eicher Good Earth Publication House with the support of Sikkim Tourism and the Department of Tourism, Government of India.
15. Even Lepchas residing in other parts of the northern district, Sikkim and the neighbouring state of West Bengal cannot purchase property and elect to reside in Dzongu.
16. The term used for Sikkim in the Tibetan language.
17. In the Tibetan language it means the hidden valley of Sikkim with its numerous treasures.
18. Entitled in the Tibetan languages as *'Bras ljongs gnas yig* or the Guidebook to the Sacred Places of Sikkim and Written by Lhatsun Jigmed Pawo (1682-1717) it is available as a block print text at the Namgyal Institute of Tibetology, Gangtok, Sikkim.
19. A Tibetan word meaning *Dharamaraja* in Sanskrit or a divine king.
20. Arora (2006b) contains a detailed discussion on secularization of Sikkim.
21. I mean the multi-ethnic population of Sikkim.
22. In the course of some interviews, some of these Tibetan refugees discussed their parents' life in Tibet and what they have heard about Tibet, the Shangri-La.
23. Refer to Arora (2006a).
24. A Sikkimese Bhutia man in his fifties whose father had been a teacher in the Enchey Monastery at Gangtok. He trained as an anthropologist at Brown University before settling in the US as a businessman with his American wife. Interested in preserving Sikkim's culture and following esoteric Buddhist Tantra, Sonam Paljor fully returned to Sikkim in 1995 and become a lama under Rev. Dodrupchen's tutelage while helping him administer the affairs of the Deorali trust.
25. For any further details the website of this institute can be consulted. See http://www.tibetology.net/
26. The traditional white-silk scarf offering made in respect and honour to people, gods and sacred sites among ethnic Tibetans.
27. ACT is the rechristened name of the Joint Action Committee, an

organization formed by the people living in the basin of river Teesta in north Sikkim in 2005. They define themselves in following terms, 'we are a group of people affected by dams on the Teesta and its tributaries in the Lepcha reserve of Dzongu in Sikkim'.

28. CLOS is a NGO based in Dzongu, north Sikkim.
29. Formed by the lamas of Dzongu in June 2007 to actively support protests against Panan and other hydropower projects located in Dzongu.
30. Concurrently, relay hunger strikes were organized by Lepcha organizations in adjoining Kalimpong and Darjeeling.
31. 'Damming the Teesta', Part 2 by L. Jishnu, *Business Standard*, 8 January 2008.
32. One of these tunnels in East Sikkim is 17 km long (Dikchu to Singtam), which means that the river will be dry for long stretches while 80-90 per cent of its water gets diverted into underground tunnels.
33. The emergence of the hyperreal is connected with the rise of media and dominance of communication such as in cinema, cyberspace, and television where reality is reduced to images. Images become self-determining, free-floating, and self-referential.

REFERENCES

Acharya, C. (1998), 'Sikkim: The Hidden Holy Land and its Sacred Lakes', *Bulletin of Tibetology*, vol. 34, no. 3, pp. 10-15.

Allen, C. (1999), *The Search for Shangri-La: A Journey into Tibetan History*, London: Little Brown.

Appadurai, A. (1986), *The Social Life of Things: Commodities in Cultural Perspective*, Cambridge: Cambridge University Press.

Anonymous (2002), *Sikkim: The Land of Mystique*, Eicher Good Earth Publications supported by Sikkim Tourism and the Department of Tourism, Government of India: Delhi.

Arora, V. (2006a), 'Text and Context in Sikkim, India', in E. Arweck and P.J. Collins (eds.), *Reading Religion in Texts and Context: Reflections of Faith and Practice in Religious Materials*, Aldershot: Ashgate.

——— (2006b), 'The Roots and the Route of Secularism in Sikkim', *Economic and Political Weekly*, vol. 41, no. 38, pp. 4063-71.

Bishop, P. (1989), *The Myth of Shangri-La: Tibet, Travel Writing, and the Western Creation of Sacred Landscape*, London: Athlone Press.

——— (1993), *Dreams of Power: Tibetan Buddhism and the Western Imagination*, London: Athlone Press.

Baudrillard, J. (1994), *Simulacra and Simulations*, tr. Shiela F. Glaser, Ann Arbor: University of Michigan Press.

Dolma, Y. and T. Namgyal (1908), 'History of Sikkim,' unpublished manuscript available at the Namgyal Institute of Tibetology, Gangtok, Sikkim.

Dodin, T. and R. Heinz (2001), *Imagining Tibet: Perceptions, Projections, and Fantasies*, Boston: Wisdom Publications.

Evans-Wentz, W.Y. (ed.) (1960), *The Tibetan Book of the Dead*, Oxford: Oxford University Press.

Foning, A. (1987), *Lepcha: My Vanishing Tribe*, Delhi: Sterling Publishers Ltd.

Gorer, G. (1938), *Himalayan Village: An Account of the Lepchas of Sikkim*, London: Michael Joseph.

Harris, C. (1999), *In the Image of Tibet: Tibetan Paintings After 1959*, London: Reakiton Books.

Hilton, J. (1933), *Lost Horizon*, New York: Simon and Schuster.

King, A. (1998), 'A Critique of Baudrillard's Hyperreality: Towards a Sociology of Postmodernism', *Philosophy Social Criticism*, vol. 24, no. 6, pp. 47-66.

Klieger, C. (1997), 'Shangri-La and Hyperreality: A Collision in Tibetan Refugee Expression', in F. Korom (ed.), *Constructing Tibetan Culture: Contemporary Perspectives*, Quebec: World Heritage Press.

———. (2002), *Tibet, Self, and the Tibetan Diaspora: Voices of Difference. Tibetan Studies: Proceedings of the Ninth Seminar of the International Association for Tibetan Studies, Leiden 2000*, Leiden: Brill.

Korom. F. (1997a), 'Introduction', in F. Korom (ed.), *Constructing Tibetan Culture: Contemporary Perspectives*, Quebec: World Heritage Press.

———. (1997b) (ed.), *Tibetan Culture in the Diaspora. Papers Presented at a Panel of the 7th Seminar of the International Association for Tibetan Studies, Graz 1995*, Wein: Verlag der Österreichischen Akademie der Wissenschaften.

Kumar, K. (2003), 'Aspects of the Western Utopian Tradition', *History of the Human Sciences*, vol. 16, no. 1, pp. 63-77.

Lepage, V. (1996), *Shambala: The Fascinating Truth Behind the Myth of Shangri-La*, Wheaton: Theosophical Publishing House.

Levitas, R. (1979), 'Sociology and Utopia', *Sociology*, vol. 13, no. 19, pp. 19-33.

Lopez, D.S. (1998), *Prisoners of Shangri La: Tibetan Buddhism and the West*, Chicago: Chicago University Press.

MacKay, A. (1997), *Tibet and the British Raj: The Frontier Cadre 1904-1947*, London: Curzon Press.

——— (2001), 'Truth, Perceptions, and Politics: The British Construction of an Image of Tibet', in T. Dodin and R. Heinz (eds.), *Imagining Tibet: Perceptions, Projections, and Fantasies*, Boston: Wisdom Publications.

Masuzawa, T. (1999), 'From Empire to Utopia: The Effacement of Colonial Markings in Lost Horizon', *Positions, East Asia Culture Critiques*, vol. 7, no. 2, pp. 541-72.

Morris, J. (1938), *Living with Lepchas: A Book About the Sikkim Himalayas*, London: Heinemann.

Reinhard, J. (1978), 'Khembalung: The Hidden Valley', *Kailash: A Journal of Himalayan Studies*, vol. 6, no. 1, pp. 5-35.

Siiger, H. and J. Rischel (1967), *The Lepchas: Culture and Religion of a Himalayan People*, Part II, Copenhagen: National Museum of Denmark.

Silverman, H.G. (1980), 'From Utopia/Dystopia to Heterotopia: An Interpretive Topology', *Philosophy Social Criticism*, vol. 7, pp. 170-82.

Van Spengen, W. (2000), *Tibetan Border Worlds: A Geohistorical Analysis of Trade and Traders*, London and New York: Kegan Paul International.

Verma, R. (1999), *Sikkim: A Guide and Handbook*, Gangtok: Rajesh Verma.

Waddell. L.A. (1899), *The Buddhism of Tibet: or, Lamaism with its Mystic Cults, Symbolism and Mythology, and in its Relation to Indian Buddhism*, Luzac: London.

CHAPTER 6

'We are the Land; The Land is Us': Land and Identity in Australian Aboriginal Culture

MALATHY A.

INTRODUCTION

Throughout the world, the cultural practices, livelihoods and knowledge systems of indigenous peoples have been threatened and marginalized by colonialist forces and more recently, by the globalization ethic. Indigenous people have been uprooted and displaced from their traditional habitats, leading to severance of traditional community bonds, destruction of age-old lifestyles and a general loss of cultural identity. This has been the common experience of indigenous people in all the continents—whether we consider the native Americans and the Inuits of North America, the aboriginal population of Australia or the indigenous people of Guatemala, Mexico, Colombia, Venezuela, Bangladesh or India.

This paper discusses the significance of the relationship with the land in constructing identity in Australian aboriginal culture. The land and the human relationship with it have always figured conspicuously in the Australian aboriginal consciousness. Traditional and contemporary narratives, song cycles and art reflect a view of human beings as totally identified with the land and the natural environment. The advent of colonialism and the fiction of 'terra nullius' disrupted this sense of aboriginal interconnectedness with the land. Against the background of the debates regarding traditional rights of aboriginals to land, native rights, and so on this paper explores Australian literary texts that document the traumatic consequences in aboriginal life of alienation from the land. Such a discussion would help in forming a deeper understanding of the sufferings caused by displacement, in emplaced and rooted indigenous communities.

This paper addresses a major issue that has been confronting indigenous peoples in different parts of the world over the past few centuries: the issue of displacement and consequent loss of identity. This issue is discussed here with special reference to displacement and identity politics of the aboriginal population of Australia. The Australian aboriginals belong to an emplaced and rooted culture, and the loss of their traditional lands has meant a loss of not only livelihoods and resources but the most valuable aspect of their selves and identities. The paper considers the political resistance movements for land rights in the context of the belief systems that make Australian aboriginals identify totally with the land and its creatures, and the incompatible views of land ownership and management in aboriginal and white settler cultures. Positioning itself at the interface between literature and the social sciences, this paper considers literary texts as representations of the subtle and intangible aspects of aboriginal bondings with the land and of the trauma created in aboriginal life by the loss of such bondings.

INDIGENOUS = MARGINALIZED?

Who are the world's indigenous peoples? Graham Griffin attempts to specifically identify the indigenous communities of the world:

> Almost 300 million people of the world, across all continents are indigenous. The term is both spatially and temporally scale-dependent (all humans are indigenous to the earth). 'Indigenous' has come to mean the original inhabitants of an area that has been subsequently occupied by migrants (Seymour–Smith, 1986). Most colonization has been by migrants from Western Europe over the last few centuries. . . . Frequently, the term is reserved for populations which occupy an economically or politically marginal role compared with later arrivals in what the 'indigenous' people regard as their own land. People not affected by recent migration but none the less having a very long history of occupation and association with land, number 1.5-2 billion. They are members of local communities practising traditional lifestyles, mostly in the rangelands of Africa, Central Asia, the Americas, the Middle East and Australia. (Griffin, 2002: 29)

A UN Report on Discrimination against Indigenous Populations defines them as peoples and nations:

> . . . which having a historical continuity with pre-invasion and pre-colonial societies . . . consider themselves distinct from other sectors of the societies now prevailing in those territories. . . . They form at present non-dominant sectors of society and are determined to preserve, develop and transmit to future generations their ancestral territories, and their ethnic identity, as the basis of their continued existence as peoples. . . . (Cobo 1982: para 379)

Different definitions of the term 'indigenous' have varying emphases, but they all suggest the marginality of indigenous peoples and cultures the world over, even at the turn of the twenty-first century. Michael Dodson points out how even governmental attempts to classify indigenous people seem to include marginality as a distinguishing criteria. In Indonesia these criteria include not matching up to the standards of development required by the government and having less ability to perform social functions, whereas in Paraguay, to be officially defined as indigenous, one had to be marginalized, outside the economic mainstream and backward. In Bolivia the indigenous Indians were identified as being illiterate, speaking only a native language and providing unskilled labour in the economy (Dodson, 2003: 29).

If colonialist forces had deprived indigenous peoples of rights over land, pushing them to the fringes of society, annihilating entire communities, often severing bonds to community and tradition, and leading to loss of language and identity, placing them in a subject position as victims of humiliating racist discrimination, then globalization and the free trade regime continue and reinforce the process of marginalization by appropriating, commodifying and commercializing indigenous knowledge, patenting indigenous practices and resources and dumping agricultural produce from developed countries on indigenous communities. The concerns of the indigenous peoples in the context of globalization are voiced in the International Cancun Declaration of Indigenous Peoples (2003):

> With the creation of the World Trade Organisation (WTO) and with the continuing imposition of the structural adjustment policies of the World Bank and International Monetary Fund, our situation, as Indigenous Peoples, has turned from bad to worse. Corporations are given more rights and privileges at the expense of our rights. Our right to self-determination which is to freely determine our political status and pursue our own economic, social and cultural development, and our rights to our territories and resources, to our indigenous knowledge, cultures and identities are grossly violated.

INDIGENOUS RESISTANCE MOVEMENTS

In her pathbreaking critique of Western approaches to the study of indigenous issues, Tuhiwai Smith points out how during the past 500 years or so, indigenous people have been primarily focusing on survival—from conflicts with the colonizers, diseases, dislocation from land—and on survival as a distinct people with a separate linguistic and cultural identity. However, there was a change in the scale and focus of the indigenous project in the second half of the twentieth century when indigenous struggles have centred around wider concerns which tended to go beyond the decolonization aspirations of particular communities, and moved towards indigenous global alliances. During this period, indigenous resistance movements for land rights, linguistic and cultural rights, human rights and civil rights happened on a global scale—in Norway, Spain, the Middle East, Africa, South America and South Asia (Smith, 1999: 107-9).

The issues of land and rights to the land are subtly related to the inherent right of indigenous peoples to self-determination. The protracted struggle of indigenous Australians for land rights, which gained momentum in the second half of the twentieth century, has to be contextualized in the worldwide indigenous peoples' resistance movements. Displacement from traditional habitats and homelands has been a major problem that indigenous peoples have been confronting from the beginning of the colonial period. If in previous centuries they had been ruthlessly deprived, by policies of colonial appropriation, of rights over their land, in the twentieth century displacement has been largely due to migration, civil wars and take-over of land by multinational corporations and other agencies for 'developmental' purposes. According to a UN report, though migration of indigenous peoples has been an ongoing phenomenon from colonial times, its effects have been most pronounced in the twentieth century. The deterioration of peasant economies, the loss of community lands and lack of productive resources have been some of the factors leading to large-scale migration. The report also mentions civil wars as another factor leading to displacement (UN, 2002: 46). Whether by forceful eviction or due to migration, displacement from traditional habitats has been for most indigenous peoples, a traumatic experience that has led to loss of identity, of traditional lifestyles, community bonds and very often a spiritual relationship with the land.

ABORIGINAL LAND RIGHTS: UNDERLYING ASSUMPTIONS

Land rights of the indigenous aboriginal peoples of Australia have been a major issue ever since colonialists began appropriating the land, assuming the fiction of 'terra nullius'. Resistance to colonial appropriation has been an ongoing process from the time of the earliest settlements, but as Kim Bullimore points out, the modern movement for indigenous rights began in the 1920s when the first aboriginal political organizations were formed (Bullimore, 2001: 1). The land rights movement in Australia witnessed strident public protests, petitioning and litigation, all of which led to several landmark legal decisions. The various protests and petitions such as the Yolngu Bark Petition (1963) protesting the government's decision to excise the land of the Yolngu people for a bauxite mine, the Wave Hill protest (1966) of the Gurindji people led by Vincent Lingiari, the establishment of the Tent Embassy, and so on, prompted the setting up of commissions like the Woodward commission (1973-4) and legislations such as the Aboriginal Land Rights Act (1976), the Mabo decision (1992), the Wik decision and recognition of Native Title (Native Title Act 1993). Native Title represents an attempt to reconcile indigenous and common law concepts of landownership and acknowledge traditional ownership of land by indigenous communities.

In addition to the settlers' project of taking over land to satisfy colonial greed for resources, a misunderstanding of the aboriginal concept of landownership and management has also been responsible for the problematic issue of indigenous land rights. Aboriginal spirituality is primarily a spirituality of place and aboriginal culture is bonded with the land physically and spiritually through the Dreaming or the time of creation when the mystical ancestors created the various features of the earth. Bourassa points out how aboriginal paintings often depict stories of the creation of the Australian landscape by the ancestors during the Dreamtime and how most aboriginal rituals are designed to maintain the landscape by recreating the actions of the ancestors (1991: 4-5). Aboriginal mapping strategies thus mapped the land not only in physical terms, as in modern scientific cartography, but also in spiritual terms. For the Aboriginal population in Australia, identity is deeply linked to land and a sense of place, which is why Fabienne Bayet-Charlton declares: 'Aboriginal people are an integral part of the Australian landscape. We are the land, the land is us'

(2003: 171). Aboriginal people see themselves as custodians rather than as owners of the land. M. Kirk points out how aboriginal people see themselves as responsible for caring for sacred sites and ensuring the well-being of the land, the plants and animals. These responsibilities, says Kirk, together with sacred sites and objects '. . . constitute in Aboriginal terms, inalienable title to the land' (1986: 38). It is the age-old bond with the land, established from the time of the Dreaming, rather than any 'common law' legislation that constitutes rights to land in the aboriginal perspective. The remark on Native Title by the Gumatj elder Galarrwuy Yunupingu in his Vincent Lingiari lecture, 'As long as we live and breathe, our rights will still exist, because land rights and Native Title are not pieces of paper: they are the Aboriginal people. Native Title is in the ground and the trees, the rocks and the water, it's in me and it's in the land. . . . You can't separate us and you can't destroy it while there is one Aboriginal person still alive who knows the law' (1998: 8) reiterates this perspective.

Bayet-Charlton explains how a key difference between aboriginal and settler culture lies in differing attitudes to the land and environment. While aboriginals see themselves as custodians of the land, the

> . . . Eurocentric work ethic held by the settlers dictated that the 'land must be toiled with your own sweat' and the environment possessed, changed and exploited to its fullest extent. To the settlers . . . natural Australia was an uncouth waste. They were programmed to change, improve, dominate, exploit. In this process, the original inhabitants were dispossessed of their land and cultural roots. The Western land ethic dictated that 'progress' and development was the ultimate justification for the dispossession of the original custodians. The Aboriginal population were perceived as savages who did not exploit the land to its potential (according to European agricultural expectations), thus Aboriginal people were considered to have no right of property ownership. The entire continent was perceived to be empty of meaningful human occupation, bringing about the term 'terra nullius': unoccupied wasteland. (2003: 173-4)

Aboriginal people knew the land differently, mapped it differently, saw it differently, and used it differently. Aboriginal and white settler attitudes to the land and the natural environment are thus founded on entirely different assumptions. David Tacey in 'Aboriginality, Landscape and the Imagination' examines the fundamental differences between the two attitudes:

Whereas the Western view sees the individual as isolated and apart from the landscape, a living self against a dead objective background, the Aboriginal conception places the landscape at the centre of everything: at once the source of life, the origin of the tribe, the metamorphosed body of blood line ancestors. . . . (2001: 230)

Another point where aboriginal culture departs widely from white settler culture is in the approach to land use and land management. The laws regarding the access of resources from the environment are fixed by tradition from the Dreamtime. The Central Land Council says:

Our land is our life. We look at it in a different way to non-aboriginal people. For us, land isn't simply a resource to be exploited. It provides us with food and materials for life, but it also provides our identity and it must be looked after, both physically and spiritually. If we abuse our land or allow someone else to abuse it, we too suffer. (1991: 15)

The fact that the colonialists and the British colonial law that encouraged the 'settling' of Australia chose to view the land as terra nullius—land that belonged to nobody since it was apparently uncultivated and not properly managed—was a clear violation of aboriginal perceptions of themselves as the custodians of the land. Stuart Banner notes how 'terra nullius' remained the law in Australia throughout the colonial period, in fact up to 1992. If the colonialists framed 'terra nullius' as a convenient justification of colonial takeover of land, the aboriginals interpret this concept differently. The Yolngu leader Yunupingu in his Vincent Lingiari lecture says '. . . their law told them a story called "terra nullius" which meant that if you go to a land where the people don't look like you or live like you, then you can pretend they don't exist and take their land' (1998: 2).

LAND AND THE AUSTRALIAN LITERARY TEXT

It is evident from the discussion in the previous section that the land and the human relationship with it have always figured conspicuously in the Australian consciousness. A spiritual relationship with place and a holistic sense of interconnectedness of man with the land have been distinctive aspects of aboriginal culture throughout the long period of the continent's history that predated European colonization. However, since Australia's history as a settler colony and a modern nation has been marked by confrontation between man and the land, between human and non-human life, writing this confrontation with the environment has been a major preoccupation of modern Australian literature. John McLaren identifies '. . . a distinctly Australian tradition which rises from the hostility of the landscape to man's effort to tame it' (2001: 45).

The texts that write the colonial experience employ metaphors of mastering, controlling, owning, possessing and manipulating a hostile environment. The metaphors of human relationship with the land thus reflect the dominant economic ideology and intellectual discourse of the settlers though at least some novels of the early twentieth century like *Coonardoo* (1929) and *Capricornia* (1938) depict, as Jennifer Strauss points out, such mastering as ephemeral and the settler's achievements as '. . . doomed to failure—natural forces are uncontrollable, their pastoral practices destroy the natural ecological balance that make the land viable . . . ' (1998: 124). Aboriginal literary texts however avoid the vocabulary of confrontation, control and mastery in depicting the relationship with the land and the natural environment, and reflect the harmony and easy understanding of the land that has always typified aboriginal culture.

The acknowledgement that the Australian land truly belongs to its original inhabitants and the traumatic consequences in aboriginal life of alienation from the land have been problematized by several writers over the years. D.H. Lawrence's novel *The Boy in the Bush*, written in collaboration with Mollie Skinner, foregrounds the typical settler vocabulary of 'going on the land', 'taking up land', clearing, reclaiming and improving the land. The advice of the character Mr. George to young Jack Grant, the protagonist, succinctly expresses the colonisers' view of land: 'Take up land, Jack Grant, take up land. Buy, beg, borrow or steal land, but get it sir, get it' (*The Boy in the Bush*: 44). Jack Grant however has an instinctive disgust for the whole business: 'He thought the land looked lovely. But he had no desire to own any of it. He never felt the possibility of "owning" land. There the land was for eternity. How could he own it' (ibid.: 47). Ultimately Jack's desire to lead an isolated life in the north-west is accentuated by a desire to break free of such associations with the 'landtakers' and their social pretensions and enter into a more meaningful relationship with the land where he could be '. . . Beyond all fences, where a man was alone with himself and the untouched earth' (ibid.: 227). Here Lawrence seems to be invoking the aboriginal spirit of place. Lawrence's more widely read Australian novel *Kangaroo* also suggests the essentially aboriginal quality of the Australian land.

Randolph Stow is another writer whose writing of place and the Australian land is often deeply bound with his interest in metaphysics and spirituality and is therefore close to the aboriginal concept of place. Stow's novel *To the Islands*, winner of the 1958 Miles Franklin award, and one of his best known works, is set in the north-west of Western Australia. Stephen Heriot is on a journey which he hopes will lead him 'to the islands'—towards death and self-obliteration. He is provoked into an unfortunate skirmish with Rex, a young black, attacks him and mistakenly believes he has killed the younger man. In an act of atonement he strikes out with the faithful black Justin to the North, the 'lost man's country' which in aboriginal lore is the land inhabited by wrongdoers and murderers like him. In an act of defiance, Heriot breaks his crucifix as if breaking free from the religion to which he had been so faithful for so long and submits himself to the spiritual influence of the land. He gives himself to the country to let it do what it likes with him. That he feels would be God's justice. Though the European place names of locations in West Australia—such as Albert Creek, Dampier and Broome find mention, it is the aboriginal sense of the place that the novel evokes. The deep attachment of the blacks to their territory, their 'country', is suggested throughout. The character Terry Dixon senses this attachment of the blacks to the land: 'The phrase "gre ngaiananggа", "my country", so often in their mouths would keep recurring to his mind' (Stow, 1995: 8). The two instances when Heriot encounters cave paintings underline the aboriginal associations of the land which are rooted in its ancient history. The journey across the wilderness is a metaphor for Heriot's search into his own inner being and Heriot submits himself to the ancient forces of the land to aid him in his self-discovery.

The central concerns of Kim Scott's novel *True Country* are representative of the issues that aboriginal writing in Australia has been involved with during the final decades of the twentieth century—displacement, linguistic dislocation, dispossession, economic and cultural deprivation and marginalization. One of the Nyoongar people of South-western Australia, Scott has been deeply involved in issues concerning aboriginal identity and their role in contemporary Australia, through activism and through writing. Aboriginal culture provides the basic texture of the Australian reality and this is a reality that is closely linked to the experience of place. In a lecture broadcast on ABC on 15 May 2001, Kim Scott said: 'The people who did create a society in Australia, were Aboriginal Australians, and that society, like its language, arose from the environment, from a sense of place'. *True Country*, Scott's first novel, is semi-autobiographical, and Billy, one of the many voices in this heteroglossic narrative, is like Scott, a school teacher in a remote community and partly aboriginal. In the remote mission town of Karnama, Billy encounters an aboriginal community that is beset with problems of modern living, yet linked to the past through slender but vital links. Belonging and identity are closely linked to a sense of place in this novel. Karnama is partly real, partly dream country. Scott himself says in the author's note to the novel that it is a fictional space created out of the topography of the Kimberley region of Western Australia, from which Scott creates a 'primary personal territory' which helps him to explore 'neglected interior space' and to consider his heritage (Author's Note, *True Country*). The basic aspects of a West Australian aboriginal community are there—an emplaced community and culture:

> And it is a beautiful place, this place. Call it our country, our country all around here. We got river, we got sea. Got creek, rock, hill, waterfall. We got bush tucker: apple, potato, sugarbag, bush turkey, kangaroo, barramundi, dugong, turtle . . . every kind. Sweet mangoes and coconuts too. (*True Country*:13)

The sacred groves and sites, the magical rites and rituals, the memory of a hunter-gatherer past, the intimate knowledge of every inch of the soil and everyone of its creatures—all evoke an aboriginal communal space.

The need to reconnect with one's place, in an attempt to re-construct an aboriginal identity, is a distinctive feature of aboriginal life writing. For many aboriginals, the journey to the traditional homeland is not only a journey to one's roots, but also a journey in search of wholeness and well-being. Sally Morgan's *My Place*, considered a classic in aboriginal life writing and a crucial text in the contemporary discourse of aboriginality, clearly links the author's homeplace, Corunna Downs with peace and well-being.

> . . . the hospital represents the most alienating and unhealthy environment in the narrative, while the natural settings of the swamp and Corunna Downs afford a healing serenity and spiritual peace. . . . The journey to Corunna Downs is crucial to Sally's insight into her aboriginality. By meeting formerly unknown relatives and being welcomed into the kinship network, by treading on ancestral soil, she discovers her 'place' both within the extended family and in connection with tribal territory, with 'country'. (De Groen, 1992: 3-5)

As De Groen rightly points out *My Place* may not represent a vehement and strident demand for land rights. The implicit critique of white injustice, however, compels readers to see the importance of healing the wounds of the past (2-3). 'Country' in aboriginal knowledge systems meant much more than geographical space. One is reminded while reading *My Place* of Deborah Bird Rose's explanation that 'country' for the aboriginal is a living entity with a yesterday, today and tomorrow, with a consciousness and a will towards life, and '. . . because of this richness, country is home and peace: nourishment for body, mind and spirit, heart's ease' (Rose: 1).

In Rosemary van den Berg's *No Options, No Choice: The Moore River Experience*, a renewal of spiritual connectedness with the land is a crucial aspect of Thomas Corbett's efforts to regain his aboriginal heritage. Again, in Doris Pilkington's much acclaimed *Follow the Rabbit Proof Fence*, Molly, Daisy and Grace escape from a white settlement and return to their family and ancestral home. The long and arduous journey of Molly, Daisy and Grace is not merely an attempt to regain a fragile personal freedom, but also a return to homeland, territory and community. The story is based to some extent at least on Pilkington's own experience of life on a settlement and separation from her mother, and is as Julia Ravell points out, all about 'reclaiming territories' (Ravell: 8).

Indigenous issues, especially land rights and dispossession have been major proccupations in the writing of Judith Wright. Throughout her prose and poetry, she apologizes for the historic wrong of displacement of indigenous peoples from their traditional homelands and the subsequent trauma in the indigenous consciousness. For instance, Wright says, '. . . to all the peoples of the old and true Australia on whose land I have trespassed and whom by being part of my own people I have wronged, I plead for forgiveness' (1999: 296). Elsewhere in the same book she expresses her '. . . deep uneasiness about the situation of Aborigines and our own part in what I was beginning to see as a country despoiled' (1999: 284). Again, in *Preoccupations in Australian Poetry*, her sense of guilt and unease are apparent when she writes that the aborigines '. . . were bound to the land we took from them, by the indissoluble link of religion and totemic kinship so that our intrusion on the land itself became a kind of bloodless murder even where no actual murder took place' (48). Wright is of the view that the antithetical views of land and environment held by the Europeans and Aboriginals are themselves responsible for the clash between the two perspectives.

The European view is embodied in the concept of landscape, a word that implies, '. . . an irreconcilable difference of viewpoint. . . . It is a painter's term implying an outside view, a separation. . . . We cannot see it against the reality of that earth–sky–water–tree–spirit–human complex existing in space–time, which is the Aboriginal world' (1985, 32). In the same essay, Wright critiques the white Australian viewpoint that aboriginals had no claim on land or title to it by cultivation, management or habitation (29). Apart from such prose writing, in poems like 'Bora Ring', 'Nigger's Leap' and 'At Cooloolah', Wright poetically engages with issues such as the white European's alienation from the Australian land and the aboriginal anguish at being spiritually uprooted from their traditional habitats.

Les Murray is another major poetic voice that has identified closely with the indigenous cause in Australia. Essays such as 'The Human-hair Thread', and poems like 'The Buladelah-taree Holiday Song Cycle', 'The Boys Who Stole the Funeral', 'The Ballad of Jimmy Governor' and perhaps most famously, the overtly political poem 'Thinking About Aboriginal Land Rights, I Visit the Farm I will Not Inherit', show deep empathy for the land rights campaign. 'Thinking about Aboriginal Land Rights' was written at a crucial period in the history of the campaign, when the Labour Government under Gough Whitlam had assumed power and the aborigines granted land rights in the Northern Territory. It is, as Adam Shoemaker points out, a '. . . personal evocation of the pain that the dispossession of land can cause. . . . Here it is implicit that Murray's feeling for the farm which he will be denied is akin to the sense of loss which has afflicted Black Australians confronted with the white encroachment into their continent' (21).

The 'Jindyworobaks', a group of poets writing in the 1930s, who attempted to revive aboriginal idiom and language in their poetry and to adopt aboriginal practices of 'reading' the environment and the land, again represent a major literary attempt to recapture the power of the aboriginal connectedness with the Australian land. This group, which included radical poets like Rex Ingamells and Ian Mudie can be seen, as Jennifer Strauss points out, as '. . . expressing an early environmentalism which, perceiving Aboriginal culture as having achieved its identity with the "primal essence" of the land, imagined that it could be appropriated and improved upon . . .' (1998: 114). Adrian Ceasar acknowledges their indirect significance for the land rights campaign: '. . . through their ambition to learn by listening to the land, and notionally at least to the land's original inhabitants, they might even be seen as distant precursors to the political impetus that has resulted in the Mabo legislation' (1998: 161).

Rachel Perkin's classic film *One Night the Moon* (2001) is a contemporary re-visioning of issues of landownership and belonging. Emily, daughter of white settler parents, goes in pursuit of moonlight and disappears into the night. Her father refuses the help of the black tracker Albert in finding her. Later on, the child's mother seeks Albert's help and he leads them to the child—but by then she is dead. Fiona Probyn and Catherine Simpson situate this film within contemporary debates about land, belonging and settler—indigenous relations. They see the film as a foregrounding of the 'unsettlement of the settler' and the aboriginals' superior knowledge of the land which suggests them as its rightful owners. The settler's envy of indigenous belonging leads to his violent denial and expulsion of Albert from the land. It is a statement of the exclusion of indigenous people throughout colonial history and an uneasy admission of their rightful ownership of the land. The duet sung by the black tracker and the settler negotiates the contrasting views of landownership. It

> . . . expresses the discordant beliefs held by the black tracker and the settler in regard to their incommensurable views of landownership. While the settler articulates a defined ownership over the land 'all the way to the old fence line' and sings his insistent and desperate refrain of 'this land is mine' the black tracker sings 'this land is me'. (Probyn and Simpson, 2002)

The distinction between what Way and Beckett identify as the proprietary relationship of non-indigenous Australians with land and the spiritual relationship of the aboriginals is poignantly represented here. For white Australians, Way and Beckett suggest, a sense of identity derives not from being part of the land, but from exercising control over it through formal rights of exclusive possession and occupation.

CONCLUSION

This paper has highlighted a major issue confronting indigenous communities throughout the world-displacement and disruption of traditional bondings with land and territory. For the aboriginal population of Australia, the relationship with land has been a major organizing principle of their culture, and the deciding factor in constructing their identity. Colonialism however has inscribed new meanings on the cultural landscape of the ancient continent, with an almost total disregard for the values ascribed to it by the original inhabitants of the land and brought new ways of reading, mapping and using the land. In the words of Gary Clark:

> The earth–sky–water–tree–spirit–human complex became fragmented, the perspective and meanings of the ocularcentric agriculturalist inscribed on the land, effacing a vast and intricate web of cultural and spiritual meanings. Like the 'outside view' of the picturesque painter, the maps of the cartographer which replaced indigenous meanings with 'tracks and fences' are a form of ocularcentrism with potent political, social and environmental consequences. (2006: 156)

The protracted struggle of the aboriginals to regain traditional rights over their lands has been an epoch-making popular movement of the previous century. There is understandably an extensive body of literature that discusses the political aspects of the land rights campaign in Australia. However, the subtleties of the aboriginal bonding with the land and the consequences of the disruption of these bondings are best captured by writers in literary texts that have overt political overtones as well as those that do not necessarily take a political stance on the land rights issue. As Shoemaker rightly points out, the essence of the land rights campaign is a relationship which requires a poetic understanding (Shoemaker, 2004: 2). Judith Wright, for instance, succeeds in expressing the destabilization in the aboriginal world that has come about as a consequence of dispossession, more powerfully than most political writing on the issue:

> The land itself was now disfigured and desecrated, studded with huts crossed by tracks and fences. The all-embracing net of life and spirit which had held land and people and all things together, was in tatters. The sustaining ceremonies could not be held, men and women could not visit their own birthplaces . . . and proper burial became impossible and injustice had to be done to the rights of the dead. (1981: 27)

Literary texts if read alongside sociological and political documents on the issue can yield a deeper understanding of the complex land rights campaign of the Australian indigenous peoples, and their efforts to regain their places, which have always sustained them and given them their unique identities.

REFERENCES

Aboriginal and Torres Strait Islander Social Justice Commissioner (1995), Native Title Report, July 1994—June 1995, Sydney: HREOC.

Banner, Stuart (2005), 'Why Terra Nullius? Anthropology and Property Law in Early Australia', *Law and History Review*, vol. 23, no. 1 Spring.

Bourassa, Steven (1991), *The Aesthetics of Landscape*, London: Belhaven Press.

Bayet-Charlton, Fabienne (2003), 'Overturning the Doctrine: Indigenous Peoples and Wilderness—Being Aboriginal in the Environmental Movement', in Michele Grossman (ed.), *Blacklines: Contemporary Critical Writing by Indigenous Australians*, Carlton: Melbourne University Press, pp. 171-81.

Bullimore, Kim (2001), 'The Aboriginal Struggle for Justice and Land Rights', *Green Left Weekly*, issue 433.

Central and Northern Land Councils (1991), *Our Land, Our Life: Aboriginal Land Rights in Australia's Northern Territory,* Alice Springs: Central Land Council.

Caesar, Adrian (1998), 'National Myths of Manhood: Anzacs and Others', in Bennett et al. (eds.), *The Oxford Literary History of Australia*, Oxford: Oxford University Press.

Clark, Gary (2006), 'The Two Threads of a Life: Judith Wright, the Environment and Aboriginality', *Antipodes*, vol. 20, no. 2, December.

Cobo (1982), *Study of the Problem of Discrimination Against Indigenous Populations*, UN Doc.E/Cn.4/Sub.2/1982/2 Add.4, para 379.

De Groen, Frances (1992), 'Healing, Wholeness and Holiness in "My Place"', Bird and Haskell (eds.), *Whose Place? A Study of Sally Morgan's 'My Place'*, Pymble: Angus and Robertson.

Dodson, Michael (2003), 'The End in the Beginning: Re(de)finding Aboriginality', in Grossman (ed.), *Blacklines: Contemporary Critical Writing by Indigenous Australians*, Carlton: Melbourne University Press.

Griffin, Graham (2002), 'Indigenous People in Rangelands', in A.C. Grice and K.C. Hodgkinson (eds.), *Global Rangelands: Progress and Prospects*, CABI Publishing.

Heseltine, H.P. (1985), 'Australian Image', in Kramer and Mitchell (eds.), *The Oxford Anthology of Australian Literature*, Melbourne: Oxford University Press, pp. 298-312.

Ingamells, Rex et al. (eds.) (1948), *Jindyworobak Review (1938-1948)*, Melbourne: Jindyworobak.

International Cancun Declaration of Indigenous Peoples, 2003. http://www.tebtebba.org

Kirk, M. (1986), *A Change of Ownership: Aboriginal Land Rights*, Milton: Jacaranda Press.

Lawrence, D.H. (1972), *Kangaroo*, Harmondsworth: Penguin.

Lawrence, D.H. and M.L. Skinner (1996), *The Boy in the Bush*, London: Penguin.

McLaren, John (2001), 'The Image of Reality in Our Writing', in Delys Bird et al. (eds.), *Authority and Influence: Australian Literary Criticism 1950-2000*, St. Lucia: UQP, pp. 43-6.

Morgan, Sally (1987), *My Place*, Fremantle: Fremantle Arts Centre Press.

Murray, Les (1994), *Collected Poems*, Port Melbourne: William Heinemann.

Pilkington, Doris (1996), *Follow the Rabbit Proof Fence*, St. Lucia: UQP Press.

Probyn, F. and C. Simpson (2002), 'This Land is Mine/This Land is Me: Reconciling Harmonies in "One Night the Moon" ', *Senses of Cinema*, May.

Ravell, Julia, 'A Place in the Past: Pilkington and van den Berg on the Moore River Settlement', http://www.api-network.com.

Rose, Deborah Bird, *Nourishing Terrains*, http://www.ahc.gov.au

Scott, Kim (1993), *True Country*, Fremantle: Fremantle Arts Centre Press.

Scott, Kim. 'Australia's Continuing Neurosis: Identity, Race and History', <http://www.abc.net.au/rn/deakin/stories broadcast on 15.05.2001, 28.9.2006

Shoemaker, Adam (2004), *Black Words, White Page: Aboriginal Literature 1929–1988*, http://epress.anu.ed.au

Smith, Linda Tuhiwai (1999), *Decolonizing Methodologies: Research and Indigenous Peoples*, London: Zed Books.

Stowe, Randolph (2002), *To the Islands*, St.Lucia: UQP.

Strauss, Jennifer (1998), 'Literary Culture 1914-1939: Battlers All', Bennett et al. (eds.), *The Oxford Literary History of Australia*, Oxford: Oxford University Press, pp. 107-29.

Tacey, David (2001), 'Aboriginality, Landscape and the Imagination', in Delys Bird et al. (eds.), *Authority and Influence: Australian Literary Criticism 1950-2000*, St.Lucia: UQP, pp. 229-33.

UN CEPAL Review, 2002.

Van den Berg, Rosemary (1994), *No Options: No Choice: The Moore River Experience*, Broome: Magabala Books.

Way, Frith and S. Beckett, 'Governance Structures for Indigenous Australians', http://www.austlii.edu.au

Wright, Judith (1981), *Cry for the Dead*, London: Oxford University Press.

——— (1985), 'Landscape and Dreaming', in Stephen R. Graubard (ed.), *Australia: The Daedalus Symposium*, Sydney: Angus and Robertson, p. 32.

——— (1999), *Half a Lifetime*, Sydney: Text Publishing.

——— (1996), *Preoccupations in Australian Poetry*, London: Oxford University Press.

Yunupingu, Galarrwuy (1998), 'We Know These Things to be True', *The Third Vincent Lingiari Memorial Lecture*, 20 August.

CHAPTER 7

Mauritian Sugar Cane Planters Struggle for Survival

P.S. VIVEK

Sugar has made the fortunes of a few and caused unbelievable misery to many more. It has inflicted sufferings on the people involved in its production. This paper is an outcome of the field study of a research project conducted in the island nation of Mauritius in 2006. The nation has been a victim of substantial and progressive decrease in world sugar prices of up to 37 per cent over a period of three years (2006-9, see Table 7.1). This is a fallout the 'sugar regime' promoted by the European Union and World Trade Organisation (WTO). An overpowering odour of molasses surrounds the island of Mauritius. It used to be the sweet smell of success when the cane sugar industry and its by-products of molasses and Rhum kept the island in relative prosperity. But changing world markets have affected the economy. Sugar is still a major export. Cane plantations cover 90 per cent of the cultivated land and use one-fifth of the labour force. But new industries have been developed and sugar now accounts for only 40 per cent of the island's exports compared with 98 per cent in former times.

The people of Mauritius have had to struggle for every single achievement of their life, even after gaining independence from the British Empire in 1968. The elected representatives started working against the interest of their voters and cheated the masses systematically. The small planters in Mauritius today are the direct descendents of the indentured labour brought from India, almost without any exception, by the British rule in the first half of the nineteenth century. The records show that they were treated as lesser humans in a country which was made be conducive for habitation by the blood and sweat of their forefathers. The British subjugated the aspirations of the

TABLE 7.1: SUGAR PRICE REDUCTIONS AS PER THE SUGAR REGIME PROPOSAL

Year	Present rate US$ Per Tonne Cane		Present Price MUR per	Present Rate per Acre @30t/ac	Price Reduction (%)	Price Mur per Tonne	Price per Acre @ 30 t/ac on Reduction	Actual loss per acre @ 30 t/ac
	Present	After						
2005-6	640	–	17,625/-	5,28,750/-	–	–	–	–
2006-7	640	608	17,625/-	5,28,750/-	5	17,595.62	5,27,868.75	881.25
2207-8	640	512	17,625/-	5,28,750/-	15	17,507.50	5,25,225.00	3,525.00
2008-9	640	406.40	17,625/-	5,28,750/-	16.5	17,410.56	5,22,316.88	6,433.12
Total					36.5			6,433.12

Notes: 1. Calculation as per the proceeds received from the 2005-6 crops.
2. EU rate of 2005 @ 640/- per tonne is assumed constant.
3. Total phase of progressive reduction of actual price of Mauritian sugar during the three years will be 36.5 per cent.

workers and the post-1968 era saw the same high-handed approach being adopted by the ruling elite and their officiating agents in disguise of elected representatives of the planters.

One of the small planters recollected his grandmother,[1] who was one of the early immigrants from India, saying, 'Please keep at least one paisa separate, out of every five paisa, in the name of the mother land, and buy a small plot; you will never die of hunger.' The small planters, who became owners of small plots of land in this manner, over the period of time, have been following their own indigenous methods of cane cultivation, without any real time help from the government. However, all kinds of taxes and insurance premiums are imposed by the authorities on the planters in the name of administrative efficiency.

In the globalized economy, sugar cane is not insured but its by-product: sugar. Compulsory global cess is collected from the planters at source to meet the expenses of 'Mauritius Sugar Production' without mentioning the actual cost of production of one tonne of sugar from the required sugar cane. Currently, more than 28,000 small planters and Metayers (hillstop sugar cane planters cultivating estate owners land in exchange for a portion of the produce) grow sugar cane in their fields that produces approximately 30 per cent of the 6,00,000 tonnes of sugar in the country (the rest being produced by a handful of miller planters). Majority of them have hand-to-mouth existence and have invariably four-five dependents to look after.

It is interesting to note that the small planters' community of Mauritius has some devoted and dedicated leaders who have the foresight and energy to struggle for attainment of social justice for their compatriots. During meetings in the villages, many planters came out with wonderments, suggestions and alternatives to combat what they see together as the emerging crisis created due to the progressive reduction of sugar price in the EU market dictated by the manoeuvrings of the WTO.

TRAJECTORY OF INDENTURED LABOUR

Under the British, Mauritius was no longer a free port. To compensate for the resulting loss in trade, the government encouraged sugar production. In 1825 Britain equalized the duty on sugar from all of its colonies, providing a strong stimulus for Mauritians to produce more sugar. Production leaped from 11,000 tonnes in 1825 to 21,000 tonnes in 1826. By 1854 production exceeded 1,00,000 tonnes. By the mid-nineteenth century, Mauritius had reached the apex of its importance in the world sugar market; it was Britain's main sugar-producing colony, contributing 9.4 per cent of the world's sugar cane between 1855 and 1859. However, production in other countries robbed Mauritius of its dominant role in subsequent years. Nonetheless, as sugar increased in economic importance, the percentage of food crop production dropped accordingly, and landownership became concentrated in large, profitable estates. Indentured workers from India replaced slaves as a source of cheap labour for the sugar plantations. Between 1834 and 1910 (the last year of Indian labourers arriving in Mauritius), 4,51,776 Indians migrated to Mauritius, the majority arriving before 1865.

An indentured servant is a labourer under contract to work (for a specified period of time) for another person or a company/corporation, often without any monetary benefit, but in exchange for accommodation, food, other essentials, training or passage to a new country. After working for the term of the contract (traditionally seven years) the servants were then free to farm or take up any trade on his own. The term comes from the medieval English term '*indenture of retainer*', a contract written in duplicate on the same sheet, with copies separated by cutting along jagged teeth. Hence, the '*indenture*' line, on the contract signed, was *meant to represent the teeth of the two parts* that could later be refitted, *to confirm authenticity*. Indentured labour was also used to grow the labour-intensive cash crop of tobacco in the seventeenth century.

Most workers came from Bengal and Madras Presidency under contract to work for at least ten years for low wages under harsh conditions. At the end of their contracts, workers supposedly had the option of returning home, but plantation owners often succeeded in eliminating this choice. Many plantation owners punished workers with beatings, hunted down those who ran away and imprisoned them, and unjustly withheld pay. In 1878 a labour law regularized the pay system, and in 1917 the indenture system formally ended. Further, a 1922 law permitted workers to choose their places of work.

By 1871 more than 68 per cent of the Mauritian overall population was Indian, of which more than 25 per cent had been born in Mauritius. In 1931 the proportion of Indians in the population was the same, but more than 93 per cent of them were natives. By contrast,

Mauritius had no immigration from Africa. The freed slaves and their Creole offspring left the plantations to become fishers, dockworkers, and civil servants and formed about 20 per cent of the population in 1931. A number of Chinese immigrated during the nineteenth century and they made up about 2 per cent of the population. The Indian rupee became the island's official currency in 1876.

DETERIORATING CONDITIONS

Deterioration in the social climate attributed to massive introduction of Indian labourers. The operation, which threatened to grow out of control, forced the government to take the decision to discontinue the granting of permission to individual planters for the introduction of Indian labourers. Suits for unpaid wages or fraud were becoming so numerous that Justices of Peace could not examine them all. It was also noted that idleness and disorder were prevalent among labouring classes.

Again as it happened in 1829, the cause of instability was attributed to the bad selection of immigrants by 'crimps' and not by *sirdar* who used to accompany the workers on the work site and who commanded respect and obedience. Motivated by quick profits made through the recruitment of a great number of labourers, emigration agents had abandoned the traditional way of contracting hill coolies through the services of a *sirdar*. Recruitment was carried on by a host of crimps employed by the great Anglo–Indian firms of merchants to procure labourers. When a planter's order arrived at the office of one of those merchants, an elaborate process had to be undertaken by the superior Indian agents in the chief towns. They in turn passed on the order to senior recruiting agents called *duffadars*. The lowest of all in the hierarchy were the *arkotties* whom the *duffadars* hired to do the actual business of obtaining labourers. The *duffadars* and *arkotties* went out into the rural districts equipped with lavish grants of money from Indian agents, and resplendent with badges of authority. They easily attracted attention of the Indian population. However, some *duffadars* even resorted to kidnapping.

The sorrows of the recruits did not stop on land, for during the sea voyage, the captains of the ships lodged the immigrants in the lower deck, among bales of rice. As a result the death rate was high.

Complaints which followed forced the deputy-governor of Bengal to appoint a committee to investigate into the abuses that were reported to him in August 1838. Pending the publication of the report the Government of India prohibited emigration to Mauritius on 29 March 1839. It was a severe blow to the Mauritian planters. The Emigration India Act of 1839, coming at the critical time of the suppression of Negro apprenticeship, roused considerable alarm among the colonists. Sir Lionel Smith, who assumed office of the Deputy-Governor of Bengal in July 1840, took immediate steps to reverse the decision of the Government of India. He undertook to visit every estate on the island and to conduct a full enquiry into the treatment of Indian labourers. He then reported that the Indian labourers were living in good understanding with their employers and that justice and good treatment were guaranteed to labourers by the appointment of Stipendiary Magistrates and the enforcement of the Order in Council regulating relations between 'master' and 'servant'. The evidence given by returning emigrants before the Bengal Emigration Committee supported the appeal of Sir Lionel Smith. Most of them testified that their treatment was on the whole satisfactory.

As can be seen from the evidence, most of the emigrants had left their wife and children in the care of their in-laws or parents. In fact, desertion of the family was one of the main obstacles to the resumption of emigration towards Mauritius. The evidence given by the Chief Magistrate Macfarlance removed that last obstacle. In a letter to the Secretary of the Bengal government, he explained that in cases where wife and children were left behind, the emigrant was either convinced that members of their family could fare by their own industry, or was relying on the family tradition whereby relatives fed those left behind on the understanding that the expenses would be reimbursed on the return of the emigrant. In fact, payment of such debt was considered a sacred duty in emigrant circles, and in cases where the emigrant did not return home, the children were honour-bound to repay the debt.

The Mauritian emigrants, especially from India, certainly girded their loins and with an indomitable will, got down to the work that eventually turned the island of barren rocks into a fertile agricultural land. People have suffered adversity during their long march in search of a better world. The descendents of the Indian immigrants who now are part of the core of the island's society are anxious and ready to make their full contribution to the building of the new Mauritian nation which has emerged after independence. The rise and development of the Indian immigrants is so intimately connected with the island's story that it is necessary to make a brief survey of the country's history up to the time when Indians began to have a decisive influence on it.

The movement of the old immigrants was in many respects similar to the challenge of the sepoys to British Rule in India. Many sepoys who had deserted the army or who had even taken part in the mutiny escaped judgement by emigrating overseas. They carefully concealed their identity, drifted to the Mauritius emigration agencies of Calcutta and Madras, presented themselves to a Mauritian requisitionist and signed their engagement as agricultural labourers. In the case of Mahadoo, for instance, who reluctantly avowed to the Commissioners of Inquiry that before coming to Mauritius, he had been a sepoy belonging to a regiment of Bombay army that mutinied at Kanpur. Integrated in the labour force of Mauritius the former sepoys must have communicated to the Indian labourers their vengeance and aspiration for independence.

Such an overall change in the mental frame of the labourers could not have been brought about without new awakening about their apathy, a growing opposition to long accepted abuses and a zeal for reform. Their growing industrial militancy was apparent in the initial stage in recurrent absenteeism, desertion and vagrancy. The economic and social crisis that spread through Indian states in the 1850s, which generated discontent and which culminated in the revolt had much in common with the economic and social crisis of the 1860s in Mauritius. In India, the sepoy revolt marked a turning point in the history of the country. The outcome was the passing on 2 August 1858 of an 'Act for the better government of India'.

In Mauritius, the stout resistance of the Indian workers to their exploitation led in the first place to the setting up of the inquiry Commission of 1872 and to the subsequent passing in 1878 of a New Labour Law whose 284 articles laid new basis for fairness in industrial relations. The Chamber of Agriculture called upon to express its views on the proposed New Labour Law concluded its report by stating that the objective of labour laws was to conciliate the protection of employees with the legitimate rights of employers. On leaving the country, Governor A.P. Phayre, referring to the labour law which had been passed during his term of office, expressed the wish that: 'Estate owners would cheerfully do their part in carrying out the law and that the result would be advantageous to property as well as to labour, since the prosperity of Mauritius wholly depends on agricultural interests.'

The labourers were part of the Indian peasantry that is traditionally passive and submissive, so it was but natural that they should accept whatever they were told to do. Men who were uprooted from their homes and made to live in strange surroundings were not happy.

SOCIAL AND POLITICAL AGITATION

When Mahatma Gandhi visited Mauritius in 1901, he saw visible signs of political awareness among his fellow Indians, so much so that he thought Mauritius was a small India beyond the seas. An account of the unhappy plight of indentured labourers settled in the island had reached him in South Africa and although they were not subject to the same political restrictions as South African Indians, Gandhi wanted to visit the island to acquaint himself with the conditions under which the Indians were living.

Gandhi's interest in Mauritius was motivated by another reason which concerned the great doctrine of his life namely, *Satyagraha*. Interestingly, in the early stages of his passive resistance campaign in South Africa, Gandhi had found in a Mauritian Indian, Tambu Naidoo, settled in Natal, a great and devoted ally who fought with him with courage, self-sacrifice and determination throughout the epic struggle.

Gandhi, who has described passive resistance 'as a method of securing rights by personal suffering', was only too aware that the Indian community in South Africa was not in a position to challenge the power of the South African government. His religious bent of mind led him to believe that eventually the forces of injustice would be overcome by non-violent means. He discussed his plans with some prominent Indians in Natal and among them was Tambu Naidoo. Of his unique contribution to the *Satyagraha* campaign, Mahatma Gandhi has recorded the following tribute:

> But perhaps the bravest and the staunchest of all is the indomitable Tambu Naidoo, I do not know any Indian who knows the spirit of the struggle so well as he does. He was born in Mauritius but is more Indian than most of us. He has sacrificed himself entirely and has sent me a defiant message, saying that, even though I may yield and accept anything less than Lord Ampthill's account, he alone will offer resistance and die in Transvaal goal!
>
> (Gandhi, 2000: 97)

The success Gandhi won in South Africa with the help of Naidoo earned him the admiration and respect of many Indians settled in Mauritius. It was therefore not surprising that he was given a rousing welcome on his arrival in Port Louis. A reception committee under the chairmanship of Hajee Goolam Hossen was formed to organize receptions to commemorate the visit. A mammoth meeting attended by leading Indians from all over the country as well as representatives of other communities was held at the Taher Bagh in Port Louis. Gandhi's visit coincided with the municipal elections and inevitably some speakers who addressed the gathering at the Taher Bagh referred to the inadequate representation of Indian interests in the political institutions of the island. In his reply, Gandhi reminded the audience that the fruits of democracy were accessible only to those who were willing to pay the price and this meant that they had to struggle hard to win their rights. This statement, which was made in good faith, was strongly resented by the conservative press of the island. Leoville L'Homme, the well-known poet, was no doubt echoing the feelings of the other sections when he wrote in the *Radical*, a daily newspaper based towards the sugar magnates, that it was only by fulfilling those conditions that the Indians could hope to participate in the public life of their country. However, it must be said to the credit of Leoville L'Homme that he modified his views when in one of his poems he wrote some time after, he regarded Indian civilization as a harbinger of peace and liberty throughout the ages (Hazareesingh, 1975: 75).

During his stay in Mauritius, Gandhi was the guest for one night of the Governor of Mauritius, Sir Charles Bruce, a great Sanskrit scholar who sympathized with the political aspirations of Indians settled in the British Empire. Gandhi's visits round the island gave him a thorough insight into the living conditions of Indian immigrants. They were in despair and no one was stretching out a helping hand to them. Gandhi, who was very sensitive to human misery, was deeply moved and decided to do all that was in his power to improve the lot of the Indians. While attending a wedding in a small Indian village in the south of the island, Gandhi was impressed by the contribution made by the guests, both in kind and in cash, to meet the costs of the function. Such a spirit of cooperation was in consonance with the conception he had of a happy village community. It was while he was in the company of these villagers that Mahatma Gandhi decided to take positive steps towards improving the lot of Indians in Mauritius.

Back in India, on 1 December 1901, Gandhi submitted to the Indian National Congress, which was then holding its annual session in Calcutta, a full report on Indians in Mauritius. It was felt necessary to set up an organization on the spot, and a few years later he arranged for Manilall Doctor, a barrister whom he had met in London and who was equally inclined to help his less fortunate brethren, to visit Mauritius with a view to promoting the welfare of the Indian community. Manilall arrived on the island in October 1907 and during the four years of his stay, laid the foundations for the emancipation of the labouring classes, thereby helping to create a society where Indians could achieve some progress and play their legitimate role in national affairs. During those four years, Manilall kept in close touch with Gandhi, who by then had gone back to South Africa to pursue the struggle on behalf of overseas Indians. There can be no doubt that Manilall's influence largely contributed to the setting-up of the Royal Commission of 1909, which helped to alleviate the sufferings of agricultural workers. Manilall was also the prime mover in the political awakening which shook the very foundations of Mauritian society.

In 1907, a political movement, 'L'Action Liberale' was launched under the leadership of Messrs. George Guibert, Edouard Nairac, R. Merandon,[2] and Dr Eugene Laurent. The Indians threw in their feeble weight in favour of it, because they expected that the agitation and representations by this group would help better their political and economic situation. In carts drawn by mules and in a 'house wagon', the followers of 'L'Action Liberale' went all over the island to preach the new gospel to the people. It aroused some attention at that time, and was looked upon as a new force supported by the masses.

The year 1907 is memorable for another incident which occurred at the Legislative Council. An elected member of the Council raised a protest against the appointment of an English official as Receiver-General. D. Cameron, who was the Acting Colonial Secretary, made some remarks in reply which were regarded as 'a flagrant breach of good manners'. His statement implied want of confidence in some members of the Civil Service and when he refused to withdraw the 'offensive' words, a full-scale campaign followed against him and he left for another colony.

To restore the finances of the colony, which by 1908 were in a very poor condition, the Chamber of Agriculture applied for a loan of £4,00,000 from the Imperial Government, repayable at a low rate of interest. Representations were also made to the home authorities for improved railways and the establishment of a Department of Agriculture. An Agricultural Bank was also created to help especially the small planters; their situation was unstable at this moment, and the new Governor, Sir Cavendish Boyle, had appointed a Commission to look into their difficulties. The report disclosed many abuses, but a proposal sponsored by the Indian small planters to establish a central cooperative sugar factory, under government control, was rejected by the Commission.

The Secretary of State rejected the petition of the Chamber of Agriculture for a loan. The position Indians held in Mauritius at that period is summarized in the memorial of the community of planters and traders presented to the Directors of the Government of India on 10 June 1839:

> Thousands of aliens of India have been settled here for very many years as planters, shopkeepers, clerks and artisans, so that the native languages of India are here all perfectly understood and fluently spoken, not only by the Creole-Indians but by a great number of European residents, and the consequence is that the habits, manners, religious feelings and native prejudices of Indians being well comprehended are universally respected. All these circumstances combined with the constant weekly and almost daily communications with various parts of India render this island almost the same to an Indian as his native land. (Memorial of Planters, published in *Cerneen*, 10 June 1839: 10)

Things went from bad to worse, and the situation was so desperate that during a debate on the current expenditure of the administration, the word 'bankruptcy' was used by Sir Graham Bower, the Acting Governor. In February 1909, the Legislative Council asked for the appointment of a Royal Commission. ' L'Action Liberale' organized agitations in favour of the Royal Commission while the conservative members of the Council opposed it altogether, as they had not forgotten the experiment of 1872. The Enquiry Commission never did any good, they said.

On 18 June 1909, the Royal Commission arrived in Mauritius. It was composed of Sir Frank Swettenham, Chairman, Sir Edward O'Malley, and H.B. Woodcock. It was a great opportunity for Indians to state their case in the sure belief that they would have a good hearing. They had not produced any leader from their own ranks who could be their spokesman before the Commission, but in the absence of a local man the work was ably done by Manilall Doctor, who had been delegated by Gandhi to champion the Indians' cause. He had arrived in the colony eighteen months earlier and was fully acquainted with all the problems of the Indian community. He was indeed a great social worker who had made up his mind to organize the Indians and to fight on their behalf. It was a momentous event in the life of the community, for it was exactly 72 years after the arrival of the first immigrants that somebody had come from India to look after them. Until then the immigrants and their descendants had accepted life submissively, as if everything which happened to them was ordained by fate.

Manilall, who came from Gujarat, was a lawyer by profession. He was also a journalist and he found that he could not serve the cause of his people unless he had a newspaper at his disposal. Four months before the arrival of the Royal Commission, he founded a weekly paper, the *Hindustani*, which displayed on the front page the motto 'Liberty of Individuals; Fraternity of Man; Equality of Races'. His programme of work was summed up in the following words:

> Everyone has a right to do what he chooses, provided he does not encroach upon the liberty of others. If in all human beings is cast the image of God, i.e. of the external nature, so that the true destiny of man is divine, one man or one race cannot morally enslave, dominate or even exploit another for mere private gain.

For Mauritius it was nothing short of a revolutionary gospel.

Manilall felt he had a definite mission to fulfil and whether he was liked or disliked, supported or let down by his own folk, he was not going to be daunted. He went ahead with his work. He went from village to village and held hundreds of meetings all over the island, and obtained a mandate from the Indians to state their case before the Royal Commission. He always spoke in Hindustani, and made fiery speeches, as will be seen from the following resolutions passed at one of these meetings:

> That an enquiry be made into the condition of the Indian Labourers, many of whom are dead or starving in the streets of Port Louis, and into the story of their being induced by false pretences to come from India, and into their present helpless position after the completion of the indenture.
>
> That the proposal to substitute maize for rice is really to break trust with the poor indentured labourers, who have been induced to come to Mauritius by misguiding touts under false promises of making fabulous fortunes, and who, at the present day, are sometimes forced to eat uneatable rice.

Manilall had arranged to bring a number of Indians before the Commission. Acting always as their spokesman, he made a number of suggestions. He asked for the appointment of English magistrates, the establishment of cooperative credit societies on the same lines as in India, and the introduction of Indian laws of succession. He also asked for the inclusion of an Indian language as a principal subject of study for Indian boys in schools. The stand taken by him before the Commission aroused much opposition in other quarters. He was by no means popular; and in answer to his many suggestions, it the Royal Commissioners stated that Indians had to fit in with the laws of the colony. Many Indians were victimized for giving evidence before the Commission. With regard to the day-to-day life of the Indian peasantry, the Commissioners remarked that they 'were struck with the happy and contented appearance of most of the labourers and their families' (Hazareesingh, 1975: 80).

The centenary of Indian immigration was a time for stock-taking, and it provided Seewoosagar Ramgoolam, the first prime minister of Mauritius, with an opportunity to raise his voice against the evils which afflicted the masses. In an article in the *Indian Centenary Book* he wrote:

> Long accustomed to a life of toil, hunger and misery the worker finds it perhaps a little difficult to grasp the meaning and significance of the celebration of the Centenary of Indian immigration. Only a few years ago—and to a great extent now—his labour was unrecognised by his masters and he himself was looked down upon as an inferior being in the scheme of life. Now with the spread of education and the shrinking of the world by scientific discoveries, the more sharp-witted among the workers are beginning to grow restless. They may even go further and make mental notes of history and accordingly draw their own conclusions and make their reservations.
>
> Today they can hold their heads high with the assurance that they and their ancestors have given their best to this little island. The past never belonged to them; but the future smiles on them.
>
> It is our duty to enunciate a clear and defined principle of farsightedness for our people and to make up our minds to put an end to the social cruelties rampant in our society, and conceive of life as something not our own but a trust dedicated to the good of our community. (cf. Hazareesingh 1975: 124)

THE WOES OF SMALL PLANTERS

Everyone concerned with the development of Mauritius would be interested in understanding and characterizing the policy process in the island nation. There is hardly any objective analysis by the intelligentsia and the political elite in this area, in spite of immense benefits such an exercise could potentially yield. The risk and complexity associated with this exercise and the murky intellectual terrain may have been some of the factors that kept inquisitive minds at bay.

Despite overall growth of the Mauritian economy revolving around the four important pillars of sugar, textile, tourism and services sector, the country's performance in the spheres of social justice, reforms, equality and human rights has been varied and generally disappointing. Explanations of lacklustre performance have but been convincing in the case of Mauritius. Mainstream analysis foisted upon the island nation has ruled out any prospect for strategic social policy leave alone trade and industrial policies. The reasons for such a stance are not always internally consistent.

It is argued that the strategic policies which have propelled the success of economy in Mauritius are the consequence of a 'peculiar' institutional deficiency. Such policies cannot be expected to succeed in the interest of the faceless, voiceless majority of the country's citizenry. Paradoxically, despite nearly three decades of *laissez-faire* reforms, aggregate social performance has not improved (Soludo, 2004: ii). More and more African nations continue to join the league of Least Developed Countries (LDC). There must be, in effect, some 'peculiar conditions' that make trade and industrial policies of all vintages not to succeed as designed.

The political economy of policy choice and implementation together with all the domestic and external factors that circumscribe such an environment like that exists in Mauritius need to be scanned minutely. In this regard, several questions beg for an answer. Why, for example, have past policies failed to benefit the small planters in Mauritius for even three decades since independence? Who designed the policies and what were the motivations of and constituency of such policies? What was the bargaining process (and the parties) that led to the present policies and how did that affect its implementation? How could one characterize the present sugar policy in Mauritius, and its dynamic evolution over time? What is the nature of institutions/ parastatal bodies that are connected with the sugar industry in Mauritius? What is the role of the government in implementing the policies? What are the current policy challenges, especially in the context of WTO and globalization? How are the policies and institutions being adapted to respond to the changes? This report in the form of a book was motivated by the need to provide answers to these and a host of other questions.

A broad set of factors, shapes policy implementation in most countries, but the extent of each factor has differed from country to country. A key feature of the policy process is the loss of policy autonomy in almost all the countries to the extent that the domestic politics and institutional capacity can affect the implementation process and the broad policy thrust is either dictated (as under the conditionality of the Structural Adjustment Programme) or have to be approved (as under conditionality for the Poverty Reduction Strategy) by the boards of the Brettons Woods institutions. Given the fact that most African countries including Mauritius are indebted and aid-dependent, the broad and specific choices of trade and industrial policies have increasingly been tailored to meet the demands of the WTO. What has therefore emerged as the broad consensus on the nature of trade and industrial policies is rather a forced consensus. Over time, since independence, nuances in the development of Mauritius have brought about the identification of actors in mapping the new influence centres.

During the 1970s, Mauritius suffered from chronic unemployment and trade deficit. As a result it had to adopt the International Monetary Fund's Structural Adjustment Programme and push for an export-oriented economy for the sake of stability. A look at the policy decisions taken over the past two decades and the nature of economic growth indicates that despite the positive role played by the government, the macro-economic management has not been efficient. The globalization of the world economy and the implementation of the WTO provisions are now beginning to have a strong impact on the Mauritian scene. The country is mainly dependent upon preferential access to major markets in the world and is now facing competition from other emerging exporters. The conditions under which Mauritius exports sugar to the European Union do not indicate that it will be able to maintain the levels for long.

The ownership pattern has not changed much in Mauritius since 1939-40 except for the fact that there is now a new generation of owners as a result of the development of entrepreneurship in the country. In fact, the proprietors of sugar cane estates and sugar factories who were of Indian origin from 1871 to 1939 were systematically dispossessed of their property and factories to make way for politically motivated landownership pattern in a bid to look down upon the toiling people of Indian origin.

The official records the landownership point out the startling fact that none of the present estate owners have ever purchased the vast stretches of land under cane cultivation. Their forefathers had grabbed it without any payment to anybody. In due course, laws were manoeuvred and documents forged to legalize the unauthorized possession of the land.

Some of indentured labourers who were paid compensation by the Governor in the 1840s in lieu of their return passage opted to become Metayer cultivators of cane in the rough terrain possessed by the estate owners. The entire family including the children would work on the land and as much as 60 per cent of the produce (in the form of sugar) given to the absentee landlord of the plot of land. Metayers of Mauritius, at present numbering 905, have been cultivating these difficult terrains land of 'absentee landlords' for over 160 years; many of these families have spent generations cultivating sugar cane.

Each family of Metayer has to enter into a legal agreement with the absentee landlord family, to agreeing to share at least 35 per cent of the sugar produced on the plot of land being cultivated by the family, in lieu of the authorization to cultivate and maintain the land lent to them. The absentee landlord is not bound to pay any amount in cash or kind toward the cultivation and other requirements of fertilizers, and cutting-loading-transport of the cane.

Surprisingly enough, more than 50 of the small planters who had leased government agricultural land under *state land lease* agreement at Riche Terre locality were served notices on 6 March 2007 asking them to vacate the land by 30 April 2007, though the lease agreement was valid until 13 July 2015. The move, apparently, was the Mauritius prime minister's plan to attract direct foreign investment of US$ 5 billion from China. Under the scheme, the Shanxi Tianli Enterprise Group from China would create an Economic and Trade Cooperation Zone in Mauritius over an extent of approximately 211 hectares (500 arpents) of land situated at Riche Terre and Terre Rouge, in the proximity of the port area. The project will bring foreign direct investment to the tune of Rs. 17 billion (US $ 500 million) spread over a five-year period at the cost of displacement of more than 400 people who have spent their life cultivating the land (since 1948). (See Appendix Parliament Debate No. 5 of 27 March 2007.) There has neither been compensation nor any alternative that has been proposed by the government to the planters in the notice served to them.

The hardships and difficulties faced by the Metayers and other small planters of Mauritius has made it very difficult for them to overcome poverty conditions. Most of them are illiterate, old and living at subsistence levels. Their main grievance is that they have no other source of income but to cultivate cane in land of absentee landlords, generally a couple of acres in size. They demand ownership of land to salvage the situation.

GLOBAL CESS COLLECTED FROM SMALL PLANTERS

The Mauritian Sugar Authority determines the global cess, presently a mandatory deduction (at source) and forced upon the small planters. It includes financing of the following organizations:

1. The Sugar Industry Labour Welfare Fund
2. The Cane Planters and Millers Arbitration Control Board
3. The Mauritius Sugar Industry Research Institute
4. The Mauritius Sugar Terminal Corporation
5. The Mauritius Sugar Authority
6. The Farmers Service Corporation
7. The Sugar Planters Mechanical Pool Corporation

A whopping Rs. 800 million is earmarked annually for financing all the above organizations. Apart from the Sugar Planters Mechanical Pool Corporation there is no other organization which provides direct assistance to the small planters. Most of the other organizations ought to have been financed by the government in the interest of the nation and prevent the small planters from exploitation, especially in the wake of global market price reduction for the sugar.

THE WAY OUT

Sugar alone brings Rs.10 billion in foreign currency as every crystal of sugar produced in Mauritius is exported to the European Community under the Sugar Protocol. The sugar industry in Mauritius is quite a complex one. The Mauritius Sugar Syndicate (MSS) has been assigned the important role of marketing all the sugar produced in the country. The sugar being sold under the Sugar Protocol could have been done directly by the local office. Incidentally, the expenses for managing the sales are not spent from the government treasury but from the planters remuneration for the price of their sugar equivalence of sugar cane produced and marketed abroad.

Mauritius Planters Association demanded a probe into the financial irregularities of the sugar barons, that is the Miller Planters. The government therefore instituted an enquiry into the affairs of the Mauritius sugar industry. In accordance with the provisions of the Mauritius Sugar Authority Act 27, a global cess has been levied on the annual proceeds from sugar exports. The global cess is used to finance the administrative expenses of not only the Mauritius Sugar Authority, but also the annual budget and capital expenditures of various organizations of the sugar industry, namely the Mauritius Sugar Terminal Corporation, the Cane Planters and Millers Arbitration and Control Board, the Mauritius Sugar Industry Research Institute, the Sugar Planters Mechanical Pool Corporation, the Farmers Service Corporation, the Farmers Service Corporation and the Sugar Industry Labour Welfare Fund.

It is astonishing to note that Mauritius' main crop, i.e. sugar cane, is *not* insured in the country. It is only the by-product of sugar cane—sugar—that is insured. Mauritius is a small country with micro-climates. The control board does the sugar sharing as per the apportionment ratio of 78:22. When the sugar price sharing ratio between small planters and the millers was 74:26, planters were getting some 80 kg of sugar for every tonne of cane supplied to the mills. Surprisingly, the planters were told that the sugar has already been shared between millers and planters in an 'objective assessment'. During that time the concerned planters lost some 3 kg of sugar per tonne of cane every crop year. The planters had produced about 2,300 tonnes of cane that year and by the loss of 3 kg of sugar per tonne of cane the planters lost some 6t 900 kg of sugar. At the rate of Rs. 15,000 per tonnage of sugar that year, the planters had lost Rs. 1,05,000.

There has been a dispute between the small planters and millers on the sharing of marketed sugar price and the quantity of sugar produced out of one tonne of sugar cane. The Sugar Milling Cost Analysis issued by various sugar factories since 1992, available with the author, mentions the inclusion of 'indirect expenses' in the cost of sugar milling. Sugar cane is weighed by the mills when it is brought to the yard by the small planters. It is these multiple players, incharge of weighing the sugar cane and sugar in Mauritius, that have been creating problems about weight at different locations of the sugar trade. The 28,000 small planters cultivating sugar cane in Mauritius over presently possess plots of about four hectares and account for 23 per cent of sugar production in the country. Similarly, the Metayer planters approximate around 1,000 in number and account for about 2 per cent of the country's sugar production. The Government Programme 2005-10 assured the survival of small planters by investing Rs. 2 billion in derocking and irrigation schemes over a period of five years, but the small planters and Metayers got nothing. The land owned by small planters, and over 5,000 hectares in the possession of Metayer planters and small planters suffer from lack of required irrigation.

250 litres of ethanol can be produced out of one tonne of sugar cane. Ideally, small planters could supply their cane exclusively to the units manufacturing electricity and ethanol. As seen earlier the government action programme proposes to maintain only four sugar factories in the four corners of Mauritius with increased capacity for manufacturing sugar. If a single sugar manufacturing unit is maintained on a cooperative basis by the small planters and Metayer planters out of the 20 per cent share held by the Sugar Investment Trust in the present (to be closed mills), then the tonnage of sugar cane could be brought by any of the shareholder planters without any restriction. Small planters can have sizeable sum in their kitty, if the anti-small planter practices undertaken by the Mauritius Sugar Syndicate and Mauritius Sugar Authority are discontinued forthwith.

One thing is certain—the sugar industry in Mauritius will continue to exist and grow as over 60 per cent of the sugar cane plantations belong to the big estate owners and a handful of Franco–Mauritians. Hence, the main question is the survival of 28,000 + 1,000 small planters and Metayers. It would be unfair and against natural justice to thrust a public policy on these people without their consent. To say that the small planters and Metayers must cultivate sugar cane will be a wrong move. It will weaken the planting community and may lead to a degradation of the economic, social and cultural climate of Mauritius. In fact, the small planters and Metayers should be allowed and encouraged to cultivate whatever produce that they think is suitable, profitable and viable for them, be it horticulture, paddy, greenhouse cultivation, dairy farming, poultry farming, floriculture, mushroom farming, vegetable cultivation, commercial outlet for cane juice, paper industry based on sugar cane straws or anything else. For these reasons and many others, it is imperative to institute afresh a Commission of Enquiry headed by a judge of the Supreme Court of Mauritius to look into the various dimensions of the present crisis in the sugar industry and make the necessary recommendations that will be all encompassing and impartial, binding on all the parties concerned.

As seen in the past, small planters and Metayers have great survival instincts. It is they who have developed almost a barren island, against all odds, in cooperation will one another, to build the sovereign democratic republic of Mauritius. It is high time that they are treated with respect and dignity by the policy makers and politicians alike.

NOTES

1. Bissoo Mungroo of Flic En Flac was vociferous and emotional while narrating the sufferings of the past and discussing present issues facing the small planters of the country.
2. Merandon retained his love for small men till the end; he lived abroad for thirty years and returend to his native land in March 1972 and spent his last days among the tillers of the field in a small village outside Port Louis. He died there shortly after and in accordance with his wishes was buried in the local cemetery among those for whom the bells did not toll.

REFERENCES

Chung Tze Cheong, M., and Jacquin, E. (2003), 'Use of the Geographic Information System to Assess the Suitability of Sugarcane Lands for Mechanized Crop Production in Mauritius', *Revue Agricole et Sucriere de Tile Maurice*, vol. 82, nos. 1 & 2, pp. 33-41.

Deerpalsing, S. (1979), *A Bibliography of Mauritian Government Publications: 1955-78*, Moka: Mahatma Gandhi Institute Library.

Farmers Service Corporation and Sugar Productivity & Competitivity Unit, (2004), 'Cost of Production–Small Sugarcane Planter', Occasional Publication, St. Pierre, pp. 2.

Foolmaun, G. (2004), 'The Block Management System as a Management Tool Towards Improving Sugarcane Growers' Productivity, Financial Viability', MSc Dissertation, Mauritius: University of Technology pp. 85.

Gunesh, T. (2004), 'Brix Monitoring—A Tool for Higher Returns', *Planters Bulletin*, Fanners Service Corporation Publication, pp. 9-10.

Jhoty, I., S. Ramasamy, D. Baggonauth, P.K. Tulloo (2002), 'Suitability of Cane Land for Mechanization', MSIRI, Occasional Report No. 29, pp. l-11.

Jhoty, I. and S. Ramasamy (2003), 'Derocking of Sugar Cane Land in Mauritius', MSIRI Occasional Report No. 30.

Lange, Matthew (2003), 'Embedding the Colonial State: A Comparative-Historical Analysis of State Building and Broad-based Development in Mauritius', *Social Science History*, vol. 27, pp. 397-423.

'Mauritius: Narrow Options', *Economic and Political Weekly*, vol. 17, no. 44, 1982, p. 1756.

'Mauritius Striking a Balance', *Economic and Political Weekly*, no. 25, 1982, pp. 1007-8.

McIntyre, G. (2001), 'The Influence of Poor, Late Sugarcane Varieties on Sugar Production', *Revue Agricole et Sucriere de Tile Maurice*, pp. 44-6.

Miesenhelder, Thomas (1997), 'The Developmental State in Mauritius', *Journal of Modern African Studies*, vol. 35, no. 2, pp. 279-97.

Nababsing, V. and R. Virahsawmy (1977), 'The Characteristics of the Small Planter Class in a Small Plantation Economy: The Case of Mauritius', Seminar Papers—'Characteristics of Island Economies', pp. 44-74.

Nixon, D.J. and L.P. Simmonds (2004), 'The Impact of Fallowing and Green Manuring on Soil Conditions and the Growth of Sugar Cane', The University of Reading, vol. 40, Cambridge University Press, pp. 127-38.

Padya, B.M. (1984), 'The Climate of Mauritius', Mauritius: Meteorological Office, p. 217

Pillay, K.P. (2001), 'Use of Fertilizers and Herbicides in Sugarcane Cultivation in Mauritius', International Extension Workshop, Mauritius: MSIRI, pp. 29-33.

Sabhrawal, O.P. (1982), 'Indo Mauritian Ties, New Phase', *Mainstream*, vol. 20, no. 43, pp. 3-4.

Samatar, Abdi (1999), *An African Miracle: State, Class Leadership and Colonial Legacy in Botswana Development*, Portsmouth: Heinemann.

Soludo, Charles, Osita Ogbu and Ha-Joon Chang (eds.) (2004), *The Politics of Trade and Industiral Policy in Africa: Forced Consensus*? New Jersey: Africa World Press. [See also www.idrc.ca/openebooks/125-6]

Shukul, H.C. (1983), 'Indian Ocean—Politics of Confrontation or Coexistence', *Indian Journal of Political Studies*.

Simpson, B.W. and R. Ng Kee Kwong (2001), The Australian and Mauritian Partnership–International Extension Workshop, Mauritius: MSIRI, 8-9 August, pp. l-7.

Singh, R.P. (1998), 'Economic Development, Sustainabihty of Farming System, and Rural Poor: Some Policy Issues', Fourth International

Programme on Strategies for Sustainable Agriculture and Rural Development in Developing Countries, November-December, Hyderabad: National Institute of Rural Development, pp. 55-84.

Umrit, G., B.W. Simpson, A. Soobadar and R. Ng Kee Kwong (2001), 'Offsite Movement of Herbicides in Sugarcane Production in Mauritius', International Extension Workshop, MSIRI, Mauritius', 8-9 August 2001, pp. 77-85

Virahsawmy, R. (1981), 'Morcellement and the Emergence of villages in Mauritius', A Case Study of Vale and Holyrood, *Regards sur le monde rural Mauricien*, University of Mauritius, pp. 23-50.

CHAPTER 8

Flogging and Marginalization of Plantation Workers in Mauritius: A Case Study

AJAY MAHURKAR

A neglected aspect of studies on globalization and the marginalized is the penal and control regimes which the marginalized are subjected to in the interface between globalization and marginality (Hughes, 1987). In the medieval times as Michel Foucault has demonstrated the penal regimes often exhibited the public flogging of the body as the means of legitimizing the state and the penal regimes themselves (Foucault, 1975). Bentham uses the concept of 'Panopticon' to express the very visible display of state power for control in the nineteenth century (O'Sullivan, 2006). Foucault has also demonstrated how state power in modern times percolates to the individuals through countless capillaries to discipline and punish. In the post-industrial society Marcuse argues that the regime of technological and political control mobilizes the individuals of these societies for total defence of these societies (Marcuse, 1996).

Foucault analyses these control regimes in order to demonstrate how a new discourse emerges in the nineteenth century to demonstrate 'discipline or punish' or 'madness and civilization' pushing the existing knowledges on these themes to the background. Marcuse on the other hand points to the increasing disconnect between the techno-political universe of the new society and what he calls the 'context'. This context he says is invariably the environmental context. The cathect between individual or this society and environment is placed in a disconnect mode.[1]

This paper on the basis of some archival evidence gathered on nineteenth-century Mauritius is placed between the Foucault and Marcuse argument. I try to argue that in the context of nineteenth-century globalization the penal discourse offers clues to links with the way perceptions on the environmental question were changing. How did this happen? I will try to outline in the following sections of the paper.

A DEBATE ON FLOGGING

I recovered this debate from the archival records and newspapers of the period between 1883 and 1886. The focus of this debate was the death due to flogging of a low caste Indian prisoner named Seechurn in the Port Louis jail of Mauritius in July 1883.[2] The debate focuses on the body of the prisoner who was flogged for violating prison discipline and tries to determine whether the prisoner died due to flogging or the heart disease from which he was suffering. Both aspects then are linked to the question of jail discipline, conditions of jail and the health context of the individual concerned. The debate in overall sense exhibited the flogged body in a manner akin to Foucault's description of medieval flogging in his 'Discipline and Punish'.

However, the debate points to the variety of opinions on the issue. It is the reports of the representatives of the state ironically which evince opposition sympathetic to the prisoner and his context and argue actually for abolition of flogging.[3] On the other hand, the newspapers and opinions of the private members of legislative council are either divided or are in favour of flogging.[4]

The interim report issued by the government medical team on this question is categorical that the flogging undergone by the malaria stricken prisoner 'was determinate in hastening his heart disease to which the prisoner had succumbed'.[5] The governor of Mauritius Sir John Pope Hennessey who had taken office in June only was 'forthright in his condemnation and referred to the Indians as being very badly treated in his legislative council speech'.[6]

Reporting on this speech on 28 Februrary *Merchants and Planters Gazette* (henceforth *MPG*) reported: 'Turning to our prisons the governor said that he had some experience in other part of the world in prison discipline, but had never seen anything so objectionable and unjust. This condition of things, he averred, prevailed despite the protests of the press and the wishes of the Downing Street.'[7] The *MPG*, a representative of the upcoming planters and the professionals itself identified this event as a 'black record' in the history of the colony.[8]

The *MPG* however clarified its stand on the penal regime in the prisons. In an editorial titled 'The Cat in the Prison: The Case of Seechurn' (Cat is the instrument with which flogging is carried out), it declared

> Now we are all agreed that punishment ought not to be inflicted on vindictive principle, but on a deterring principle. But on this principle to be effective it must be painful. It need not be, nor should it be, cruel. Men after conviction have to conform to prison regulations. This is essential, but no unnecessary pain should be inflicted even in the attainment of this object.[9]

In this the *MPG* was echoing Lord Kimberley, the British secretary of state for colonies who had put on record 'my regret that in 40 out of 50 cases flogging had been administered for insignificant prison offences. I notice the large number of stripes being administered.'[10]

The *MPG* further argues

> now let us ask as to what was being done in respect to these admonitions of Kimberley? Absolutely nothing, we fear, calculated to check this practice. Indeed we have heard it alleged that members of the prison committee knew nothing of these rebukes administered by the secretary of the state. Then on whose shoulders rests the responsibility for making a state secret of the matter? On the government of the day of course.[11]

The *MPG* while pointing to government of the day clearly makes a distinction between the governor and his administration. The governor as we saw above was being seen by *MPG* as the man who condemns flogging and the bad treatment of the prisoners in jail.

The 'who' in question then boils down to those interests in the administration and their sympathizers who favour flogging. In the press the man who is identified with this opinion is the 'senior, unofficial member of the legislative council'[12] and a wealthy influential planter who had reported to the secretary of the state that he 'personally differed' from the result of the inquiry and that 'the prisoner was flogged mostly on the breaches and not the back'.[13] This was Mr. Cecilcourt Antelme who is also identified as a defender of the French legal system and culture in the colony of Mauritius.[14]

This private opinion was clearly shared by a section of the administration. The press seems to be aware of the existence of this private and vindictive opinion within the Mauritius administration. A letter to the *MPG* on 27 February 1884 blames individuals in the government being responsible for the flogging. Titled the 'Prisons Scandal' it said, the public desire to know who is responsible for having instituted the abominable practice of causing documents to be signed by the prison committee; authorizing the infliction of corporal punishment on convicted prisoners charged with breaches of prison discipline when the member in the question had not assisted at the investigation of the charges and was ignorant of the details. The report of the special committee informs us now that the practice has been discontinued, but who inaugurated it?[15]

The *MPG* further report that Mr. Cecilcourt Antelme the private (unofficial member) of the legislative council expressed his apprehension to the secretary of the state regarding the question of abolition of flogging. Pulling back the governor to the private interests he argued, 'I admit the *sociable* qualities of Sir John Pope Hennessey, but I fear that the governor's generous feelings are likely to raise difficulties.'[16]

THE PROTAGONISTS

Apart from Antelme, the private unofficial member of the legislative council who else could have been the supporters of this private opinion in the administration. Here we need to go back in Mauritius history a little. Prior to coming of the British, Mauritius had been a colony of the French. It was in fact the French who had settled the colony with the planters invited from France.[17] Richard Grove points out that these were called the 'labouring Proles of the Metropole' (Grove, 1995). These were settled through elaborate land grants called 'concessions'.[18] To assist them in cultivation mostly slave labour was used. Now with the settlement an elaborate judicial and financial system was built which was based on 'physiocratic' principles.[19] Now as pointed out in the vast literature of the political economy of this time, the physiocrats believed that the only labour capable of producing surplus value was the agricultural labour.[20] Any labour outside this conception was unproductive, vagrant and in the French understanding was the *marron* or run away labour. In this sense even the planters brought for the French plantations in the colony was 'productive labour'.[21]

To uphold this an administrative, judicial and legal system was built which would enable this productive labour to function.[22] In a sense this was a world-view which was founded in the process of establishing the colony. Vagrant, *marron* or otherwise labour dissociated with this conception was to be kept under a strict penal regime. The slaves who had been brought from Africa were then unavoidable *instrumentum mutuum* (voiceless instrument) to keep this productive labour in operation.[23] Deserters and run aways were hunted and punished.[24] Upholding this world-view was dissemination of French language and culture taken forward by people like Mr. Cecilcourt Antelme.[25]

Now under the Treaty of Paris in 1810 under which French transferred effective power to the British, the interests of this productive labour which had now become a planter aristocracy were to be upheld and protected.[26] The British who took over Mauritius in their home context of slavery abolition movements found it hard to dislodge this legacy.[27] However, they found the key to establishing control in the colony in the control of labour supply to the plantations. So, therefore, in 1832 slavery was abolished in Mauritius and by protracted negotiations a more model form of labour, the contract 'indentured' labour was introduced. This were mostly Indian, though not totally low caste in composition, but comprised of castes designated by the British as being fit for agricultural work.[28]

By variety of ordinances and legislations successive British governors sought to establish control over the Mauritius administration by controlling this labour supply.[29] The British to strengthen themselves also enacted regulations countering the financial and credit system of the French by creating credit cooperatives and credit networks of the Indians. As Richard Allen has pointed out, this also meant countering the network of the *baileur-du-fonds* who used their personal ties with the French families of the colony to advance crop loans which sustained the plantation economy in Mauritius.[30]

This then was an attempt to control the system of Mauritius administration. The British however were obliged under the treaty of Paris to keep the interest of the planter aristocracy intact and therefore could not go very far. So then, as Marina Carter has noted, there was a compromise between the French private interest and the British interest.[31] This was most starkly reflected in the compromises on vagrancy legislations.[32] Since the plantation economy continued to recognize only agricultural labour to be productive, any attempt by Indians to diversify into small trades, vending, shop keeping, etc., was regarded as vagrant behaviour by the French planters.[33] Meanwhile, since the system of French laws continued in the Mauritius Supreme Court and since the French culture was upheld as the dominant culture by the French community, the British found it difficult to get away from the French definitions of vagrancy.[34] Besides, the British too wanted to implement their notions of industrial efficiency and discipline to keep in check the growing Indian labour in Mauritius.[35] As a consequence by 1860s a compromise had been effected on the question of the penal regimes for the plantation and the vagrant labour. This compromise though, was challenged by several enlightend governors and officials, could not be easily shaken. It is this compromise then which is being mentioned in *MPG* as interests of private individuals and opinions.[36]

This compromise with the private interest now formed the 'reverse world'[37] to the world which Sir John Pope Hennessey is advocating for his administration. In Hennessey a former Irish reformist member of parliament of the Tory Party in Britain, a range of possibilities were opened up for the Mauritius people.[38] His stance on abolition of flogging, his support to a middling group of planters, professionals like doctors and lawyers and the Indian community gave him a *social* space to counter the compromise lobby.[39] The *MPG* in this period was supportive of this group. It is here that the governor found support for his anti-flogging stance. Later in advocating for elected Indian representation in the legislative council the governor converted this stance into a political campaign.[40]

THE 1880s CONTEXT

The 1880s provided a peculiar flash point for the clash of the two world-views mentioned above. The context was basically the link between the penal regime and the forest policy which had been enacted in the Woods and Forest ordinance of 1882.[41] In the spirit of anti-vagrancy laws the forest policy enacted by this ordinance punished even 'picking up small brush wood' by the Indians.[42] The penal regime created to ensure this by the ordinance of the 1882 actually then led to increase in the population of Indian inmates in the Mauritius prisons by the 1880s.[43] Sir John Pope Hennessey was quite perturbed by this development since as he put it, 'only the poor Indians' went to jail who were actually just picking up brush wood and forest wood for their daily needs.[44]

In this context he asked for the forest laws to be amended and for prevention of overcrowding in the prisons.[45] He argued that

> because a large number of prisoners are contravenors of forest legislation and the legislation is under consideration and I hope that it may be possible

to make such amendment in the laws as which lead to a considerable decrease in the number of prisoners who have been provided for under the present system. Secondly, there are advantages which could follow a separation of persons imprisoned for such contraventions as I have alluded to from the really criminal classes. Thirdly, I believe that the really criminal class of prisoners is small and I am inclined to think that the best plan will be to retain the present or district jails for short sentence prisoners and to provide the central prison accommodation for the really criminal class only.[46]

Hennessey further argued, 'I found this legislation (the forest Legislation) had come upon the Indian population like a hurricane, sending those men, women, and children to prisons, who had been well conducted and industrious'.[47]

It is in this spirit of countering the anti-vagrancy legislation that Hennessey pushed against expansion of prison space in Mauritius. Here he met with opposition both from secretary of the state and the influential planter lobby.[48] However, Hennessey continued to emphasize the link between the countering of anti-vagrancy forest laws and the reform of the penal regime.[49] On 13 May 1884 he clarified to the secretary of the state that 'the report of the superintendent of prisons referred to the recent decrease in the number of prisoners and prison offences owing mainly to the alteration of forest laws, to abolition of hawking license on sale of food and to the substitution of proper discipline in place of cruel punishment in the prisons'.[50]

This then is the outline of the world which Sir John Pope Hennessey is trying to build in Mauritius. By the 1880s the Indians constituted about 62 per cent of the population.[51] The old emigrants and the indentured expired amongst them had by now settled in the plots bought from the parcelling estates of the French plantocracy.[52] A large number had become what M.D. North Coombes calls 'allotment workers'.[53] These people worked on their small plots part of the week and for a few days of the week they worked on the French plantations. Some of their family members had become small time vendors and hawkers of food and other items.

These were the people who were constrained by requirements of 'passes' and 'hawker licenses', which Hennessey says he had abolished. A similar plea was made later on in the decade by Sir Ashley Eden that in the name of anti-vagrancy the industrious classes of the colony should not suffer.[54] It is thus that the penal regime which had come up in the name of anti-vagrancy was sought to be countered.

THE LINK TO HEALTH

The legitimacy for the Woods and Forest legislation of 1882 was also derived from the way forests were linked to health in the physiocratic world-view. It was Quesnay, the founder of the physiocrats, who formulated the doctrines which transferred the anxieties of health to nature. In the context of 1880s this was being done through the forest policy.[55]

As noted above, the interim report on Seechurn's death had pointed out that the prisoner had a history of malarial disease. Malaria in fact had been raising itself as an epidemic from 1866 onwards claiming a large mortality amongst the Indians and other classes of the colony.[56] The dominant wisdom in Mauritius on malaria from 1860s to 1880s was that it was carried by *air*.[57] As Dr. Bruce Reilly reported in the Fever Enquiry Committee report of 1867, 'the probability of carrier of malaria is very much the *wind*—the vehicle which in the other countries has been found to carry malarious fever many miles and also to non-malarious localities'.[58] Reilly argued that in 1867 malaria had spread due to destruction of forest cover by a hurricane. This forest cover he had argued had earlier acted us a barrier between the fever stricken and the non-fever districts. But with the barrier gone, *wind* carried malaria into other non-malarial localities.[59] Charles Meldrum who was in-charge of the meteorological observatory in Mauritius wrote a report in 1880s titled 'Weather, Health and Forests' which was a little more advanced. The report argued 'though deforestation did not bring meteorological changes which were determinant in bringing disease and fever, yet it is likewise evident that the effects of abnormal weather with respect to health and agriculture are mitigated by forests and aggravated by their destruction'.[60]

This outlook was reflected in the penal regime as well as in its prisons. The *MPG* in 1884 put it clearly,

> the official theory, as recorded in the administration report is that unhealthiness of the jails must be to a great degree *due to the unhealthiness of the country generally*, rather than to any *defects in the jails themselves*, the diet and treatment of the prisoners or to the work upon which they are employed; and in support of this contention, the fact of sequel to fever is cited; and this is held to be sufficient proof that the heavy jail mortality is due to ordinary causes affecting the free as well as the *immured* (jailed) population, and not to any defects of the jail system.[61]

Sir John Pope Hennessey is precisely trying to reverse the thrust of this administrative report. His contention is that it is precisely the treatment of the prisoners (as in the case of Seechurn's flogging) and the internal conditions of jail like lack of sanitation due to overcrowding which point to the crux of the health problem in Mauritius. Mauritius records also show that he is in tune with the section of opinion in the colony which is advocating sanitation, drainage, diet and treatment of the body as the crucial factors in the health reform of the colony for tackling diseases such as malaria.[62]

Highlighting of Seechurn's death brings out the then presumed connection between malaria and heart disease. Seechurn's inquiry report mentions that he had been suffering from malaria as well as heart disease. However, Sir John Pope Hennessey's take on malaria seems to be different from the upholders of 'air borne' theory of the epidemic of the 1882 Woods and Forest legislations. There is evidence that Sir John Pope Hennessey was aware of Dr. Patrick Menson's researches which linked malaria to the anopheles mosquitoes from his Hong Kong days.[63] However, it is still *not clear* as to what exactly caused malaria.[64] It is this aspect which was noticed by Ronald Ross who authored a report on malaria in Mauritius in 1908. Ronald Ross mentions that the emphasis on drainage and sanitation had been advocated in Mauritius since the Fever Enquiry Report of 1867 but

> it has been more frequently neglected . . . this has been due to many causes—to the expense of drainage: to the small *political* influence of the medical profession; to faulty public education and not the least to scepticism regarding the truth of the dogma owing to the *absence of full explanation of it*. . . .[65] [emphasis added]

It is this absence of the 'full explanation' for the cause of malaria which Sir John Pope Hennessey is trying to overcome. In this process he puts forward his own environmental perspective. Highlighting Seechurn's death enables him to make the connection between malaria, sanitation and treatment of the body with the disease in a dramatic way and in a sense he uses the episode for the public education for his reforms. He then takes the debate to a political level when he points out in September 1884 'I believe flogging will be abolished when the intelligent opinion of the island is more directly represented in the council'. A year later he was asking 'for a free vote on the question of flogging in the legislative council'.[66]

It is thus Sir John Pope Hennessey distances himself from the physiocratic premises of the environmental and penal policies embodied in Woods and Forests ordinance of 1882. In the process he put forward his own environmental perspective. It is this sense of historical transition on the environmental question, effected through a debate on the penal regimes, which seems to be missing in the Foucault and Marcuse accounts.

NOTES

1. Herbert Marcuse, *One Dimensional Man*, Boston: Beacon Press, 1996, pp. 76-7. Similarly studies on Foucault have recently demonstrated how he neglects the environmental context. See Jeremy W. Crampton and Stuart Elden, *Space, Knowledge and Power: Foucault and Geography*, Aldershot: Ashgate Publishing Ltd., 2007, p. 75. It has also been argued that 'Foucault leaves the door open for an environmental critique despite his own disinterest in the natural world . . . (therefore) a Foucaldian should not say that since Michel Foucault did not love nature, or was not concerned with nature, I will not waste my time applying his work to environmental issues.' See Brian Solis, 'Foucault and the Defense of Deep Ecology' working paper at the Department of Government and Politics, University of Maryland-College Park. On the Net.
2. *Interim and Final Report into the Enquiry of circumstances connected with the death of a prisoner, Seechurn and into certain matters concerning prison discipline. (1884) No. 1941, 1942*, Mauritius Archives (henceforth M.A.). See also *Merchants and Planters Gazette (MPG)* from July 1883 to the end of 1884 in M.A.
3. No. 1941, 1942, M.A.
4. *MPG*, 11 February 1884.
5. No.1941, 1942, M.A.
6. *MPG*, 27 February 1884.
7. *MPG*, 11 February 1884.
8. Ibid.
9. Ibid.
10. *MPG*, 28 February 1884.
11. Ibid.
12. *Governor's Despatch to the Secretary of State, S.D.145*, M.A.
13. Ibid.
14. Ibid.
15. Ibid.
16. Ibid.
17. J. Fowler, 'Mauritius as a Problem in Crown Colony Administration, 1849-57', M. Phil thesis, University of London, 1970.
18. Richard Grove, *Green Imperialism*, London: Oxford University Press, 1995, ch. on Mauritius.

19. Ibid.
20. See Karl Marx, *Theories of Surplus Value*, Moscow: PPH, 1977, section on physiocrats.
21. Richard Grove, op. cit. Also see the Vagrancy Registers in the Immigration Archives in Moka in Mauritius.
22. Richard Grove, op. cit.
23. Richard Grove, op. cit. And the vagrancy registers.
24. Marina Carter, *Servants, Sirdars and Settlers: Indians in Mauritius, 1834-74*, Delhi: Oxford University Press, 1995, pp. 151-93. Also the *Report of the Royal Commission on Labour in Mauritius*, 1875.
25. *MPG*, 28 February 1884.
26. See the newspapers *Le Cerneen* and *Le Mauricien* for various years from 1870-84 (M.A.).
27. M.D. North Coombes, 'From Slavery to Indenture: Forced Labour in the Political Economy of Mauritius', in K. Saunders (ed.), *Indentured Labour in the British Empire, 1834-1920*, London, 1984.
28. Marina Carter, op. cit., pp. 41-53.
29. Ibid.
30. Richard Allen, 'Creoles, Indian Immigrants and the Restructuring of Society and Economy in Mauritius, 1767-1885', Ph.D. thesis, University of Illinois, 1983. Also his forthcoming book.
31. Marina Carter, op. cit., p. 199.
32. Ibid.
33. Ibid.
34. Ibid.
35. Ibid.
36. *MPG*, 27 February 1884.
37. I have taken the term from Karl Marx, 'Debates on Laws of Theft of Wood', in *Marx and Engels Collected Works*, vol. 1, Moscow: PPH, 1978.
38. *MPG*, 11 February 1884.
39. *MPG*, 28 February 1884.
40. No. 1941, 1942 (M.A.).
41. *Commercial Record*, 14 January 1882 (M.A.).
42. R. Thompson, *Report on Forests of Mauritius*, 1880, M.A. No. 867, *Annual Police Report*, 1883, M.A.
43. *MPG*, 28 February 1884.
44. Ibid.
45. Ibid.
46. No. 1941, 1942, September 1884 (M.A.).
47. *S.D. 145*, M.A.
48. Ibid.
49. *S.D.* 13 May 1884 (M.A.).
50. Ibid.

51. K. Hazareesingh, *History of Indians in Mauritius*, London, 1975.
52. See Richard Allen, op. cit.
53. M.D. North Coombes, 'From Slavery to Indenture: Forced Labour in the Political Economy of Mauritius', in Kay Saunders op. cit.
54. *R.A. Records*, M.A.
55. Richard Grove, op. cit. *Quesnay's Medical Writings*, see Peter D. Groenewegen, *Physicians and Political Economy*, Routledge, 2004, p. 93.
56. *Fever Enquiry Committee Report, 1867* (M.A.).
57. Ibid.
58. Ibid.
59. Ibid.
60. Charles Meldrum, *Weather, Health and Forests*, 1881 (M.A.).
61. *MPG*, 13 March 1884.
62. See *MPG*, throughout 1884 and *Commercial Record* for the year 1884 (M.A.).
63. See the Transactions of Royal Society in Mauritius, at the Mauritius Sugar Research Institute, Reduit. Esp. years 1884-6.
64. Ibid.
65. Ronald Ross, *Report of Malaria in Mauritius*, London, 1908.
66. *MPG*, September 1884.

REFERENCES

Foucault, Michael (1975), *Discipline and Punish*, Paris: Gallimard.

Grove, Richard (1995), *Green Imperialism*, London: Oxford University Press.

Hughes, Robert (1987), *The Fatal Shore*, London: Pan Books.

Marcuse, Herbert (1996), *One Dimensional Man*, Boston: Beacon Press, pp. 76-7.

O' Sullivan et al. (2006), *Collected Works of Jeremy Bentham*, Oxford: Clarendon Press.

CHAPTER 9

Agrarian Development, Marginalization and Unionization of Peasants in Meerut

A. SATYANARAYANA

The agrarian movements of the 1990s in India have attracted the attention of many scholars both in India and abroad. Two contrasting viewpoints are prevalent about the social composition of the participants in such movements in the literature. One stream of scholars have characterized the movement as articulating the interests of rich farmers (Dhanagre, 1995) and agrarian elite (Banaji, 1995), as in the case of Shetkari Sanghatan in Maharashtra, and agrarian capitalists (Hassan, 1989) in the case of Bharatiya Kisan Union (BKU). Omvedt (1995) analysed the same Shetkari movement and interpreted the social composition of the movement as rooted in petty commodity production. Gill (1995) in the case of Punjab, Haryana and Uttar Pradesh (UP) observed that the BKU attracted support from every peasant stratum and from retired military and bureaucratic personnel with rural background. Lindberg (1995) found the BKU movement in UP as led by middle peasants. Given such contrary interpretations of the agrarian movements, an endeavour has been made here to comprehend the nature of agrarian development, interactions of cultivators with proliferated middlemen and subjective interpretations of such interactions in the continuous drought period and aggregation of initially manifested grievances in the form of BKU in the Meerut Commissary on the basis of data collected though observations, interviews, and listening to the discussions among collectivities in different collective actions and participants in different *kisan* (peasant) panchayats.

PATTERN OF AGRARIAN DEVELOPMENT IN THE COMMISSARY

On the basis of the logic propounded by Mellor (1976) and Torri (1976), the data on size of landholdings in the Statistical Bulletins of the Commissary of 1985 and 1995 are categorized into three main categories: holders of less than two hectares, two to five hectares and more than five hectares. These categories can be termed as poor, middle and rich peasants, or small, medium, and large landholdings, respectively. The analysis of the Statistical Bulletin data of 1985 and 1995 reveals that the proportion of poor peasants' landholdings increased from 77 per cent in 1983-4 to 82 per cent by 1991, while the middle peasants' share of landholdings declined from 18 to 15 per cent in the same period. The proportion of landholdings of rich peasants too declined from 5 to 3 per cent in the same period. The poor peasants experienced an increase in the quantity of ownership of cultivable land from 35 to 45 per cent. However, the amount of landownership in the hands of middle peasants declined nominally from 40 to 37.7 per cent and that of rich peasants' share significantly declined from 25 to 17.7 per cent (Statistical Bulletin, 1985; 1995). These facts indicate fragmentation of landholdings rather than concentration of land in fewer hands—a general trend observed in the Commissary (Satyanarayana, 2004). Friese (1990) analysed the data on landownership pattern from 1948, 1971 and 1981 and also found no trend of concentration of land in fewer hands in the area. Analysis of data on the size of landholdings of households in the Tyagi village, mentioned by Dube (1958), from 1954-94 reveal that small and marginal landholders not only increased in number but also increased the area under their ownership. The number of big size of landowners declined not only in the proportion but also absolutely. The area under their ownership also declined drastically (Satyanarayana, 1996; 2005). Thus households with smaller landholdings are gaining importance in terms of landownership and numerical preponderance at the expense of middle and rich peasants' households in the Commissary. As the size of landholdings is becoming smaller, cultivators with smaller size of landholdings are compulsively producing crops for the market (Bharadwaj, 1986) by adopting HYV seeds, and increased intensity of double and triple cropping in order to cope with subsistence needs. However, the size of landholdings is not coterminous with class status. In order to comprehend the agrarian class structure, we have to look into the ownership, control of land and use of labour (Beteille, 1974) in the organization of production of agricultural produce, i.e. social units, technology and relations between the social units involved in major agricultural operations of predominant crops in an area along size of landownership.

Let us look at the organization of production of major crops in the Commissary. There are two major crops in the area. Wheat, under HYV, occupies 40 per cent of the total cultivable land followed by sugar cane with 30 per cent of total cultivable land (Statistical Bulletin, 1985). Analysis of organization of production of different operations associated with these two crops reveals that reciprocal exchange of farm tools, cattle, and labour among kin, factional members, and neighbouring landowners, supplemented occasionally by wage labour or *naukars* or sharecroppers is the predominant form of production organization observed in the Commissary. Rich and middle peasants employ one or two extra-family labour for a period of ten months or for a season or for a month's duration with advance payments without interest (Satyanarayana, 1985 and 2005). Depending on the size of landownership and ownership of farm implements the organization of production varies in the intensity of use of extra-family labour. But in general the landowner is also a co-worker, not a manager looking after only organizational activities as employment of *nigamaans* by landowners in coastal Andhra Pradesh (ibid., 1985). From these facts it can be derived that familial mode of organization of production is predominant, i.e. more homogeneity in terms of organization of production.

Paddy (7.6 per cent of the total cultivable land) is mostly cultivated under sharecropping or with extra-family labour in the transplantation, weeding, harvesting and threshing seasons. Maize (covering nearly 1/6th of the total cultivable land) is cultivated mostly under sharecropping. From these facts it can be derived that organization of production in the Commissary is predominantly homogeneous, with minor variations in form. Landless labourers are mainly dependent on domesticated animal husbandry as their major continuous source of livelihood. The landless acquired milk cattle either from their in-laws or from the landowners through the *saajhi* system or purchasing from the cattle market (Field observations and interviews with landless in Jhabiran, Rasana, Phugana, Baoli, Akkhapur). Under the *saajhi* system the landowner gives the buffalo aged less than 2 years to a poor family to raise till it reaches the stage of milking. Both the parties share the milk equally and thereafter one of the partner acquires the buffalo after paying half of its value to the other partner. Pradhan (1966) too found a similar pattern. Landless labourers labour for the sugar cane cultivators and receive the tender parts of the harvested sugar cane as payment in kind nearly for eight months in a year. They use the tender parts as fodder for their milk cattle. For the remaining four months in a year, women of the landless labourers collect grass from the ridges of the landowners' land while their male counterparts look after the non-agricultural jobs in the nearby urban areas. Girl children and women of landless households play a crucial role in fetching grass. Many conflicts between landowners and the landless women revolve around the issue of allegedly or really cutting crops from the fields rather than collecting grass from the ridges. This is often linked to the atrocities committed by the landowning group on the landless women of lower castes in general.

Nearly 80 per cent of the total cultivable land in the Commissary secured irrigation facilities in 1983-4 (Statistical Bulletin, 1985). Out of the total irrigated land, the area under canal irrigation declined from 31 to 25.60 per cent while the proportion of irrigated of land dependent on tube wells increased from 67 to 71 per cent in the period 1983-4 to 1991-2 (Statistical Bulletin, 1985 and 1995). The traditional sources of irrigation like wells, Persian wheels, tanks and others have lost their importance in the irrigation of land in the Commissary (Whitcombe, 1971). These facts indicate that the state's investment on the maintenance and extension of canal networks for secured irrigation facilities is declining while the role of private investments in secured irrigation facilities has become greater than before. It is striking to note that even the owners of small size of land-holdings with irrigational facilities had adopted the high-yielding varieties (HYV) of wheat by the 1980s (Singh, 1987). The small landholders might have lagged behind in the initial phases of the Green Revolution because of their 'resource constraints' (Singh, 1987) and 'subsistence ethic' (Scott, 1979). The HYV of seeds require more quantity of seeds per hectare than the traditional varieties of seeds (Trazler, 1990) to have insurance against poor germination. It also reflects a complementarity between good plant stand and inputs such as fertilizers and water. As the vegetative growth of HYV seeds is of a shorter duration, 65 per cent of the total cultivable land in the Commissary is under double cropping while 30 per cent of the cultivable land is under sugar cane for more than two consequent years. The consumption of chemical fertilizers has increased from 20 kg per hectare in the mid-1960s to 122 kg per hectare in 1991 (Statistical Bulletin, 1995).

Intensive rotation of crops requires more capital to purchase chemical fertilizers, pesticides, insecticides and commercial energy for irrigation (Alam, 2000). The smaller landholders could overcome such initial constraints through the joint ownership, maintenance and use of tube wells, diesel engines, threshers and the like. Landholders with less than 2.87 hectares owned more farm assets like farm cattle and farm machinery per hectare in value than the larger landholders. The landholdings above 2.87 hectares show a relative advantage only in irrigation facilities (Singh, 1987), besides they too could overcome disadvantages in irrigational facilities through multiparty ownership and use of irrigational technology. Leaving aside tractor to some extent, farm cattle and other components of farm technology associated with the HYV of wheat seeds became size neutral through multiparty ownership and use of technology or through reciprocal exchange of farm tools, cattle and labour among kin to a certain extent. Cultivators in 30 per cent of the villages avail repair services of farm implements either from within the village or within a distance of 1 km from their villages while the remaining travel more than 3 km in order to avail the repair, maintenance and purchase of spare parts for the farm implements (Statistical Bulletin, 1985). Thus urban capitalism has emerged as a major force in the supply and repair of farm implements like diesel engines, electric motors, tractors, tillers, threshers, rubber tyres, tubes, electrical bulbs and other simpler farm implements and their spares. Thus the volume of capital requirements, both industrial, financial and usury, has magnified. This has affected the relations between agriculture, commerce and industry and also between town, city and country in general and more specifically in the drought period.

The contribution of human labour in agriculture has nominally declined from 35.2 to 32.2 per cent in the period of 1955-6 to 1970-1 (Rastyannikov, 1981). The decline of hired labour use is more pronounced in the case of owners of less than 2 hectares of land. The proportion of hired labour to the total labour has gone up on all size groups above 4.72 hectares and remained more or less constant in all size groups between 2.88 and 4.72 hectares. The owners of more than 4.72 hectares of land are opting for increased leisure preferences (Singh, 1987). From this we can derive that the owners of more than 5 hectares are using more hired labour. In the Commissary the proportion of owners of more than 5 hectares of land is shrinking both in numbers and in proportion to total landowners, as found in the analysis. Simultaneously, land under their ownership is also declining. In such situations household members contribute labour for various agricultural operations (Satyanarayana, 1985). Srivastava (2000) compared labour use in western UP with eastern UP and found the predominant use of family labour in the western half than in the eastern. Bardhan (1970) too observed significant contribution of household labour, to the extent of three-fourths of the total required labour, in the agricultural production process in western UP. Thus from these studies it can be derived that familistic organization of production is predominant in the Commissary rather than the farmer type of organization of production.

The pattern of agrarian development in the Commissary can be summarized as experiencing fragmentation of landholdings rather than centralization and concentration of land in fewer hands. The possibility of concentration and centralization of ownership of land is bleak given the policies of land ceiling, distribution of common village land to landless and the policy of not allowing the non-agriculturists to purchase cultivable land from cultivators, besides the slower rate of absorption of rural population into non-agricultural urban occupations. Thus lesser population is absorbed in non-agricultural economy and continued dependency of higher proportion of population on agriculture resulting in convergence of the roles of owners, controller and worker in the organization of production. Moreover the employment of wage labour in comparison to the labour of the household members is very less as the crop cycle is continuous with a variety of crops cultivated on adjacent plots of land. Though production of commercial crops like sugar cane is basically oriented for the market but the cash acquired from the sale of the produce is significantly spent on subsistence needs. Accumulated savings are spent on events like marriage, death and legal suits. Class relations and relations of production in agriculture acquire importance only when ownership, control on land and use of labour are separated (Batra, 1978). However, only those relations of production that are subject to contradiction of interests emerging from the way they are related to the means of production are termed as classes (Rudra, 1978). This form of organization of production projects classlessness within agriculture, i.e. contradiction of interests in agriculture are undermined, and class-based relations with the groups associated with urban capitalism with whom they are interacting (Batra, 1978) are highlighted. In such interactions Lipset propounded the emergence of populist ideology (Lipset, 1950).

AGRARIAN GRIEVANCES BEFORE THE FORMATION OF BKU

Such a pattern of agrarian development compels the cultivators to interact with proliferated middlemen associated with agricultural inputs like farm implements and their spares, commercial energy, pesticides and chemical fertilizers, seed markets and agricultural produce markets in order to cope with their subsistence requirements. Two illustrations are chosen to bring out the grievances prevalent in the area during severe and continuous drought before the formation of the BKU. The illustrations are electricity as an agricultural input, and sugar cane as an agricultural produce produced for the market.

Electricity-Linked Grievances

There was one electrified tube well per nine cultivators in the Commissary in 1984-5. However, the intensity of dependency of cultivators on electrified tube wells (ETW) extended further as some of the siblings and other co-sharers owned, maintained and used the ETW jointly while others leased the services. Thus the intensity of dependency on electrified tube wells was relatively more than the facts indicate in the normal conditions of monsoon and more so in the drought period. Thus in severe drought periods, supply of electricity, repair, maintenance and its charges acquired relatively more importance as the erratic and irregular supply of electricity failed to cope with the irrigational requirements of the cultivators. Besides, the groundwater table sank to deeper layers that resulted in drying up of many ETWs in the region. As most of the cultivable land was under HYV seeds, lack of irrigation facilities further reduced the productivity and the subsistence of the cultivators. Owners of ETWs, *kolhus* (sugar cane crushers) and flourmills owners, household consumers of electricity in the villages and powerloom owners in the urban areas of the Commissary were affected, as the supply of electricity was irregular and erratic. Thus, comprehension of the issues associated with electricity will provide us a base to recognize the range of grievances prevalent in the severe drought conditions in the Commissary prior to the comprehension of the formation of the BKU.

Traditionally, peasants of this area had kinship relations and bought milk cattle from Haryana (Rastyannikov, 1981). They also participated in the Serve Khap Panchayat meetings organized at Khanjawala, Haryana, in the contemporary period, to express their protest against the distribution of common village land to the cumulatively deprived sections of the society (Friese, 1990). Besides, the farmers of this region, in the contemporary period, have further extended their relations with the cultivators of Punjab and Andhra Pradesh for the purchase of old tractors (Satyanarayana, 1985; Chauhan, 1989). Thus, the cattle markets, kinship relations and modern technology along with the spread of mass communication and transportation have resulted in the augmentation of frequent functional interactions with people in other states. These frequent functional interactions has brought more awareness among cultivators of this area, about the existing disparities in matters of electricity tariffs between states. Collection of electricity charges even prior to August 1986 by the Uttar Pradesh State Electricity Board (UPSEB), based on the horsepower capacity of motors installed in the tube wells was Rs. 22.50 per month, which was significantly higher in UP than in Haryana (Rs. 16.00 per horsepower), Punjab (Rs. 15.00 per horsepower), and Andhra Pradesh (Rs. 14.50 per horsepower). That means a cultivator in UP, after selling one quintal of wheat at state-regulated prices, could utilize, lesser quantum of horsepower units of electricity than the cultivators availing electricity in Haryana and Punjab. Thus electricity as an agricultural input became relatively costlier in UP than in other states even prior to August 1986. An interview with a retired chairman of the UPSEB revealed that the utilization capacity of power plants is not only low but that the transmission losses are relatively high. The prevalence of corruption in the electricity board has further contributed to the higher rate of power tariff in UP. According to the chairman, the Board is playing the role of a mythical cow in the hands of politicians and bureaucracy. Increase in power tariff from Rs. 22.50 to Rs. 30 in August 1986, has further accentuated the existing disparities between states, as other states have retained the older rates of power tariff.

In addition to this, supply, repair and restoration of burnt transformers were not undertaken promptly, not even after two to three months after their damage, without bribing the concerned personnel in the electricity department. The engineers serving in the Commissary concede that they paid a higher premium for transfers to the area and were collecting extra-constitutional charges from the tube well owners in order to recover the premiums paid for the transfers. Such a hike in the power tariff might not have resulted in the aggregation and mobilization of agrarian categories for collective actions, if the electricity board had agreed to renegotiate the terms of the contract at least for the drought period and provided the services promptly without corruption. For instance, on an earlier occasion in 1977–8, when sugar cane was sold at throwaway prices, the cultivators of this area preferred to burn the standing crop without any collective action during the Janata Party rule at the centre. In the contemporary collective actions cultivators not only spent a huge amount of resources but also faced coercion from the state, and lost significant amount of time in aggregating and mobilizing the peasants for collective actions. They perceived the earlier situation as a consequence of their own mistake as they could not allocate their land rationally to different crops. Peasants perceived the prevailing contemporary trouble as imposed on them through the policies of the state and its agencies.

Let us see, in brief, the issues related with the electricity tariff. In the 1970s each electrified tube well had an electric meter to record the actual amount of electricity the tube well owner availed. Thus electricity tariff was collected on the basis of the actual amount of electricity availed. Later, electricity meters at the ETW were removed and the tariff was collected on the basis of horsepower capacity of the motor installed at the tube well. Such a change compelled the ETW owners to pay the electricity charges for the entire year and on the horsepower capacity of the motor installed at the tube wells, irrespective of its use or non-use. In a normal monsoon year, according to the cultivators, ETW had been used for a maximum period of 120-50 days, even in the context of prompt repair and replacement of burnt transformers in a normal monsoon year. Once a transformer is burnt, it takes months for its replacement/repair in this area, as each cultivator with ETW/co-sharers in the ETW has to contribute their own share in the service charges to be paid to the employees of the electricity board. The owners of ETW could not use electricity in the period of replacement of burnt transformers, besides the normal rainy season. However, flat rates were collected for the total year. Neither the state nor the UPSEB took measures or build-in mechanisms in the contracts to waive off the power tariff at least for the drought period or in the period of replacement of burnt transformers. Thus, cultivators in this area perceive that the UPSEB had imposed unilateral contracts on individual peasants over the last decade and converted them into powerless and 'under dog' positions. However, the peasants previously never articulated their grievances in a collective form on the issue of electricity tariff, but paid the dues in time, though, individual cultivators and users of electricity expressed their grievances in daily interactions through different forms like abuses, manhandling, etc. Users of ETW services perceived the decision to hike the electricity tariff in place of its waiver in the context of drought as an indicator of further loss of their power. It indicated that cultivators in the region are sensing an under-dog position to the proliferated middlemen and to the bureaucratic components of the state. In addition to this, the electricity board does not apply universal norms based on equality between the rural and urban consumers of electricity. Electricity charges in urban areas are collected on the basis of actual amount of electricity availed as indicated in the meters, but in rural areas the collection is on the basis of flat rates, even in the context of non-supply of electricity. In the rural areas, the non-supply or irregular and erratic supply of electricity in the drought period affected not only the productivity of crops but also the fulfilment of contracts with sugar mills and commitments related with their subsistence as well.

Change in the calculation of electricity tariff came into existence on the logic of prevalence of intensive and extensive power thefts and the arduous work the electricity employees have to perform in the collection of electricity meter readings from distantly located ETW. Electricity thefts are still rampant though they have undergone a change in form, like installing a motor of higher horsepower capacity than the approved ones and paying the tariff at the rate of sanctioned capacity of motor. Secondly, the owners of ETW receive electricity connections illegally in alliance with the electricity board employees at the local level. Thirdly, the owners of ETW violate the undertaking given to the board and operate *kolhus* and threshers with the motor installed at the tube well (personal field observations in Bawali, Phugana, Bora Kala, Rasana villages). These factors enhance load on transformers and burns the electric bulbs and motors of ETWs repeatedly. Thus, cultivators' produce is diverted to the repair and replacement of these burnt items for the owners of ETW, flourmills, and household users of electricity. It means more proportion of the cultivators' produce is spent as 'replacement fund' (Wolf, 1966). Under the conditions of burnt transformers, electricity cannot be supplied to the owners of flourmills and household users of electricity even though they have paid the power bills promptly. Thus, the owners of ETWs, cultivators hiring the services of ETWs for the irrigation of their land, rural household users of electricity, owners of flourmills and *kolhus* have developed a common grievance emanating from the electricity. Thus, the electricity-linked grouses were common to all users of electricity in rural areas in general. They compare not only the supply of electricity in rural areas with urban areas of UP but also the electricity tariff prevalent in UP and in other states. Such comparisons result in negative outcomes to the individual peasant and lead to the emergence of egoistic relative deprivations.

The electricity-linked issues acquired relatively more importance for the operation of *kolhus*, electrified tube wells, flourmills, and rural lighting and differentially affected the life chances of rural population on the basis of their class position. The rich peasants were making more investments to deepen their tube wells in order to draw more ground water. For this, they used their own savings or took loans from formal credit institutions. Some of the middle and poor peasants, who owned and operated the ETWs jointly, looked for finances in order to cope with the sinking ground water level. Such cultivators were worried about the prevailing situation of unsecured supply of electricity, and irrigation facilities through canals. Some of their ETWs became defunct as the ground water table sank to deeper levels. The state could not make effective steps either to reduce the electricity tariff or to provide relief in the form of waiver of electricity tariff in the drought period. In successive drought conditions, peasants in general anticipated benevolent relief from the rulers just to cope and maintain subsistence needs. Non-receipt of relief is considered as unjust.

Sugar cane–Associated Grievances

Sugar cane is a major commercial crop cultivated under contract system with the mills in the Commissary. The contract system has brought vertical integration of dispersed sugar cane cultivators with the sugar mills. Cultivators bear all the risks related to investment under the contract system. In visualizing the nature of grievances associated with the crop, the production, pricing and marketing of the produce are of paramount importance.

Sugar cane cultivators make individual contracts with the primary cane society for the supply of an estimated quantum of sugar cane in a crop season. The cultivators receive pesticides and fertilizers and loans for the cultivation of sugar cane from the society. The household members of sugar cane cultivators' contribute their labour mainly in the sowing, watering and harvesting of sugar cane. Their labour is supplemented by the landless and help from neighbouring landowners. The extra-family labour is mainly paid for in kind. For tying the shoots of cane and weeding operations, payments are made in piece rates (Satyanarayana, 1985). During the harvesting season, cultivators receive slips from the cane society which contain the name of the cultivator, and the quantity of cane to be supplied within a particular time. However, the socially embedded primordial relations with people in the sugar cane society are affecting the issue of sugar cane supply. If the cultivator fails to supply the specified quantum of cane in the contract, then the deducted amount remains with the society and the quantum of sugar cane to be supplied for the next year is determined on the fulfilment of the previous contract. Non-payment of arrears, even after the supply of the specified quantum in the contract, constitutes one of the major sources of grievance for farmers in this area. Thus hundreds of millions of rupees remain unpaid with the cane society. It implies that the cultivator of sugar cane, who is supplying the produce to the mills, is facing a double disadvantage. The cultivator borrows loans on interest from moneylenders or formal financial institutions not only to cope with the contingent expenditure but also to make investments in and the maintenance of farm tools, commercial energy and other inputs needed in the cultivation though he has balance payments on his account with the society. The balance amount in the society yields no interest to the cultivator while he pays interest on the borrowed loan amount. Thus it is a double disadvantage to the cultivator.

The issue of non-payment of arrears acquires more importance every now and then and manifests in the form of collective action. For instance, the Kisan Sabha of CPI launched an agitation in January 1978 to manifest the interests of sugar cane cultivators in matters of payment of arrears, and hike in the prices of sugar cane. More than 800 *kisans* courted arrest and finally forced the millers to pay the arrears (Surjeet, 1986). In successive drought situations, issues like deductions and non-payment of such earlier deductions acquired relatively more importance in the accumulation of grievances prior to the formation of BKU but these grievances got lesser attention in the initial phases of aggregation of grievances than the electricity.

In normal monsoon years the excess production of sugar cane is absorbed by *kolhus* and provides a continuous flow of cash to the sugar cane growers to cope with their subsistence needs and also to make informal payments to the position holders in the formal institutions and middlemen to receive the services of critical agricultural resources on priority. Thus, the supply of excess sugar cane to the *kolhus* provided some help in coping with subsistence needs and other requirements of immediate concern to the cultivators. However, the state through its various policies promoted the dismantling of *kolhus* and further intensified the vertical integration of sugar cane cultivators with the sugar mills. Such a process is illustrated here.

Under conditions of low productivity of sugar cane in the drought periods and the payment of higher prices for sugar cane by Khandasari units in 1986-7, the UP government imposed two sanctions on the *kolhu* owners: the government announced that the licenses of the *kolhu* owners purchasing sugar cane at prices higher than the state-regulated prices will be cancelled. Secondly, electricity connections to such plants will be disconnected. Besides these sanctions, nearly 20 types of taxes were imposed on the products produced from the *kolhus* involving the same number of formal institutions. Such proliferation of formal institutions resulted in the slower growth rate of Khandasari units and even their continuity became difficult. As a consequence of the above-mentioned constraints, many *kolhus* were dismantled and the sugar cane harvest prolonged beyond May in 1988 to crush 402 lakh quintals as against 391 lakh quintals in 1987 though productivity declined nearly by 35 quintals per hectare on average (Hassan, 1989). Thus, the state government made systematic endeavours to reduce the dependence and integration of sugar cane cultivators with Khandasari units that were acting as a safety valve in the continuous supply of cash to the cultivators. Such anti-*kolhu* policies resulted in no option to the cultivator but to depend only on sugar mills. It strengthened the subordination of sugar cane cultivators to the mill owners in terms of issue of slips, payment and the duration of waiting at the mill gates/purchase centres to get the produce weighed (Personal interviews with former *kolhu* owners and sugar cane cultivators). These former *kolhu* owners mainly belonged to the category of rich peasants (*maldars*) who had their interests anchored in the urban trade of *gur* (jaggery) and the purchase of sugar cane from cultivators at prices dictated by the market forces. Thus, the power of the rich peasants seems to be on the decline in rural areas, as one of their sources of control on cultivators became weak.

The functioning of cane purchase centres is another source of grievance for the sugar cane cultivators. These purchase centres are usually located at a distance from the mills. The purchase centres serve as a nodal point to a cluster of villages not only in distributing slips to the cultivators but also weighing their produce. The clerks entrusted with the roles of issuing slips, weighing the produce and the specifying the variety of crop, allegedly commit irregularities. For instance, cultivators under the centres Khodana, Rasana, and Patni villages allege that the weighing clerk remains absent for 4 to 5 days in a week and tries to complete the backlog within a day. The cultivators wait at the centres for 4 to 5 days for the clerk, with sugarcane-filled trolleys. Labour of one family member is wasted in this process and the person faces severe weather conditions of both cold and summer and additional expenses in the form of cash are incurred for his diet. In addition, they face humiliation from the clerk on the following grounds: firstly, he refuses to weigh the produce on the pretext that the working time is over. Secondly, he refuses to weigh the produce with the help of a balance on the pretext that the balance is not working. Thirdly, he underestimates the weight of a trolley/buggy of sugar cane by nearly 2 to 3 quintals. Fourthly, CJ 64 variety of sugar cane, an early maturing variety, which gets an incentive of Rs. 3 per quintal than the ordinary variety of cane is allegedly clubbed with the ordinary variety. Finally he demands service charges at the rate Rs. 25 to 30 for the issue of fresh slips worth of 25 to 30 quintals.

Collectivities of peasants while participating in various collective actions after the formation of BKU compared their position with artisans, agricultural wage labourers, industrialists, politicians, and employees in government and private organizations and traders and felt cumulatively deprived in matters of power, status, honour, and freedom. The unilateral imposition of contracts by the cane society and sugar mills on the cultivators and the corruption of the electricity boards reflects the lack of negotiating power of the cultivators in relation to their partners in the contract. These facts and perceptions reflect that the cultivators are placed in an 'under dog' political position and marginalized, which corroborates with the arguments of Shanin (1971), Wolf (1966) and Moore (1966).

Thus, in smaller groups such economic and political conditions and day-to-day events are interpreted in terms of their cultural meanings of crude equality, trust, reciprocity, patronage, power, self-respect, status and honour in various collective actions organized by the BKU later. These cultural meanings are linked with the moral notions of justice and injustice. These interpretations depict that the cultivators felt multiple deprivations of egoistic nature in comparison with urban individuals. These multiple deprivations are highlighted to promote consensus among *kisans* of different castes and classes and cohesion among the formed collectivities is manifested by observing non-cooperation and by not selling wheat to the government purchase centres at state-regulated prices at a later stage of the movement.

FORMATION OF BKU

The historic electoral victory of Congress and the defeat of opposition candidates in the Assembly and Lok Sabha elections after the assassination of Smt Indira Gandhi though the area was a stronghold of independents and opposition parties. Secondly the L.D. was experiencing the problem of succession to Chowdhary Charan Singh while on death-bed. Thirdly the populist policies of Haryana government under the leadership of Devi Lal became a reference point for the cultivators in the Commissary. Fourthly rural population in general mistrusted the political leaders. The Khanjhawala unit of BKU leaders, on their visit to Baraut, made concerted efforts to contact the leaders of BKU unit at Baraut in 1986 but in vain. They met Chowdhary of Desh Khap (clan/lineage/exogamous social unit), a rich peasant. The Haryana leaders shared their experiences of collective actions in the redressal of peasants' grievances in their state and various programmes initiated by the Haryana government for the welfare of *kisans*-like old-age pension, electricity tariff, sugar cane prices, waiver of loans, and so on. They pressed the Chowdhary of the Desh Khap to call a meeting of *kisans* of his area in their presence. In the meeting, the *kisans* aired their individual problems associated with escalating indebtedness, lowering ground water table, and problems related with the supply of electricity, its tariff, and replacement of burnt transformers. Individually the participants in the meeting approved the relevance of the Kisan union to resolve their grievances as done by the BKU unit of Haryana and the trade unions of Modinagar and Modipuram. Thus the sharing of individual grievances in smaller collectivities transformed individual worries into public concerns (Mills, 1959) and social facts (Durkheim, 1982). Prior to the formation of smaller collectivities the individual peasants used to compete for scarce agricultural inputs among themselves. These smaller collectivities perceived that their troubles are the consequence of the structural conditions of the development. However, their negative perceptions, according to the respondents from Bavali and Baraut, towards their Chowdhary constrained the revival of the BKU unit at Baraut. Thus, the lack of trusted leadership postponed the collectivization of *kisan* grievances into a union.

Later the Desh Khap Chowdhary called a meeting of Chowdharies of all Khaps in the area at Baraut. Some important persons who participated in the meeting were the Chowdharies of Baliyan and Chaugama Khaps, some active members of Chaprauli and Ghatwala Khaps, a retired High Court judge, and others. However, no organized political party leader participated in the meeting. The participants in the meeting too expressed their individual grievances and complained of rising indebtedness, drought, electricity supply, replacement and repair of burnt transformers and tariff, sinking ground water table and scarcity of drinking water. Thus, individual *kisans* shared their problems in a wider geographical and social space. The participants in general asserted the relevance of a non-political union for *kisans*. They also decided to form units of *kisans*' unions, initially in each district and to extend them to village level at a later stage. However, the Baliyan Khap Chowdhary argued that the prevalence of intense hostilities and factional conflicts within each village would impede the organization of *kisans* at the district and village levels. He gave the illustration of his own Khap's capital village, Sisauli, where he was unable to resolve the intense factional conflicts even as its Chowdhary. Some of the participants accompanied the Desh Khap Chowdhary, the latter had kinship relations with the Baliyan Khap Chowdhary, visited Sisauli and made endeavours to resolve the factional conflicts in a Panchayat but in vain. Thus, there was a prevalence of common grievances in this area even before the formation of the BKU in September 1986. The peasants meetings organized by Khanjhawala *kisans* promoted the sharing of such common grievances. Nevertheless, the primordial loyalties based on Khap and factions, inter-Khap rivalries, and the perceptions about their Khap Chowdharies impeded the aggregation of peasant interests. The chance for the formation of union of peasants was further hampered by caste rivalries, which can be substantiated with the role of the Gujars of Kairana.

The Gujar Khap Chowdhary in Kairana area made concerted endeavours, independently, to mobilize the peasants of his own Khap. His younger brother shifted political affiliation from LD to Congress in 1984 as one of his political rivals joined the LD. The Congress leaders of UP state considered the younger brother of the Chowdhary as a close associate of the Jana Morcha leader, V.P. Singh who shifted from Congress and formed Jana Morcha. Under such conditions, the younger brother of Gujar Khap Chowdhary of Kairana was inducted into the government to reduce his chances of joining the Jana Morcha. Once his brother got a berth in the UP cabinet, the Chowdhary became inactive in the mobilization of peasants, at least initially. In the latter phases, he tried to counter-mobilize peasants of his Khap area against BKU's activities. The perceived erosion of political identity and domination of Gurjar led to the power struggles between castes that impeded the formation of *kisan* unions. Thus, primordial loyalties could succeed at least in the formation of smaller groups where they shared their individual sufferings but coordination could not be achieved at a broader level though they were eager to do something collectively in order to redress their grievances.

The opposition party leaders of the area, who lost the 1984 assembly and parliament elections, too called meetings of *kisans* in 1986 to aggregate the interests of peasants in this area. The *kisans* responded indifferently to the meetings as they developed an attitude of aversion and distrust towards the political leaders. The leaders of political parties, according to the *kisans*, shifted their stand on agrarian issues with their changing political affiliations and their relations with the party in power. *Kisans* also allege that the members of legislative assembly and parliament are unable to protect the interests of *kisans* and act more or less as power brokers. Such perceptions about political leaders has contributed to the apathetic response from the *kisans* to the meetings of opposition party leaders.

At the level of civic collectivities, the villagers of Haryana, claiming their affiliation with the Haryana unit of BKU, visited the villages near Sisauli and Shamli along with two *kisans* of Shamli. They collected

BKU membership fees from the *kisans* with the help of an Ayurvedic doctor of Bora Khurd village. The doctor was a rich peasant with a symbiotic relationship between the agrarian and the urban interests, the owner of a *kolhu*, a tractor, a thresher, and living with his unmarried brother and widowed mother, his wife and two children. Change in the government policy on *kolhus* affected the interests of the doctor as a *kolhu* owner. The collectors of membership fees were later found to be cheats. The contributors of membership dues were in turn inquiring about the activities of the BKU in the drought period for them. The homeopathic doctor met the Shamli residents and collected a portion of the contributions from them and returned it to the contributors. Thus, aliens with civic identities were, though initially, treated with trust as they were accompanied by local *kisans* but such trust could not be prolonged for long.

After such experiences from the civic identities, the doctor, a post-graduate aged below 35 years and head of a complex household, established contacts with peasants in the nearby villages and discussed the problems of *kisans* in smaller collectivities in the absence of *goonda* (anti-social), *neta* (leader), and *pradhan* (village panchayat president). *Kisans* of this area consider these three categories of people as exploiters, power brokers and usurpers of peasants' surplus. In these smaller collectivities, *kisans* discussed their individual problems related to the irregular supply of electricity, sinking ground water table, drought, *kolhu* plant policies, growing indebtedness, corruption and humiliation at the hands of the bureaucratic elements in their everyday interactions. The aggregator of peasant grievances proposed for the non-payment of loans borrowed from the formal financial institutions, operation of *kolhu* plants without renewal of licenses up to December 1986. He proposed for the withdrawal of individual savings from banks and to uproot the electricity poles standing on the peasants' lands, if the government opts for coercive actions. The collectivity of cultivators became conscious that the grievances were general in nature rather than of a particular individual and of a particular village. The collectivity felt such deteriorating conditions need to be changed not by individual effort but through collective action. Though the participants agreed on the commonness of the goal they differed with the aggregator of *kisans*' grievances on the means to end the grievances. In addition to this, they also looked at the aggregator of *kisans*' interests with distrust, as he was also an exploiter of cultivators. The participants in the meeting called the aggregator of *kisans*' interests as *paagal* (mad) and went back to their respective villages. Though consciousness is a prerequisite (Weber, 1961) for the formation of a union to organize collective actions, structural constraints like trusted leadership hinder the process of unionization of *kisans*. Further, the formation of a *kisan* union could not occur, as the aggregator was younger in age within his own lineage. Besides this, the principle of gerontocracy, respect and honour of different levels of Chowdharies is observed in the Khap areas. In addition to this, traditional leaders of some importance either at Khap, or Khamba did not attended the meeting. However, the attempt contributed in the realization of collective action as a prerequisite to redress similar structural sources of grievances.

Two peasant leaders of Khanjhawala unit of BKU revisited Baraut under the instructions of the Haryana BKU leadership in September 1986 in order to comprehend the various problems associated with the formation of a BKU unit in the Meerut Commissary. The homeopathic doctor in the presence of the Haryana BKU leaders called an indoor meeting of the *kisans* of his village at his residence. Twelve peasants belonging to different castes and categories of peasants attended the meeting. The participants in the meeting resolved: (1) to bestow the district-level BKU leadership to an honest, trustworthy, and assertive Chowdhary of a Khap. They thought that the leadership at the Commissary- and state-level could pass slowly into the hands of those persons who lived up to the expectations of *kisans* and fought for their interests. Thus, they decided to bequeath the leadership role to primordial identities rather than to political and civic identities. Secondly, they resolved to deposit the union membership fees in the local banks against the union's account in order to avoid misappropriation of funds. Thirdly, they considered politicians and corrupt people as enemies of the union. Finally, the participants decided to operate *kolhus* without renewal of licenses up to December 1986. These decisions reflect an attitude of reverence and trust towards the patriarchal authority. In addition to this, the interests of the *kolhu* owners were manifestly articulated in the meeting.

The doctor after contacting the *kisans* of different villages adjoining Sisauli called a meeting of peasants at Sisauli in October 1986. Nearly 2,000 *kisans* attended the meeting. Two retired army persons, a primary school teacher, and a respected *kisan* of this area, a retired High Court judge, the Ayurvedic doctor and the Desh Khap Chowdhary were some of the prominent persons who attended the meeting. The participants in the meeting requested the Baliyan Khap Chowdhary, chairperson of the meeting, to lead the peasants of Muzaffarnagar district in the redressal of their grievances. The chairperson again declined to lead the peasants, as he was unable to resolve conflicts within his own village. Then the collectivity not only refused to accept the hospitality of the chairperson but also sat on fast. Such behaviour in general reduces the status and honour of the host, and more so in a group where honour and self-respect are highly appreciated. Under such compulsive circumstances, the Chowdharies of different *patties* (divisions of a village into a smaller unit) of Sisauli village met separately and conceded not only to resolve the factional conflicts amicably but also to extend their cooperation in the aggregation and articulation of the interests of peasants. Thus, the Muzaffarnagar district unit of BKU came into existence on 17 October 1986 after sorting out internal factional disputes. One of the retired army people was nominated as its president, the chairperson of the meeting as treasurer and the primary school teacher as its secretary. Thus the formerly competing lineages or groups/factions within a lineage merged in mutual alliance against outside oppression in order to accomplish their instrumental interests.

The participants after announcing the formation of the BKU, aired their grievances individually. Aggregation of such grievances constituted the first charter of demands of the *kisans*. These demands are described as their rights. The rights were:

1. Withdrawal of hike on the power tariff
2. Withdrawal of extra-charge for the bulb fixed at the tube well
3. Location of electricity tariff collection centres at places nearer to villages
4. Need for the prompt repair and restoration of disconnected and loose electric wires
5. Need for regular and continuous supply of electricity for tube wells, flourmills and *kolhus*
6. Parity in matters of electricity supply between rural and urban areas
7. Action against corrupt personnel in the electricity department
8. Continuous supply of power to those cultivators, who either failed to pay the dues in time or those who became defaulters over time
9. Non-imposition of penalty in the event of late payment of power tariff

10. Not to collect security from the new aspirants of power connections to tube wells and finally
11. Parity between the power supply and the tariff charged.

An analysis of the demands depicts that the collectivity was mainly composed of electricity consumers. The consumers of electricity in rural areas are mainly owners of electrified tube wells and flourmills; electrified *kolhus*, and households. *Maldars* (rich peasants) and *khaate-peete log* (middle class peasants) are the owners of electrified tube wells and *kolhus*. However, cultivators with less than 2 hectares of land with secondary sources of livelihood or the owners who got land through inheritance, or the purchasers of small pieces of land too own and use tube wells jointly. Thus the issues related with electricity, in general, were the similar structural sources of grievances against the state government in the initial phase of the formation of BKU.

Thus the pattern of agrarian development in the Commissary is predominantly capital intensive, with commercialization and mechanization, but the organization of production is predominantly familial in nature. Such agrarian development promotes intensive and extensive relations with proliferated middlemen to avail the scarce agricultural inputs and to ensure relative priority for the sale of agricultural produce at reasonable prices. Such organization of agricultural production has contributed to the marginalization of *kisans* and to the development of class-based relations with groups outside agriculture and classlessness within agriculture. Sharing such private worries in smaller collectivities has converted private worries into public concerns and facilitated the formation of BKU.

Acknowledgements: The author acknowledges the financial assistance that he has received from the CAS research funds of the department for the pursuance of fieldwork on this theme in western Uttar Pradesh. The author further expresses his sincere gratitude to Professor T.K. Oommen, Professor Brij Raj Chauhan, Professor V.K. Srivastava, Professor R.C. Tripathi, Professor Janak Pandey, Professor E.S.K. Ghosh and many others who encouraged and took keen interest in the study.

REFERENCES

Alam, A. (2000), 'Farm Mechanization: Rising Energy Intensity', in *Hindu* (ed.), *Survey of Indian Agriculture 2000*, pp. 181-92.

Banaji, J. (1995) 'The Farmers' Movements: A Critique of Conservative Rural Coalitions', in Tom Brass (ed.), *New Farmers' Movements in India*, Essex: Frank Cass and Co. Ltd.

Bardhan, P. (1970), 'Trends in Land Relations', *EPW*, pp. 261-6.

Batra, R. (1978), 'Modes of Production and Agrarian Imbalances', Meeting on Comparative Research on Urban-Rural Interactions, New Delhi, 19-22 September.

Beteille, A. (1974), *Studies in Agrarian Social Structure*, New Delhi: Oxford University Press.

Bharadwaj, K. (1974), *Production Conditions in Indian Agriculture*, Cambridge: Cambridge University Press.

Brass, T. (1995), *New Farmers' Movements in India*, Essex: Frank Cass and Co Ltd.

Chauhan, B.R. (1967) (1999), *A Rajasthan Village*, Udaipur: A.C. Brothers.

——— (1990), *Rural Urban Articulations*, Etawah: A.C. Brothers.

Dhanagare, D.N. (1995), 'The Class Character and Politics of the Farmers' Movement in Maharashtra during 1980's', in T. Brass (ed.), *New Farmers' Movements in India*, Essex: Frank Cass and Co. Ltd.

Dube, S.C. (1957), *India's Changing Villages: Human Factors in Community Development*, New Delhi: Allied Publishers.

Friedman, H. (1978), 'Simple Commodity Production and Wage Labour in American Plains', *Journal of Peasant Studies*, vol. 6.

Friese, K. (1990), 'Peasant Communities and Agrarian Capitalism', *EPW*, vol. 25, no. 39 (29 September).

Gill, S.S. (1995), 'The Farmers' Movement and Agrarian Change in the Green Revolutionary Belt of North-west India', in T. Brass (ed.), *New Farmers' Movements in India*, Essex: Frank Cass and Co. Ltd.

Hassan, Z. (1989), 'Self-serving Guardians: Formation and Strategy of *B.K.U.*', *EPW*, vol. 24, no. 45.

Lindberg, S. (1995), 'New Farmers' Movements in India as Structural Response and Collective Identity Formation', in T. Brass (ed.), *New Farmers' Movements in India*, Essex: Frank Cass and Co. Ltd.

Lipset, S.M. (1950), *Agrarian Socialism*, Berkeley: University of California Press.

Marx, Karl (1967), *Capital*, vols. I & III, Moscow: Progress Publishers.

Mellor, J.W. (1976), *The New Economic Growth*, Ithaca: Cornell University Press.

Mills, C.W (1959), *The Sociological Imagination*, New York: Oxford University Press.

Moore, B. (1966), *Social Origins of Democracy and Dictatorship*, Boston: Beacon Press.

Omvedt, G. (1995), ' "We Want the Return of Our Sweat": The New Peasant Movement in India and the Formation of a National Agricultural Policy', in T. Brass (ed.), *New Farmers' Movements in India*, Essex: Frank Cass and Co. Ltd.

Pradhan, M.C. (1966), *The Political System of the Jats of Northern India*, Bombay: Oxford University Press.

Redfield, R. (1956), *The Little Community and Peasant Society and Culture*, Chicago: University of Chicago Press.

Rudra, A. (1978), 'Class Relations in Indian Agriculture-I', *EPW*, vol. V, no. 28, Review of Agriculture (March).

Satyanarayana, A. et al. (1989), 'Emergence of Bhartiya Kisan Union and its Interactions with Khap and Sarve Khap', *Indian Book Chronicles* (Nov.-Dec.).

Satyanarayana, A. (1985), *Technology, Work and Social Relations in Agriculture*, Meerut: Sociology Workers Sangam.

——— (1996), 'Changes in Landownership Pattern in Jhabiran Village over 40 Years', paper presented at Kolhapur, All India Sociological Conference.

——— (2004), 'A Paradigm of Peasant and Farmer: The Study of Meerut Commissary', in Yogesh Atal and Rajesh Mishra (ed.), *Understanding the Social Sphere: The Village and Beyond*, Jaipur: Rawat Publications.

——— (2005), 'Patterns of Peasant Mobility in a Tyagi Village-1954-94', *The Eastern Anthropologist*, vol. 58, no 3-4, pp. 573-92.

Scott, J.C. (1976), *The Moral Economy of the Peasant*, New Heven: Yale University Press.

Shanin, T. (ed.) (1971), *Peasants and Peasant Societies*, Harmondsworth: Penguin.

Sidhu, D.S. and D. Byerlee (1991), 'Technical Change and Wheat Productivity in Post-Green Revolution Punjab', *EPW*, vol. 26, no. 52(Dec.), pp. A159-A166.

Singh, A.K. (1987), *Agricultural Development and Rural Poverty*, New Delhi: Ashish Publishing House.

Sorokin, P., C.J. Zimmerman and C.J. Galpin (1930), *A Systematic Source Book of Rural Sociology*, vol. I, New York: Russel and Russel.

Srivastava, R.S. (2000), 'Rural Labour in Uttar Pradesh: Emerging Features of Subsistence, Contradictions and Resistance', *Journal of Peasant Studies*, pp. 162-215.

Statistical Bulletin (1985), *Meerut Commissary*, State Planning Institution, Economics and Statistics Department, U.P., Meerut: Meerut Commissary.

Statistical Bulletin (1995), *Meerut Commissary*, State Planning Institution, Economics and Statistics Department, U.P., Meerut: Meerut Commissary.

Stavenhagen, R. (1975), *Social Classes in Agrarian Society*, New York: Anchor.

Surjeet, H.S. (1986), 'Kisan Sabha Leads Struggles', in A.R. Desai (ed.),

Agrarian Struggles in India After Independence, New Delhi: Oxford University Press.

Torri, M. (1976), 'Economic Policy and Political Gains: The First Phase of India's Green Revolution (1966-71)', *Asia Quarterly*, vol. 1.

Whitcombe, E. (1971), *Agrarian Conditions in Northern India*, vol. I: *The United Provinces Under British Rule, 1860-1900*, New Delhi: Thompson Press (India) Ltd.

Wolf, E.R. (1969), *Peasant Wars of the Twentieth Century*, New York: Harper & Row.

CHAPTER 10

Why the Marginalized Protest: Environmental Movements as a Critique of Dominant Development Discourse

SUBHASH SHARMA

The objective of this essay is to provide an overview of globalization and its discontents at a macro level in terms of weakening of the sovereign nation state, deregulation, liberalization, privatization and marketization. Second, we would present the grand narrative of the 'Dominant Development Discourse' (DDD) with its perceptions and priorities, vision and model, especially in the context of India. Third, we would analyse as to why the marginalized people protest in their everyday life. Finally, we would try to explore as to whether there emerges an 'Alternative Development Paradigm' (ADP) in a manifest or latent form. We divide our essay in these four sections for convenience.

GLOBALIZATION AND ITS DISCONTENTS

Historically speaking, the long span from 1600 to 1950 was a period of colonialism and imperialism wherein economic interests were accompanied by grabbing direct political rule. The phase of 1950s and 1960s was described by the West as *'development decades'* and the 1970s as *'the lost decade'* but actually there emerged neo-liberal globalization (strategic-economic interests at the centre) in early 1980s. Globalization is actually a grand narrative with a packaged process of inter-connectedness going beyond the borders of nation states. But its essence is not compatible with real internationalization as it does not question the multi-dimensional unequal relations of contemporary world order. Hence one has to take an inter-disciplinary critical disempowerment approach to understand globalization and its discontents. Global economic inequality (as the world was never flat and even now is not flat, though Thomas Friedman presumes so) perpetuated by the dominant transnational corporations (TNC), technological advancement, escalating militarization (going beyond 'balance of power' and 'balance of terror'), cultural fusion (remixing in music), and the decline of sovereignty of nation states are its salient features.

Undoubtedly globalization is America-centric in letter and spirit. As Jan N. Pieterse (2004: v) correctly remarks: 'The most recent globalization project, neo-liberal globalization, is the deluxe model of Pax Americana that combined economic unilateralism with political multilateralism.' In fact, neo-liberal policies add to the globalization package (of informatization, flexibilization, regionalization and reconfiguration of states) are supplemented by neo-liberal policies of *to* (a) deregulation (liberalization, privatization), (b) marketization (unleashing of market forces), (c) financialization and securitization (conversion of assets into tradable financial instruments), and *the ideology of* a lean government (Pieterse 2004).

Interestingly while the Western developed nations pressurize the developing countries for relaxing import laws, charging user fees for irrigation, health and education, and for reducing agricultural subsidies (on irrigation, water, electricity, fertilizers, insecticides/pesticides, seeds, and so on), they tighten their own import laws in the name of sanitation and phyto-sanitation (SPS) and increase agricultural subsidies in one or other form under Blue Box (as provided in the WTO Agreement on agriculture). For instance, agricultural subsidies in Europe and US are to the tune of \$1 billion per day, which amounts to six times to the annual aid to developing countries.

If we look at the world, we find that though the ratio of poor people in the total world population is reducing, yet the gap between the richest 20 per cent and the poorest 20 per cent is increasing over the long term (Table 10.1).

Second, as per UNDP's Human Development Report (1990), the net worth of 358 richest people is equal to the combined income of the poorest 45 per cent of the world's population—2.3 billion people. Third, L. Eliott and C. Denny (Pieterse, 2004) estimated that the richest 1 per cent of the world have income equivalent to the poorest 57 per cent. But, unfortunately, instead of adequately helping the

TABLE 10.1: GLOBAL POVERTY SCENARIO (1820-1997)

Year	Gap between richest 20% and poorest 20%
1820	3:1
1870	7:1
1913	11:1
1960	30:1
1970	60:1
1997	74:1

Source: UNDP, HDR, 1990.

poor of the developing countries, the US prefers to attack them in order to preserve its hegemony. Thus globalization does not come to the rescue of the poor people and poor nations.

Further globalization brings in borderlessness but only for capital, communication, travel and consumption. Actually labour faces border restriction policies, not allowing free migration of labour. For example, US visa (H1B) is restricted to only 60,000 in a year for the whole world and within three hours of its opening this meagre quota is over like a share on the stock exchange! Again globalization has weakened the power of the nation states, hence the latter are unable to control crimes and conflicts. Thus globalization has many positive outcomes for the rich and for the capital but more negative outcomes for the poor and the labour class. The global inequality in terms of technology, geopolitics and economy have led to several kinds of conflicts—manifest or latent. Geoff Mulgan (1998), linking technology and politics, argues that the heavy technologies of industrialism in the mass production phase were paralleled by heavy command and control politics; standardized production was matched by standardized administration and regulation, standardized politics and coalitions. These involved top-down hierarchical relations between government and the governed, and within bureaucracies, parties and trade unions. Usually the technologies of work, war and politics are 'intertwined but their interrelations are uneven within and across countries' (Pieterse, 2004).

The Western dominant view is to prefer 'high tech' with 'flexible production' and 'smart war'. No doubt, technology matters but technological determinism is not acceptable as it is only an enabler—a necessary but not a sufficient condition for action. For technology human capability, political will and contextuality are equally significant. In practice, it is seen that propaganda about profitability, speed, less risk, economy of scale, less drudgery, more output, and so on is spread. Second, often the politics of representation becomes decisive in matters of purchase, use, maintenance and sale of technology. Third, the politics of violence involves a play of technology or capability differentials across terrains and social contexts (during the colonial period 'we have got the Maxim gun and they have not' was the motto). Fourth, a Western nation state wants a level of technology that enables it 'to effectively monopolise the means of coercion' (Pieterse). That is why most of the developed nations focus more on providing training for better capacity-building of human resources in developing countries but ultimately do not share the nitty-gritty of latest technology. But a Chinese saying correctly explains the problem: instead of giving fish to the poor, tell him how to catch the fish.

DOMINANT DEVELOPMENT DISCOURSE

Development means different things to different scholars, groups, organizations and establishments. Neo-classical economists equate development with economic growth measured in terms of gross domestic product and per capita income. Hence they desire an increase in per capita income to ensure better purchasing power. But it is only one aspect of development as the UNDP talks of 'human development' with three aspects: income, school enrollment and adult literacy, and longevity. Amartya Sen expands it to include 'development as freedom'. However, the conception of social development is very comprehensive and takes a holistic view about the real progress of a society in the economic, social, demographic and political arena.

Various social scientists formulated a modernization theory for the 'catching-up development' following the path adopted by the West. They differentiated between 'traditional' and 'modern' societies in terms of their social value systems, psychological motivations, attitudes and aptitudes, and economic capital accumulation. For instance, T. Parsons, focusing on behavioural orientation, made dichotomies of pattern variables like ascription-achievement and role diffusedness-specificity, where the former of each pair represents the traditional societies and the latter modern ones (Webster, 1990). Parsons' dichotomization is actually based on that of earlier sociologists like Tonnies' gemeinschaft-gesselschaft (community-association) and Durkheim's 'mechanical solidarity' and 'organic solidarity'.

In 1960, W.W. Rostow wrote a book *Stages of Economic Growth: A Non-Communist Manifesto* wherein he declared: 'it is possible to identified all societies, in their economic dimensions, as lying within one of five categories: the traditional society, the preconditions for take-off, the take-off, the drive to maturity, and age of high mass-consumption' (Webster, 1990). There are five key elements of the modernization theory: evolutionism (change through a fixed set of stages), unilinearity (all societies to pass through the same route and in the same order), internalism (crucial changes are internally generated), exposure and diffusion (of Western ideas, values and technology), and recapitulation (to follow the path of developed countries). Rostow went beyond the dichotomy syndrome of Parsons by stating five stages. His key concept is 'take-off' stage of economic growth when barriers to economic growth are removed, especially by the onset of an adequate rate of capital investment so that growth becomes a normal condition.

But the modernization theory does not stand the test of ground reality in most developing countries. It may be criticized on the following main grounds:

First, all societies cannot be dichotomized as 'traditional' or 'modern' because (a) all societies with pre-Newtonian science had a wide range of differences in their economy, technology, values, policies and political order; (b) a developing society may be having one modern sector (say, manufacturing) with another traditional sector (say, agriculture) at the same point of time; (c) even the so-called modern societies themselves are not in the same stage, say, the age of high mass consumption—only the US may be put in that stage in the real sense; (d) some developing societies had indigenous industrialization, though non-Western, before the onset of Newtonian science and technology; e.g. India in the seventeenth and eighteenth centuries; (e) even a modern society like Japan practices ascriptive criteria (family background, age and sex) in promotion of employees who were appointed on the basis of achievement criteria of skills and education (A.G. Frank in Sharma, 1998). Further, gender discrimination is very much evident in many developed countries of the North.

Second, it ignores the historical fact of imperialism and colonialism which were, to a large extent, responsible for the underdevelopment of Third World countries; e.g. the process of 'de-industrialization' in India by the British Empire in nineteenth and early twentieth centuries.

Third, the theory confuses pre-industrial and non-industrial paths of development, and wrongly puts the two together.

Fourth, even modern technologies and facilities may contribute to reinforcement/resurgence of old traditional religions/ethnic values and attitudes; for instance, *purdah* by women during the Islamic Revolution in Iran, or Sikh separatist activities in Punjab (north India) associated with the Green Revolution. Further, new modern transports facilitate visits to religious places like Mecca by foreign Muslim devotees or Mathura and Ayodhya by Hindu Non-Resident Indians. So is the case of extended families, caste and ethnicity.

Fifth, it makes a grand generalization at a theoretical plane at the cost of concrete reality in a specific country.

Sixth, the theory ignores the contribution of religious values in the growth of capitalism. For instance, Max Weber did a pioneering work to show the relationship between 'Protestant ethic' of salvation and growth of spirit of capitalism in post-sixteenth-century western Europe.

Seventh, it suffers from the 'tragedy of psychologism' blaming all the peoples of the Third World as fatalist, passive, other-worldly, superstitious, backward-looking against the modern Western peoples as forward-looking, creative, scientific, innovative, and entrepreneurial. Actually the attempts of the West to diffuse through aid has resulted in debt crisis, political oppression, militarization, trans-boundary wars and war psychology, and racial discrimination against the developing countries which have become the 'victims of development'.

Finally, and most significantly, it has created a mad race for overuse and exploitation of natural resources in the name of development. Its *productionist* view sees problems like poverty, illiteracy, hunger, malnutrition and famine as those of production or lack of development. However, as Amartya Sen has correctly shown, the crux of the problem lies in people's entitlement or being able to command food supplies than in its production or supply. Thus, the modernization thesis neither emphasizes on entitlement nor on ecological sustainability, rather nature is wrongly seen as of only instrumental/use value, not intrinsic value.

Some neo-liberal social scientists have reformulated the modernization thesis in terms of 'Transfer of Technology' (TOT) where development is seen as a modernizing force—a blueprint intervention—from research stations to extension services to farmers. Second, the superiority of 'rational science' is assumed. Third, farmers are seen merely as 'adopters' or 'rejectors of science', not originators of technical knowledge/improved practice, which is discredited and undervalued. Fourth, this thesis does not empower the farmers, rather sees them as a part of the problem of backwardness. Finally, its 'menu' is fixed, not open with alternative choices (Robert Chambers). These are depicted in Table 10.2.

As far as the major question of development of large dams is concerned, scholars are divided. Large dam or 'major project' is defined in India as one with a cultivable command area of more than 10,000 ha, 'medium' one between 2,000 and 10,000 ha and 'minor' one below 2,000 ha (as per Government of India). There are three major opinions regarding the construction of large dams: development optimists, conditionalists, and negativists. Table 10.3 gives a comparative picture of the three categories.

The following points learnt from the Indian experience are relevant to note here:

1. Genuine objective environmental impact assessment (EIA) of large dams is not made, and if anyhow made at all, the team has neither the courage nor morality to advise the government concerned not to build such dams. Moreover, 'the main motivation for commissioning the objectives of environmental assessments is to rationalize decisions which have already been made' (Goldsmith and Hildyard). In the Sardar Sarovar Project (SSP) dam, prior

TABLE 10.2: COMPARISON OF TOT THESIS AND ALTERNATIVE PARADIGM

Dimension	TOT thesis	Alternative Paradigm
Primary goal	Transfer of new technology	Empower the people critically —recognizing power relations
Needs/priorities	By outsider experts	Critical interaction between farmers and experts
R&D location	Experiment station, lab, greenhouse	Farmers' fields and conditions
Contents' transfer	Precepts, messages and package of practices by experts	Contents' mutual conflict-resolution
Menu	Fixed blueprint	Open ended
Science *vs.* traditional knowledge	Superiority of science	Respect for traditional knowledge in addition to adapting of suitable science

TABLE 10.3: VARYING VIEWS ON BUILDING LARGE DAMS

Categories	Scholars/Activists	Views
Development optimists	Neo-classical economists (World Bank)	Catch up development with West, modernization, cost effective, multipurpose, to increase per capita water storage easily—larger the size of population, more the need for big reservoirs
Conditionalists	R. Blackwelder, Philip Williams, Barbara Bramble, Bruce M. Rich, Shekhar Singh et al.	Environmental Impact Assessment, to benefit large population, labour-intensive work, for food production, not to compromise public health, not to affect national parks/heritage, scientific and educational systems, rainforests and endangered animal species, not to silt for 100 years, no salinity, long-term sustainable resource enhancement, to ensure project affected persons' life better than earlier, not to build dam in seismic/landslide zones, not to damage estuarine/ocean fisheries, not to harm environment of a neighbouring country—these conditions to be met.
Negativists	E. Goldsmith and N. Hildyard, S. Sanghavi, A. Kothari and R. Bhartari, Smitu Kothari and P. Parajuli	No objective EIA, no social impact assessment, landlosers not beneficiaries, not labour-intensive, dams encourage growing of cash crops, create diseases/epidemics, damage more plant/animal species, water logging and salinity, large displacement, associated with earthquake—not to be constructed.

Source: Prepared by the author.

EIA was not made, and SSP was started even before the approval by the Planning Commission of India. Actually, in the case of SSP, the state government of Gujarat commissioned an ecological impact study by Maharaja Sayaji Rao University after the project had been sanctioned; the university could not do adequate fieldwork and, therefore, mostly relied on the data from government sources rather than empirical data (Kalpavriksha, 1985). Further conditional approval was given by the Ministry of Environment and Forest (Government of India) and those conditions were not fulfilled before actual work started.

2. In SSP, for instance, the electric power to be generated is to be used mainly by the industries, rich farmers and urban consumers (of Gujarat and Maharashtra) while the land losers are generally Madhya Pradesh's small peasants, in rural areas, whose production mode (food crop for subsistence) and consumption pattern is different from those of the former. So the question arises whether government can acquire the lands of people without their consent? In India, for instance, since the 1950s 1,600 major dams and thousands of medium and minor dams have displaced 10-12 million persons (Kothari, 1996). Under the Land Acquisition Act 1894 (a colonial legacy serving the interests of the ruling class) anybody's land may be acquired for the so-called 'public purpose' that in reality is nothing but the government's purpose or industrialists' and urban elites' purpose—thus private or state purposes far exceed public purposes. Unfortunately even the Supreme Court of India has declared such purpose and right of the state as the ultimate power of sovereignty on the principle of *'eminent domain'*. Thus common property resources belonging to the people is not recognized at all. So is the case in most of the developing countries.
3. Large dams are incompatible with labour-intensive activities like agriculture or handicrafts or small-scale industries. Large dams have not been economically successful in the developing countries. Maintenance and operational costs far exceed the revenue earned from water taxes and electricity charges. For instance, in India, in 1979-80, the total national loss on irrigation projects was about Rs. 3,480 million, which was ultimately met by the Government of India (Bandyopadhyay, 1986).
4. Most dams encourage growing of cash crops to earn foreign exchange for the loan taken as well as to finance other projects. For instance, in the case of SSP, Gujarat's rich farmers are planning to grow sugar cane, and licenses for sugar factories have already been issued. Even the productivity after dam irrigation does not necessarily; increase rather in the case of Tawa dam in MP, the yield of wheat and maize declined in the post-dam period in 1978-9 (Mishra, 1986).
5. Big dams also create diseases and epidemics like malaria, bilharzia or schistosomiasis, as has been found in many large dams.

6. Big dams affect the rare rainforests along with rare medicinal plants (e.g. SSP) and endangered species of animals.
7. Since rivers in tropical areas in the developing countries carry high quantities of silt, it cannot be guaranteed that dams like the SSP will not silt up within 100 years.
8. Canal irrigation during the British rule in India resulted in both waterlogging and salinity. As a study noted, 'increasing salinity in irrigated soils on arid lands is practically universal' (V. Kovda, cited in Goldsmith and Hildyard, 1984), hence it is not sustainable in the long run. In Madhya Pradesh itself, the Tawa dam scheme caused waterlogging of 800 ha of fertile land. There is every likelihood of the same happening in the case of the SSP. In India as a whole, irrigation water has caused waterlogging of 10 million ha and another 25 million ha are threatened with salinity (Bandyopadhyay, 1986).
9. Almost all big dams displace a large number of local people. The SSP has displaced 1,50,000 persons mostly the marginalized people. Unfortunately there is no 'social impact assessment' (SIA) of most of proposed/planned dams to study how the critical life chances of local people will be affected—from livelihoods to cultural heritage.
10. Dams are also associated with, if not cause, earthquakes. Many areas of developing countries like India are in the seismic zone, and are hence more prone to earthquakes. As a former environment commissioner of Madhya Pradesh warned about the SSP: 'a chain of reservoirs on Narmada could create seismic aftereffects' (Kalpavriksha et al., 1986).
11. Large dams cause inequality, indebtedness and corruption (in inflated estimates, payment of compensation and rehabilitation). In Africa, too, this experience is common: 'Africa's history of large dams is filled with tragedy. Many have caused indebtedness, political inequalities, widespread environmental degradation, and have sapped resources from more appropriate, smaller scale development projects' (Horta and Pottinger, 2008).

Thus the perceptions and priorities of different quarters differ. For instance, the Save Narmada Movement's 'perception from below' differed from the 'perception from above' of the policy makers, financing agencies, contractors, political representatives and industrialists. This is clearly shown in Table 10.4.

TABLE 10.4: CONTRASTING PERCEPTIONS ON SSP

Perception from above (Dominant development)	Perception from below (at whose costs and for whom?)
(a) To provide irrigation—5 million ha	(a) Power for use of rich farmers, industrial and urban dwellers. (b) Irrigation water mostly for farmers in Gujarat but peasants mostly from M.P. to lose lands along with others in Maharashtra and Gujarat—37,000 ha of lands in 3 states to be submerged, loss of biodiversity.
(b) To check floods	(c) Dam will cause floods and earthquakes, and submerge forests (a source of people's livelihood) and cause silting.
(c) Employment generation	(d) Temporary employment at the cost of losing permanent and secure livelihood—displacing 1,50,000 persons, plus 1,40,000 others to be affected by canal and irrigation system. (e) Wrong data produced without specifying villages and urban centres to be provided drinking water.
(d) Water for domestic and industrial use	(f) Tourism for the rich, at the cost of the submergence of temples, graves. (g) No faith in government regarding compensation and rehabilitation, as land to be given for the land lost is not available—90 per cent of land survey numbers given by Gujarat for rehabilitation are non-existent.
(e) To promote tourism	(h) Ecological impact study commissioned by Gujarat government after the initiation of the project to justify it, over-estimation of benefits and under-estimation of environmental and social costs. (i) Loss of tribals' cultural identity.

Source: Prepared by author.

Despite such contrasting perceptions of the people, on the one hand, and that of the state, industrialists, rich farmers and contractors on the other, large dam construction has been in practice in developing countries for long. Why is there so much gap between the perceptions of the rulers and the ruled, between the prosperous and the marginalized? The first reason is 'damming the river and damning the people', i.e. 'promise a dam and win an election' syndrome. In India, there are more than 300 unfinished irrigation projects, initiated under the illogical and undue pressure of some political representatives of the people decades back. Jawaharlal Nehru talked of dams as 'temples of modern India', but they are now 'unholy monuments of waste and greed', a 'grand political statement', a great scandal 'sucking money faster than a tubewell depletes ground water' (Halarnkar, 1998).

The second reason is an opportunity for making money by many technocrats, bureaucrats, contractors, politicians, suppliers and traders. There is massive corruption in it in different ways: inflated estimates of the projects, expenditure on unnecessary items, commission in purchase of construction materials, nepotism in awarding contracts, revision of estimates, payment for materials not supplied and used, and so on.

The third reason is the role of financing agencies as 'big brothers', usually seeing large dams as symbols of the 'grand narrative of achievement', 'big is beautiful', 'visible is successful' and 'only concrete is real'.

Finally, many aspects of dams become standardized, uniform and universal—rather than specific, diverse and local—so that no extra efforts in terms of time and labour may be required of the officials and technocrats concerned in conducting specific field surveys, preparing estimates as per local conditions, and checking these. This will also make supervision, monitoring and evaluation easy. Thus, it duly fits in their 'book view of reality' as per 'dominant development discourse' (DDD)—a 'perspective from above', though, of course, at the cost of 'field view of reality'—a 'perspective from below'. This has been depicted in Table 10.5 (prepared by the author).

WHY THE MARGINALIZED PROTEST?

Here we take up four case studies:

(a) Damming of the Narmada River (MP)
(b) Sale of Neera River with Deogarh dam (Maharashtra)
(c) Drying of Kosi River (Uttarakhand)
(d) Closure of Muhane River (Bihar)

(A) DAMMING OF THE NARMADA RIVER (MP)

About 20 million people live in the Narmada (1,300 km length) basin, depending on the river for survival. Out of its 41 sub-rivers,

TABLE 10.5: CONTRASTING PERCEPTIONS ABOUT LARGE DAMS

Dimensions	Dominant Development Discourse (North, financing agencies, national governments in South)	Alternative Development Paradigm (Environmental movements in South)
I. Negative outcomes:		
(a) Number of persons displaced	Less (than beneficiaries)	More (than beneficiaries)
(b) Forests and bio-diversity submerged	Less area (than stated by movements)	More areas (than formally notified)
(c) Agricultural areas submerged	Less Area	More area
(d) Socio-cultural monuments submerged (religious places, graves, schools, health centres, festival/fair places)	Less Area	More area
(e) Submerging of houses	Less number	More number
II. Positive outcomes:		
(a) Water supply for domestic use in urban areas	More areas	Less areas (at the cost of land losers)
(b) Irrigation of agricultural lands	More areas	Less areas (landlosers not benefited)
(c) Flood control	More areas	Less area
(d) Generating electricity	More consumers' demand to be filled	Electricity supply to other areas at environmental, social and economic costs born by people displaced
(e) Tourism promotion	More visitors, more trade, more money	Graveyards don't inspire for life
(f) Employment-generation	More employment	Anti-livelihood
III. Vision of development	Grand narrative, big is beautiful, only concrete is real, river water as a saleable commodity, macro level	Small is beautiful, social harmony and peace, river water as life, is real, micro level
IV. Model of development	Standardized, uniform, reductionist quantitative and universal—techno-centric model from above	Local, diverse, specific, qualitative, holistic, eco-friendly, people's model from below

39 meet in MP. Out of its flow area of 98,796 sq km, 89,850 sq km falls in MP. More than 80 per cent of the people live in villages and amongst whom a large number are tribals (Bhils, Gonds, Baigas and others). But the basin is backward with low agricultural yield, low literacy, low life expectancy, and lack of medical, educational and banking facilities. The Narmada Valley Development Project has planned to 'develop' the region with 30 major, 135 medium and 3,000 (plus) minor dams of which 10 major, 20 medium and 893 minor dam projects have been completed. This may be seen in Table 10.6.

Claude Alavares has called the Narmada Valley Project the 'world's greatest planned disaster'. Ironically, the World Bank agreed in 1985 to lend $ 450 million for the Sardar Sarovar Project (SSP) dam and its canals but due to the pressure of international NGOs, the Bank gave a signal to the Government of India to withdraw the project. Hence, the Indian government terminated the contract in March 1993 but by then the World Bank had disbursed $280 million. Since then the S. Kumar group has been constructing the dam. Local marginalized people under the banner of Narmada Bachao Andolan (led by Medha Patkar) have been protesting against it for decades because it has displaced about 1.50 lakh people of whom 60 per cent are tribals. These people come from 243 villages of which 193 fall in MP. Similarly, the Indira Sagar Project Dam on the Narmada has submerged 249 villages in MP. A old town of 700-years-old town, Harsud, with 5,600 families also submerged, rather was 'destroyed' by the state apparatus, says Ravindra Shah (Tiwari, 2005). Unfortunately both the Congress and the Bharatiya Janta Party (BJP) state governments, observes Ravindra Shah, while raising fingers at each other, 'did not give priority to the issue of rehabilitation'. The state government of MP submerged Harsud on paper on 30 June 2004 by creating an artificial flood there by releasing water from the Bargi Dam in order to terrorize the people in Harsud and it was announced through loudspeakers: 'The compensation of Rs. 25,000 would be

TABLE 10.6: PROFILE OF DAMS ON THE NARMADA RIVER

No. of proposed and planned dams		No. of completed dams	No. of dams to be constructed
(a) Large	30	10	20
(b) Medium	135	20	115
(c) Minor	3,000+	893	2,107

given only to those who will destroy their homes in the same night' (Arundhati Roy in Tiwari, 2005).

But at Harsud a mass rally by different people's movements resolved to firmly fight for people's right over forests, lands and rivers. Resettlement and rehabilitation of project-affected persons (PAP) in SSP is not satisfactory (*as found by the Tata Institute of Social Sciences*) in five localities: Somaval, Dekati, Amoni, Roswa and Amlibari (Singh and Banerji, 2002):

(a) Land allotted to PAPs is not agricultural—rather it is forest land, again environmental damage in the name of rehabilitation.
(b) Many PAPs have not got actual possession of land, and the allotted land has been encroached by others.
(c) Housing materials like roofing tiles and bamboos have not beens supplied to PAPs.
(d) Many PAPs have not got compensation for trees and houses in the submerged areas.
(e) Five per cent reservation for oustees to ensure employment to educated PAPs not followed.
(f) No streetlights have been provided in their colonies.
(g) Non-parity of rehabilitation package across MP, Gujarat and Maharashtra.
(h) In Gujarat land for rehabilitation is bought in the open market, but in small bits/pieces. Even 30 families cannot resettle in one location—families from 19 villages are resettled in over 175 locations, causing disharmony.
(i) Displaced persons from MP and Maharashtra are not willing to settle in Gujarat due to different cultural and language backgrounds.
(j) It has caused deprivation to a group of people that has lived beyond the 'development' strategies for centuries.

(B) Sale of Neera River with Deogarh Dam (Maharashtra)

One major aspect of globalization is privatization, hence we would show how the impact of globalization has resulted into privatization of Shivnath River in Chhattisgarh (2002) and Neera River in Maharashtra. Earlier at Haridwar Ganga water was sold to a French company for supplying to the Sonia Vihar colony in Delhi.

Neera River flows in the Pune and Satara districts of Maharashtra, with a flow area of 208 km. Neera–Deogarh project was planned in

1984. The Maharashtra Krishna Valley Development Corporation (MKVDC)(corporate development?), under the Government of Maharshtra's Water Resources Ministry, floated in November 2007 an expression of interest 'with a minimum reserve of Rs. 1,000 crore (Rs. 10,000 million) against which five private responded. The Neera–Deogarh project has a capacity to irrigate 43,000 ha of land. Actually 95 per cent of the Deogarh dam is complete, hence the highest bidder will have to complete only 5 per cent, canal work of 164 km and the water distribution structure.

Interestingly against the original estimate of Rs. 2 crore, Government of Maharashtra has spent Rs. 450 crore—Rs. 196 crore on dam, Rs. 93.6 crore on canals, Rs. 87 crore on land acquisition, Rs. 21 crore in rehabilitaion of PAPs and Rs. 50 crore as 'other' expenditure. In 2001-2 MKVDC assessed that Rs. 910 crore was further required. In November 2007 the latest requirement was Rs. 1,000 crore (Dutta, 2007).

The local farmers have been protesting against the privatization of the Neera River through the Deogarh dam on the following grounds:

(a) The private company will impose high water tax on use of river water;
(b) The irrigation water may be used by the company for industrial purposes also;
(c) Only rich farmers will be able to buy the river water;
(d) The facilities for tourism and water sports would reduce the availability of water for irrigation;
(e) Water is a fundamental right of the people and it is the social responsibility of the state—how can state permit a private company to earn profit from it? asks Shripad Dharmadhikari. Ramaswamy R. Iyer, former Secretary, Ministry of Water Resources, Government of India, rightly observes: 'Economic rights of some people should not be permitted to endanger the fundamental rights of others.' (Dutta, 2007). However, the minister of water resources, Government of Maharahstra, Nayak Nimbalkar had a different perception: 'I hail from that region, so I know the needs of people from there. They want water' (Dutta, 2007). But at what cost? His response is that he is simply implementing the Maharashtra Government Notification (GR No. BOT/702, 425/2002 MP-1)!

It transpired that World Bank has been behind the Neera River Project in the name of 'economic reforms'. The Government of Maharashtra received a loan of $325 million from the World Bank. Thus, it is clear that the World Bank, the Government of Maharashtra and private firms are in favour the privatization of Neera River while the local people have been protesting against it as their critical life issues are at stake.

(C) Drying of Kosi River (Uttarakhand)

People of Kumayun and Garhwal regions of Uttarakhand undertook long foot marches for saving the rivers from (1-16 January 2008). They all met in Ramnagar (Nainital) on 16 January 2008 under the banner of 'Nadi Bachao Andolan' (Save Rivers Movement). Thus the spirit of the Chipko Andolan (Hug the Tree Movement) of the early 1970s in the region is being repeated. NBA started with the drive for the saving of Kosi River which is not a glacier-based river. Rather it originates at a height of 2,340 m at Panidhar in Kausmi from an source underground and ends at Ramnagar (Nainital) where it meets with the Ramganga.

In 1994 the flow of the Kosi River was 994 litres per second, which declined to 65 litres per second in 2003 and continues to decline, as per Prof. Jivan Singh Rawat, a hydrologist (Tiwari, 2008). If the same trend continues, the Kosi may dry up by AD 2020—the deadline of 'India: Vision 2020' prescribed by the ex-President of India, A.P.J. Abdul Kalam. According to Rawat, the recharge level of the Kosi River is on an average 12 per cent but it should be 31 per cent—therefore it is continuously drying up. While in Banj forests the recharge level is 23 per cent, in the barren land it is only 5 per cent and in urban lands it is safely 2 per cent on an average. Prof. Rawat has further pointed out that about 40 years ago the length of perennial rivers (meeting the Kosi River) was 225.6 km but their network has shrunk to merely 40 km. Since afforestation helps recharge levels in 40 to 50 years, it is pertinent to construct more water reservoirs. Earlier in the radius of 1 km of every small river there used to be 3-4 indigenous water mills facilitated by check dams. But now due to the prevalence of electric water mills, the reservoirs required for indigenous water mills (which help recharge) are non-existent. The table of underground water in Kosi range has gone down more than the water table of other rivers.

Activists are generating mass awareness through folk songs sung by the local people's poet Girda (who sang during the Chipko Andolan too)—'Heard from grandmothers and grandfathers

About flowing of healthy Kosi
But alas! it has become as tiny as a little finger
our Kosi is lost.

It is notable that in the Saryu Valley of Uttarakhand four villages are submering and 78 families are being displaced due to two dam projects at Patali Bagar. People are protesting through relay hunger strikes, demanding agricultural fields, not dams. As an activist Radha Bahan remarked, agriculture in the region depends on the Kosi River and if this 'life line' dries up, where would the local residents go? Further, Shamsher Singh Bisht of the Uttarakhand Lok Vahini observed that the government was not making projects to conserve water and to increase the water table, instead hand pumps had been installed but 60 per cent of the handpumps do not work due to further depleting of the water table.

(D) Closure of the Muhane-Nonai River (Bihar)

For centuries the Muhane-Nonai River had been flowing to a length of about 165 km (mainly in the Nalanda district of Bihar. Local people used its water to irrigate 1 lakh ha of their agricultural fields spread over more than 1200 villages through 365 irrigation channels (*pynes*) in four districts of Bihar (Nalanda, Gaya, Jahanabad and Patna). Its water was also used for drinking by humans and animals. The Government of Bihar in 1967 constructed a 6 feet high weir-water reservoir at Uderasthan at the cost of about Rs. 12 crore (Rs. 120 million). Since then rain has not been allowed passage into the river. In fact, the Muhane-Nonai should not be called a river now as it has no water and most of its long bed has been encroached. A popular anecdote is notable about Gaya town is 'Hills without forest, men without brain/river without water, road without drain'! About 2,50,000 people were affected due to the reservoir (wier), which only helped farmers in thes Ghosi block in Jahanabad district through the Nataur branch, at the instance of the influential local MLA (Jagdish Sharma then of the Congress). Due to closure of the river, the water table has gone down. Some areas (Patna-Gaya Road) are often flooded while in 1,200 villages in Nalanda, Gaya, Jahanabad and Patna there is drought due to non-availability of water for irrigation.

At the time of its construction the local people were assured that a sluice gate will be constructed there through which water will pass to Muhane-Nonai River but it has remained a mere promise. Local people have protested against the river's closure for long. In the beginning the protest was unorganized but from 11 October to 23 December 2002 it was well-organized by the local Muhane-Nonai Sangharsh Samiti (led by Sadhu Sharan Singh, the local *mukhia* or village head) and the Ekta Parishad (led by Ravindra Pratap and Pradip Priyadarshi) wherein about 5,000 persons participated directly in *dharnas* (sit-ins) and rallies. Lobbying by the movement led some people's representatives to raise the question in the Vidhan Sabha/ Parishad in December 2002 where the Government of Bihar (of Rashtriya Janata Dal) at first justified the construction of the dam wier and closure of the Muhane-Nonai River. However, after a long debate in the Vidhan Parishad a committee was constituted with the experts of the Water Resources Department and those nominated by the movement organizations (2 January 2003). The new government of JD(U) and BJP in Bihar has laid foundation (January 2006) for a new barrage there to ensure flow of water into the river, but nothing has come up there even after lapse of several years.

Thus, it transpires that due to financing by multilateral agencies as well as the government's policy of liberalization and privatization, interventions into these four rivers have had many negative consequences:

(a) Displacement of local people due to damming of river by the government (Narmada);
(b) Privatization of river water by the government, depriving the masses of their fundamental right to water (Neera);
(c) Financing by multilateral agencies like the World Bank leads to a neo-liberal technocentric model of 'development from above' in favour of the rich and against the poor (Narmada, Neera);
(d) A wide gap between the marginalized people's view and their political representatives—while the former see dams as anti-people, the latter see it as necessary and developmental (Narmada, Neera);
(e) Dominant development discourse, in the name of so-called development, takes steps resulting into permanent closure of a river (Muhane-Nonai).

This may be vividly seen in Table 10.7.

TABLE 10.7: PROFILE OF DOMINANT DEVELOPMENT IMPOSED ON FOUR RIVERS IN INDIA

Dimension	Narmada River (MP)	Neera River (Maharashtra)	Kosi River (Uttarakhand)	Muhane-Nonai River (Bihar)
Traditional use	Irrigation, socio-cultural functions, drinking by humans/animals	Irrigation, socio-cultural functions, drinking by humans/animals	Irrigation, socio-cultural functions, drinking by humans/animals	Irrigation, socio-cultural functions, drinking by humans/animals
Perception of technological intervention	Dam for more irrigation, electricity, flood control, water supply for urban-industrial purposes	Dam for more irrigation	Dam for more irrigation, hand pumps for drinking water, electric water mills	Dam for more irrigation
Financing agency	From World Bank, corporate group, govt.	From World Bank, state govt. and corporate group	From World Bank, state govt.	From state govt.
Negative outcome	Huge displacement, submergence of biodiversity, houses/heritage	Displacement, privatization of river water	Displacement, drying of river, lowering of water table	Full closure of river leading to non-irrigation of fields, lowering of water table
Pol. representatives' view	Necessity of dam	Necessity of dam and privatization (due to lack of govt. fund)	Necessity of dam, hand-pumps and electronic water mills	Necessity of dam weir
Marginalized people's view	Dam as anti-people	Dam and river's privatization as anti-people	Dam, large number of hand-pumps/electric water mills as anti-people	Dam as anti-people

Source: Prepared by the author.

Thus it transpires that the causes of the marginalized people's protest are various kinds of their disempowerment:

(A) *Economic Disempowerment:* As the main sources of livelihood of the marginalized people (agricultural lands, forests, common property resources) are lost, they become economically disempowered, unable to meet their basic needs of food, shelter, clothing, health and education.

(B) *Social Disempowerment:* Due to displacement, the PAPs are resettled in new locations, thus their old neighbourhood and community life is lost and, therefore, it creates problems. Further, often new locations provide the challenge of new language (displaced persons from MP are not willing to be resettled in Gujarat) also, leading to incapacities. On the other hand, due to dislocations, often their mother tongues/dialects are in disuse, leading to their slow death. Losing old homes and social ties lead to homelessness in the real sense.

(C) *Environmental Disempowerment:* This is due to physical isolation in terms of remoteness, pollution at new places, lack of access to natural resources like forests, water reservoirs, pasture, etc., and new climatic conditions.

(D) *Political Disempowerment:* If the state apparatuses are unfavourable to the marginalized people, they become powerless. Often there is no proper political process, channel or opportunity structure to address their political claims. Further due to displacement their political constituencies also change from equal participants to '*less than equals*'.

(E) *Cultural Disempowerment:* Since the PAPs lose their religious places of worship (temples, mosques, etc.), or their ancestors' graves or funeral places, places of fair and weekly markets, they feel rootless at new places of resettlement. Further due to dislocation the ill effects of globalization, liberalization and privatization are more perceptive upon the new generations of PAPs because of age, new contacts with outsiders (especially traders), new patterns of consumerism and casualization of jobs. Thus physical dislocation also leads to cultural dislocation.

ALTERNATIVE DEVELOPMENT PARADIGM

An alternative development paradigm (by the environmental movements) may be seen in Table 10.8.

TABLE 10.8: ALTERNATIVE DEVELOPMENT PARADIGM OF ENVIRONMENTAL MOVEMENTS

Theme	Alternative Development Paradigm
Economy	Mixed economy, or even eco-socialism, decentralized planning, development with people
Polity	Democratic socialism, full participation of the excluded
Science and technology	Small scale, labour-intensive, mix of indigenous and public-interest scientific knowledge, appropriate technology, moderate rate of change
Culture and consumption pattern	Limited consumption, rejection of superstitions and irrational practices, equitable and just culture
Linkage to world economy	Critique of globalization, liberalization and privatization, focus at local level—think globally, act locally;—weak linkage to world economy

Source: Prepared by author.

CONCLUSION

From the above discussion we find that most environmental movements emphasize on 'collective empowerment'—i.e. some kind of development *with people*, not *for the people*. In fact, environmental movements, more or less, believe in the credo of Y.C. Yen of the Rural Reconstruction Movement in China in the 1920s (Sharma, 2009):

(a) 'learn *from* the people, plan *with* the people and work *with* the people';
(b) 'not to conform but to transform';
(c) 'not relief but release'.

The environmental movements aspire for genuine participation of the marginalized people in the decision-making process at all stages and at all levels, from village to nation, with a flexible and dynamic process approach rather than a 'blue print' approach. The ultimate goal of real social development is 'collective self-reliance' and critical empowerment with the critical adaptation of *'think globally, act locally'* praxis. This may be done in three ways, as D.R. Gadgil rightly pointed out long back and was appreciated by Schumacher (1993):

(a) improvement of traditional technology;
(b) adjustment and adaptation (not adoption)
(c) innovative experiential research—going beyond (b)

Further, unlike the credo of '*expansion in consumption and enhancement of welfare*' (Cohen, 1985), in DDD, we have to limit our consumption to the extent of necessity only and go beyond welfare (under industrialization and urbanization) to social development (being in harmony with nature, culture and equity) in letter and spirit, otherwise our ecological epoch of Holocene would be renamed as 'anthropocene epoch' (due to increasing human population and economic activities), to use the term coined by the Nobel laureate Paul Crutzen. We should also learn from the indigenous ecological practices of various groups and communities like the Bishnois (who gave their lives for saving the *khejari* trees in Rajasthan) and tribals who have learnt well to live in harmony with nature for centuries. In our ancient tradition there is the concept of the *panch mahabhutas* (five basic elements) that constitute our being and the universe: *kshiti* (earth), *jal* (water), *pavak* (fire), *gagan* (space) and *sameer* (air). Thus river and its water are considered sacred in India and are essential as much as air for humans. Thinking globally-acting locally, as well as sustainability in outcome (rather than big size that does not matter) should be the guiding ethos in all kinds of development. That is, small is beautiful—micro irrigation and hydro-plants at the local level to suit the needs of people without displacement and disaster of ecology be given the top priority. Only then would there be social, economic, political, cultural and inter-generational equity and ecological sustainability through a dialogical relationship between nature, labour and culture. The environmental movements share with M.K. Gandhi's firm belief: 'Earth has everything to fulfil everybody's need but not anybody's greed.' With this credo the environmental movements provide a *'paradigm shift'* in development and technology for liberating the marginalized people rather than enslaving them. Unfortunately the DDD based on large dams and the culture of consumerism is more enslaving than liberating as it takes a myopic view with immediacy ('here and now' as the phenomenologists term) at the cost of *ecological sustainability*. Hence an alternative development paradigm with specificity, locality, diversity, equity, quality (not quantity), collective self-reliance, critical empowerment and sustainability, as propounded and practised by the environmental movements, is the need of the hour. This is possible through a new 'science of quality' or 'science of relationships', as F. Capara (2008) correctly terms:

> The planet is a collection of ecosystems that regulates and organises itself. Life evolved according to certain principles, such as forming networks, sharing resources, cycling matter, developing diversity, and so on. Endeavours to create sustainable societies should be led by an understanding of how nature has done it for billion of years.

The marginalized people have protested in developing countries like India against the DDD imposed from above with a grand narrative that size matters, big is beautiful and only concrete is development. Environmental movements have shown that people's needs are different from the greed of the elite consumers and the industrialists. Further these movements have an alternative vision and paradigm of development that takes care of local needs, social equity, sustainability and economic development, That is, an ecologically sustainable and egalitarian (inter-generational, inter-class, inter-locational equity) social development is called for by according due weightage to the marginalized people as well as the ecology.

REFERENCES

Bandyopadhyay, J. (1986), 'The Economics of Large Dams in India', in E. Goldsmith and N. Hildyard (eds.), *The Social & Environmental Effects of Large Dams*, vol. II, Cornwall: Wadebridge Ecological Centre.

Baviskar, Amita (1997), *In the Belly of River*, New Delhi: Oxford University Press.

Capara, F. (2008), 'Consciousness is an Aspect of Life', *Times of India*, 5 March 2008.

Cohen, J.L. (1985), 'Strategy or Identity: New Theoretical Paradigms and Contemporary Social Movements', *Social Research*, no. 52(4), Winter.

Dutta, S. (2007), 'Hajar Crore Rupaye Mein Kharido Nadi', *Outlook Saptahik*, 24 December 2007.

Foster Carter, A. (1985), *Sociology of Development*, Lancashire: Causeway Books.

Goldsmith, E. and N. Hildyard (eds.) (1984), *The Social and Environmental Effects of Large Dams*, vol. I, Cornwall: Wadebridge Ecological Centre.

——— (1992), *The Social and Environmental Effects of Large Dams*, vol. III, Cornwall: Wadebridge Ecological Centre.

Halarnkar, S. (1998), 'The Dam Scam', *India,Today*, no. 25, June, pp. 16-22.

Horta, K. and L. Pottinger (2008), 'Africa's Dams Not Helping Poor Communities', *The Hindu*, 24 January.

Iyer, Ramaswamy R. (2008), 'Water: A Critique of Three Concepts', *Economic & Political Weekly*, 5-11 January 2008.

Kalpavriksha et al. (1986), 'Narmada Vallley Project: Development or Destruction', in E. Goldsmith and N. Hildyard (eds.), *The Social and Environmental Effects of Large Dams*, vol. II, Cornwall: Wadebrdige Ecological Centre.

Kalpavriksha (1985), 'Narmada Valley Project: Development or Destruction', *The Ecologist*, pp. 1595-6.

Kothari, S. (1996), 'Whose Nation?: The Displaced as Victims of Development', *Economic & Political Weekly*, vol. XXXI, no. 24, 15 June.

Mishra, A. (1986), 'The Rawa Dam: An Irrigation Project That has Reduced Farm Production', in E. Goldsmith and N. Hildyard (eds.), *The Social and Environmental Effects of Large Dams*, vol. II, Cornwall: Wadebridge Ecological Centre.

Mulgan, G. (1998), *Connexity*, London: Vintage.

Pieterse, J.N. (2004), *Globalization or Empire*, New York: Routledge.

Roy, D. and G. Sen (1992), 'The Strength of People's Movement', in G. Sen (ed.), *Indiginous Vision*, New Delhi: Sage Publications.

Sanghavi, S. (1994), 'Nation, Nationalism and Mega Projects', *Economic & Political Weekly*, vol. XXIX, no. 10, 5 March.

Schumacher, E.F. (1973), *Small is Beautiful*, London: Abacus.

Sharma, S. (2009), *Why People Protest: An Analysis of Ecological Movements in Third World*, New Delhi: Publications Division, GOI.

Singh, Shekhar and Pranab Banerji (eds.) (2002), *Large Dams in India*, New Delhi: IIPA.

Stiglitz, J. (2002), *Globalization and Its Discontents*, London: Allen Lane.

Tiwari, Rakesh (2008), 'Panidhar Bane Sukhapani', *Jansatta*, 9 January.

Tiwari, Vijay Mohan (2005), *Harsud, 30 June*, New Delhi: Rajkamal Prakashan.

UNDP, (1990), *Human Development Report*, New York: Oxford University Press.

Webster, A. (1990), *Introduction to Sociology of Development*, London: Macmillan.

III. MARGINALIZATION OF DALITS, TRIBE, MINORITIES AND CHILDREN IN A CHANGING WORLD

CHAPTER 11

Globalization and Livelihood: Increasing Marginalization of Dalits and Tribals in India

JOSE KALAPURA

INTRODUCTION

Adopted as the New Economic Policy in 1991, globalization has been vigorously pursued in India. While it has tapped resources and increased productivity, it has also displaced millions of people from their natural habitat, enhanced unemployment, and further widened the chasm between the rich and the poor, especially among dalits and tribals.

The dalits, numbering some 167 million, are a broken people, struggling against economic, social, cultural, religious, and political oppression. Similarly, the tribals numbering some 84 million are marginalized as their lands have been taken over for industrialization without adequate share in the benefits of industrialization.

Dalits and tribals, comprising the largest segment of India's poor, are increasingly being marginalized due to globalization and its ugly forms: inflation, deindustrialization, unemployment, loss of livelihood, worsening food security, destruction of environment, growing inequality, suppression of democratic rights and de-culturation.

This paper is an attempt at understanding the ill-effects of globalization on dalits and tribals. At stake is the issue of livelihood and increasing marginalization of these two communities. The main argument of the paper is that decreasing livelihood sources and increasing marginalization of dalits and tribals have been impacted by anti-people, insensitive pursuance of economic globalization in India.

Thematically my paper is divided into three sections: (1) understanding globalization in India with its implication for the poor, (2) the impact of globalization on dalits, (3) the impact of globalization on tribals, and concluding considerations on major challenges and possibilities.

UNDERSTANDING GLOBALIZATION

Globalization as a concept is complex and controversial. The views on this issue vary from country to country depending on their economic status, cultural ethos, and socio-political and religio-cultural compulsions. The phenomenon of globalization is going to stay with us for a long time whether we like it or not. As a process and a project, globalization has a chain effect with wide repercussions, especially for us in Asia and for other developing countries all over the world. Globalization has many facets and has affected many aspects of life and living. Its main entry points are economic and cultural. In turn it is supported by politics.

Globalization is no longer a theoretical concept; it is a glaring reality, impinging upon almost every aspect of human existence—economic, political, environmental, cultural and the like (James David, 1998a: 17). The world is made to shrink into a 'global village', an expression that has gained much currency and acceptance in every lexicon. The most striking manifestation of globalization is the omnipresence of transnational corporations. These are the engines driving the world towards commonality, speeded by mass communication, transport and travel.

Globalization operates on the following principles:

(*i*) *Liberalization:* It means that a country, which has accepted globalization, has to open the doors for the transnational corporations to carry on their trade without any restriction.
(*ii*) *Privatization:* It means that the state must withdraw itself from industry and business and allow the private companies to manage the entire affairs on their own. The reason given is that the public sector is inefficient.
(*iii*) *Deregulation:* It refers to a policy of dismantling government controls on business activities, so that the market forces have a free hand in regulating the economy.

Globalizers believe in one, free, interconnected, united and democratic world which makes rapid economic progress (growth) by the integration of the economies of the nations into one global economy. This is achieved via the free international flow especially of financial capital, technology and information and then of goods, services, labour and culture to all the world's resources and markets. These markets operate as one, free, global, transnational market.

Globalization in History

Globalization is not a new phenomenon: It began in the late fifteenth century with the rise of capitalism and its overseas expansion under colonialism. The conquest and exploitation of Asia, Africa and Latin America and the white colony settlements in North Africa and Australia were all instances of 'globalization' (James David, 1998a: 17). Trade and capital movement were generally free until 1913. Even the movement of labour across countries was without restriction. For example, the conquistadors skilfully crafted colonization through indentured labour. This practice also existed in the US (import of slave labour from Africa) and in the West Indies, Mauritius, South Africa, Myanmar, Malaysia and Fiji. Indian labour was indentured by the British to exploit the resources of these countries for the benefit of Britain.

In fact, globalization was far more prevalent until the First World War. The main differences between 1900-10 and 1985-95 are the restrictions on cross-country movement of capital and labour and the revolution in communications that has made the whole world a sort of 'global village' (James David, 1998a: 18).

India and Globalization

The Bretton Wood institutions have been the main instrument to spread globalization. However, globalization came to be adopted by every nation state in the form of some kind of local initiative, euphemistically called as Reforms. The conditionalities accepted as a rescue package were declared here as economic reforms by the government. These economic reforms launched in July 1991 in India were in the nature of a crisis management response to the economic and political crises that erupted in early 1991. The economic crisis comprised a steep fall in the foreign exchange reserve, galloping inflation, large public and current account deficits and mounting domestic and foreign debt.

In politics, the fall of two governments in a short span of four months, from November 1990 to March 1991; deferment of presentation of the Union Budget, fairly long political interregnum till the elections, the assassination of former prime minister Rajiv Gandhi in their midst and the emergence of a minority government with a leader sans charisma, reflected an unprecedented crisis. These events led to a sharp erosion of confidence in India among lenders, downgradation of India's credit rating and consequently snapping of international credit lines from private or commercial sources.

Indian reforms thus, were

> essentially of a 'crisis driven' variety. They did not represent strategic choice with a vision of long-term development of Indian people. The blue print for the reforms was provided by the combination of macro-economic stabilization and Structural Adjustment Programme (SAP) of the International Monetary Fund (IMF) and World Bank (WB) respectively, which had been adopted by many countries before in similar situations. (Bhatt, 2005: 165)

The underlying economic philosophy of these programmes stems from the theories of neo-liberalism that propounds the rule of market, reduction in the role of state, cutting public expenditure on social services and eliminating the concept of public good; deregulation, and general replacement of public with private. It is based on the premise that the public sector leads to inefficient allocation and utilization of economic resources and that the enterprise of private sector overcomes it through the dynamics of free market (Bhatt, 2005: 166).

Globalization and the MNCs and TNCs

The central forces behind the present level of globalization are the multinational corporations (MNC) or transnational corporations (TNC) which dominate and control investment, production and trade. A TNC can be defined as 'a corporation or enterprise that owns and controls productive activities in more than one country' (Raju, 1999: xxv). It will source its inputs of manpower, capital, raw materials and intermediate products from wherever it is best to do so, and it will sell its goods and services in each of the main markets of the world. The corporations are huge and bigger than many national economies in terms of the productive assets they own.

The main motives of TNCs are maximization of profit and global control of resources. As the global economy becomes increasingly integrated, countries of the world, especially the Third World countries, have to open their economies and play host to TNCs. The size and power of the TNCs do indicate transnational influence in the socio-economic, political, cultural and environmental spheres and they are certainly interlinked with each other. In the ultimate analysis, the TNCs have furthered their growth on a significant scale and tend to exert considerable influence on many countries. In developing a new world, managers of firms like General Motors, IBM, General Electric, Shell, Volkswagen, Exxon and a few hundred others make daily business decisions which have more impact than most sovereign governments on where people live, what work—if any—they will do, what they will eat, drink and eat and wear . . . and what kind of society their children will inherit.

TNCs over the past 20 years have shown substantial quantum growth and have become a dominant force in the world economy. Presently, between 350 and 500 TNCs relatively control an enormous portion of the world's production, distribution and marketing processes through their subsidiaries or affiliates.

The number of TNCs has shot up from 7,000 to 37,000 in the past two decades. However, only a hundred or so of the top TNCs control about one-third of the total foreign direct investment. The power and influence of these TNCs has been further consolidated by their close alliance with the multinational banks (MNB) which in turn collaborate with international institutions like the WB and the IMF. These powerful industrial and financial interests are increasingly in conflict with the interests of civil society. While the spirit of liberalism is committed to fostering competition, the G-7 macro-economic policy has in practice supported a wave of corporate mergers and acquisitions as well as the planned bankruptcy of small and medium-sized enterprises (David, 1998a: 19).

All those countries who are against TNCs attribute the phenomenon to 're-colonization'. In 1998 out of the world's top 100 economies, 51 were corporations and 49 were countries. In the year 2000, of the world's top 100 economies, 54 were corporations and 46 were countries. Out of the top 500 corporations listed by *Fortune*, US dominates with 185 slots followed by Japan with 104 corporations, together accounting for 58 per cent of the top 500 corporations. Further, of the top 100 economies in the world, 47 are corporations—each with more wealth than the 130 developing countries.

The world economy is marked by the relocation of a substantial share of the industrial base of the advanced countries to cheap-labour locations in developing countries. The development of the cheap-labour export economy was launched in South-East Asia in the 1960s and 1970s, largely in labour-intensive manufacturing. Initially limited to Hong Kong, Singapore, Taiwan and South Korea, the development of off-shore cheap-labour production gained impetus in the 1970s and 1980s. This process is based on the destruction of national manufacturing for the internal market in individual Third World countries and the consolidation of a cheap-labour export economy (David, 1998a: 21). Production for the internal market and import substitution have become obsolete concepts.

Globalization is being accomplished in two ways, that is, through the creation of a seamless, borderless global order with increasing de-nationalization of the nation state and its sovereignty whilst steadily and critically altering the nature of the state itself with aggressive interventionist measures in favour of capital. It also involves the integration of the market and economies through trade, investment, finance, new labour skills, knowledge and technology, the trans-nationalization of production and standardization of consumer wants. These processes have accelerated with the completion of the Uruguay Round of GATT and the establishment of the World Trade Organization (WTO) (Murickan, 1998: 10).

Under such a dispensation the world is reduced to the status of economic territories to be exploited by transnational capital without any accountability or obligation to the nation state. This process has changed significantly the balance of power between TNCs and governments. TNCs today influence the major economic decisions of the world, such as what to produce, how much to produce, where to produce, when to shift from one region/country to another in search of a better profit margin, and so on. These decisions significantly determine the current and future control of the world's resources.

Production increasingly takes place in a global factory where different phases of production are performed in different countries.

> When an American buys a Pontiac Le Mans from General Motors for $10,000, $3,000 goes to South Korea for routine labour and assembly operations, $1,750 to Japan for advanced components, $750 to West Germany for styling and design engineering, $400 to Taiwan, Singapore and Japan for small components, $250 to Britain for advertising and marketing services and about $50 to Ireland and Barbados for data processing. (David, 1998b: 29)

What are the consequences? There is a frenetic pace to produce more goods and services. To create more desire and greater demand thus becomes a by-product. The TNCs have developed advertising into a fine art for manipulating the mind of the masses. Once used for establishing links between scattered consumers, advertisements now dominate 'all external life from presidential elections to the consumption of ties and cigarettes' (David, 1998a: 21). It is often assumed that production is geared to answer the 'demands of the market'. Tacit subservience to cultural imperialism follows from the dictum 'the market demands'. Even the most advanced countries do not escape its reach.

Globalization Process and Marginalization of the Poor

As noted above, there is a radical reorganization of the manufacturing activity. The manufacturing process is transnationalized, fragmented and dispersed across many countries. It becomes extremely capital intensive and constantly replaces labour. It is not industrial but finance capital which dominates the scene in the stage of globalization. Speculation then becomes more important than manufacture. There is an unprecedented emphasis on the fashion, entertainment/leisure and culture industry along with basically non-essential consumer perishables. Marketing including advertising itself becomes an important economic activity. There is a dispersal of industry within the country as well, along with a fragmentation of the production process. As collective production is dispersed, the working class is splintered, scattered and forced into a decline. Its weight in economic, political and social terms as a class decreases. It is weakened in the face of capital. Capital also dodges its responsibility to labour by these mechanisms since it becomes free of any obligations towards wage increases, employment benefits, welfare measures, social security, redundancy payments, and so on (Murickan, 1998: 11).

Forests, lands and minerals have always been valuable resources. The compulsions of international competition now create ever greater pressures to exploit these at tremendous speed and with 'efficiency'. There is already a trend towards greater concentration of these resources, a move towards concentration and accumulation. The victims of this accumulation will obviously be small landholders, women, dalits, *adivasis* and members of other oppressed castes (Murickan, 1998: 11). The new development will also increase the demand for water and electricity, which means even further displacement of people as new hydel and other infrastructural development projects are executed. Cash crops for sale in international markets will replace mass consumption crops, leading to a scarcity of necessities and increased vulnerability. Agriculture will also, under the new auspices, acquire corporate logic. The resultant mechanization and rationalization will spell reduced employment for the sections dependent on agricultural labour. The overall vulnerability of agriculture increases in the era of dependence on global markets. This brings about the doom of small landowners. The new techniques and seeds demanded by the new agricultural practices will render impracticable traditional methods of earning livelihood.

Privatization in the industrial sector spells similar disasters for the weaker sections. Reservations will become irrelevant with the shrinkage of the public sector. Lack of assets and creditworthiness will prevent the poor from entering the new order (Murickan, 1998: 11). Shrinkage of employment will mean that they will not find any gainful employment even as wage slaves. The available employment will in all probability be in demeaning and degrading jobs which are created by the consumerist new order. The burgeoning tourism and entertainment industry will for example lure women as sex workers and will make child labour even more obnoxious than it is today.

The withdrawal of the state from the realm of welfare, social entitlement and public service spheres also has negative impacts on the weaker sections (Murickan, 1998: 12). Their food security is affected adversely. Their access to health care services, education and employment will become even more restricted. Housing and transport facilities will go beyond their reach. With liberalization the problems become more complex as rapid economic growth unaccompanied by a social safety net increases disparities as only small sections of society benefit. The economic onslaught is accompanied by political, ideological and cultural offensives which create a sense of powerlessness and a loss of identity and autonomy.

Poverty under globalization has assumed newer dimensions. Globalization and marginalization go hand in hand. Under the market-friendly regime, the poor, the marginalized who have no entitlements (land, other income-yielding assets, social securities, employment) are kept out of the market. This leads to the fragmentation of collectivities, communities and traditional support systems.

Globalization as a disguised form of the imperialist strategy of capitalism in crisis was implemented in India through the programmes of the IMF, WB and WTO. Adapted as NEP by India some 17 years ago, globalization has been wrecking havoc on dalits and tribals. Even the well-meaning analysis of the impacts of globalization completely ignored the dalits and tribals who constitute more than one-fourth of the Indian population. This is our concern in the following sections.

DALITS AND GLOBALIZATION

Dalits are the most oppressed group in India. They are a people broken by and struggling against social, cultural, religious, economic and political oppression. On account of centuries of oppression, they still remain the least educated. A careful analysis of our social system explains that the caste system has divided Indian society into hierarchically arranged castes. Dalits being at the lowest rung of the caste hierarchy have suffered crippling social handicaps.

The term 'dalit' refers to a situation of subjugation and brokenness. But the term is loaded with political, cultural and social connotations. The term 'dalit' empowers those who designate themselves with it, as they perceive a new identity of their own (Wilfred, 2007: 9). Other expressions such as 'untouchables' or 'ex-untouchables' indicate the ritual position of the dalits in the Hindu hierarchial socio-religious order. Gandhi and other Hindu reformers spoke of them as 'Harijans'—Children of God. This has been found very condescending by the dalits whom, ironically, Gandhi wanted to honour by elevating them to the status of the children of God. Today the term 'Harijan' has acquired even a pejorative and contemptuous connotation. The British colonizers referred to them as 'the Depressed Classes'. In the context of the Constitution of India a neutral terminology is used to refer to the dalits—Scheduled Castes. This expression is widely used in connection with the issues of reservation and process of parliamentary democracy, and in legal parlance. The etymology of the term 'dalit' however recalls their original situation of being the Dravidas and Adi-Dravidas who were subjugated and oppressed by others.

Dalits, as a very distinct social group belonging to a broad class of have-nots, suffer an additional disability of social oppression. Economically, most of them are still the poorest of poor. The balance minuscule minority has managed to escape poverty limits and to locate itself on to a continuum ranging up to a reasonable level of prosperity. According to Anand Teltumbde, the main factor that has catalysed this transition is the reservation policy, which has provided the dalits an opportunity to enter the modern sectors of economy (Teltumbde, 2003: 25-6).

In social terms, however, all dalits, irrespective of their economic standing, still suffer oppression. This social oppression varies from the crudest variety of untouchability, still being practised in rural areas, to sophisticated forms of discrimination encountered even in the modern sectors of urban areas. Although the statistics indicate that dalits have made a significant progress on almost all parameters during the five post-Independence decades, the relative distance between them and non-dalits seems to have remained the same or increased.

More than 75 per cent of the dalit workers are still connected with land; 25 per cent being marginal and small farmers and balance over 50 per cent are the landless labourers. In urban areas, they work mainly in the unorganized sector. Out of the total dalit population the number of dalits in services is less than 1 per cent.

Earlier they were ostracized by the caste-ridden society, but now they experience genocide by the whole process of globalization. In globalization competition is the name of the game. People who are more or less at an equal level can compete with one another. The handicapped, the weak and the socio-economically oppressed are left out, unable to compete, for they have no chance in the rat race of competition. This is the fate of dalits. The values of globalization are based on greed, injustice, exploitation, oppression, profit, and selfishness, whereas dignity, equality, justice, freedom and hard work are the values for dalits, which are consistently violated by the values of globalization. Since the entire argument of globalization with respect to the poor is based on the 'trickle down' effect, it is admittedly not oriented to benefit the dalits. Poverty is the cumulative result of deprivation on many counts. Thus each micro move of globalization can be discerned to be directly hurting poor people. Dalits are the most vulnerable even among the poor, naturally so they are being hit the hardest.

Globalization and the Violation of Dalit Human Rights

The General Assembly of the United Nations adopted the Universal Declaration of Human Rights (UDHR) on 10 December 1948.

These rights also find a place in the Indian Constitution. The UNO defines human rights as 'those rights which are inherent in our nature and without which we cannot live as human beings. Human rights allow us to fully develop and use our human qualities, our intelligence, our talents and our conscience to satisfy our spiritual and other needs' (Dev, 1996: 10).

The UDHR spells out the aspiration of humankind to make this world a just and humane one where people will enjoy their basic human rights. Though these rights are guaranteed in the Indian Constitution, they are widely violated because of the policy of globalization. As a result the majority of the dalits remain poor and oppressed.

It was thought that globalization would entail spread of modernity in society so as to bury caste-based discrimination and oppression (Teltumbde, 2003: 32). On the contrary, there is a good deal of evidence of caste discrimination getting accentuated during the globalization period. The caste atrocities that best represent this menace show significant rise during the globalization period as compared to the pre-globalization period as shown in Table 11.1.

Globalization, Dalits and Livelihood Issues

Right to life does not mean mere animal existence but includes the right to livelihood because no person can live without the means of livelihood. Under globalization the state is providing industries with subsidized infrastructure. At the same time millions of people lack proper food and clean drinking water and are living in unhygienic conditions. This is violation of dalit rights to livelihood and dignity.

Over 81 per cent of the dalits still live in rural areas of whom about 50 per cent are landless labourers and about 25 per cent are cultivators with marginal farms. The dependency relationship of dalits with the upper caste has been a significant factor in shoring up the economic basis of caste. As only land reforms could feasibly break this relationship, they constituted a progressive agenda all through the post-Independence years. Globalization has not only eclipsed this agenda of land reforms but also substituted it with corporatization of farming for the global agricultural market (Teltumbde, 2003: 27). Globalization goes beyond the skewed distribution of land among people and rather takes advantage of it to consolidate farms for

TABLE 11.1: AVERAGE NUMBER OF ATROCITIES PER ANNUM ON DALITS DURING PRE-REFORM AND POST-REFORM YEARS

Year	Murders, Injury, POA	Serious under Section	Rape	Arson	Others	Crime	Total
Pre-reform years 1981-90	534.9	1477.8	714.1	866	11896.1	15182.8	30365.7
Post-Reform years 1990-2000	548	3472.7	922.1	421.9	14159.1	8307.6	21877.8
Difference between the two period	13.1	1994.9	208	–444.1	226.3	–6875.2	–8487.9

Source: Computed from the figures from the reports of National Commission for SCs and STs.

capitalist agriculture. Globalization has undone the ceiling on land-holdings in state after state to allow corporate super farms for luxury production for international markets.

The policy thrust of the WB–IMF–WHO combine has always been clearly for the abolition of the land ceiling laws and for liberalizing investment in agriculture. For example, Karnataka was one of the first states to amend its Land Reforms Act (1961) that aimed at removing the land ceiling for aquaculture in the Uttara Kannada and Dakshina Kannada districts and also for horticulture, floriculture and agro-based industries. Food growing land is being diverted to non-food crops such as flowers or luxury commodities such as shrimp. Corporatization of agriculture, which is being pushed under trade liberalization as a successor of the Green Revolution is leading to new poverty for small farmers as unequal and unfair contracts lock them into new forms of bondage (Teltumbde, 2003: 27).

There is a close nexus between caste and capital in Indian society. 'Today 77 per cent of the Dalits are employed in the agricultural sector of which 50 per cent are landless and agricultural laborers' (Kurian, 1994: 121). But under globalization more and more areas under cultivation of wheat, rice and maize are replaced by cultivation of cash crops and agricultural land is purchased on a large-scale for non-agricultural purposes due to which dalits have lost their livelihood without alternatives for survival.

The right to life also includes the right to live with human dignity. In the feudal system, the dalits were ill-treated by the landlords, but at the same time the dalits knew that they were indispensable and without them society would not function. But with globalization the poor, particularly the dalits, are told in many ways that they are not wanted. They are considered a burden to society because they do not have enough purchasing power. This harms the dalits' sense of self-worth and dignity. Thus globalization blatantly violates the dalits' right to life.

Violation of Dalits' Rights to a Standard of Living

Globalization also violates the dalits' right to a standard of living. After India opted for the implementation of the SAP, there has been a steep increase in the prices of essential commodities. However, the wages of the dalits have not gone up much. Hence, the percentage of people living below the poverty line jumped from 35 to 41.7 per cent during 1991-2. The National Family Health Survey (NFHS) estimates that 47 per cent of the children in India below the age of five were malnourished in 1998-9. Similarly, a study by the Indian Council for Medical Research and the Institute of Population Studies estimates that 53 per cent of children in that age group are undernourished. Tripathi rightly concludes that globalization has created conditions in which the life of the common people has become miserable (Tripathi, 1996: 6). Table 11.2 presents the comparative picture of incidence of poverty among the households of the SCs,

TABLE 11.2: PERSONS BELOW POVERTY LINES, 1993-4 (ALL INDIA PERCENTAGE)

Household Type	ST	SC	Other	All
Self-employment in agricultural households	47.12	37.71	25.57	29.04
Self-employment in non-agricultural households	44.70	33.14	29.49	31.95
Agriculture labour households	63.86	60.00	52.64	56.78
Other labour households	51.69	41.44	35.59	39.59
Other households	31.39	29.65	20.19	22.47
All households	52.17	48.14	31.29	37.09

Source: National Sample Survey on Consumption Expenditure.
Note: Other: Non-Scheduled Tribe/Scheduled Caste.

STs and others to highlight the miserable condition of the dalits (Teltumbde, 2003: 20).

Poverty is the cumulative result of deprivation on many counts. As for the rural population, the declining public investment in agriculture, trade liberalization in many agricultural products, declining rural employment, sharp rise in prices of food items and the government's abdication of the responsibility to provide food security to people by performing 'funeral rites' of the public distribution system (PDS), all under the dictates of globalization, have been mainly responsible for the increase in poverty.

Violation of Dalits' Right to Employment

The problem of dalits' unemployment has worsened in the process of globalization. Due to lack of education, dalits find it extremely difficult to create a space for themselves in the commercial sphere. Secondly, with growing mechanization and computerization, the skill of the dalits finds no market value. Thirdly, competition is possible only among equals. The socially and economically oppressed dalits have no chance for survival in the rat race for success through competition. In the government sector also the trend of downsizing, outsourcing and freeze on recruitment is being followed in order to adhere to the 'minimalist state' dictum of globalization (Teltumbde, 2003: 26). There will be fewer government jobs for the dalits in the future. Moreover, the exit (retrenchment) policy which was advised by the WB reduced the workforce in different sectors in order to make way more profit.

The rural employment growth fell to an alarming 0.67 per cent during the 1993-4 and 1999-2000 period; urban employment growth fell equally sharply to 1.34 per cent over the same period. These are far below the annual growth of population of job seekers, thus causing huge unemployment year by year [RUPE (30 and 31) 2001a: 153]. The pro-rich bias of globalization has aggravated existing the inequality world over (Teltumbde, 2003: 23). Table 11.3 gives a picture of unemployment in India.

Violation of Dalits' Right to Health

The health of the dalits is worst hit by globalization. The SAP demands that the government reduce its spending on health. As a result the Public Health Care (PHC) is the first to get axed. This goes against

TABLE 11.3: EMPLOYMENT RATE FOR MALES
(PERCENTAGE OF EMPLOYED TO TOTAL POPULATION)—ALL INDIA

Year	Scheduled Caste				Others (Non-SC/ST)			
	UPS	UPSS	CW	CD	UPS	UPSS	CW	CD
1977-8	63.50	NA	56.15	52.50	56.05	NA	55.42	53.61
1983-4	62.24	64.00	54.24	50.14	56.96	58.20	56.19	53.93
1993-4	54.90	52.90	52.30	51.60	54.00	54.50	54.10	53.40
1999-2000	52.90	50.30	48.60	45.80	51.40	51.80	51.30	49.90

Source: National Sample Survey, 1977-8, 1983-4, 1993-4, 1999-2000.
Note: UPS: Usual Principal Status, UPSS: Usual Principal Subsidiary Status, CW: Current Weekly Status, CD: Current Daily Status.

the Alma Alta Declaration of 1978 which says, 'Primary health care is essential care, based on practical, scientifically sound and socially accepted methods and technology made universally acceptable to individuals, and families in the community through their full participation and at a cost that the community and country can afford to maintain.' With globalization a sharp cut took place in the preventive disease control programme as a result of which diseases like malaria and TB have increased in the rural areas.

In major cities and towns dalits work under very unhygienic conditions. As a result most of them suffer from communicable diseases. The situation is no better in rural areas. Extreme poverty and under-nutrition are reducing the dalits' resistance to diseases. Instead of concentrating on the government hospitals and PHC centres which take care of the poor, the government slashed the budget allotted to them and went for privatization of health care. As a result today private hospitals are coming up, which take approximately Rs. 6,000 to treat a TB patient. With more than 40 per cent of the population living below the poverty line, very few poor people, especially dalits, can afford the private health care system. The following data (Table 11.4) reveals the health condition of the people in India (Roy Choudhury, 1999: 269).

Thus globalization systematically violates the dalits' access to health care. The policy of 'health for all by 2000' has become a mere rhetoric. Globalization in its present form is a 'recipe for suicide'. It offers nothing for the poor but death.

Globalization Deprives Constitutional Provisions

The constitutional space for dalits comprises mainly the provision of reservation in state-aided educational institutions and employment

TABLE 11.4: SOME INDICATORS OF POOR HEALTH CARE IN INDIA

Only 20 per cent of Indians have access to modern medicine.
40 per cent of our children suffer from malnutrition.
23 million children are born every year.
2.5 million of these children die within the first year.
5,50,000 Indians die of TB every year.
9,00,000 Indians get infected by TB every year.
Only 2.1 per cent of government funds are spent on health.

in the government and public sector undertakings (PSU). Globalization has constricted this space. As a result without any actual change in the Constitution, reservations have come to an end.

Deprived of Reservation in Jobs

With the wholesale privatization of the public sector and massive retrenchment of government jobs, the question of reservation in the sphere of jobs has become irrelevant. And as the private sector has no job reservation policy, the job opportunities that had been available to dalits during the past three decades will now totally dry up. The general population is facing the horrors of unemployment and this will be more deeply felt by the dalits. In addition, the government, which has been systematically cutting expenditure on the people's welfare at the behest of the WB–IMF, has also cut its expenditure on the dalits. The outlay for SC welfare has declined from 8 per cent in 1990-1 to 6.7 per cent in 1994-5.

Reservation in services relate with the larger question of employment. If there is more employment than sjob seekers, there will not be any necessity of reservation. What does globalization entail in terms of generating employment? Notwithstanding the protagonists' apologetic claims that globalization will create huge job opportunities in the service sector (away from the traditional manufacturing sector), the answer is obviously dismal, as the vast empirical data all over the world would testify (Teltumbde, 2003: 26).

The winds of privatization within the globalization package have already shaken the very foundations of reservations. Even without actual privatization of the PSUs, the kind of ethos it unleashed in the PSU managements under the plea to prepare themselves for competition in the free market regime has been grossly oppressive to dalit employees (ibid.: 25).

Deprived of Reservation in Education

Education is another vital factor in the emancipation project of dalits as reflected in all their movements. Mahatma Phule, for instance, had attributed the miserable plight of the shudras and ati-shudras (dalits) to the denial of education to them by brahmins and had therefore opened schools for them. Every other leader who championed the cause of dalits has stressed the importance of education. Babasaheb Ambedkar placed education foremost in his agenda, as his *mantra—educate, organize and agitate*—reflects. As a result of these reform movements and particularly because of the Ambedkar's role model many dalits took to education as a key to their emancipation and made some progress during the post-Independence decades (ibid.: 28).

Education in its comprehensive instrument in an emancipation project: its role in providing individual and social competencies is much bigger than as a means in economic production. Fundamentally this paradigm is negated under globalization, which has given impetus to the 'human capital' discourse that measures education system exclusively in economic terms particularly in responding to market needs. This discourse is fraught with several implicit dangers not only to dalits but also to the overall constitution of civil society. As for dalits, it totally demolishes the extra-market rationale for giving them preferential access to and certain concessions in education (ibid.: 28).

Higher education, thus, is to be entirely market oriented and clearly out of bounds of the commoners, not to talk of dalits. The framework has clearly advocated literacy for the masses and education for the classes. During the past decade of globalization, we clearly see the impact in terms of a far more elitist orientation in education than ever before. In accordance with one of the globalization virtues, the state in the attempt to contain its fiscal deficit has been throttling its funding to education. As a result, some elite institutions that had demand in the education market have increased their fees to be self-supporting. Many foreign universities have tied up their programmes with Indian universities and denominated their fees in dollars; many self-financed new schools and colleges have opened up a new tribe of brokers that mediate in educational transactions have cropped up in this mega-business (ibid.: 28-9).

The increasing cost of education on one hand and the drying up of the motivation for education because of no job prospects created by globalization on the other, is fast proving the reservation in education to be meaningless. In addition the generally pervading ethos of globalization has marginalized the discourse of reservation. The recent court judgements removing the reservation to SCs and STs in the minority-run educational institutions can be a good example of this trend. Globalization has created a neo-caste divide in education which is pushing the dalits back into the dark times (ibid.: 25).

The thrust of the change can be discerned in terms confining the government's role to literacy so that people do not fall out of the market net (as illiterates they would not be able to read the advertisements!) and leave higher education entirely in the private domain for the select few who can afford its 'commercial' costs (ibid.: 24).

Dalits who have barely been able to afford schooling with the aid of freeship and scholarship are squeezed out from both ends. Firstly, education has become increasingly inaccessible and unaffordable to them. Even if they persist with it, they have to face several hurdles on the way to get education that would get them gainful employment. The increasing opportunity cost of schooling is dissuading many dalits from education, resulting in increasing number of dropouts (ibid.: 29).

The literacy rate for dalits is around 36 per cent, which means that only a small fraction of them are educated, while millions of them are not even able to enroll themselves in schools. Globalization has created a new, neo-caste divide in education which is pushing the dalits back into the dark ages. The privatization and commercialization of education neutralizes the constitutional provisions for dalits.

With primary education itself becoming an insurmountable barrier and higher education becoming a virtual taboo, dalits are literally getting left out of the educational arena. The impetus that privatization and commercialization of education received during the globalization period is pushing education out of the public sphere and thereby neutralizing the constitutional provisions for dalits. Left out of education, the only future that could be in wait for them is alienation, lumpenization and criminalization (ibid.: 25).

Alienation is a Result of Globalization

With the advent of globalization dalits have been alienated from various other spheres of life.

Alienation from Land Leads to Migration

Around 22 per cent of the urban population of the cities live in slums. According to the government reports, Chennai has 1,750 slums and Delhi has about 30 lakhs of people living in slums and this population is increasing everyday. This is mainly due to globalization which has caused massive urbanization of cities, mass land acquisition by the MNCs and TNCs, the cultivation of cash crops for export, the drastic cuts in agricultural subsidies and the mega-developmental projects.

Socio-Cultural Alienation

The biggest attack of globalization is on the local culture of the dalits. The culture of globalization invades the culture of the local people. Through various media, the culture of accumulation, technology, wasteful consumerism, beauty parlours and fashion parades are bombarding the innocent minds of the dalits. The cultural hegemony of globalization poses a serious threat to the specific local culture because of its wider geographical coverage (Raj, n.d.: 192). The worst victims of this denial of culture are the dalits.

IMPACT OF GLOBALIZATION ON THE TRIBALS

The recent globalization has negatively affected the tribal economy and identity. Soon after Independence the STs were given special provisions. The Constitution laid down special directives for the development of the tribals. The first prime minister Jawaharlal Nehru laid down a principle of development called *Panchsheela* for the tribal areas. The *Panchsheela* was aimed primarily at preserving, protecting and promoting the genius and environment of the tribals along with their distinctive culture.

The common English terms in India for members of the *adivasi* community are *tribals*, *girijan* (hill people), *vanjati* (forest dwellers), *adimjati* (original tribe), animists, and so on. The Constitution of India uses the term STs in its English version and *Anusuchit Janjati* in its Hindi version. These terms have a paternalistic, discriminatory and derogatory connotation. The tribal community uses the Hindi/Sanskrit term for *adi* (first or original) and *vasi* (dweller or inhabitant). Literally it means the first, original or aboriginal dwellers (Bijoy, n.d.: 211). This self-identification as *adivasi* has found widespread acceptance among the members of the tribal communities all over the country.

The tribal population of India (67.6 million) stands at around 7 per cent of the total population. No other country in the world has such a large population of indigenous people. If all the tribals of India had lived in one state, it would have been the fifth most populous state after Uttar Pradesh, Bihar, West Bengal and Maharashtra.

The essence of 'we-feeling' of the tribals is based on the sharing of their symbolic meanings, myths, memories and values. Love for nature, fellow-feeling, simplicity, truthfulness, mythical thinking, community life, simple rituals, physical labour, equality, freedom, hunting, music, song and dance are some of the basic characteristics of tribal culture. These values are opposed to greed, injustice, exploitation, oppression, private profit, selfishness, and corruption, which are the values promoted by globalization.

Tribal Economy and Identity Host Due to Globalization

Today globalization and its non-tribal agents coming into the tribal areas through the MNCs and TNCs is threatening the very existence of the tribals. Because of this the tribals are forced to assert their identity which is essential for their survival as a distinct ethnic and cultural unit within the larger pluralistic Indian society. Therefore time and again we see a number of movements, demonstrations and protests against government policies and private companies.

The ill-effects of globalization, especially in the area of industrialization and modernization of tribal lands, have been devastating. Some of these are increasing materialism, consumerism, greed for power and money, use of violence, lack of concern for others, dishonesty and trampling ruthlessly upon the rights of the poor, the weak, women and children. These are directly opposed to the tribal values of honesty, simplicity, hard work, community living, solidarity, equality and hospitality. All these are signs of socio-cultural degradation of the tribal communities under the impact of globalization.

The Constitution assures the tribals protection. There are many committees and commissions under the central and state government for their development and upliftment. But still the tribals rate very low on the three most important indicators of human development: health, education and income. All the more the condition of the tribals has worsened economically, politically, culturally, and socially. Today because of globalization they face the challenge of becoming extinct. For a focused study, let us take the case of the tribals of Jharkhand state.

Tribals in Jharkhand: Victims of Globalization

The state of Jharkhand is spread over an area of 79.71 thousand sq km and has a population of 26.91 million as per 2001 census. This land of the tribals is rich in mineral resources. The economy of the tribals depends on land, forest, and various minerals. In the name of development of the tribal areas, many developmental projects have been launched by the MNCs, TNCs, WB and IMF that have been approved by the central and state government for the improvement of the economy. However, the economic development of the tribals has been destroyed over the recent years. The rights of the tribals over the land and forest have been affected by globalization.

Economy of Jharkhand Ruined by Globalization

The present trend of economic globalization pursued by the MNCs in collusion with the state government may be noted from Table 11.5.

Deforestation and Greed of Globalization

At the time of Independence in 1947 the total forest land in Chhota Nagpur and Santal Parganas amounted to 54 lakh ha. This amount has been reduced to 3.1 lakh ha, according to the 1981 census. Contractors in collusion with the police and forest officials rapidly carried out the ruthless cutting down of forests. As a result the traditional rights of the villagers over forests were blatantly flouted as the government became the owner. The tribals of this region have thus lost their secondary source of income.

Nowadays there is massive deforestation to exploit the natural resources and establish new developmental projects (Jain, 2001: 170). All these things are happening because of the impact of globalization. The reforestation programme of the government is not popular among tribals due to fear resulting from their past experience. Besides, the trees planted are commercially oriented and not bolstering the economic condition of the tribals.

TABLE 11.5: A LIST OF MNCs GIVEN RECOGNITION PERMIT BY THE JHARKHAND STATE GOVERNMENT

Name of Company	District	Area (sq km)	Mineral
Anglo-American Exploration	Gumla, Ranchi, West Singhbhum	472	Nickel
De Beer's India Pvt. Ltd.	Palkot, Gumla	2015	Silver
" " "	Simdega	2189	"
Jiyo Mysore Services, India	Ranchi	220	Gold
" " "	E. Singhbhum	1540	Gold
" " "	Saraikela, Kharsawan	840	"
" " "	West Singhbhum	770	"
" " "	Saraikela, Kharsawan	970	"
" " "	" "	860	"
" " "	East Singhbhum	295	"
" " "	" "	–	"
Suvernarekha Minerals Resources Co	" "	930	"
" " "	" "	460	"
" " "	West Singhbhum	2160	"
VHP Minerals	" "	1688	--
" "	Saraikela, Kharsawan	390	--
Doj Explorations	Tamad	860	"
India Pvt. Ltd. Minerals	East Singhbhum	1869	Copper
Anglo-American	Chaibasa, Kharsawan	3033	Gold
Exploration India	Saraikela	–	Copper

LAND ALIENATION IS THE OUTCOME OF GLOBALIZATION

The Chhota Nagpur Tenancy Act of 1908 and the Santal Pargana Tenancy Act of 1949 prohibit the transfer of tribal land to non-tribals. With the advent of globalization we see the violation of these acts: non-tribals are inheriting tribal land by marrying tribal women as second or third wives. In the name of work, outsiders come and occupy the land. Mega projects and factories are built on tribal land, thanks to MNCs and TNCs (Raju, 1999: 68). The tribals are alienated from their own land in various ways. Developmental projects and housing cooperatives also contribute to their alienation. All the more the Jharkhand Domicile Issue has further alienated the tribals from their own land. All these realities are due to the impact of globalization (Ekka and Asif, 2000: 95). Table 11.6 gives an idea of the amount of tribal land acquired in the name of development.

TABLE 11.6: TOTAL LAND ACQUIRED FOR DEVELOPMENT SCHEMES IN JHARKHAND (ACRES)

Category of Project	Private Land	%	Common Land	%	Forest Land	%	Total Land	%
Water resources	3,64,646.00	71.7	94,808.00	18.7	48,498.00	09.6	5,07,952.00	34.0
Industries	98,525.59	56.1	63,786.68	36.3	13,435.91	07.6	1,75,730.18	11.7
Thermal Power	2,598.45	43.1	2,534.38	42.1	894.04	14.8	6,026.87	0.4
Mines	1,84,169.00	35.7	1,56,341.19	30.4	1,74,614.40	33.9	5,15,124.59	34.4
Defense Estd.	22,543.61	20.1	11,134.93	09.9	78,610.57	70.0	1,12,289.11	07.5
Misc. Schemes	1,52,000.65	85.0	8,941.21	05.0	17,882.43	10.0	1,78,824.29	12.0
Sub-total	8,24,483.30	55.1	3,37,528.39	22.6	3,33,935.35	22.3	14,95,947.04	100.0
Missing Schemes	27,550.00	55.1	11,300.00	22.6	11,150.00	22.3	50,000.00	
Grand Total	8,52,033.30		3,48,828.39		3,45,085.35		1,545,947.04	

Source: Computed by Regional Theology College (RTC) Gyanodaya, Patna.

Inhuman Development and Displacement: Products of Globalization

The mineral resources of Jharkhand are exploited by the state and central governments at the cost of the local people. The richness of natural resources being exploited in Jharkhand is illustrated in Table 11.7.

National development cannot be carried out at the expense of any segment of the population when resources are found in their soil. The sons of the soil have the right to develop on par with the rest of the country. They cannot be sacrificed at the altar of national development.

Tribals strongly feel that outsiders are grabbing the benefits of development and industrialization in this region. In the last four decades the displacement of tribals has been due to the emergence of large-scale irrigation and power projects, steel plants, forest-based industries, national parks, game sanctuaries and biosphere reserves. Now the local labourers in the coal mines number only 24 to 26 per cent.

The displacement due to large power projects and irrigation dams is most common. The Koel-Karo Dam Project would submerge 50,000 acres of land, of which 25,000 to 30,000 acres will be farmland and the other 20,000 to 25,000 acres forests on which the tribals

TABLE 11.7: MINERAL RESOURCES IN THE JHARKHAND AREA

Minerals	Estimated Reserve (million tons)	Production (1998-9)
Coal	65,205.4	76,349 (1000 tons)
Hematite	2,967.0	12,003 (1000 tons)
Asbestos	403.5	NA
Graphite	533.2	9,906 tons
Feldspar	345.2	8,093 tons
Quartzite	317.3	17,771 tons
Copper	113.8	6,47,844 tons
Kainite	113.5	4,993 tons
Bauxite	64.1	12,42,001 tons
Fire Clay	52	20,944 tons
Manganese	2.29	NA
Mica	9,64,917 (tons)	925 tons
Gold	NA	505 kg

Source: Indian Bureau of Mines, March 2002 (cf. Mahato, 2006).

have traditional as well legal rights. This project alone would displace about 16,350 families of which 70 per cent tribals. A rough estimate shows that about 12,000 households are displaced by the Subarnarekha Multipurpose Project. Similarly the Damodar Valley Corporation, the Tenughat, Chandil Dam and Chandrapura Project have also displaced thousands of people and rendered them homeless.

There are so many projects coming up in the tribal land sponsored by WB, IMF and implemented by the state and central governments. These agencies along with the MNCs and TNCs are also investing money. The people accept that development should go on, but some groups of people should not become victims of development. Between 1991-5 because of industries and other infrastructure 15,03,017 tribals were displaced in the Jharkhand region. Factories at Ranchi, Jamshedpur, West Bokaro and Patratu have uprooted 115 villages displacing 54,800 tribals. Nationalization of coal mines in 1971 resulted in throwing thousands of local tribals out of jobs. In their place labourers from other states were brought in. These factors have adversely affected the tribals (Ekka and Asif, 2000: 67). Table 11.8 indicates the extent of displacement, especially of the tribals.

Globalization Demands Privatization of Public Sector Enterprises (PSE)

One of the ways of globalization in India is disinvestment or privatization. Many PSEs are being sold off to the private sector with the objective of raising revenues to meet the fiscal deficits and to improve efficiency. Profit-making enterprises like BALCO have been privatized and soon NALCO will see the door. PSEs in the tribal belt were beneficial to tribals, giving them employment and livelihood. Now they are rendered jobless.

Destruction of Tribal Socio-cultural Life by Globalization

Maintenance of socio-cultural pluralism has been one of the cherished national goals of India. Diversity is our strength as a nation. The culture of the tribals over the years has attained distinctiveness by fostering a balance between nature and culture, egalitarianism in social structure, accommodative history, equal economic sharing, secularism in religious pursuits, a democratic political thinking and a people-oriented art and literature. These are marks of a truly viable modern culture.

TABLE 11.8: THE NUMBER OF PEOPLE DISPLACED DURING THE PERIOD 1991-5 IN JHARKHAND

Type of Project	STs	%	SCs	%	Others	%	Total
Water Resource	1,75,127	75.2	17,554	07.5	40,287	17.3	23,22,958
Industries/Quasi Industries	22,483	34.0	15,006	22.7	28,548	43.2	66,087
Mining: Coal	79,568	29.6	42,268	15.7	1,46,752	54.6	2,68,588
Mining: Non-coal	3,975	–	21,084	–	73,324	–	1,34,294
Defense Establishment	2,37,147	89.7	18,529	07.0	8,677	03.2	2,64,353
Wildlife Sanctuaries	80,867	15.8	87,601	17.1	3,39,266	66.5	5,09,918
Infrastructure development	13,800	27.6	5,900	11.8	30,300	60.6	50,000
Total	6,20,372		2,12,892		6,76,575		15,03,017

Source: Computed by Regional Theology College (RTC) Gyanodaya, Patna.

Globalization tries to eliminate this diversity of culture and language in favour of one language or culture in the name of the 'global village' credo. The prevailing tribal social and cultural patterns also get challenged. One's cultural identity can be best expressed in one's own language which is a carrier of the values of that culture. Hence, people who lose their language lose their identity as well. Elite tribals in many metropolitan cities have lost their culture and language. So is the case of migrant tribals in cities, thanks to economic deprivation effected through globalization. Thousands of tribal women are forced to seek low-paid employment as domestic help in several urban centres of India.

CONCLUSION

We have seen from the available data and the discussion above the extent of marginalization of the poor caused by globalization. Summing up, we see how badly globalization has impacted dalits and tribals in every aspect of their living and how if persisted, it will lead to their extinction. It is a great challenge to sort out the right remedy.

Globalization, contrary to the claims of its protagonists, has been a total failure even in generating growth and increasing productivity. It has created unprecedented inequality in every possible sphere. The poor people experience the ill-effects of globalization in the form of inflation, deindustrialization, casualization of labour, unemployment, worsening food security, growing inequality, depeasantization, destruction of environment and agriculture, suppression of democratic rights and pollution of culture.

David Rockefeller hoped that the free market forces were capable of transcending national boundaries to serve broad human interests. We are also often reminded that globalization builds a global village. And we were told that the 1990s would be years of economic recovery. Yet, the facts have betrayed such prophecies. In 1993, the profits for the 500 largest US manufacturing and service corporations grew 14 per cent but the benefits did not necessarily trickle down. The same companies cut back 10 per cent of their workforce despite the ongoing economic recovery! (David, 1998b: 38).

The former UN Secretary-General, Kofi Annan further pointed out that in the developing world as well, globalization is very far from having delivered all it has promised (David, 1998a: 26).

The benefits of globalization are not always apparent to the poor, the hungry and the illiterates. Over 60% of the world's population must subsist on $ 2 or less per day. A hundred of the world's countries are worse off today than they were 15 years ago. An increasing disparity between the rich and the poor countries remains a serious threat to stability and to long-term economic growth. (David, 1998a: 26)

This is indeed a very serious indictment! In fact, one can even ask whether globalization really benefits the poor and the marginalized—except perhaps on quite a long-term basis (David, 1998a: 26).

Globalization as implemented today is nothing but a new expression of the discarded dispensation theory which advocates the annihilation of the 'useless people for development'. It makes the rich, privileged consumers and sends the rest to slums or to prison. It treats the poor as disposable commodity. It has sacrificed the act of living, celebrating and conserving life in all its diversity—in people and in nature for the sake of progress in which the sanctity of life has been substituted by the sanctity of science and development. Globalization tells the dalits and tribals 'to buy or to die' because a human being is a consumer: 'I buy, therefore I exist'.

What could be a way out for the dalits and tribals? Even for positive discrimination in their favour, dalits and tribals need to unite with others in a common struggle against imperialism.

Concerned social scientists have suggested certain strategies to undo the ill-effects of globalization today. Critically oriented individuals and activists from various action groups, mass organizations, people's movements and political formations must acquire a theoretical understanding and analysis of the trends and impact of globalization on the people of India, its democratic traditions and sovereignty. They must develop a critical outlook, resist co-option and evolve alternative transformative strategies (Murickan, 1998: 12).

According to James David, we also have to think of globalization as the inevitable consequence of increased communications and contacts, and in its manifold cultural forms. In spite of all its pitfalls, we must therefore accept globalization, fight it, transform it where necessary, and make available its numerous potential benefits (David, 1998a: 26). It is true that globalization was, and is, disastrously used by the dominant Western powers to promote their vested interests. But Third World countries have to get better organized and put their case in a more convincing and forceful manner. The world must learn to evolve an equitable and dynamic strategy to deal with global trade and cash flows. It must learn to hold mutually enriching exchanges in the economic, political, ecological and cultural fields. All this is undoubtedly very difficult, but it is also historically imperative for the progress and even survival of the whole of humanity. Hopefully, the prevailing doctrine of the twenty-first century will not be capitalism, nor socialism, nor nationalism, but genuine and equitable globalization or globalism (David, 1998a: 27). This will probably be fostered by all those who believe in a Universal Civilization (truly based on the common good and other shared values, a global economy and a worldwide parliament), while cherishing all forms of legitimate diversities and pluralisms.

What may be suggested is a broad-based anti-globalization struggle which alone can shelter specific dalit and tribal interests as well as accomplish their emancipation.

REFERENCES

Baxla, F. (2003), 'Birsa and Freedom Struggle', in *Sevartham*, vol. 28.

Chathanatt, John (2000), 'Globalisation Virus: An Ethical Scanning', in *Third Millennium*, III (2000) 3, pp. 6-23.

David, James (1998a), 'Globalisation: Past, Present and Future', in James David and John Desrochers (eds.), *Dimensions of Globalisation*, Bangalore: Centre for Social Action.

———. (1998b), 'The Backlash Against Globalisation', in *Dimensions of Globalisation*, Bangalore: Centre for Social Action.

David, James and John Desrochers (eds). (1998), *Dimensions of Globalisation*, Bangalore: Centre for Social Action.

Dev, A. (ed.) (1996), *Human Rights: A Source Book*, New Delhi: National Council of Educational Research and Training.

Dietrich, Gabriele (1978), *Culture, Religion and Development*, Chennai: Centre for Social Action Publications.

Ekka, Alex and Mohammed Asif (2000), 'Development-induced Displacement and Rehabilitation', in *Jharkhand*, New Delhi: Indian Social Institute.

Fernandes, Walter and Anupama Dutta (1999), *Colonialism to Globalisation: Five Centuries After Vasco da Gama*, vol. 1, New Delhi: Indian Social Institute.

Jain, P. (2001), *Globalization and tribal Economy*, New Delhi: Rawat Publications.

Jha, Avinash (2000), *Background to Globalisation*, Mumbai: Centre for Education and Documentation.

Kurien, C. (1994), *Global Capitalism and the Indian Economy*, New Delhi: Orient Longman Limited.

Mahta, B.K. (2006), *Jharkhand: Ek Adhyayana*, Agra: Sahitya Bhawan Publication.

Michael, S.M. (2007), *Dalits in Modern India: Vision and Values*, New Delhi: Sage.

Muricken, Ajit (1998), 'Globalisation—Overview', in *Dimensions of Globalisation*, Bangalore: Centre for Social Action.

Pinto, Ambrose (1997), 'Dalits and Globalization', in *Integral Liberation*, September.

Raju, I. (1999), *Transnational Corporations as Agents of Dehumanization in Asia*, Delhi: ISPCK Publication.

Raju, Mohan J. (1999), *Transnational Corporations as Agents of Dehumanization in Asia*, Delhi: ISPCK.

Rawat, V.B. (2005), *Dalit Movement at the Cross Road*, countercurrents.org, August

Roy Choudhury, A. (1999), 'Globalisation and Accentuation of Inequalities', in *Social Action*, July-September, vol. 49, no. 3.

Samel, Swapna (2004), *Dalit Movement in South India (1857-1950)*, New Delhi: Serial Publications.

Shah, Ghanshyam (2004), *Social Movements in India*, New Delhi: Sage.

Teltumbde, Anand (2000), 'Impact of New Economic Reforms on Dalits in India', in P.G. Jogdand (ed), *New Economic Policy and Dalits*, New Delhi: Rawat Publishers.

Vanaik, Achin (1998), *Economic Globalisation: Myth or Reality?*, New Delhi: People's Publishing House.

Wilfred, Felix (2007), *Dalit Empowerment*, Bangalore: National Biblical Catechetical Liturgical Centre.

CHAPTER 12

Locating the Prospects of Dalits in the Era of Globalization

ASHISH SAXENA

THE BACKGROUND

Development involves complex processes and procedures of institutional changes and the redistribution of economic and political power for a more egalitarian society. It must be broadly conceived as the expansion of opportunities and the enhancement of human capacities. The reduction of mass poverty, unemployment and inequality are the concomitant of development so conceived. Indian state in the post-colonial period has assumed the role of an interventionist to bring about social transformation. Enactment of land reforms, reserved constituencies, adult franchise, Panchayati Raj Institutions (73rd Amendment) are considered to be vital agencies in bringing about structural transformation in the social and political framework, both at the regional and the national level. Social transformation, which calls for analysing social forces in the historical and cultural contexts, raises questions like—in which direction society

*Here dalit has been used in a broader sense as referred by Shah (2001) In a way, the word 'dalit' is of relatively recent origin of the 1960s. The word gained currency in public sphere during the SC-Caste Hindu riots in Bombay in the early 1970s. The Dalit Panthers, an organization of the SCs in Maharashtra, used the term to assert their identity for rights and self-respect. Later, the term has been used with a wider connotation. It includes all the oppressed sections of society—ST, landless and poor peasants, women and others. It does not confine itself merely to economic exploitation, it also relates to suppression of culture and more importantly, the denial of dignity. For some, it connotes an ideology for fundamental change in the social structure and relationship.

is transforming? What is the role of the state in bringing about transformation? Which are the dominant agents that set direction for transformation?

If we look at the development landscape of India, it has transformed from nation state sponsored politico-economic development to the present era of global economy and polity. India accepted the principle of planned growth after it became an independent nation. The five-year plans became the tools for development. Broadly speaking, the first seven five-year plans focused on industrialization and increasing agricultural production. The Nehruvian model of development was characterized by a highly interventionist state, which was supposed to radically transform the economy and society, but that intervention was still within the territory, or the nation state. The Eighth Plan that commenced in April 1992 saw the entry and adoption of words like New Economic Policy, Structural Adjustment Programme, liberalization, and privatization. These processes henceforth became the focal points of growth and development in India. Thus the early 1990s brought into being a resolution which broke the sacred barrier—it exposed India to the world market; it unleashed competition; it made Indian one of the world players.

But this restructuring was the felt need at the time; and it was inescapable (due to financial crisis arising from adverse balance of payment from March-September 1991). Presently, globalization is the most burning issue in social science, and it has gained prominence since the second half of the 1990s. The institutional innovations that globalization has introduced into society are: market, trade and finance, communication and media, science and technology, migration and inter-cultural transaction. Thus with the introduction of the free-market economy and globalization, there is the radical departure from the earlier models of development. In social-structural terms, globalization is a historical process of transition from the agrarian-industrial, post-industrial and finally the stage of the information society (Singh, 2000).

ABOUT THIS PAPER

The effect of globalization on Indian society has been felt since the 1990s. Gradually, Indians have started to feel the intensity of its effect. The effect of globalization on economy, media and sometimes on general society are almost regularly analysed and debated in various forums. Mahbub-ul-haq (1998) had warned back in 1998 that developing countries must learn to manage globalization in their best interest or they would get drowned by its cross-currents. If globalization were superimposed on a poorly educated and poorly trained labour force with poor governance and infrastructure, it would neither lead to growth nor reduce poverty. According to Kurian (1997: 122), globalization is not a remote experience or removed from the lives of the ordinary people of India. If foreign capital brings in new technology, it may either increase employment, or more likely reduce employment. New capital that comes in is likely to go into the production of goods that cater to the needs of those who have high purchasing power because the profits are likely to be higher in such spheres. This may create an impression that there is growth and prosperity, but the needs of the bulk of the population may be neglected. There will be no sense of accountability to the Indian people in this process. The local manufacturers and workers may be replaced. This is happening to the handloom weavers in different parts of India. Kurian also mentions that globalization usually benefits people who can play the game, but the chances are that the many who are resourceless, uneducated, and making a living through traditional production activities will come under various kinds of pressures. So he advises that we educate people about the nature and implications of globalization and its different impact on different sections of the Indian population. We also need to formulate popular strategies to influence state policies. He emphasizes the need to wipe out illiteracy, to develop educational facilities, and to train young people in skills needed in the globalized world.

Keeping in view the above cautions, the point of focus of the present paper is the implications of this paradigm shift for those who are weak, poor, marginalized and downtrodden (like Scheduled Castes). Can the Indian nation state tackle the 'social concerns' (welfare goals) of dalits in the globalization era? To put it differently, what would be the implication of globalization on eradication of social inequality and other forms of disparities (especially for dalits)? Would the globalization process protect and promote human rights of the dalits? In a nutshell what are the major implications of globalization for dalits in the Indian context?

It is presumed that globalization has dual implications for the dalits population, both negative and positive. Here I would like to follow the proponents of 'critical globalism' who take a neutral view of the globalization process. According to Scholte (1996: 53) 'globalization has often perpetuated poverty, widened material inequalities, increased ecological degradation, fragmented communities, marginalized subordinated groups, and deepened crisis of democracy; they also see that it has had a positive effect . . . various subordinated groups have grasped opportunities for global organization'. Before discussing the pros and cons of globalization, let us first try to understand the idea of globalization.

'GLOBALIZATION': A CONCEPTUAL ANALYSIS

Like so many concepts in social science, globalization is a word of lay language and everyday usage. The term used by Theodore Levitt in 1985, has today assumed variable shades of meaning and many connotations. But as a concept of social theory, globalization should have a precise meaning. It should be usable in empirical investigation and it should have a variety of possible applications. Although the understanding of globalization cannot be confined to one dimension and its conceptual delimitation is unmanageable, let us try to mention a few conceptual frameworks as given by various social scientists for getting acquainted with this phenomenon.

At the outset, to address the broadly defined parameters of globalization in its singular form, it might be useful to describe it as a historical and geographical condition. The characteristic features of this universal condition can be summarized as follows:

- It means increased political and military interdependence of a set of sovereign nation states and the expanded and strengthened set of organizations involved.
- It means the increased economic interdependence of a set of national or sub-national economies and their relevant multilateral as well as international public and private organizations.
- It means an expanded flow of individual persons among societies through socio-economic migration, travel and political expulsion. Here 'state' and 'individuals' are the subjects being discussed.
- Globalization means the expanded interdependence of expressive culture through intensified global communication.

To be accurate, let us observe the analysis of prominent social scientists on the issue. According to Giddens (1990: 64) globalization is the 'intensification of worldwide social relations which link distant localities in such a way that local happenings are shaped by events occurring many miles away and vice versa'. However, to Robertson (1992) globalization has been used in scholarly literature as a catch-all phrase to include an array of processes such as: time-space compression; technological commercial and cultural homogenization; and a general intensification of the consciousnesses of the world as a whole. In his simple explanation he speaks of globalization as a process by which the world is becoming more and more a 'single village'. Similarly, Alberto Martinelli (2003) conceptualizes globalization as a set of related processes which interconnect individuals, groups, communities, states, markets, corporations, international governmental and non-governmental organizations in complex web of social relations.

In a nutshell we may characterize globalization as following:

- First, economic globalization defined by both growing structural power and mobility of capital in production and financial markets is articulated with neo-liberal policies of privatization, deregulation and structural changes in national bureaucracies, welfare programmes and public services (Gill, 1995).
- Second, economic globalization, defined by the liberalization of trade and monetary policies, the growth of transnational networks of investment, finance, advertising and consumption market as well as rise of transnational networks (Strange, 1995).
- Third, conventional institutions such as the nation state, national military, police force, political parties, legislature now faces new challenges posted by this interactive, mobile transnational network (Held, 1991).
- Fourth, the rise of regional economic and political bodies as well as supranational bodies introduces new agents into the decision-making process with which the conventional centres of political power have to negotiate and contend.
- Fifth, the growing influence of electronic media in everyday life has the net affect of creating multiple forms of imagined communities (Anderson, 1992: 13).

Under such diversified ideas of universal and plural manifestation of globalization, Robertson (1995) rightly argues that the problem is not to choose one or the other, but rather to 'spell out the ways in which homogenizing and hetrogenizing tendencies are mutually implicative. The condition of globality facilitates the interaction between global and local forces, and it needs to be examined in concrete localities (Robertson, 1995: 27).

Now it may be clear from the above references why globalization should be taken in plural, as it involves a number of substantive social processes and more than one procedural dynamics. In brief, globalization is a multi-form, multi-faceted and multi-dimensional process.

'GLOBALIZATION' *VS* 'DALITS': THE EMERGENT POSSIBILITIES

Globalization is a complex phenomenon and process by which the world becomes a 'global village'. It affects different aspects of any country—economic, political, social, and religious. It is a concept used to convey a wide variety of processes, possibilities, and positions. It is, therefore, capable of being interpreted differently. Hence one cannot define one's response to it until the concept is adequately specified. The challenges posed by globalization to existing non-global forms of civic rights and collective action vary fundamentally along two axes with regard to position in the social structure and with location in the geography of globalization, i.e. context and space. Two questions—Who you are? Where you are?—make crucial differences and give very different grounds and possibilities of action.

Globalization can affect the social space of actors (here the SCs) from two angles: effect from the top, i.e. by directly changing their given social location in terms of consumerism, competition and development, or effect from below, i.e. by opening new avenues from rest of the world. Thus, globalization being a central driving force behind the rapid social, political and economic changes can reshape modern societies and world orders and no society can escape from its reach as it recasts traditional patterns, creates new hierarchies, and most crucially reshapes the power, functioning, authority and objective of nation states.

Regarding the implications of globalization on dalits, Vivek Kumar (2007: 327) rightly says that the dalit diaspora has used the internet to unite the dalit world over. There are about 51 sites which provide information about dalits in India and abroad. A few important ones are www.ambedkar.org, www.dalitusa.org, www.dalitstan.org, www.

dalitawaj.com, and www.dalitindia.com. Similarly dalits also run e-magazines like Dalit-International@yahoogroup.com, dalit@ambedkar.org, Buddhistcircle@yahoogroup.com. In general, we may say that globalization has enhanced the democratic space for dalit population.

Keeping in mind the above discussions, let us try to analyse the possible pessimistic (here dysfunctions) and optimistic (here functions) implications of the process of globalization on dalits of developing countries like India.

Dysfunctional Aspect of Globalization on Dalits

Globalization has had an adverse impact on all social groups, which have already been pushed down by centuries of oppression. It is a fact that in the last one decade the livelihood of dalit communities has become miserable. Under the old economic policies of the Indian government, dalits were given minimum protection and support in the field of education, land, capital and employment. Till the 1980s there was a visible growth and development among the dalits in these fields. One can observe decrease in unemployment, increase in wages and fall in poverty mainly due to high expenditure of the government on the welfare sector, particularly in the rural areas. However, in the present era of privatization, the state's indirect withdrawal ('disinvestment' from the public sector, huge cuts in welfare spending and privatizing of the services and work places) from 'welfare' of service sector people, particularly dalits, became vulnerable. Further the shift of decision-making power into the hands of transnational institutions like the WTO, IMF, WB and others has severely reduced the sovereignty of the national government and resulted in a very serious drift. In this context the struggle for dignity and social equity has to be the principal issue among dalits, so that they are well equipped to contribute from their perspective and experience to the struggle against globalization. The civil society groups working among the dalits are so overwhelmed by local issues that they hardly get to link the pressing issues of identity and dignity with the larger issues of globalization. This can be understood in terms of 'new social movements' at the global level. In all these processes many dalits on the one hand are losing their jobs in public sector industries and factories and on the other hand they are not able to find any new jobs in the 'open' market which is highly privatized and requires capital and specialized skills. Lack of reservations in the private sector debars dalits' entry into the competitive world. In this regard we find that the dalits are at the lowest end of the economic and social ladder and are quite obviously at the receiving end of the elitist culture promoted by globalization. Economically, the small gains made earlier through reservations have been, in essence, reversed; and socially the elitist culture (Hindutva) which marginalizes the poor generally will now have a double impact on dalits.

Teltumbde (1996) in this regard rightly says that

> In social terms however, all Dalits, irrespective of their economic standing, still suffer oppression. This social oppression varies from the crudest variety of untouchability, still being practiced in rural areas, to the sophisticated form of discrimination encountered even in the modern sectors of urban areas. Although the statistics indicate that Dalits have made a significant progress on almost all parameters during the five post-independence decades, the relative distance between them and the non-Dalits seem to have remained the same. More than 75% of the dalit workers are still connected with the land; 25% being the marginal and the balance over 50% are the landless labourers. Out of the total dalit population of 138 million, the number of Dalits in service falling in the domain of reservation does not exceed 1.1 million, a mere 0.8%. They are in the category of dual disabilities, i.e. socially and economically. The rate of growth of employment in the organized sector dropped from more than 1.7% per annum in the late 1980s to 1.2% in 1991-92 and to 0.6% in 1992-93. Thus these reforms had an adverse impact on different aspects.

Similarly S.K. Thorat (2002) in 'Newsletter Conference for ASF' said,

> The structural adjustment programme was reversing the economic policies of India that were built up as a result of the national movement. The Dalits were given special protection under the old economic policies in the fields of education, land, capital, employment etc. In the 70s and 80s there was a decrease in unemployment, increase in wages and a fall in poverty mainly due to high government expenditure in the rural areas. However, in the present era of privatization and withdrawal of the State, the unemployment especially among the scheduled castes has increased manifold. The Dalits are at a crossroads with the reversal of the minimum support policy of reservation affecting the working and health conditions of the marginalized.

Taking another dimension, Shiva (1998) said that

> The present process of globalization threatens to undermine aspects of agricultural policy. The transnational corporations (TNC) are not guided by

any philosophy of welfare of the marginalized. Liberalization emphasizes competition, efficiency and providing commodity for the market. Such an approach goes against the prevalent practice of poor farmers who produce for their own use and their methods are based on traditional wisdom. Land has been transferred to TNC's who produce luxury and non-food crops (cash crops) for export rather than staple food. There is also diversion of cereals from domestic market to export, resulting insecurity and inflation. The farmer's suffers from food insecurity as he has lost his land, resources and is unable to buy them from the market.

Contract farming, which is promoted as a part of globalization has had adverse effect on the farmers in general and rural dalits in particular. The contract made with illiterate farmers is one sided. Further traditional societies emphasize cooperation, harmony and accommodation, with personal relations being regulated *jajmani* and other caste-based systems. But globalism emphasizes on efficiency and competition. Thus it appears that for the majority of 'dalit' and poor, globalization has meant further deprivation. Singh (2000) too agrees with the above comment and adds that markets are the vital mechanisms through which globalization extends its reach. Some of its effect upon the regional culture may be modernizing but there are significant areas where it has a disruptive influence upon the local cultures. It has not only disrupted the autonomy of folk cultures, but also destabilized the life of artisans by creating a new network of competition and price war. In Indian context, the social costs of economic globalization and the neo-liberal policies related to it have already been very high. The dalits, the landless, the *adivasis* will be the worst hit. Besides this economic reversal, the process of economic globalization has created a serious challenge for the democratic decision-making processes. In political terms the process of globalization has triggered off forces of change which have set people rethinking about the political institutions under the growing forces of globalization (Kothari, 1995).

The Vikas Adhyayan Kendra (VAK) report in 1997 brings out many realities of India. For example, the reduction of fertilizer subsidies has most severely affected the marginal peasants who cannot afford the higher prices. Agricultural as well as industrial unemployment has increased, especially in the rural areas. The mechanization of agriculture through use of tractors and harvesters displaces labour. So the workers will sell their labour power cheaply. Migrant labour is also increasingly used. Unemployed *adivasis*, dalits, and OBCs are given small advances during lean periods and are then compelled to work as seasonal migrants at very low wages. Thus nearly 8,00,000 cane harvesters from all over Marathwada are employed as an army of semi-bonded labourers by sugar factories. Thus bonded labour is the outcome of globalization.

Relying and quoting from relevant data from website of peoplesmarch.com, let us specifically analyse the impact of globalization on the status of dalits in different spheres of life as mentioned below:

(i) *Impact on Workers/Labourers*

As per Peoples March Group analysis more than 75 per cent of the dalit workers are still connected with land, only 25 per cent of which are marginal and small farmers, while the balance is landless labourers. It was found that at all-India level (1999-2000) about 41 per cent of all rural labour households owned some land, by the proportion of SC rural household passing land was only 34 per cent. In the urban areas, they work mainly in the unorganized sector. As per the Rural Labour Enquiry Report of 1987-8, over 63.14 per cent of the total rural households were wage labour households as compared to 31.16 per cent for others. In the same year, half of the dalit population was below the poverty line as against 39.06 per cent for others. The incidence of poverty was 55.12 per cent for the neo-Buddhists among them. It was 60.5 and 50 per cent for agriculture labourers and for the non-agriculture labourers, respectively.

In the urban areas, the poverty ratio among dalits was higher at 57 per cent as compared to 37.21 per cent among the non-dalits. It was as high as 73.45 per cent among the casual labourers and 87.23 per cent for the neo-Buddhists in the urban areas. On the other hand, in the rural agrarian sector, dalit farmers, cultivators and wage labourers are facing exclusion from their fields. At one level the government itself denies dalits access to land by not distributing the surplus lands as promised in the Land Reform Acts. In a state like Andhra Pradesh which has a 'perfect' Land Reform Act, 16 lakh acres of surplus lands identified lies undistributed. The situation is not different in other parts of the country. This clearly reflects the miserable condition of all categories of dalit workers.

(ii) *Impact on Dalits in the Economic Sphere*

The economic dimension of India can be seen through agriculture land and related issues. In the Indian situation as the bulk of dalits are without land, land reform is a key solution for their development.

Here globalization has not only eclipsed this agenda of land reforms but it has substituted it with corporatization of farming for the global agricultural market. The thrust of the WB–IMF–WTO combine has always been clearly for the abolition of the land ceiling laws for liberalizing investment in agriculture. Land reform has openly been opposed. If we see the situation of dalits in agriculture we find that they will not be immediate beneficiaries. According to Haq (1998), diversification of small farms is often suggested as a means for rapid rural development in India. He emphasized on the need for commercialization and diversification of small farms within and outside agriculture and their proper integration with local and global markets. This is intended not only to liberate the small and marginal farmers from the poverty trap, but also to meet the country's growing demand for fruits, vegetables, milk and milk products, meat, fish, eggs, and so on, which generally show rising trends with increasing levels of per capita income in the economy. However, the moot question today is how do we achieve the goal of diversification of small farms by overcoming various technological, infrastructural, institutional and policy constraints. The agricultural census data as well as various micro-level studies conducted in different regions indicate that the small and marginal farms adopt diversified farming, despite very limited space and low sizes of holdings. Further it is the affluent categories of farmers mainly who are going in for diversified farming and not the dalits in majority. Thus we have to improve the over all structure of the society to attain the justified fruits of globalization.

This relationship cannot be altered till the dalits get land. Thus, what impact would the new regime have on the socio-economic setting of Indian villages? Can the new regime afford the economic empowerment of the dalits? Can it, for instance, grant them land? The answer to all these questions will be in negative. Instead of talking about land reforms, the new regime will promote depeasantization of Indian agriculture and consolidation of their holdings to start corporate farming. Thus the privatization and free market components of the reforms are certainly affecting adversely the livelihoods of dalits. The impact of the reforms has already made the dalit society more insecure and no doubt it will uproot the entire community if we allow things to continue in the same fashion.

(iii) *Impact on Dalit Education*

As a result of the various reform movements and particularly because of Ambedkar's role, many dalits took to education. This is now negated under globalization. In the context of globalization the education system is exclusively shaped by economics, particularly in responding to market needs. The *New Policy Framework for Reforms in Education*, 24 April 2004 drafted by a committee (of PM's Council on Trade and Industry constituted as a special subject group on policy framework for private investment in education, health and rural development) convened by Mukesh Ambani with Kumarmangalam Birla as members, seeks to drive privatization and introduce rampant commercialization of higher education along the lines of the USA. It envisages foreign direct investment in education, progressive reduction of government funding for universities and making them adopt the route of self-sufficiency, and concurrent development of a credit market for private finance to meet the cost of higher education. The latter is a clear smoke screen to diffuse the elitist intentions, as everyone knows that more than half the population of this country is not creditworthy. Higher education, thus, is to be entirely market oriented and clearly out of bounds of the commoners, not to talk of dalits. The commercial ethos that has entered the education field through globalization has further created a divide between the haves and have-nots. The 'pay seats' in the educational institutions have fortified the class basis of education. Dalits who have barely been able to afford schooling with the aid of freeships and scholarships are now being squeezed from both ends. Firstly, education has become increasingly inaccessible and unaffordable to them. Even if they persist with it, they have to face several hurdles on the way to getting education that would get them gainful employment. The increasing opportunity cost of schooling is dissuading many dalits from education resulting in increasing numbers of dropouts. Even if they crossed all the hurdles as an exception, they would face a far bigger hurdle in the job market that tends to value family background more than scholastic performance.

The general population is facing the horrors of unemployment and this will be more deeply felt by the dalits. In the market economy, education is a saleable commodity. After liberalization all the educational institutions including universities, IIMs and IITs, have suddenly turned into *gurukulas* of Hindu age, where there is no entry for dalits. All the higher education institutions are showing 'budget cuts' and 'fund crunch' as a reason and raising their fees, which is not affordable to any dalit. Further, in this era of globalization there is a gap between natural language and the language of technology (through computers). In the formal sector of education, literacy in the mother tongue is losing value in the context of demand for English and computer literacy. One can imagine the level and medium of education that the dalits are getting today and how difficult it must be for them to overcome such hurdles.

(iv) *Impact on Employment of Dalits*

In the sphere of jobs the privatization of the public sector and the massive retrenchment of government jobs makes the question of reservation in the sphere of jobs irrelevant. As the private sector has no job reservation policy, the job opportunities that had been available to dalits during the past three decades will now totally dry up. Unfortunately, some intellectuals are giving a very rosy picture of globalization and constructing castles in the air, as if privatization is readily accommodating every dalit. The convent-educated, urban-oriented, second-generation intellectuals talk about 'new opportunities, new openings, and new environment', but it is a fact that there is no new wine in the age-old bottle. Dalits should understand the caste–class relation of capital. Liberalization is neither liberal to encourage dalits into 'new openings' nor strong enough to break the caste domination of the Indian employment market. In addition, the government, which has been systematically cutting expenditure on people's welfare, has also cut its expenditure on SCs and STs. The outlay for SC, ST and OBC welfare has declined from 8 per cent in 1990-1 to 6.7 per cent in 1994-5. Thus the dalits have tough times ahead in the field of employment.

(v) *Social Impact on Dalits*

Caste has often been viewed as the defining feature of the 'traditional social order' of India. Dalits in contemporary India bear the anguished burden of a long unbroken legacy of the deepest social degradation. They usually fall at the bottom of almost any parameter relating to economic well-being or quality of life. Starting from *achhut* (untouchable) to 'Harijan' they have fallen into the category of SCs after Independence. But from the 1970s, the term 'dalit' has become increasingly popular, with its connotation of active anger, assertion and pride. The word 'dalit' literally means poor and oppressed persons. It not only includes SCs but also includes tribals, woman, bonded labourers, minorities, and so on. As mentioned earlier, for the purpose of this paper, we will confine our usage to the popular interpretation of term as SC. 'Dalits' were placed right at the bottom of the social structure, below the ritually sanctioned 'line of pollution'. In terms of location in the global geography they are placed under the category of developing nations.

Parallel to this issue, Beteille (2000) has rightly said that while ideologically caste has considerably weakened and the older form of untouchability is receding, atrocities committed against dalits by the local dominant castes have in fact increased. This is supported by Thorat's (2002: 572) study that says that in rural areas the social behaviour of the high caste Hindus is still governed by norms and codes of the traditional caste system. Even the incident of Chakwara village in Jaipur where assertive dalit men and women along with human rights groups organized a two-day march to protest against the continuing social and economic boycott of Bairwa community of dalit on 22 September 2002 who were deried access to the water tank and temple and excluded from general communication interaction. While in another incident related to the Hindu social order, an ordinance was passed by the state government of Tamil Naidu to check proselytization. This is an attempt to retain dalits in the Hindu order, help the upper castes retain their majority and continue with their political manipulations. The sixth report of the commissioner of SCs and STs, 1990-2000 and 2000-1 lists 23,742 cases of atrocities against dalits in the year 2000 alone. It thus becomes evident that despite the constitutional safeguard, liberalization, globalization and saffronization of dalits, atrocities against them continue unabated.

The above analysis suggests that still the space of dalits is graded lower with respect to local and global network. It is assumed that in the era of global network of exchange, there will be one-way transmission of goods and services, i.e. the developed countries will be the transmitters of services and the developing countries will be the acceptors. This will cause elements of the dominant cultures of Europe and the United States to penetrate the urban and rural areas of India and lead to further inequality.

In brief, we see that dalits too are victims of globalization in various sphere of life and so they too constitute an important force in the anti-globalization, anti-imperialist struggle in the country. We may in brief say that the major social concerns of dalits in the era of globalization are massive structural unemployment, greater employment instability, lower wage rates and casualization of labour. There is a need to look into these issues because it is the oppressed who are going to loose the most because of globalization. However, there is always the other face of the coin, the brighter aspects of globalization that the dalits can look forward to.

FUNCTIONAL ASPECT OF GLOBALIZATION

In principle, the process of globalization ultimately leads towards homogenization of world culture. To quote Hannerz (1996: 17) 'In the most general sense, globalization is a matter of increasing long-distance interconnectedness, at least across national boundaries, preferably between continents as well.' We can say that these processes of linkages across borders include a restructuration of spaces for 'dalits', leading to the disappearance of fixed links of them to villages, towns and national frontiers. In this regard, Waters (1995: 136) points out that the process of globalization specifies greater connectedness and de-territorialization simultaneously. If we look at it in positive terms then it tries to break the barriers, i.e. de-capsulization of communities and identities. In the longer run this may lead to disappearance of inequalities, because it is not possible for an ethnic identity to survive without a specific territory or place. This situation will have a positive impact on the people who are marginalized as against the dominating categories in specific territories. In this framework it may be perceived as a welcoming process for the dalits, as it will not only put them out of the hands of the high castes but also ensure they get a fair scope for economic empowerment and social mobility which they can't get in the earlier stratified system. Further, globalization policies will increase free flow in the international market of labour, goods, ideas and capital. Quoting Deliege (1999), one can say that 'today in this global world Dalits aspire to more comfortable material circumstances and demand more dignity'. This global/international mobilization will provide the dalits the opportunity for global solidarity and for upholding human rights. In this regard, Jogdand (2000) has rightly argued that the much cherished principle of growth with justice, social responsibility, accountability, equity and self-reliance have been rendered obsolete with the new slogan of liberalization and globalization. Here, Buell's (1994) arguments stand valid that 'Tighter integration (due to globalization) has thus paradoxically meant, and continues to mean, proliferation of asserted differences'. To add, Mendelsohn and Vicziany (1998: 1) too point out that dalits will almost everywhere become much more assertive about their human and political rights. An example to support the argument is the establishment of organizations like the World Social Forum (WSF) and specifically the Asia Social Forum (ASF), which provide advocacy on issues regarding neo-liberal globalization and its impact on discriminated communities. To quote Vivek Kumar (2007: 326) on the issue of dalit diaspora and social solidarity

> Dalits settled abroad did not remain aloof from each other. . . . They created their own organizations to develop social solidarity with different Dalit communities. . . . The Federation of Ambedakarite Buddhist Organisations (FABO) and Voice of Dalit International (VODI) are also working in UK to uplift Dalits back in India. . . . A more organized effort came in the US from literate NRI Dalits when they formed Volunteers in Service to India's Oppressed and Neglected (VISION) in 1975.

If we try to put the above discourse on the measuring scale, we may arrive at the conclusion that globalization is worse for dalits but one can't negate the brighter side of the picture. As 'critical' globalism we should welcome the mixed impact of globalization on the dalits. Further, the pathetic condition of dalits in contemporary society can be supported by the fact that quantitative and politico-economic changes are observed and implemented rapidly in comparison to qualitative changes, and assimilation and adaptation take time. Individually, the Indian society has to fight the problems of poverty, illiteracy, cultural oppression and ethnicity that are deep rooted in the society and impede the growth of new development. For imbibing and continuing globalization one has to be really global in personality terms so that he/she can reap the benefits of globalization in the true sense.

CONCLUSION

Globalization is the intensification of worldwide social relations which links distant localities in such a way that local happenings are shaped by events occurring many miles away and vice versa. Indigenous or local groups will suddenly find themselves being catapulted from their traditional ways of life into tension and conflict, both within their own group and in their interaction with other superior groups at the global level. Sociologically, globalization may be understood as a process of 'universalization' whereby the parochial elements disappear. In utopian sense it may lead to a stage when society will be more or less homogenized and where there will be no outsiders (as territories breaks down) and everyone will share similar norms. It may bring more transparency, de-territoralization and homogenization in which the concept of private or ethnic belongingness will be marginalized.

Globalization depicts both manifest and latent functions of the society. Economic liberation is observed as the manifest consequence but it may lead to several latent consequences like decline of nation states, threat to cultural identity, uniqueness, and so on. With reference to dalits it may show differential impact. In optimistic terms the process involves tremendous exposure of local and regional entities to a new orientation. It enhances the consciousness of these identities at the global level. It orients them to the forces of market and finance on one hand, and on the other side access to revolutionary means of communication and media. Thus instead of being a threat to such identities, it may become a means for their identity construction. By appropriating strategies of representation, organization and social change through access to global system, local communities and marginal interest groups can both empower themselves and influence the global system. In this sense, the appropriation of global forms of culture may free one from local forms of dominance and oppression or at least provide the tool for a different kind of identity formation. Further we can perceive the process of global village or single village through the process of globalization in terms of an ideal village-community, where informal flow of information is very rapid. We can interpret that in the era of globalization, information flow will be rapid and everybody will be aware of every event or happening in any corner of the world. For instance, if the dalits are being oppressed in any corner, there will be rapid flow of information and this will result into their association and coalition at the global level and the concerned interventionist, for example, the ASF may find a quick remedy for the situation. Further, we can't deny the role of the dalit diaspora, which can aid and support the native dalits from a distance. At the end we may say that the dalits in collaboration, with the Media, NGOs and civil society can transform their fate in the globalized world.

REFERENCES

Anderson, B. (1992), 'The New World Disorder', *New Left Review*, no. 93, 13.

Beteille, A. (2000), 'The Scheduled Caste: An Inter-regional Perspective', *Journal of Indian Schools of Political Economy*, vol. XIII, 34.

Buell, Frederick (1994), *National Culture and the New Global System*, Baltimore, London: Johns Hopkins University Press.

Deliege, R. (1999), *The Untouchables of Hindu Organization*, New York: Berg Press.

Giddens, A. (1990), *Consequences of Modernity*, Stanford: Stanford University Press.

Gill, S. (1995), 'Knowledge, Politics and Neo-liberal Economy', in R. Stubbs and G.R. Underhill (eds.), *Political Economy and the Changing Global Order*, Fernwood: Halifax.

Hannerz, Ulf (1996), *Transnational Connection: Cultures, People, Places*, London: Routledge.

Held, D. (1991), 'Democracy, the Nation-State and the Global System', in D. Held (eds.), *Political Theory Today*, Cambridge: Polity Press.

Jogdand, P.G. (2000), *New Economic Policy and Dalits*, New Delhi: Rawat Publications.

Kothari, R. (1995), 'Globalization and Revival of Tradition: Dual Attack on Models of Democratic Nation Building', *Economic and Political Weekly*, 25 March.

Kumar, Vivek (2007), 'Governance and Development in the Era of Globalisation: Understanding Exclusion and Assertion of Dalits in India', in Kameshwar Choudhary (ed.), *Globalisation, Governance Reforms and Development in India*, Delhi: Sage.

Kurian, C.T. (1997), 'Globalization—What is it About?' *Integral Liberation*, vol. 1, no. 3, September, pp. 122-40.

Mahbub-ul-haq (1998), Quoted in 'Foreword' by Khadija Haq in *Report on Human Development in South Asia 2001: Globalization and Human Development*, New York: Oxford University Press.

Martinelli, A. (2003), 'Market, Government, Communities and Global Governance', in *International Sociology*, vol. 18 (2).

Mendelsohn O. and M. Vicziany (1998), *The Untouchables: Subordinates, Poverty and the State in Modern India*, Cambridge: University Press.

NCDHR (National Campaign on Dalit Human Rights) (2003), 'Swadhikar Rally', *Newsletter*, 4-5.

Robertson, R. (1992), *Globalization: Social Theory and Global Culture*, London: Sage.

——— (1995), 'Glocalization: Time-space and Homogeneity', in M. Featherstone (ed.), *Global Modernities*, London: Sage.

Scholte, J.A. (1996), *Beyond the Buzzword: Towards a Critical Theory of Globalization: Theory and Practice*, London: Pinter Press.

Shah, Ghanshyam (2001), *Dalit Identity and Politics*, New Delhi: Sage, p. 17.

Shiva, V. (1998), *Globalization of Agriculture, Food Security and Sustainabilities*, New Delhi: Research Foundation for Science and Technology.

Singh, Y. (2000), *Culture Change in India: Identity and Globalization*, New Delhi: Rawat Publication.

Strange, S. (1995), 'The Limits & Politics', *Government & Opposition*, no. 30 (3).

Teltumbde, A. (1996), 'Impact of New Economic Reforms on Dalits in India' Paper presented in the seminar 'Economic Reforms and Dalit in India', University of Oxford, 8 November.

Therborn, G. (2000), 'From the Universal to the Global', *International Sociology*, vol. 15, no. 2, p. 149.

Throats, S.K. (2002), 'Oppression and Denial: Dalit Discrimination in the 1990s', *Economic and Political Weekly*, vol. XXXVII, no. 6.

Waters, Malcolm (1995), *Globalization*, London: R&KP.

People March websites link http// www.peoplesmarch.com/publications/ globalisation/Chapter 14, 2003.

Vikas Adhyayan Kendra website link http://www.vakindia.org/index.html, 1997.

CHAPTER 13

Social Exclusion and Marginalization of Poor among Tribals in Village Democracy

D.C. SAH

INTRODUCTION

Rapid agricultural growth—despite the falling share of agriculture in the GDP— still fascinates the imagination of researchers and policy makers in India.[1] Agricultural growth, along with some other measures, reduced rural poverty[2] from over 57 per cent in the early 1970s to less than 26 per cent in 1999-2000. The growth strategy in the last half a decade has revolved around high farm-gate prices to producers and low prices to consumers; high subsidy to farmers for fertilizers, irrigation and power; market controls in the form of levies on sugar and rice; and controls on storage, transport and credit. As tribals have remained untouched by this growth strategy, poverty in these areas is still very high at it about 50 per cent (Sah, 2007a). The important question is whether state withdrawal, due to liberalization, shall have any impact on the tribals. It is argued that the exclusion of tribals from agricultural technology, markets, and social sector investment is absolute. This, along with growing dissent against their marginalization would result in a process where decision-making in village democracy will be controlled by a small elite group.

After Independence, three important processes have brought considerable change in constitutive ideas and behavioural expectations of tribals of south-western Madhya Pradesh. Factors like development interventions by state, political decentralization and seasonal migration have influenced the tribals' social and economic outlook. In order to appreciate the struggles between continuity and change, each of these processes has to be located within the cultural construct that tribals employ to interpret them. Development for tribals brings, in its train, images of large projects, displacement and associated hardship.[3] Otherwise, large sections of the tribals have missed the fruits of post-Independence development interventions, which have been poor in terms of both coverage and quality. Except elementary education and public distribution system (PDS), other amenities like access to electricity, all-weather roads, health services, drinking water and sanitation, irrigation, agricultural extension and rural cooperatives, are poor. In fact, their remoteness to administration and civil society institutions is overriding enough not to allow these facilities to reach the needy areas. What has, however, reached them is the fear of displacement due to development projects and the administrative insensitivity that accompanies them. Presence of administration—in the form of police, forest and revenue officials—is synonymous with corruption, repression and exploitation.[4] The experiences of development in tribal consciousness have left behind a trail of mistrust towards non-tribals, caution and apathy towards state interventions, and loss of land and natural resources for the tribals.

Change in the form of technologically-driven agriculture, though restricted to a small subset of area, is not entirely an outcome of state intervention either. It happened because of seasonal migration. Seasonal migration for tribals is not coping with scarcity alone;[5] it is experiencing development that has by-passed them.[6] What a migrating tribal learns during his stay as a labourer either on irrigated farms of *Nimar* plains or on the farms of irrigated HB cotton growers of Khandesh or on the fields of irrigated paddy and sugar cane growers in south Gujarat is a main source of agriculture technology transfer. How to energize the well and distribute water, how to grow irrigated fertilizer-responsive cotton, soyabean and wheat, and utilization of post-harvest technology of these market-oriented crops is learnt during seasonal migration. No matter how much the Adivasi Mukti Sangathan (AMS) discredits it, this process of production of knowledge is creating space for non-tribal institutions that is inducing conversion of subsistence way of agriculture to a market driven agriculture.[7] This process is internalized without any state support. In irrigated areas, the *bania* is providing agricultural credit without any security. The tribals are also able to repay the loans promptly, at least during good agricultural years. But in the process, tribals have started attaching a high degree of dependence on non-tribal institutions they loathed the most, the *market*. This is an ideological contradiction that is the handiwork of modernity. This emerging consciousness about technological change, along with conditions of larger tracks of poor quality of land, produced a feeling in which the *bania* finds that land as a source of exploitation is not as remunerative for the money-lending business as it used to be during pre-Independence years.

The third important process that is imprinting the tribal consciousness is the process of decentralized governance. The logic of decentralized governance is to bring decision-making nearer to the masses. In the last eight years of its working in the region, decentralization has brought about considerable transformation. Traditional leadership and its social dominance have given way to elected leadership; many a role that the village *Patel* used to play have become redundant with the identity of the *Patel* being subsumed in the position of *sarpanch*. But when *Patels* are unable to establish themselves as elected leaders, especially in multi-village panchayats, decentralization has become a ground where traditional ideology would assert to re-establish itself. This has resulted in divides and fractions in village polity. Social interests that used to be supreme are giving way to economic interests. Generation divide has sharpened with older people being sceptical of all economic changes, whereas the younger generation is receptive and adaptive to interventions and economic changes. Both sides with their experiences—marginalization and exploitation *versus* modernity and economic affluence—have stood to their ideological stand. But the divide is apparent.[8] Both the agents, the *Patels* with their social power as well as the elected representatives with their political influence and reach up to the high echelons of administration, are playing their respective roles. Changes are accepted slowly in tribal society and with caution.

The above discussion clearly reveals that tribal society is as stratified on political and economic lines as non-tribal society. It becomes pertinent to explore whether a group among tribals is systemically excluded from state policies, programmes and economic and political institutions. If so, it would be worth understanding the implications of marginalization and exclusion in the decision-making for development. The paper argues that the lack of formal institutional structure and lack of development have not discouraged the formation of social capital [9] in this region. The recently acquired awareness—with the help of the civil society—has strengthened the social network's capabilities in terms of associational activities, trust among the social groups and individuals, and collective actions for shared goals. The social capital in this tribal region manifests itself through social hierarchy and moves to the political domain, though with varying intensity. In relatively less remote areas, the stratifications created by political and economic processes have displaced the social hierarchy. But in remote rural areas where the economic hierarchy is fragile and gets reshuffled within a short span,[10] the social elites get an upper hand even in non-social affairs. While the bonding social capital helps in fighting the crisis (like draught, crop failure, sickness, migration, dealing with outsider, etc., the bridging social capital when manifested brings economic opportunities to individuals. In remote tribal areas, the well-to-do are able to develop these bridges and control development decision-making at the grassroots level.

This study is based on both qualitative and quantitative data from three predominantly tribal villages in Badwani district of Madhya Pradesh. The qualitative data[11] is collected from villages Kirchali and Pospur whereas the quantitative data is generated from Kirchali and Chikalkuan.[12] The paper is divided into four sections, including this introduction. The second section reviews tribal marginalization, exclusion and dissent that helped the dormant social capital to manifest. The third section presents the creation and manifestation of social capital in this tribal belt as well as the role played by bridging social capital in village development and decision-making. The last section presents conclusions based on the major issues discussed in the paper.

MARGINALIZATION, EXCLUSION AND DISSENT

Tribal marginalization is not a new phenomenon; historically, the British and their interest in the forests started it. In the process, tribals were increasingly excluded from the forest and their customary use rights were restricted. Even after Independence, the situation of the tribals did not improve. The pattern of development adopted is responsible for fundamentally altering three crucial bases of tribal livelihood: water, land and forest. Development, environmental sustainability and governance have different meanings for the tribals and the state. This mismatch in the definition is contested by everyday practices; violent sometimes but in more sublime ways bring out the contradictions of state actions relating to access to natural resources. State, as the authority of development, rationalizes its action through projects of national interest and through interventions that rest on obsolete modes of land acquisition, which makes the tribals all the more powerless. The struggles against the state are placed within the discourse of ecology and development as is the case with the Narmada Bachao Andolan (NBA) or are located against state's force and repression as in the case of the AMS. These struggles are able to mobilize the tribals of the region. The success of these initiatives is, however, mixed in terms of weakening of state repression and bringing transparency in development initiatives.

A critical analysis of tribal mobilization by NBA and AMS (Sah, 2007) reveals that these movements were able to create awareness about state repression among the tribals of south-western Madhya Pradesh. The effect of the two agencies within the tribal community of *Nimar* has been binding. The campaigns helped in intensifying the dormant social capital in the form of closer ties between the communities, despite serious economic differences within the community. Within this scenario, it will be worth appreciating the extent of stratifications in the society and social exclusion within the tribal community. For, the economic and political hierarchies are crucial agencies in the political economy of decentralized governance. Although both the study villages (Pospur and Kirchali) are independent parts of group panchayats, political leadership in both locations is highly corrupt. What really differs between the two is the nature of economic stratification: while the remote Pospur is economically homogeneous, the less remote Kirchali is highly stratified on economic lines.

ECONOMIC AND POLITICAL HIERARCHIES

Economic stratification in Kirchali is well-developed and visible when one moves in the village during the early *rabi* season. The 200+ household-village looks deserted and unmanned, except for about 30 households that are engaged in wheat and gram cultivation; pre-sowing irrigation and sowing of crops are the major activities that engage some of the family members. These households have perennial source of irrigation, obtained at a very high cost and risk. Kirchali is an un-electrified village enclosed from two sides by Ramkula and Surana villages that have electric connections. Individual initiatives have resulted in intensive investment in irrigation and energizing the farms in order to reap economic gains. Two families—the Patels and the Bhagats—took the early initiatives in investment in agriculture in Kirchali. They have strong political clout and could get cheap institutional credit for the risky agricultural investment of digging wells and energizing them. Demonstration of economic gains attracted others to come forward for such an investment; a substantial investment is involved in such transfer of agricultural technology that includes digging wells in rocky terrain, drawing electricity line from some distance, investment in new seed varieties and yield-increasing fertilizers. All the money needed for this has to be borrowed at a high interest and sizeable risk.[13]

The risk involved in the digging of a well in Kirchali is high. But economic incentives in the form of cropping pattern changes and increase in yields keep the desire alive to invest. Half of the wells in Kirchali provide water only up to November. The perceptions on size and certainty of economic gains of investment attract new entrepreneurs; as such, there are individual attempts to draw electricity even from a distribution point that lies 2 km away.

The community in Kirchali is stratified on economic lines; there are about 25 wealthy families with perennial irrigation while 100 poor households have less land and no irrigation facility. The middle group constitutes of farmers of average size of land. Each group has its own agenda; the rich want cheap labour, modern yield-increasing inputs and investment so that their agricultural income is protected. The poor, on the other hand, want employment and labour opportunities nearby so that they don't need to migrate.

Such economic stratification has not yet developed in Pospur. The failure of irrigation well is very high in Pospur, and its implications—repayment of loan to *bania* at an exorbitant interest rate—are disastrous. Consequently, there are only a few irrigated farms in Pospur; largely, the economic homogeneity of the community is undisturbed.

POVERTY AND SOCIAL EXCLUSION

In a community like the tribals of south-western Madhya Pradesh, where a sizeable population lives in poverty, it becomes important to recognize that movements in and out of poverty are associated with access to economic opportunities. But chronic nature of poverty[14] may be associated with social exclusion of the poor as a group from public services and economic and political institutions. Investigating social exclusion in its analytical form assumes significance because it makes disparities visible. This not only ensures possibility to reach the excluded groups but also curb tendencies of violent dissents.

Despite all-round claims of the state, a significant proportion of the poor in south-western tribal Madhya Pradesh continues to experience exclusion from necessities. Chronic poor are three times more likely to be excluded from literacy drives than others are. As a result, the opportunities for education have been seized by the non-poor (Table 13.1). Also, the poor ignore their sickness and are able to bear only a third of the expenses for health care compared to the non-poor. Their exclusion from health care services is indicative of the meagre accessibility of these services to poor households. Failure to access land and labour market forces a sizeable proportion of labour to remain surplus among the poor than the non-poor. Consequently, chronic poor are twice more likely to be migrants compared to other households; in this process, they remain disconnected from the bulk of social, economic and political institutions. Access to the PDS is dismally low, and an insignificant proportion of cereal consumption of poor is supported by PDS supplies. Nor the benefits from state programme and schemes like Sampurn Gramin Rojgar Yojna (SGRY), Swarn Jayanti Gramin Swa-

TABLE 13.1: POVERTY AND SOCIAL EXCLUSION AMONG TRIBALS

Factor	Income Poverty		Chronic Poverty		Interaction with Remoteness	Nature of the Role of Remoteness in Explaining Chronic Poverty
	χ^2	Odd ratio	χ^2	Odd ratio		
Asset	6.5*	2.8	5.1**	3.3	Significant	Higher assets in less-remote areas significantly reduces chronic poverty than in remote areas
GCA	6.5**	2.5	NS	1	NS	–
Irrigation	6.8**	3.0	6.8**	5.0	Significant	No irrigation in remote areas significantly increases chronic poverty than in less-remote areas
Agricultural production	7.7*	2.5	5.6*	2.5	Significant	Production growth in remote areas significantly reduces chronic poverty than less-remote areas
Labour in village	NS	1	NS	1	NS	–
Family size	45*	0.41	NS	1	NS	–

Years of existence	NS	1	NS	1	NS	–
Literacy	9.2**	3.0	4.7*	3.3	Pure relation	Higher literacy rates in both remote and less-remote areas reduce chronic poverty
Agricultural debt	NS	1	6.8**	0.07	Significant	Higher debt in remote areas increases chronic poverty significantly more as compared to less-remote areas
Other debt	NS	1	NS	1	NS	–
Migration	4.25*	0.5	4.9*	0.5	Significant	Chronic poor in remote areas are more likely to migrate as compared to less-remote areas
Panchayat benefits	NS	1	NS	1	NS	–
PDS dependence	NS	1	NS	1	NS	–
Organization membership	NS	1	NS	1	NS	–
Sickness Expenses	12**	0.3	NS	1	NS	–
Remoteness	NS	1	4.8**	3.3	See next column	

Source: Sah and Bhatt (2004).

Notes: 1. NS: Not significant. Significance level: 10%*, 5% ** and 1% ***

2. Odd ratio of being economically poor.
3. Odd ratio of being chronic poor.
4. Odd ratio of an event is the probability it occurs divided by the probability it does not occur.

If odd ratio = 1 than probability of even taking place is same

If odd ratio > 1 than probability of event taking place is relatively more than not taking place, and vise versa.

In a 2 × 2 contingency table

	poor	not-poor
Rural	26	74
Urban	56	44

Odd of urban poor rather not = 26/74 = 0.35

Odd of rural poor rather not = 56/44 = 1.27

Odd ratio = .35/1.35 = .259

The probability of being poor rather not in urban area is .36 times that of being poor in rural areas.

Alternatively, 1/.359 = 3.86. This can be interpreted as: the probability of being poor rather than not in rural areas is 3.86 times more than urban areas.

Rojgar Yojna (SJGSY) and drought relief reach the poor equitably (Table 13.1).

The above evidences show that poor and chronic poor as a group are excluded from various state interventions. However, their exclusion from political decision making in gram panchayats is worrisome. The poor among tribals have lost faith in village democracy as a process of development and change. The decision-making, of late, has become highly centralized, where the poor, as a group, have no role to play. The poor as a group do monitor as to how the governance is neglecting them. However, it does not get enough opportunity to register its protest about such mal-governance. Moreover, the poor have no freedom in the process of planning programmes they need. The blame for this unfreedom to decide what and how the local development should take place falls at various levels (Sah, 2007; Sah and Bhatt, 2004). First, the process of centralization at the panchayat level is too overpowering for the community to exert pressures for the participatory process to begin. Secondly, the quantum of financial allocation is too meagre to meet the demands of the community. Third, the desire of the bureaucracy and the elected representatives at higher echelons to control the activities and finance of the gram panchayat does not allow needed independence to the panchayat. Lastly, existing laws that govern the natural resources obstruct the process of giving control to the community.

POVERTY, CULTURE AND DEVELOPMENT

This brief recapitulation reveals that social exclusion is multidimensional and is a process that keeps poor out from public goods and services on the one hand and denies their access to social, economic and political institutions on the other. This being an institutionalized process may also have implications for social relations. It can be argued that this may not be detrimental in the case of relations within the community, but this exclusion would certainly have implications so far as the relations with outside world are concerned. Interpreting social exclusion in this manner allows us to ponder over the notion of social capital that allows bonding within community as well as building bridges with the outside world. Sah (2007) has shown that the pattern of settlement in tribal villages is one of the important supports for development of social capital.[15] This apart, three other processes are instrumental in awakening the dormant social capital:

first, the presence of left-oriented civil society that helped ease economic repression; second, dependence on informal community legal structures that bind together people; lastly, lack of development of the region and livelihood struggles that give space to social elites to oversee emerging political and economic leadership.

The civil society organizations, namely NBA and AMS, took advantage of development-induced displacement, depletion of natural resources and repression of tribal rights by the state[16] to mobilize tribals. The presence of NBA and AMS not only made the community aware about its rights[17] but also sceptical to outsiders in their villages.[18] Notwithstanding the catalytic role of civil society in creating social capital, the relationship between civil society and governance, as would be discussed, could be vicious as well as virtuous. The question is under what conditions the social capital manifests itself in the political domain in a virtuous pattern. The remoteness of the region with respect to legal, constitutional and administrative structures[19] helped the community to create its own informal institutions. These institutions exercised their power through social hierarchy and further strengthened social bonds within the community. At times, there was an extension of formal structures with the informal institutions.[20] However, in locations where economic stratification has set in, owing to economic compulsions, economic hierarchy dominates the social hierarchy;[21] otherwise the social hierarchy dominates.

The state and market failures have influenced differently the life and livelihood of the tribals in the tribal region. Where agriculture is unsustainable, a sizeable section of the community is engaged in livelihood struggles that force them to seasonally migrate for seven to eight months in a year.[22] In order to optimize their family labour, agricultural land is pushed in short-term arrangements like leasing, renting or mortgage.[23] Land under such arrangements[24] engenders a symbolic presence of migrants in the village. In the process, land in exchange engenders a symbolic presence of the migrant household in the village[25] and his representation in the social hierarchy without his being physically present.[26]

Social capital in relatively remote tribal villages seems to be developing and providing dominant support to traditional social hierarchy to exert its power on political hierarchy. In the process, programmes that could have positive economic implications for the well-being of the community are resisted. This is something to admire as well as to criticize. Does it not mean that the social capital, in its negative aspect, makes people from the outside world and development aloof? This seems to be keeping the community frozen in time and deny the social capital a space in development. This criticism seems to be partially true. Inasmuch as state repression and access failure to common resources are the basic constraints in well-being, the importance of emerging social capital cannot be overemphasized as an important force behind their united struggle. But the desire for change is also present. This has resulted in diverting the social trust and solidarity in the community in the form of emerging organizations that take advantage of non-tribal ways: technology, markets and development initiatives.

The increasing popularity of self-help groups (SHGs) in relatively remote areas is an indication of parallel leadership that is emerging in society. The first is the traditional social leadership that helps the social capital preserve natural resources by blocking explorative non-tribal entry in the village. Another is organizing tribals to take advantage of existing government programmes through SHG,[27] that too against the wishes of the traditional social elites. Though both processes have extended social base, the latter is not the legitimate successor of the former. Despite the fact that both forms of social leaderships are exploring new dimensions of social relations, the latter does not directly contest the supremacy of traditional social elites and their ways of employing the social capital. It is unlikely that various forms of leaderships would come together in the near future. But there is a possibility that the traditional leadership may be influential only in social processes; the economic processes may be governed by the newly emerging leadership. It shall, however, be difficult to define the operation of SHGs as an indicator of social capital formation because these groups do surrogate the interests of individuals. This, in fact, is seen as a process that erodes homogeneity that is a prerequisite for social capital to manifest.[28]

The social capital as it manifests in Pospur may not be operationalized by indicators like community engagements with various organizations and associations. It has to be observed in day-to-day involvement of community in the affairs of the village. The social hierarchy has a potential to create space for community involvement in politicizing a debate. But it does not ensure participation in the decision-making. For, a vibrant social structure is present in these areas but it is only in relatively remote villages that one witnesses the manifestations of social capital. Moreover, the way the social capital is employed, strengthens the fact that (a) social capital may not necessarily manifest in virtuous imperatives; (b) all associations may not create trust and cooperation in the society while some, like SHGs with inbuilt economic interests, may even stratify the society.

These findings are at variance with what Pai (2001) has tried to establish. She observes that social segmentation emerges as a significant context determining development of trust and social capital between groups. Findings of this study reveal that trust and social capital within the tribal context are omnipresent. Economic segregation and its intensity play a dominant role in the manifestation of social capital. It remains unutilized under some conditions, is used in a virtuous pattern in some and viciously in others. These findings, however, corroborate the observations of Rudolph (2000) that not all associations are likely to create trust and cooperation with positive implications.

As seen in above analysis, social capital in the form of trust and bond within the tribal context is omnipresent. Its utilization in development decision-making and, more importantly, its pattern of manifestation would be contextual to the milieu where it is operational. Our analysis also reveals that: (i) factors like the pattern of settlement, importance of social norms, and failure of state have helped perpetuate trust and cooperation in the community, (ii) civil society has played a significant role in making this capital available for wider use, and (iii) complexities of economic stratification and efficiency of decentralized governance are contextual to social capital to manifest.

Three different types of elites have emerged in this tribal society: the traditional, the emerging economic elites and the political elites. All the three have created their own spaces in the community. But their relevance is contextual to their ability to deliver. The efficiency and working of political decentralization is not different in different tribal areas and the political leadership is unable to use social capital for improving the conditions of the people. Not so much because of the nature of the leadership but because of the policy and programmes it has introduced that are inappropriate and ineffective. What, however, is different across villages is individual economic efforts in some areas (less-remote villages) that have created sizeable benefits as compared to remote villages. The dormant social capital in development decision-making in former areas is significantly influenced by intense economic segregation that has given a strong message to community that well-being is a function of individual efforts. In contrast, in economically homogeneous remote villages, the social capital is much more vibrant.

But the trust and concerns for fellow members in both the villages are in perpetual conflict with the political hierarchy that is self-serving. In remote villages, this conflict has expressed itself in a vicious as well as virtuous pattern of social capital. On the other hand, in relatively less remote areas the social capital has remained un-invested and dormant. Despite the fact that the social capital has positively influenced non-social events since the early 1990s, its manifestations in governance have been marginal. One wonders as to why the social capital could not be transferred to the sphere of governance. Answer to this question could be found in an analysis of (a) the nature of benefits that decentralized governance could potentially give to the community; and (b) is it worthwhile to put so much faith in a process that can never address the livelihood problems of the marginalized. Community at large finds the benefits not worth wasting their days' labour.[29]

Economic stratification also affects trust in institutions, agencies and individuals. By and large, trust and faith in relatives, tribals, and people from gram panchayat or belonging to *jati* panchayat is still high. On the other hand, a large proportion of respondents do not trust Panchayati Raj Institutions. Teachers and health workers are trustworthy but government officers like foresters, police and outsiders like MLAs, MPs have failed to gain trust of the tribals. If we try to establish association between chronic poverty profile and level of trust (Table 13.2), we find that there is no significant difference in the level of trust between chronic poverty groups when it comes to trust within the community. This bond[30] within the community does not vary owing to social, political and economic stratification. But the trust for outsiders like police, forester or Janpad CEO is significantly high (revealed by significant and positive correlation coefficient) in the case of always non-poor whereas chronic poor do not trust the outsiders. It can be argued that the well-off (socially, economically and politically) are trying to reach significantly more to outsiders. Their increasing trust on these agencies is a product of their desire to economically benefit from the newfound association. On the basis of such bridges, the always non-poor and transitory non-poor receive benefits of government schemes. But the chronic poor, owing to their inability to bridge, have failed to get economic benefits. It will now be easy to understand why it was that the always non-poor and the transitory non-poor were receiving significantly

TABLE 13.2: CORRELATION BETWEEN TRUST[1] ON AGENCY AND CHRONIC POVERTY PROFILE[2]

Agency	Correlation Coefficient
Bonds within the community[3]	Strong and not significantly different across poverty profile
Bridges Outside Community:	
Police	+ 0.28 ***
Forest Officials	+ 0.26 **
Janpad CEO	+ 0.26 ***
Teacher, *bania*, Health worker, MLA, MP, Civil society like NBA, AMS	Weak and not significantly different across poverty profile

Source: Sah (2007).

Notes: 1. Trust is operationalized in a four-point scale with 1-never trust to 4-always trust.
2. Chronic poverty profile is as follows.
1: chronic poor; 2: poor; 3: transitory poor and 4: always non-poor.
3. Relatives, *jati* panchayat, gram panchayat, gramwasi, panchayatwasi, adiwasi, sarpanch, panch.
4. Significance level – **: 5%; ***: 1%

more proportion in the resource redistribution in the area than what they actually deserved.[31]

These evidences indicate that social relations are central to the governance outcome. They also reject the idea of *cultural determinism*, which rationalizes that some communities are encumbered with cultures that restrict them from progressing. Culture in our construct is, thus, a form of relationship that influences and is being influenced by socio-political and economic features. Two important issues in this context need some elaboration. First, despite dissent within the community against repressions and strong bond within, there are relational forces in the form of bridges outside the community that lead towards a fractured conformity. This conformity redefines the power relationship within the community. Secondly, some people use social relations to enhance their position and also reproduce the processes that influence governance outcome. In a sense, bridging the social capital of the groups engenders ability to exert and fulfil their aspirations, disregarding all the dissent. These two contesting forces coexist and help in redistributing the opportunities created by development. Those who are influential in exploring bridging relations could fulfil their aspirations whereas those who are less fortunate remain in square one despite having strong bonds within. The ray of hope for equity lies in the capability of bonding social capital's capability to dissent. A conferment between the two may result in bonding social capital to dominate the bridging social capital.

Then why does not confrontation between the two is take place? We need to answer if there is a sort of modality between bonding and bridging social capital that indicates if one type of trust increases, the other shall reduce. Findings of Table 13.2 reveal that it is not necessary that bond within members of one's own community reduces trust in people from outside. On the contrary, the always non-poor provide clear evidence that it is possible to trust outsiders without losing or reducing trust within the community. Trust within, in the form of bond, is important to cope with the remoteness. But bridging the distance with outsiders provides economic opportunities; those who are well-off, benefit from governance by dictating development decision-making, disregarding all the equity norms. What it, however, denotes is that participation is subordinate to bridging relational outcome. Unless these social realities are recognized, community participation in decentralized governance may remain a distant dream.

CONCLUSION

Central to the debate on impact of culture on development is a much misunderstood and deterministic notion that some societies are encumbered with cultures that hinder them from participating efficiently in non-traditional, market-driven institutions. In other words, cultures of these societies are stumbling blocks in their assimilation with non-traditional economic and political institutions and processes. In the final analysis, their cultures force them to remain underdeveloped. Evidences indicate that social relations are central to governance outcomes. Rejecting the idea of ***cultural determinism***, it is argued that culture needs to be located in socio-political domain as a form of relationship that is influencing and at the same time gets influenced by economic transformation the community is experiencing.

Despite difference of opinion within the community[32] and also exclusion of poor, there are relational forces (bridges constructed by some well-to-do in the community with outsiders like foresters, police, *taluka* officials and Janpad CEO) that lead to an apparent symmetry of opinions. Below the surface, there is a feeling of anger because, in the process, the well-to-do are able to corner a sizeable gain of development. Moreover, as some people use relations to enhance their position, they are able to reproduce the processes that influence governance-outcome. These two contesting forces, bonding and bridging social capital, coexist and help in redistributing the opportunities created by development. Those who are influential in establishing bridging relations could fulfil their aspirations whereas those who are less fortunate remain so despite having strong bonds within.

In the last two decades, development and sustainability have transformed into a new politics of environment whereby development and sustainability mean different things to different people. What the state and bureaucracy see as development is, in fact, destruction to some. This is being contested at different levels. At one level, it is responsible for politicizing the rights and interests of the people. Ethnicity, in this construct, emerges as a political process, within mixed societies, for protecting interests of groups. The bonding social capital in this political process results in forming new identities. The new identity formations help the communities first to organize themselves and then protest against the sort of development that has been forced upon them. Then why is a confrontation between the two social capitals not taking place? We need to answer if there is a sort of modality between bonding and bridging capitals that indicates when one type of trust increases, the other shall reduce. Evidences show that it is not necessary that bond within members of one's own community reduces trust in people from outside. On the contrary, the always non-poor provide clear evidence that it is possible to trust outsiders without losing or reducing trust within the community. Trust within, however, is clearly an important mechanism to cope with the remoteness. But bridging with outsiders provides economic opportunities; those who are well-off derive benefit from governance by dictating development decision-making.

This, however, implies that participation in development decision making is subordinate to bridging relational outcome. Unless these social realities are recognized, community participation in development decision-making may remain a distant dream. Moreover, cultural capital need not always bring efficiency in governance; it could work viciously, obstructing options that are virtuous in nature. In economically homogeneous and relatively remote rural areas, the bonding cultural capital is much more vibrant. Transfer of this capital from the social to the political sphere is possible only if gains of governance are large and equitable. This also indicates that like in rest of the country, in remote tribal areas community is stratified on economic, social and political lines. The trust and concerns for fellow members is in perpetual conflict with political and economic hierarchy which is self-serving. These stratifications also create variance in the ways people see the world around them. A grand unified policy intervention towards their welfare will, therefore, not work. The ambiguity in use of 'community participation' in development decision-making only reflects naïve acceptance of homogeneity in communities located in remote rural areas. This perception, in its turn, helps the state to design a blanket intervention for development. The cultural capital and its varied manifestations make policy interventions by-pass a large section of the community.

NOTES

1. The importance to agriculture is for the following reasons. First, over half of the rural masses are net purchasers of food grains, hence they depend on policies that influence food grain availability. Consequently, politically it is incorrect to have an open market policy for agriculture. Second, there is a misconception in the policy making circles that Indian agriculture is driven by incentives. As a result trade protection, marketing controls, state investment, price support and input subsidy remain important interventions in regulating the pace and pattern of agricultural growth in the country. Lastly, experiences of the late 1960s, when India was dependent on food-aid to survive, are hard to forget. From those haunting years of scarcity, India has grown to become self-sufficient in food and the growth of agricultural production has eliminated the threats of famine. This growth has increased the employment opportunities for rural labour and we have seen a rise in real wages.
2. Economic policies are not made in vacuum; serious investigations have guided the policy makers in formulating appropriate interventions. Poverty policies are also influenced by writings of social scientists. In fact, in the last forty years, three important conclusions were instrumental in shaping Indian poverty-alleviation policies. It was Ahluwalia (1978) whose seminal work repositioned Indian poverty-debate from estimating poverty to explaining it. Ahluwalia tried to establish that the years when growth in agricultural production slows down are also the years when rural poverty worsens. Saith (1981) and Narain (1985), independently, brought another important explanatory aspect in this debate—agricultural prices. They tried to provide support to the thesis that the years when agricultural

prices are high, other things remaining same, are the years when incidence of poverty increases. These researchers argued that as a large section of the rural population, including producers, are net purchasers of food grains, an increase in prices of agricultural commodities reduces their purchasing power and shrinks their consumption basket, thus, pushing people into poverty.

Taking a clue from these findings, the Indian planners developed a two-pronged strategy for poverty alleviation: providing a favourable environment for rapid growth in agricultural production and creating low and stable prices of food grains. The strategy, during the 1980s and early 1990s, saw no significant departure till Sen (1996) tried to impel the hypothesis that apart from these two factors, state investment in the social sector weakens forces that accentuate poverty. Thus, the three major planks of Indian poverty-reducing interventions remained rapid growth in agricultural sector, stable price environment for rural consumers and social sector investment. The strategy did significantly influence Indian rural poverty; the poverty ratio reduced from around 57 per cent in 1970-1 to 26 per cent in 1999-2000.

3. The Indian experience with R&R of large project-affected PAPs lacks completeness and had been apathetic to local needs and resources. The R&R policy is forced and its implementation creates visible and invisible ruptures in the social fabric in the short run and impoverishment in the long run (see Sah, 1999).
4. Revenue officials are remembered for their extortion in land sales which cost the seller about Rs. 4,000 per acre or land transfer to a son that could be registered only after a bribe of Rs. 2,000 per entry. The police have dual images. First as an institution for settling disputes in such a way that each affected party has to bribe in order to resolve the dispute in its favour. Its second image is of a state apparatus that is used in intimidating involuntary relocation of PAPs. The forest officials connote a bureaucratic set-up that has denied *Barelas* access to natural resources. But if one can bribe them, limited access may be granted.
5. The agricultural technology transfer in tribal areas is driven by what migrants learn from irrigated agriculture as migrant farm labour. Use of high-yielding seeds with fertilizers under-irrigated conditions, marinating plant health during growth stage, use of irrigation and harvesting equipment and post-harvest management are introduced to tribals due to migration. As the state machinery has bypassed the tribal areas, the process is internalized without any state support.
6. In drought-prone areas, migration also works as an asset formation device. Successive droughts render agriculture an unsustainable livelihood option and forces even large farmers join the queue for doles. The marginal farmers and landless labourers accumulate assets due to their access to labouring options owing to migration.

7. This may also break the distrust syndrome with respect to non-tribals as noted above.
8. Nimar tribal belt is an economically divided lot. For example, in Pospur village in Pati *taluka* of Badwani district a group of young farmers is ready to take risk and associate itself with schemes like group financing and SHG activities. But the older generation wants no outsider, especially state intervention on schemes like social forestry and soil and water conservation activities on common property, because these further constraint their already constrained access to natural resources (for details see Sah et al., 2003).
9. Social capital comprises systems of norms, institutions and organizations that promote trust and cooperation in a community. It is considered a form of capital because it helps in accelerating the process of well-being and healthy decision-making in the community. Putnam (1993) is the best-known exponent of the concept, though both neo-institutional economists like north and sociologists like Bourdieu were early proponents of this concept. Durston (1998) argues that there are five important features of social capital. In economic exchange, social capital reduces transaction cost arising when dealing with outsiders in unregulated environment; it helps in honest and efficient governance. Social capital strengthens each time it is activated; social capital, like culture, is perpetuated and it could take a virtuous or a vicious path. Repeated social interaction, virtuous or otherwise, strengthens civic participation or non-participation; and social capital developed in cultural or religious spheres is transferable to political or economic spheres.
10. Agriculture being the main economic activity, division of family due to marriage of a son, leads to the weakening of economic hierarchy. The newly-formed households are relatively resource deficient and rely on social network for support not only in social interactions but also for economic survival; also see, Sah and Shah (2003) for details.
11. Macro findings have identified the south-western tribal belt of Madhya Pradesh as one of the economically poorest regions in the country. Badwani district in the region was selected for in-depth study to understand why and how people in remote rural areas are trapped in chronic poverty. Two *janpads*, one relatively developed Sendhwa and one resource poor Pati, were selected for the study. One village from each of the selected *janpads*, Pospur from Pati, and Kirchali from Sendhwa, were selected based on the relative remoteness; Kirchali is relatively less remote compared to Pospur. The paper derived its evidences from both qualitative and quantitative methods. The qualitative data, using case study method, compared two communities in Kirchali and Pospur. For detailed write-up on the background, demography, social structure and brief history of communities, see, Sah and Shah (2003). The quantitative data was generated from 94 randomly selected house-

holds from Kirchali village of Sendhwa *janpad* and Chilalkuan village of Pati *janpad*.

12. As access to quantitative data was denied by villagers in Pospur, for in-depth study this village was replaced by Chilalkuan.
13. The remoteness of Pospur and poor agricultural base has resulted in a relatively large population to rely on migration as a coping mechanism compared to less remote Kirchali (Sah and Shah, 2003). In Kirchali, individuals have invested over Rs. 20,000 for digging wells in a rocky terrain with a high risk of failure and in drawing electricity line from the nearest distribution point. There are about thirty individuals who have such connections. This process, though it brought economic success to individuals, has stratified the society on economic lines. Remoteness of Pospur, its difficult terrain, high risk and initial failures in such investment have made the village more homogeneous. For details on relative importance of remoteness and investment, see Sah (2005).
14. Of the two different approaches to measuring income poverty, either based on per capita calorie intake or on per capita annual expenditure, the former was not considered an appropriate indicator of poverty. This is so because food consumption does not change significantly under distress situations in comparison to non-food items. In this research, instead of calorie intake, we have tried to estimate the incidence of poverty based on annual expenditure. The official norm for identification of households that are poor is Rs. 245 per capita per month. This implies that any household that spends less than Rs. 2,950 per capita annually can be treated as poor. Among poor households, those that have less than Rs. 2,000 per capita per annum expenditure have been treated as severely poor.

    The poverty categories can further be re-categorized by incorporating the time dimension of poverty. One way to reach chronic dimension of poverty is comparing the consumption expenditure over time. The major problem in employing this method is non-availability of a panel of data that fixes the chronic nature of poverty. Sah and Shah (2003) have used variations in cereal consumption from normal as an indicator of chronic poverty. But identification of chronic poor using fall in cereal consumption from normal may provide underestimation of chronic poverty. This is because experience shows that cereal consumption is relatively inelastic to shocks. Alternatively, Krishna (2003) has identified that in sequence of changes if there is deterioration in land asset and increase in leasing-in small tracts of land, fall in food intake or clothing over time or if debts have remained un-serviced or leaky roofs have not been repaired, it is sign of chronic poverty. Since variations in the quality of clothing over time were not caught properly in our sample and the house repair has only labour component using local material, it is not desirable to include these two indicators of identification of chronic poverty. It was also found that short-term land transactions in the form of leasing-in land was more a function of market failure and brought agencies together than a pure indication of sequence of change that points a deterioration in the quality of life of a tenant (Sah, 1999). Thus, in this analysis we have proposed that if the household had lost silver in the last ten years, or could not service its old debts or did not get even the *rab* (cereals boiled in buttermilk) and hence missed both the meals, the household is a transitory household either chronic poor or transitory non-poor. The two categories of income-poverty—poor and non-poor—thus can further be categorized as poor with chronic tendency, poor without chronic tendency, transitory non-poor and always non-poor.

15. In fact, caste panchayat along with traditional village panchayat are the two tribal institutions that promote community participation in all social decision-making. See Sah and Shah (2003), chapter 3, for details.
16. Conflicts over natural resources between the state and the community in this tribal belt have a long history. However, the exploitation of natural resources is also from within. But the solidarity created by *outside* (state and *bania*) exploitation did bind the society. Two of the most active NGOs that are mobilizing the tribals in the area are the NBA and the AMS. While the former is mobilizing the tribals on the failures of the development paradigm adopted by the state, the latter is organizing them against natural resource depletion, state repression and their rights. See Sah and Shah (2003), chapter 3, for details.
17. A discussion with the Chief Executive Officer of Pati *taluka*, where the AMS is active, brings out the fact that awareness about tribal rights has grown in the area significantly over last 7-8 years. Earlier a tribal would come to the taluka panchayat always accompanied by the activists of AMS, now they come for any work on their own.
18. Even during the fieldwork of the study, because of the nature of the investigation where land, assets and livelihood were being discussed, the community was apprehensive of outsiders' presence. There was a perception, in both Kirchali and Pospur, that such investigation is part of state activities to understand pre-submergence situation so that resettlement package can be identified for individual households. In Kirchali, the community accepted the team after discussions on the nature, scope and implications of the study. But in Pospur, as been mentioned earlier, the situation became ugly and at one stage the social leadership forced the team to abandon its work. In no uncertain terms it was told to the team that the community is happy in Pospur living the way it is earning its livelihood based on meagre agriculture, some on-farm labouring and migration. Fortunately, a group of economic leaders, especially those who have had benefits of SHG, could feel that

the study is not for acquisition of land. The social hierarchy in Pospur had a strong message: 'Please leave us as we are. We do not need any outside help for our livelihood. We are content with our life and livelihood despite poor agriculture, hard labouring and degrading migration. Do not disturb us.'

19. This is especially true for forest guards and the police. What is commonly discussed in the village is that traditional local conflict resolution methods are far more just for, the police will settle the dispute by taking money from both the parties and would be biased against the group that has given less bribe.
20. Eight committees deal with decisions relating to agriculture, health, infrastructure, education, social justice, defence, development, and assets. The political decentralization has accepted the role of traditional leaders in both Pospur and Kirchali. Traditional leaders are a crucial part of the Village Security Committee that deals with all disputes emerging in the village.
21. The individualistic approach towards economic prosperity, which consolidates productivity gains, is regarded more important than social processes. The community initiatives do not pose any challenge to economic leadership. In Kirchali, individuals are investing over Rs. 20,000 for digging wells in rocky terrains with high risk of failure and in drawing electricity from the nearest distribution point. There are over thirty individuals having such connections. This process, though has brought economic success to individuals, has stratified the society on economic lines. Remoteness of Pospur, its difficult terrain, high risk and initial failures in such investment have made the village more homogeneous.
22. The remoteness of Pospur and poor agricultural base has resulted in a relatively large population relying on migration as a coping mechanism compared to the less remote Kirchali. For details, see Sah and Shah (2005).
23. Tribal economy is based on reciprocity. Apart from performing economic transactions under market failure conditions, the short-term land transactions, especially sharecropping and fixed rent, also create social trust that works as a metaphor for social return in exchange for economic gains. This latter (social) function of the exchange is as important as its formal (economic) function of exchange.
24. A sharecropper, Ramesh, said that he will have to look after the aged parents of his close relatives in their absence in any case, but he will have to bring a doctor and spend Rs. 30-50 for an injection or two in case he has leased-in their land.
25. A large number of variations exist when the contracts are agreed upon. With sharecropping at one end and mortgage of land at the other, a

large number of fixed rent contracts fall in the middle. Depending upon the bargaining power of different participants, urgency of the deal to materialize, and perception of cost of enforcing the contract, terms and conditions vary even in a village.

26. Moral hazards are involved in sharecropping. The tribal who is leasing out land would like to ensure that the tenant, as agreed, has applied labour and inputs on the field for he has to share the out-of-pocket cost. Similar is the case when the crop would be harvested and shared for, the landowner has to ensure that he receives the crop output portion as agreed. For enforcing these, the landowner migrant has to either make a number of visits to the village or leave all these monitoring in trust on the other party. In this area the first option is more prevalent, not because of lack of trust but because it re-establishes ties with the community.
27. In Pospur, seven 'SHGs' comprising around 10 members each are in operation. Members of these groups contribute Rs. 50 to 100 per month. One of the groups has provided a loan of Rs. 20,000 to a farmer in order to get his mortgaged land back from a trader. Another group has over Rs. 20,000 in a nationalized bank and is in the process of receiving a loan of Rs. 0.3 million for goat rearing.
28. It has been argued that associations that draw on inherited identities and solidarities need to be taken into account as associations that may generate social capital. Rudolph (2000) suggests that only those organizations that are egalitarian, non-interest oriented and voluntary would create collaborative and cooperative conventions that can and do mediate between individual and society or individual and the state.
29. Migration keeps a sizeable workforce out of the village for over 6 to 7 months. Moreover, iniquitous distribution of benefits and unfulfilled expectations of the community from the decentralized governance make them empathic towards the institution. See Sah and Shah (2003), chapters 6 and 7, for details.
30. Widmalam (2004) identifies trust within as bond and trust on outsiders as bridges.
31. In poverty-ridden areas, welfare schemes like pension, Indira Awas Yojana, SJGSY, SGRY and irrigation development are meant to transfer public resources to most vulnerable sections. What we find is that such redistribution is not done equitably; both poor and non-poor receive benefits though always the non-poor receive more resources from redistribution than the rest (for details see Sah and Bhatt, 2004).
32. These differences originate from a strong bonding social capital and is vocal against unequal access to developmental gains. We are inclined to use this process in the cultural context though Bourdieu (1997) clearly distinguishes between cultural and social capital.

REFERENCES

Ahluwalia, M.S. (1978), 'Rural Poverty and Agricultural Performance in India', *Journal of Development Studies*, vol. 14 (2).

Baviskar, A. (1995), *In the Belly of the River: Tribal Conflicts over Development in the Narmada Valley*, New Delhi: Oxford University Press.

——— (2001), 'Written on the Body, Written on the Land: Violence and Environmental Struggles in Central India', Berkeley: Institute of International Studies, University of California.

Breman, J. (1985), *Of Peasant, Migrant and Pauper*, New Delhi: Oxford University Press.

Bowles, S. and H. Gintis (2000), 'Social Capital and Community Governance', (mimeo), Massachusetts: Department of Economice, University of Massachusetts.

Bourdieu, Pierre (1997), 'Forms of Capital', in A.H. Hasley, H. Landere, P. Broen A. and Wells (eds.), *Education: Culture, Economy and Society*, New York: Oxford University Press.

Dubey, K.C. (1998), 'Tribal Uprising and Social Movements in Madhya Pradesh', in K.S. Singh, *Antiquity to Modernity in Tribal India*, Volume 4: *Tribal Movements in India*, New Delhi: Inter India Publications.

Durston, J. (1998), 'Building Social Capital in Rural Communities', Santiago: Social Development Division, UN Economic Commission.

Govinda, R. (2003), 'Dynamics in Decentralised Management in Primary Education', in R. Govinda and R. Diwan (eds.), *Community Participation and Empowerment in Primary Education*, New Delhi: Sage.

Krishna, Anirudh (2003), 'Falling into Poverty in High Growth State: Escaping Poverty and Becoming Poor in Gujarat', *Economic and Political Weekly*, vol. 38 (49).

Narain, Dharm (1985), reported in Gunvant M. Desai, 'Trends in Rural Poverty in India: An Interpretation of Dharm Narain', in J.W. Mellor and G.M. Desai (eds.), *Agricultural Changes and Rural Poverty: Variations in Themes by Dharm Narain*, Baltimore: Johns Hopkins University Press.

Pai, S. (2001), 'Social Capital, Panchayats and Grassroots Democracy: Politics of Dalit Assertion in Uttar Pradesh', *Economic and Political Weekly*, vol. 36, 24 February.

Putnam, R.D., R. Leonardi and Y.N. Raffaella (1993), *Making Democracy Work: Civic Traditions in Modern Italy*, Princeton: Princeton University Press.

Rudolph. S.H. (2000), 'Civil Society and the Realm of Freedom', *Economic and Political Weekly*, vol. 35, 13 May.

Sah, D.C. (1997), 'Second Generation Problems of Involuntary Migration', *Indian Journal of Agricultural Economics*, 52 (4).

——— (1998), 'Avoiding Impoverishment Risks', *Review of Development and Change*, vol. 3 (1).

——— (1999), 'Pressure on Land, Employment and Migration', *Review of Development and Change*, vol. 4 (2).

——— (2002), 'Crop Commercialisation and Migration', in G. Shah and D.C. Sah (eds.), *Land Reforms in India*, Volume 8: *Performance and Challenges in Gujarat and Maharashtra*, New Delhi: Sage.

——— (2003), 'Social Capital and Governance', *Review of Development and Change*, vol. 8 (1).

——— (2007), 'Environment, Culture and Development', in Y. Atal and D.C. Sah (eds.), *Exploring Social Frontiers*, Jaipur: Rawat Publications.

——— (2007a), 'Chronic Poverty in Tribal Areas', *Indian Journal of Agricultural Economics*, vol. 62 (2).

Sah, D.C. and Amita Shah (2003), 'Chronic Poverty in Remote Rural Areas of Southwestern Madhya Pradesh' (mimeo), Ujjain: MPISSR, and Ahmedabad: GIDR.

——— (2005), 'Migration in Remote Tribal Areas', *Indian Journal of Agricultural Economics*, 60 (2).

Sah, D.C. and A. Bhatt (2004), 'An In-depth Study of Chronic Poverty: Evidence from Southwestern Madhya Pradesh' (mimeo), Ujjain: MPISSR.

Saith, A. (1981), 'Production Price and Poverty in Rural India', *Journal of Development Studies*, 17 (2).

Sen, Abhijit (1996), 'Economic Reform, Employment and Poverty', *Economic and Political Weekly*, 31 pp. 35-7.

Sen, Amartya (1999), *Development as Freedom*, Oxford: Oxford University Press.

Srivastav, P.N. (1970), *West Nimar: Madhya Pradesh District Gazetteers*, Bhopal: District Gazetteers Department, Government of Madhya Pradesh.

Wade, R. (1988), 'Why Some Indian Villages Cooperate', *Economic and Political Weekly*, vol. 33, 16 April.

Widmalam, Sten (2004), 'The Utility of Bonding Social Capital' (mimeo), Uppsala: Department of Government, Uppsala University.

CHAPTER 14

Group Rights of Minorities: A Critical Reflection

MOKBUL ALI LASKAR

It is being argued that collective legal identity and rights of groups' may be absolutely essential for resolving many tensions in today's world. Recognizing rights of groups is considered a basic tool of peace (Barsh). Political theorists are increasingly interested in a whole range of groups, in group-based nature of society, in the status of group rights, and in the sorts of rights groups should be granted (Eisenberg and Jeff Spinner-Halev, 2005: 1). For Dahrendorf, 'defence of minority rights is certainly the litmus test of liberty and the rule of law; more than that, it is in a sense what they are about' (1984: 79). Inherent conflict, however, exists between rights of the individual and collective rights of minorities; and this is a formidable conceptual barrier for realization of group-specific collective rights. Universal human rights perspective is that 'we human beings are all much the same'; but much more plausible understanding is that we are *diversely different* (Sen, 2006: xiv). Major argument against group-specific minority rights is that these rights inevitably curtail individual human rights of minorities, i.e. internal minorities or minorities within minorities. In view of these conflicting arguments and counter-arguments, it is desirable that we understand group rights of minorities in a broader perspective. We need to analyse the main currents of theoretical-philosophical debates on minority rights, group rights and human rights. The objective of this paper is to understand the group nature of minorities. It examines whether minority as a group can claim rights; and, if so, whether there is any clash between human rights and group rights of minorities. Besides, the paper makes a critical analysis of minority rights in India.

GROUP NATURE OF MINORITIES

Historically, human beings are social and cultural in nature; they inherently exhibit tendencies to live in groups characterized by certain common group features. The Aristotelian view of human sociality recognises that human beings are marked by *esprit de corps*—feeling of loyalty that exists between members of a group. Traditional Western political thought always accepted the existence of groups and classes as natural building blocs of society. Natural societal divisions in traditional societies (such as Greek and Roman) recognized the existence of plurality of group or class interests, factions and other group features. However, in the contemporary globalized world, we see resilience of group identity, which is being intrinsically linked to the issue of 'equality'. Groups of people are claiming equality in a much stronger sense: they do not simply want equality but claim that they are entitled to it (Dworkin, 1999: 268). Historically subordinated and marginalized (minority) groups are now demanding equality, and demanding it as a *right* (Kymlicka, 2002: 1-25). Contrarily, inequality is a fundamental reality of the modern world-system (Wallerstein, 2003: 650). Finding morally defensible and right way to treat people equally is difficult. Group inequalities in incomes, wealth and access to services or political power mobilize individuals for collective action (Bangure, 2006: 299-325); leading to violent ethnic and communal conflicts.

Now before moving further, let us have a brief idea as to who are minorities and what constitute minority communities/groups. The term 'minority' has been conceptually treated in various discourses on human rights, social justice and equality but without properly defining it. Etymologically, the term is derived from the Latin word *minor* which means *less*, *lesser*, or *smaller* and *minuere* which means to *reduce and diminish* (Coontz, 1986: 155). It also comes from the French word *minorite* which means *to be in a condition of defeat* (ibid.). It was used to describe either a *condition or fact of being smaller, inferior, or subordinate;* status of *non-age* that has some bearing upon the legal status of so-called minors; relationship between larger and smaller numerical values; and number of votes cast for a political party in a democratic election (ibid.). Minority community that first appeared in the socio-political discourse is the religious minority. The scope of minority communities was gradually expanded to include linguistic and ethnic groups; and, further, this has again been expanded by an innumerable number of minority groups based on different cultural and other criteria. For some women, children, immigrants, migrant workers, refugees or other disadvantaged/non-dominant groups (such as people with socially unacceptable sex orientations) are also minorities. Helen Hacker is of the view that minority groups can be such persons who are denied rights to which they are entitled according to the value system (ibid., 163). Minority Rights Group International (MRG International) defined 'minority' as 'a group of people who believe they have a common identity, based on culture/ethnicity; languages or religion, which is different from that of a majority group around them'. In 1945, Louis Wirth tried to give a sociological interpretation of the term 'minority' defining minorities as 'a group of people who, because of their physical or cultural characteristics, are singled out from the others in the society in which they live for differential and unequal treatment and who therefore regard themselves as objects of collective discrimination' (ibid., 162). Existence of a minority in a society implies existence of a corresponding group enjoying higher social status and greater privileges. A minority, according to MRG International, is often, but not always, defined as such with reference to their position within a country, but can also be defined with reference to a wider (e.g. regional) or narrower area (e.g. province). What matters, according to MRG International, is whether minorities lack powers—i.e. the ability to affect decisions that concern them. In most probability, minorities play a ***minor role*** in decision-making.

Finding a universally acceptable and legally binding definition of 'minority' is, however, very difficult. With regard to the determination of a (minority) community, as per the meanings of various minority treaties/declarations made under the auspices of League of Nations, Permanent Court of International Justice adopted following criteria:

> existence of a group living in a given country or locality, having a race, religion, language and traditions of their own, and united by the identity of such race, religion, language and traditions, maintaining their own form of worship, securing the instruction and upbringing of their children in accordance with the spirit and traditions of their race and mutually assisting one another.

According to Francesco Capotorti, the former UN Special Rapporteur of the Sub-Commission on the Prevention of Discrimination and Protection of Minorities, 'an ethnic, religious or linguistic minority is a group numerically smaller than the rest of the population of the State to which it belongs and possessing cultural, physical or historical characteristics, a religion or a language different from those of the rest of the population' (1991). For him, to claim minority status a group must fulfil two basic conditions simultaneously: group membership should be *numerically less* than the rest of the population and the group must be in a *non-dominant position* compared to the rest of the population. Dominant numerical minority (such as the erstwhile British in India) or non-dominant majority groups (such as Blacks in South Africa) cannot claim minority rights.

For Kymlicka, cultural diversity is the coexistence within a given state of more than one nation, where 'nation' means a historical community, more or less institutionally complete, occupying a given territory or homeland, sharing a distinct language and culture. The smaller cultures in a multi-nation state form 'national minorities' (Kymlicka, 1995: 11). Henrard talks about certain distinguishable *objective* and *subjective* components involved within the minority concept (2001: 78-98). Objective components of the minority concept can be listed as possessing ethnic, religious or linguistic features which are different from those possessed by rest of the population, that is comprising less than 50 per cent of the total population, and fulfilling the so-called 'non-dominance' requirement, namely that the minority should not have a dominant position over the rest of the population (ibid.). Subjective component refers to the collective wish of the minority group to preserve and develop its own separate identity (ibid.). Thus, for Henrard 'a minority is a population group with ethnic, religious and linguistic characteristics differing from the rest of the population, which is non-dominant, numerically smaller than the rest of the population and has the wish to hold on to its separate identity' (2001: 41-61). Ramaga highlights the relativity of the minority concept with the help of numerical factors, geographical or jurisdictional context, social and socio-economic contexts, and qualitative factors (such as non-dominant status) (1992: 104-19). Ramaga is of the view that the number of the group in relation to the geographical area in which it lives was emphasized by Capotorti as it was difficult to establish universal principles for states, the evolutions of whose distinct societies are not identical. The Ohrid Conference (of 1974) emphasized *sufficiency in number to pursue group aims*, but numerical inferiority to the rest of the 'people'. The question of minority protection may not arise if the 'rest of the people' again consist of many other groups, each having distinct ethnic, religious, and linguistic characteristics; and demography is such that groups comprising the rest of the people do not individually outnumber the group claiming minority protection and minority rights. In such a scenario, if there is an argument for special protection for a minority group, the numerical factor may be irrelevant; the need for requirement of such protection may be sufficient. For Junckerstorff, too small a number of individuals is not worth forming a minority in the sociological sense; minority must include an adequate number of persons sufficient by themselves to develop significantly their traditions and characteristics (1961: 30).

Many contemporary commentators are, however, of the view that minority has nothing to do with numbers. It has to do with the ability of one segment of a society to dominate another segment or a minor role played by a segment/group in the affairs of the country (society). For them minority group status is determined by the presence of distinguishing features such as discrimination. According to Dinstein, 'if we continue to use the familiar term "minorities", it is worthwhile bearing in mind that the test for the existence of a minority entitled to protection under international law is not always numerical'. Perhaps we can think of a minority in the sense that such a group plays a minor role in the affairs of its country (1976: 102-20). In many Asian and African countries where population is highly segmented into religious, ethnic and numerous sub-ethnic groups, it is often impossible to determine which groups are dominant and which are disadvantaged. An Indian Muslim is likely to regard Hindus as dominant majority but vast majorities of the Hindus (low-caste, especially Scheduled Caste (SC)) definitely belong to non-dominant/ disadvantaged groups.

In brief, the concept of minorities as disadvantaged groups is valid in many countries and there is no sense to argue about its usage. From a proper definitional point of view, minorities are both numerically small and non-dominant/disadvantaged groups. Otherwise, minorities are social constructs only; and the term 'minority' can be applied to any group which perceives itself and/or is perceived by other groups as minority. Its disadvantaged or non-dominant status is only a matter of qualification or analysis within the wider context of existing social, political and other forms of stratification. Typically, members of a minority group share a sense of solidarity and a desire to preserve their culture, traditions, religion, or language. Central features characterizing a minority group are: its members suffer multiple disadvantages, generally at the hands of a dominant group; members broadly share identity of 'interest' and 'affinity'; and identification with national identity is generally problematic, particularly so when national identity has a mono-cultural construct. 'Deprivation', 'neglect' and 'discrimination' are some of the common connecting grounds for minorities to construct separate identities.

CAN MINORITIES CLAIM GROUP RIGHTS?

When we speak of minority or minority rights, there arises a group concept. Thus, it is pertinent to know what rights are and what the basis of group rights is. Joseph Raz, who subscribes to an *interest theory of rights* defines rights in following terms: 'X has a right if and only if X can have rights, and, other things being equal, an aspect of X's well-being (his interest) is a sufficient reason for holding some other person(s) to be under a duty' (Jones, 1999b: 80-107). The interest theory of rights recognizes and protects the interests of right-holders (Wellman, 1999: 13-40). (There are, of course, many instances where it is reasonable to see that rights necessarily protect someone's interest rather than rights-holders only, e.g. parents' rights over their children protect the interests of children.) According to Raz, to have a right to something is to have an interest in that something; although having an interest itself is not enough to create right (Jones, op. cit.). An interest translates into right only if it is an interest of sufficient moment to justify imposing a duty upon another (ibid.). Joel Feinberg urges us to recognize the importance of being able to claim that to which we have a right [claim right]; claiming is so valuable because it allows for self-respect, dignity, and respect for others that would be difficult, if not impossible, without rights (Wellman, op. cit.). For H.L.A. Hart, one has a right just in case one's choice is protected (ibid.) [liberty-right]; it involves standing in an advantaged position of bilateral choice.

Legal theorist Wesley Hohfeld introduced four elements into the conception of rights (1919)—'claim', 'liberty', 'immunity', and 'power'. The term 'right', under Hohfeld's argument, might refer '(1) to a *claim* of A against B, in respect of which B owes A a correlative duty, e.g. A's right to be repaid by B; or (2) to a *liberty* in which case A's right to do X refers simply to his having no duty to do X; . . . (3)

to a *power*, that is the ability to change a legal relation, as in the right to get married or the right to get divorced; or (4) to an *immunity*, to not being subject to another's power' (Jones, 1989: 69-96). Stoljar argues that a right is essentially a claim and a claim is something put forward not merely as a demand but as a demand accompanied with a justification indicating that that demand should me met (ibid.). Stoljar further holds that rights, in their primary sense, are not only claims to something but also claims against someone and are therefore accompanied by correlative duties . . . that A's right to X (e.g. to non-interference or to a sum of money) entails B's duty to provide X, but also that a correlative duty falls upon some C (usually a government or a community) to uphold that right (ibid.). Liberty-rights are most likely to be asserted when someone is challenged [say about his/her dress code, customs, traditions, etc.]. According to Carl Wellman, who advocated a *dominion model of rights* (Wellman, op. cit.), the nature and value of each right will vary, depending upon which Hohfeldian element is at the right's core. Common to all rights, however, is that each puts the right-holder in a 'privileged position of dominion' over some second party (ibid.). It means, 'A's right against B necessarily gives A freedom and control over A's relation to B' (ibid.). For Wellman, the language of rights is not some *respected choice* (as Hart points out); the language of rights is our *language of conflict adjudication*, and the right-holder is the party whose will would prevail in a potential conflict (ibid.). The advantage of occupying a privileged position of dominion involves freedom and control, and therefore every right must include liberties and power.

A right is a group right only if it is borne by a group or an individual as a member of a group. If individuals who form a group hold rights as separate individuals, their separate individual rights do not add up to a group right (Jones, 1999b); similarly, a right may have a content that relates to a collectivity without it being a group right (ibid.) (e.g. students' rights to access library). It is, of course, very difficult to explicitly determine the boundary between collective and individual rights. Jean-Bernard Marie held that 'all rights are individual because held by individuals and are collective by the process of their recognition, their mode of exercise and their means of protection' (cited in Ramaga, 1993: 575-88). Peter Jones provides two conceptions of group rights—*collective conception* and *corporate conception* (1999). Collective conception does not require us to give a moral standing to a group that is separate from the moral standing of each of its individual members; right is held only by the group, but interests that make the case for separate, yet identical interests of the group's members. Moral standing necessary for any claim of right is provided by moral standing of several individuals who make up the group. Claim of right is justified only when it is in the interest of the members. The corporate conception of group rights is used to describe rights which ascribe moral standing to a group (and not individuals who jointly hold the group); the holder of rights is group conceived as a single, integral entity (ibid.). Right is held not jointly by several individuals who make up the group, but by the group as a unitary entity.

There is a general argument that groups cannot be rights-holders. Contrary to this, some would, however, argue that groups have necessary features to become rights-holders. For Mitnick 'rights *inherently* exhibit collective traits'. Mitnick is of the view that individuals living under law are necessarily joined collectively and systematically in various ways. To quote Mitnick, 'rights generate collective, plural and complex spheres of membership. They take account of our group differences, help define us as members of our social and political communities, and acknowledge our common humanity'. Groups may hold rights when the joint interest of a number of individuals provides sufficient justification for imposing duties upon others (ibid.). Raz lays down the following formal conditions for having a group right:

> First, it exists because an aspect of the interest of human beings justifies holding some person(s) to be subject to a duty. Second, *the interests in question are the interests of individuals as members of a group* in a public good and the right is a right to that public good because it serves their *interest as members of the group*. Thirdly, the interest of no single member of that group in that public good is sufficient by itself to justify holding another person to be subject to a duty. (ibid.) (italics added)

In the moral context, one group could claim a right against another (Wellman, op. cit.). Let us take, for example, the case of peoples' rights to self-determination (i.e. rights to secede from the colonial powers and colonial domination). Here, each individual actually voices the claim for self-determination and each individual stands in a position of dominion only because of his or her position within the group. According to Dyke, 'if individuals have any right in connection with self-determination, it is to participate in the decision of the group. The right belongs to the group, and it is the fate of the group that is determined' (1982: 21-40). Christopher Wellman is of the view that for a group to be rights-holder it should come into conflict with other parties; and should also have the organizational structure necessary for agency (to claim rights). He is of view that three significant aspects of our moral environment would be either lost or obscured if we denied group agency and group rights—*dynamics of group conflict*, *social nature of persons*, and *responsibility of collectives.* Wellman says '. . . without conflicts there would be no need to resolve conflicts, no need to determine whose will occupies a position of dominion over another in a potential conflict, and thus no need for any talk of rights' (ibid.). Human beings are social in nature; they are nurtured and influenced by familial, filial, cultural, political and other societal allegiances emphasizing the need to recognize group agency and therefore group rights. Effective agency is, however, hard to create particularly when the group is likely to be large, politically and economically diverse, geographically dispersed, partially mixed with other groups, divided by factions, schisms and competing political visions, and lacking in a comprehensive system of formal membership (Nickel, 1997: 235-56). However, if we fail to recognize group agency, it will be costly as it precludes group responsibility. If groups cannot have rights because of lack of agency essential to rights, then we may have to agree that groups cannot be held liable for collective actions (such as ethnic cleansing, genocide, crimes against humanity, etc.) as moral responsibility would also require agency.

MINORITY RIGHTS *VS.* HUMAN RIGHTS

There are varieties of demands for treating individuals in some special way in virtue of their membership to some culturally defined group. These rights of such individuals, according to Barry, cannot be called as the rights of groups (2001: 112). For Barry, if we define 'group rights' such that they are 'self-government rights and means (for communities) to protect their religious and cultural practices', then we have to say, with Yael Tamir, that such rights are 'either dangerous or of little importance. They are dangerous if they can be turned inwards to restrict the rights and freedom of members; they are of little importance if they can only be bestowed upon groups which treat their members with equal concern and respect' (ibid.: 128). For Gordon P. Means 'the system of group special rights does involve considerable social costs and is a rather crude strategy for inducing social transformation' (cited in Glazer, 1998: 431). Post-Second World War, liberal theorists were of the view that minorities would be protected by guaranteeing basic civil and political rights to all individuals regardless of group membership (Kymlicka, 2001: 71). Basic human rights such as freedom of speech, association, and conscience, while attributed to individuals, are typically exercised in community with others, and so provide protection for group life (ibid.). Kymlicka, however, is of the view that group-specific rights for ethnic and national minorities are needed to ensure that all citizens are treated with genuine equality (1998: 104). Accommodation of differences is the essence of true equality, and group-specific rights are needed to accommodate our differences (ibid.). Contrary to the fundamental principle of liberalism, Kymlicka, a liberal political theorist, gives the most extensive defence of minority rights. He and many others (including some liberals) now argue for 'special legal or constitutional measures, above and beyond the common rights of citizenship' to defend the culture, religion or identity of a minority group (Loobuyck, 2005: 108-35). Peter Jones, however, says,

> Kymlicka does not recognize group rights of any sort as fundamental moral rights. The fundamental units of his morality are individual persons. His principle concern is to argue that vulnerable cultural minorities require 'group-differentiated' or 'community-specific' rights if their fundamental interests are to be provided for on terms equal with other cultural groups. These group-differentiated rights can be invested either in individual members of the group or in the group as a collectivity. . . . He is clearly wary of group rights and unhappy that they should enable a group to regiment the lives of its own members; rather, he argues, group-differentiated rights should be externally directed and should aim to protect or promote individuals' cultural interests against the outside world.

This, according to Peter Jones, is more consonant with the *collective conception* of group rights than with the *corporate conception* (Jones, 1999a: 353-77). It is argued that the granting of human rights, which are mostly perceived as individual rights, does not in itself provide sufficient protection to minority cultures. 'Minority needs special means—i.e. group-differentiated rights—to provide it with significant involvement in the protection of the individual rights that it ostensibly possesses' (Saban). According to Moore, the purpose of protecting group rights is to enhance individual well-being and while recognizing rights of groups it is often presumed that individual well-being is often dependent on the well-being of groups (2005: 272). Moore, however, agrees that there are exceptional circumstances as well whereby protecting group rights might not be adequate to protect the interests of individuals (ibid.). Dworkin has a different view. He says that if individual citizens in a democracy have rights to any specific kind of liberty, like freedom of speech or religion or political activity, then the idea that these individual rights may lead to overall utility and that the community will be better off in the long run, may or may not be true (Dworkin, 271). In fact, it is irrelevant to the defence of rights as such; 'because when we say that someone has a right to speak his mind freely, in the relevant political sense, we mean that he is entitled to do so even if this would not be in the general interest' (of the community) (ibid.). For Dyke, it is clearly untenable to say that rights belong only to individuals and not to groups. He says that groups identified by various characteristics, including race, language, and religion, in fact, have rights: 'a group has certain rights *if in fact the rights go to individuals* in their capacity as members' (1974: 725-41). For him, groups identified by race, language, or religion often have special legal status and legal rights as collective entities. For Dyke, groups that enjoy rights fall into two categories—one is characterized by weakness that calls for protection or disadvantage that calls for compensatory action (in order to promote equality) and other is characterized by a shared sense of a community of interest that is relatively fundamental, important, and enduring. Survival of interests of distinct group calls for certain groups rights. Dyke, however, recognizes that the fact that groups have rights—and most particularly the fact that groups identified by race, language, or religion have rights—creates a problem in theory and philosophy as well in law. Potential contradiction obviously exists between the proposition that individuals are entitled to equality, without 'distinction' as to race, language, or religion, and the proposition that groups identified by these characteristics may have special legal status and rights. It is also very difficult to identify some common criteria of recognizing group entitlement to rights. In fact, the groups that possess rights vary widely in their characteristics, and the sets of rights that they possess vary too.

The above readings concur with Chandhoke's argument that members of minority groups possess both individual as well as group rights (Chandhoke, 1999: 289). Group-differentiated collective rights are means by which group-based characteristics, such as language, culture, religious practices and traditions, etc., can be protected. Languages and cultures are entities of a collective production, and are meaningful only when viewed collectively. Languages and cultures are such that they can rarely be claimed or enjoyed by an isolated individual, who is all alone. There are many instances where universal individual rights (commonly referred to as human rights) have been linked with group-specific 'community rights' [Examples of human rights documents that (clearly or arguably) ascribe rights to groups include: Convention on the Prevention and Punishment of the Crime of Genocide of 1948 [Art. II]; ILO Convention 107 of 1957; UNESCO Convention of 1960 against Discrimination in Education [Art 2(b) & Art 5(1) (c)]; Art 2(2) of the 1965 UN Convention on the Elimination of all forms of Racial Discrimination; ICCPR [Art. 1]; ICESCR [Art. 1]; Vienna Declaration and Programme of Action, Pt. 1, Art. 2; Declaration on the Rights of Indigenous Peoples. The African Charter on Human and Peoples' Rights also catalogues several rights of peoples, but Peter Jones argues that it presents them as rights that are distinct from, rather than encompassed by, human rights.] Most of the third generation or 'solidarity' human rights (such as rights to peace, development, healthy environment, etc.) and the fourth generation human rights (such as rights of indigenous people) are collective in nature. In fact, if we are willing to extend rights to non-human animals even human rights will be rights unique to a particular group (Jones, 2008).

Minority rights protect non-dominant (or minority) groups in two ways. First, they are granted equality in treatment with the majority. Secondly, they are granted a measure of differential treatment in order to preserve their basic characteristics—those characteristics that distinguish minorities from the majority of the population (Chandhoke, 1999: 290). If minority groups lack effective agency needed to exercise and tend their group rights, then there are two main options. One is to avoid granting or recognizing group rights for groups that lack effective agency (Nickel, op. cit.). Sometimes, part of the work that group rights would have done can be accomplished by giving individual rights to members of the group (we might call this 'privatization' of group rights) (ibid.). The other option is for minorities to try to create clear identity, effective agency, and legitimated leaders that are needed for effective exercise and management of their rights (ibid.). In this regard, minority groups may be assisted by the national government that will be the main addressee of group rights (ibid.). In order to construct clear identity and effective agency, a group will need to have means of encouraging its members to participate and contribute.

Group rights assume importance in a deeply divided society, where divisions among groups are most violent. However, whenever group rights become important for minorities the scope of these rights will be controversial. The majority will act on their own notions of what these rights really are; they will disagree with many of the claims that a minority makes (Dworkin, 205). It may be right that a community's claim of group-differentiated rights hampers the realization of individual rights of members of another community(ies); but when group identity and communal and ethnic prejudices deeply permeate a society (this is perfectly the case in India), group rights of inferior groups assume particular importance. Glazar, thus, critically writes, 'if in a society the groups are sharply divided from one another, so that their boundaries are clear, are firmly set by law or custom, are not expected to become permeable; and if they live in a long historical tradition in which group identification has been used and is used for purposes of discrimination and separation, there may be no alternative: special preferences may be necessary to protect the inferior group and to foster intergroup harmony' (1998: 431). However, Glazar says, 'if inferiority and difference are being overcome, we must consider the negative consequences of selecting the path of group rights and preferences, and we would wish to avoid them if possible'. *In toto*, it is difficult to consider human rights alone without recognizing certain collective rights of people having racial, religious, linguistic, ethnic and other cultural backgrounds. However, we still have to maintain a delicate balance of recognizing individual human rights and group-differentiated minority rights. The rights of an individual should not be necessarily put at risk in the interests of a disadvantaged minority group. The group rights of minorities would be easy to recognize if the rights in question are in the interest of individuals constituting the group.

MINORITY RIGHTS IN INDIA

Minorities in India are scattered all over the country. Historically, minority groups have different cultural basis including language, ethnicity, religion, and so on. Caste, tribal, linguistic as well as religious groups define themselves as minorities in India (Sinha, 2005: 355-

74). Some of them have been officially recognized as minorities, while many others are still claiming recognition. The Sub-Committee on Minorities within the Constituent Assembly had initially identified Anglo-Indians, Parsis, plain tribesmen in Assam, Indian Christians, Sikhs, Muslims, and SCs as minorities (SCs were considered minorities because of their relative backwardness, compared to other Hindu communities). Religious identity was the primary basis of aggregating people and identifying minorities (Mahajan, 1998: 106). Nation remained the reference point of all categorization of majority and minority; communities that were minorities at the national level were considered for safeguards at both the central and the provincial levels (ibid.: 87). The Report of the Sub-Committee on Minorities recommended political and other safeguards for minorities, including reservations to certain religious minorities; but the Constituent Assembly at the time of the final adoption of the Constitution abolished all reservations for religious minorities, effectively removing religious minorities from the purview of any specific political safeguards and, thus, retaining reservations only for the SCs and Scheduled Tribes (ST).

Since the adoption of the Constitution, the context and meaning of the term 'minority' has been changing from time to time, more particularly through judicial interpretations. Though the term 'minority' has been mentioned in two articles (Articles 29 and 30) of the Constitution of India, the word has been left undefined. If we go by the text of two articles, there appears to be three categorizations of minorities in India—linguistic, religious and cultural. The word culture has again been left undefined, thus creating more confusion in defining cultural minorities. Culture may mean anything, and any particular cultural group is entitled to claim minority status based on the culture it possesses or it may intend to define for itself! Language is a part of culture and linguistic minority is considered to form a cultural group as well. Like culture, 'religion' and 'language' have also been left undefined. It is not clear whether language should be well developed with its own grammar and script or whether a spoken language will be sufficient to claim linguistic rights. In the case of DAV College, Jullunder *vs* State of Punjab (AIR 1971 SC 1737), the Supreme Court of India observed: a linguistic minority for the purpose of Article 30(1) is one which must at least have a separate spoken language. It is not necessary that that language should also have a distinct script for those who speak it.

In the case of religion, it is not clear whether religious denominations, sects, emerging new religious beliefs, etc., can also be considered, although the judiciary has accepted (in certain cases) religious denominations or sects (such as Arya Samaj, Brahmo Samaj, etc.) within the purview of religious communities.

After the state of Madras was divided into Tamil-speaking and Telugu-speaking states of Tamil Nadu and Andhra Pradesh in 1953, the States Re-organization Commission embraced the linguistic principle and recommended drastic revisions in state boundaries along linguistic lines in 1955. In the absence of any linguistic majority (no linguistic community constitutes more than 50 per cent of the total population of India), linguistic minorities emerged as a strong political force in the early 1950s; it was so strong that it ultimately led to complete reorganization of the states in India on linguistic basis. The reorganization on linguistic basis provided space for the growth of many regional languages (Mallikarjun, 2004), having far-reaching impact on the other categories of minorities, particularly the religious one. Since linguistic communities mostly did not overlap with religious identities, the demarcation of regions on the basis of a shared language, created new majorities and minorities. As one linguistic community became a majority within a region, others were reduced to the status of (regional) minorities (Mahajan, 1998: 106). With the emergence of linguistic minorities in the political discourse the traditional distinction between majority and minorities became more problematic. The linguistic reorganization created linguistic majority and minority within each region.

After the linguistic reorganization, the Supreme Court ruled that linguistic minorities in a region or more appropriately, in a state, are entitled to the safeguards provided under Article 29 and 30 of the Constitution (ibid.: 88). For example, the Supreme Court in Kerala Education Bill (AIR 1958 SC 976-7) held that when a Bill is passed by a state legislature, which extends to the whole of the state, the minority must be determined by reference to the entire population of the state. It amounted to a determination of minority status within a context smaller than the whole (Indian national) context (Ramaga, 1992: 104-19). In the cases of DAV College, Jullunder *vs.* Punjab (AIR 1971 SC 1737, 1742) and Patroni *vs.* Kesevan (AIR 1965 Kerala 75, 76), the Court pronounced judgements on the line with the 1958 Kerala judgement. In the case of DAV College, Jullunder *vs.* Punjab, the Supreme Court held that minority status should be determined 'in relation to the particular legislation which is sought to be impunged, namely that if it is a state legislation, these minorities have to be determined in relation to the population of the state'. In the matter of TMA Pai Foundation and others *vs.* State of Karnataka [Writ petition (Civil) No. 317 of 1995] the Court defined the term 'minority' within the meaning of Article 30, which provides right to the minorities to establish and administer educational institutions, as follows: '. . . for the purpose of determining the minority, the unit will be the State and not the whole of India. Thus, religious and linguistic minorities, who have been put at par in Article 30, have to be considered State-wise'. In the same case, the Supreme Court also argued that since re-organization of the states in India has been on linguistic lines, therefore, for the purpose of determining the minority, the unit would be the state and not the whole of India.

This judgement clearly says that both linguistic and religious minorities have to be defined state-wise. Under the National Commission for Minorities Act, 1992, the Government of India notified (by its notification dated 23-10-1993) Muslims, Christians, Sikhs, Buddhists and Zoroastrians (Parsis) as minorities. (The notification of the Government of India, however, does not include Jains as minorities. In fact, Article 25 of the Constitution of India, the Hindu Code Bill and some other legal documents still treat Buddhists, Sikhs and Jains as 'Hindu', which is generally considered as the majority community.) As per the 2001 Census, these communities constitute about 18 per cent of the total population of India (numbering about 18.94 crores). The First Report on Religion Data (Census of India, 2001) categorized religious communities in India into Hindus, Muslims, Christians, Sikhs, Buddhists, and Jains. Thus, while the National Commission for Minorities failed to include Jains as minorities, the Census Report on Religion has not included Zoroastrians (Parsis) under its categorization of population by religion (although it deserves to be included). As per the First Report on Religion, at the national level, of the 1,028 million population of India, 828 million (80.5 per cent) have returned their religion as Hindus followed by 138 million (13.4 per cent) as Muslims and 24 million (2.3 per cent) Christians. While 19 million (1.9 per cent) follows Sikh religion; 8 million (0.8 per cent) are Buddhists and 4.2 million (0.4 per cent) are Jains. In addition, 6.6 million belong to 'Other Religions and Persuasions', including tribal religions. About 7 lakh (0.7 million) persons have not stated their religions. State Minorities Acts have again their own definition of minorities, some of which have defined

Jains as minorities. Besides, India contains numerous linguistic minority groups. However, linguistic minority groups have not been properly identified and notified. It is important to mention here that all the states of India have different linguistic composition and all languages are minority languages in some states or other according to the number of speakers in that particular state. As per the 2001 Census, languages that returned 10,000 or more speakers each at the all India level were 122, including 22 Scheduled languages and 100 Non-scheduled languages (often referred to as minority languages). Within these languages, there are again different variations in mother tongues. As per the 2001 Census, there were 234 identifiable mother tongues which returned 10,000 or more speakers each at the all India level.

Constitutional rights of minorities. The Constitution of India inserted certain fundamental rights for the religious, linguistic and cultural minorities. The religious rights of the minority communities (in the form of right to freedom of religion) have been mentioned under Articles 25, 26, 27 and 28 of the Constitution—all persons are equally entitled to freedom of conscience and the right freely to profess, practise and propagate religion (Art. 25(1)); freedom to minorities to manage religious affairs (including right to establish and maintain institutions for religious and charitable purposes) (Art. 26); no person shall be compelled to pay any taxes, the proceeds of which are specifically appropriated in payment of expenses for the promotion or maintenance of any particular religion or religious denomination (Art. 27); freedom to attend to religious instruction or religious worship in educational institutions (Art. 28). Minority rights in the field of culture and education have been provided under Articles 29 and 30. Article 29 states: (1) Any section of the citizens residing in the territory of India or any part thereof having a distinct language, script or culture of its own shall have the right to conserve the same. (2) No citizen shall be denied admission into any educational institution maintained by the state or receiving aid out of state funds on grounds only of religion, race, caste, language or any of them. Article 30 provides minorities the rights to establish and administer educational institutions of their choice and also mentions that the state shall not, in granting aid to educational institutions, discriminate against any educational institution on the ground that it is under the management of a minority, whether based on religion or language.

Articles that are meant to protect the interests of the linguistic minorities include Articles 29, 30, 347, 350, 350A and 350B. Article 347 makes special provision relating to language spoken by a section of the population of a state (declaring a language as official language of the State). Under Art. 350 every person is entitled to submit a representation for the redress of any grievance to any officer or authority of the union or a state in any of the languages used in the Union or in the state, as the case may be. Articles 350A and 350B, which were inserted by the Seventh Amendment Act, 1956 provide facilities for instruction in mother tongue at the primary stage and for the appointment of a special officer for linguistic minorities. Besides, Article 15 prohibits discrimination on grounds of religions, race, caste or any other such grounds. Similarly Article 16(2) lays down that no person can be discriminated against in the matter of public employment on grounds of race, religion and caste.

It is, however, important to mention that the minority rights mentioned in the Constitution are general in nature; there is no specific provision for minority rights. The constitutional entrenchment of (group) rights of minorities is also not a strong proposition for a country like India, which is characterized by innumerable number of minority groups (including minorities within minorities and minorities within majorities). Thus, while constitutionally minority groups were given the freedom to establish religious institutions and manage religious affairs, to establish and administer educational institutions and to preserve minority languages and cultures, they were not granted a constitutional entitlement to state support. The constitutional provisions for the safeguards of minority interests should, therefore, not be treated as certain special provisions of the rights of minorities; instead, we must understand that the minority rights mentioned in the Constitution are very much a part of fundamental (human) rights, fundamental to any liberal democracy. Religious minorities enjoyed certain political rights (including reservation) in pre-independent India, but the constituent assembly (responsible for making of the Constitution of India) has undone all such rights. Religious minorities today enjoy cultural rights only, whereas, linguistic and ethnic minorities (including the tribal communities) enjoy both cultural and political rights. In fact, with the reorganization of the Indian federation on the linguistic basis and because of various judgements of the judiciary (declaring that minorities and their rights have to be defined state-wise) the issue of minority protection and minority rights has become more complex.

The Indian federal structure has led to the cascadization of minorities and minority problems. Now, there are minorities in almost all provinces/units of India. Because of different state laws with regard to minorities, the same set of minorities is being treated differently in different states. The Indian federal structure has put religious/non-territorial minorities into a more disadvantaged position as compared to linguistic or cultural minorities.

The recent creation of a new Ministry of Minority Affairs may be one of the major steps in safeguarding minorities and their rights and interests. The same needs to be replicated in all states. All the ministries of minority affairs (central and state level) may be given enough space to work as 'safeguard houses' for minorities at their respective levels. The Sachar Committee Report has come out with some bold arguments (with empirical facts) underlying the needs for some special measures for socio-economic and educational upliftment of one of the most backward minority communities (i.e. the Muslim). It has come out with some practically sound suggestions and recommendations, which governments (both central and state) can take into account in their policy considerations. Some other recent policy measures such as National Commission for Minority Educational Institutions (NCMEI); National Commission for the Socially and Educationally Backward Sections among the Religious and Linguistic Minorities, etc., Prime Minister's 15-Points Programme for the Welfare of the Minorities; Equal Opportunity Commission; etc., are some other important steps for the safeguard of the interests and rights of minorities. However, there is a need for effective implementation of all these initiatives taken. There is also a need to maintain balance between minority rights protection at the level of state governments and the level of the government at the centre. Nation should remain the reference point for defining religious/non-territorial minorities; and the same yardstick of minority protection and minority rights needs to be considered at the central and provincial levels.

CONCLUSION

There is an inherent conflict between rights of individuals and collective rights of minorities. It has been argued that human rights are not inherently individualistic and posses certain group features as well. There are, in fact, certain rights which men are entitled to claim as a group; these rights emanate from the 'supreme natural order' and may be referred to as natural rights. The natural order created by the family and many other group features and customs can be located prior to state. Becoming a member of an enduring community other than the state provides security and satisfaction to the members of a minority group. Thus, group rights (including group rights of minorities) have an autonomous sphere of their own. The group rights of minorities, which the natural order of law has already recognized, cannot be undone by positive human rights laws created by state. In fact, it is difficult to consider human rights alone without recognizing certain collective rights of people having racial, religious, linguistic, ethnic and other cultural backgrounds. Group rights of minorities are essential to protect minorities from any future discrimination and also to place members of their communities on an equal footing with members of the majority community.

In India, rights for minorities assume greater significance because of the segregation among different communities (based on language, religion, cultures, and so on). The minority rights mentioned in the Constitution of India are very much a part of the fundamental (human) rights, fundamental to any liberal democracy; these are general in nature and do not talk about any specific minority rights. There is no mention of any exclusive state support for the realization of the minority rights mentioned in the Constitution.

In brief, the solution to minority question lies in not giving more importance to group-based recognition of rights but on a collectivity of civic rights, human rights and individual rights with special sensitivity to members of the minority communities. Group rights may be recognized only in the rarest of the rare cases, and that too based on merit and emergency requirements. Giving more importance to group-rights of minorities may be problematic in the future—it may not be helpful to solve the rights of minorities within minorities and minorities within majorities. It may create more communal ill-feelings, more groups (though smaller in number) may come forward and demand special group-specific rights and when numbers of such minority groups increases there is always a likelihood of unequal treatment to different groups.

REFERENCES

Bangure, Yusuf (2006), 'Ethnic Inequalities in the Public Sector: A Comparative Analysis', *Development and Change*, vol. 37, no. 2.

Barry, Brian (2001), *Culture and Equality: An Egalitarian Critique of Multiculturalism*, Cambridge: Polity Press.

Barsh, Russel Lawrence, 'Evolving Conceptions of Group Rights in International Law', http://www.ibiblio.org/obl/docs3/Barsh.doc (accessed 14 August 2007).

Capotorti, Francesco (1991), *Study on the Rights of Persons Belonging to Ethnic, Religious and Linguistic Minorities*, New York: United Nations.

Chandhoke, Neera (1999), 'Negotiating Collective and Individual Rights', in Neera Chandhoke, *Beyond Secularism: The Rights of Religious Minorities*, New Delhi: Oxford University Press.

Coontz, Phyllis D. (1986), 'The Etymology of "Minority" and Women in International Law', in Satish Chandra (ed.), *International Protection of Minorities*, Delhi: Mittal Publications.

Dahrendorf, Ralf (1984), 'Minority Rights and Minority Rule', in Ben Whitaker (ed.), *Minorities: A Question of Human Rights?*, Oxford: Pergamon Press.

Dinstein, Yoram (1976), 'Collective Human Rights of Peoples and Minorities', *The International and Comparative Law Quarterly*, vol. 25, no. 1.

Dworkin, Ronald (1999), 'What Rights Do We Have?', in Ronald Dworkin, *Taking Rights Seriously*, Delhi: Universal Law Publishing Co. Pvt. Ltd.

Dyke, Vernon Van (1974), 'Human Rights and the Rights of Groups', *American Journal of Political Science*, vol. 18, no. 4.

——— (1982), 'Collective Entities and Moral Rights: Problems in Liberal-Democratic Thought', *The Journal of Politics*, vol. 44, no. 1.

Eisenberg, Avigail and Jeff Spinner-Halev (2005), 'Introduction', in Avigail Eisenberg and Jeff Spinner-Halev (eds.), *Minorities within Minorities: Equality, Rights and Diversity*, Cambridge: Cambridge University Press.

Glazer, Nathan (1998), 'Individual Rights against Group Rights', in Gurpreet Mahajan (ed.), *Democracy, Difference & Social Justice*, New Delhi: Oxford University Press.

Government of India (2004), *Census of India 2001: The First Report on Religion Data*, New Delhi: Registrar General and Census Commissioner, India.

——— (2006), *Social, Economic and Educational Status of the Muslim Community of India: A Report, Prime Minister's High Level Committee, Govt. of India (also referred to as Sachar Committee Report).*

Henrard, Kristin (2001), 'Language Rights and Minorities in South Africa', *International Journal on Multicultural Societies (IJMS)*, vol. 3, no. 2.

——— (2001), 'The Interrelationship Between Individual Human Rights, Minority Rights and the Right to Self-determination and its Importance for the Adequate Protection of Linguistic Minorities', *The Global Review of Ethnopolitics*, vol. 1, no. 1.

Hohfeld, Wesley (1919), *Fundamental Legal Conceptions*, New Haven: Yale University Press.

Jones, Peter (1989), 'Re-examining Rights', *British Journal of Political Science*, vol. 19, no. 1.

——— (1999a), 'Group Rights and Group Oppression', *The Journal of Political Philosophy*, vol. 7, no. 4.

——— (1999b), 'Human Rights, Group Rights, and Peoples' Rights', *Human Rights Quarterly*, vol. 21.

——— (2008), *The Stanford Encyclopedia of Philosophy*.

Junckerstorf, Henry K. (1961), *World Minorities*, Kolkata: Bookland Private Limited.

Kymlicka, Will (1995), *Multicultural Citizenship: A Liberal Theory of Minority Rights*, Oxford: Clarendon Press.

——— (1998), 'Multicultural Citizenship', in G. Mahajan (ed.), *Democracy, Difference & Social Justice*, op. cit.

——— (2001), *Politics in the Vernacular: Nationalism, Multiculturalism and Citizenship*, Oxford: Oxford University Press.

——— (2002), 'Multiculturalism and Minority Rights: West and East, *JEMIE: Journal on Ethnopolitics and Minority Issues in Europe*, Issue 4.

Loobuyck, Patrick (2005), 'Liberal Multiculturalism: A Defence of Liberal Multicultural Measures without Minority Rights', *Ethnicities*, vol. 5(1).

Mahajan, Gurpreet (1998), *Identities and Rights: Aspects of Liberal Democracy in India*, New Delhi: Oxford University Press.

Mallikarjun, B. (2004), 'An Exploration into Linguistic Majority-Minority Relations in India', *Language in India* 4(8).

Mintnick, Eric J., 'Taking Rights Spherically: Formal and Collective Aspects of Legal Rights', *Wake Forest Law Review*, vol. 34.

Moore, Margaret (2005), 'Internal Minorities and Indigenous Self-determination', in Avigail Eisenberg and Jeff Spinner-Halev (eds.), op. cit.

Nickel, James W. (1997), 'Group Agency and Group Rights', in Ian Shapiro and Will Kymlicka (eds.), *Ethnicity and Group Rights*, New York: New York University Press.

Ramaga, Philip Vuciri (1992), 'Relativity of the Minority Concept', *Human Rights Quarterly* 14(1).

——— (1993), 'The Group Conception in Minority Protection', *Human Rights Quarterly*, vol. 15, no. 3.

Saban, Ilan, 'Minority Rights in Deeply Divided Societies: A Framework for Analysis and the Case of the Arab-Palestinian Minority in Israel. http://www.law.nyu.edu/journals/jilp/issues/36/36–4–Saban.pdf (accessed 12 January 2007).

Sen, Amartya (2006), *Identity and Violence: The Illusion of Destiny*, New Delhi: Penguin Books.

Sinha, Manoj Kumar (2005), 'Minority Rights: A Case Study of India', *International Journal on Minority and Group Rights*, no. 12.

Wallerstein, Immanuel (2003), 'Citizens All? Citizens Some! The Making of the Citizen', *Comparative Studies in Society and History: An International Quarterly*, vol. 45, issue 4.

Wellman, Christopher Heath (1999), 'Liberalism, Communitarianism, and Groups Rights', *Law and Philosophy*, vol. 18, no. 1.

CHAPTER 15

Double Colonization for the Marginalized Children: A Literary Delineation

NANDINI SAHU

INTRODUCTION

The objective of this paper is to focus on the structurally defined roles of the marginalized children in India since time immemorial by making a literary analysis of two most famous novels by Mulk Raj Anand and gradually redefining some social issues in modern India. Change is the spice of life, the grassroot of civilization. But are we really changing? According to the UNICEF and International Labour Organization (ILO), around the world today, some 250 million boys and girls between the ages of 5 and 14 are exploited in perilous labour conditions. Most of these children live in the developing world, but even in industrialized countries such as the United States, hundreds of thousands of under-age boys and girls are at work in sweatshops, farms, brothels and on the street. It is estimated that about 5.5 crore (55 million) children in India between the ages of 5 and 14 are labourers. India has the ill fame of having the largest number of child labourers in the world. It is really unfortunate that one in every four working children in the world is an Indian. The UNO has prescribed several rights for children out of which how many are really practised is the matter of concern and dialogue here. Children's rights include:

- Right to be loved;
- Right to nutritious food and good health;
- Right to education;
- Right to entertainment coupled with proper physical growth;
- Right to get his/her nationality in his/her name;

- Right to get other's attention in distress;
- Right to relief in cases of natural calamities;
- Right to nurture and develop their inherent skills and abilities so as to be a useful member of the society;
- Right to nurture humanitarian values and goodwill in others; and
- Right to guard against forces dividing the country on caste, religion and other grounds.

In this paper I would be discussing how literature contributes towards the process of social development of the marginalized. How are the structurally defined roles of the marginalized sections of the society redefined by writers like Mulk Raj Anand who are rather social reformers setting their pen towards a social movement and the empowerment of the marginalized. Due to limited scope, only two important novels by Anand—*Untouchable* and *Coolie* would be discussed in the paper.

II

Writing in the realistic mode, Mulk Raj Anand tries to use English in a nativized way. The intention of the writer is to bestow sympathy on the poor, the untouchable and the marginalized. By doing so Anand suffers resistance to both the forces: the forces of conventional society which colonized the poor and the untouchables from a religio-social-superstitious attitude, and the forces of the political colonizers who never had any sympathy for the marginalized. Anand evidences and illustrates the forces of double colonization and reveals a humane and sympathetic attitude towards the marginalized. By doing so, Anand was not only trying to represent India from a much more realistic perspective, but also trying to highlight a new concept of identity which was emerging because of the dehumanizing condition generated by colonization. Anand tries to illustrate a national identity bedecked with sympathy, but also attempts at championing the causes of the marginalized in a larger perspective so that a universal construct of the marginalized could be established and followed. It is for his adherence to an indigenous value system that Anand could champion the causes of the marginalized in his fiction and attempt to save these marginalized ones from the uncanny forces of double colonization. This is how, by representing the nation he was trying to go beyond the nation.

There was a socio-political background to the making of this great writer. From his peasant mother he derived his rationality, his sense of the ache at the heart of Indian civilization, and his understanding and compassion for the waifs, the disinherited, the lowly, the lost, *Daridranarayana* (the poor and the downtrodden, who is close to the heart of God), the one visible godhead omnipresent in the Indian subcontinent. Somerset Maugham has written in his *Notebook* about the marginalized in India: 'it wasn't the Taj Mahal, the *ghats* of Benaras, the temple at Madurai or the mountains of Travancore that had moved me; it was the peasant, terribly emaciated, with nothing to cover his nakedness but a rag round the middle. . . . That was the sight that had given me the most poignant emotion in India' (Bald, 1974). The 1930s were the seed-time of modern independent India—the Gandhian salt satyagraha movements of 1930 and 1932, the three Round Table Conferences, the passing of the Government of India Act of 1935, the preamble of Provincial Autonomy in 1937, the Gandhian movements of Harijan uplift and basic education, the organization of Marxist parties of diverse hues (the Congress Socialists, the Royalists, the Communists), the involvement in the War in 1939, the rupture in the Congress leading to the removal of Subhas Chandra Bose and his eventual escape to Germany and Japan—it was a packed decade. Although resident in England, Anand was tempted to respond to the impact of those events in Indian society and literature. With him, as with Bankim Chandra, the political actions took the form of writing novels. He wrote about the people, for the people, and as the one in charge of the common people, the marginalized Indian. His early novels reveal an endeavour and a sense of direction much as a deluge or a flood that shows viciousness of thrust, a pouring of strength, a motivating rush towards the goal. His first five novels appeared in the following sequence—*Untouchable* (1935), *Coolie* (1936), *Two Leaves and a Bud* (1937), *The Village* (1939) and *Across the Black Waters* (1940). There are several other novels and collections of short stories: *The Sword and the Sickle, The Barber's Trade Union, The Big Heart, The Tractor and the Corn Goddess, Seven Summers, Private Life of an Indian Prince,* and *Morning Face*. Anand's concentration on social themes continued in *The Coolie* and *Two Leaves and a Bud*, which relate the tribulations of working-class life in India. Critics assert that in his early work Anand employed a markedly polemical style when attributing India's social problems to the caste structure, British rule, and capitalism. His approach and thematic focus shifted to more psychosomatic and humanistic interpretations in such later works as *The Private Life of an Indian Prince* (1953) which explores the emotional and mental corrosion of a young royal who neglects his duties in pursuit of an affair with a peasant woman—and in the autobiographical novels comprising his *Seven Ages of Man* series, in which he relates the events of his life through the character Krishan Chander. The first volume in the series, *Seven Summers* (1951), spans the first seven years of the author's life and explores the relationship of actuality and imagination inimitable to childhood. In *Morning Face* (1968), Anand recounts the meagreness of his early education and the cruel behaviour he and other students endured at the hands of their schoolmasters, memories that led the author in later years to fight for educational transformation in India. *Confession of a Lover* (1984) explores the sting of a vanished love during the author's college years. *The Bubble* (1984), which covers his way of life as a student and juvenile writer in London, includes much dialogue of his connection with the Bloomsbury Group writers.

In the setting of the late 1920s and the early 1930s, the Indian air was filled with the dust of politics and infected with the smoulder of man's callousness to man, but it was not completely pessimistic. In his special Preface to the second Indian edition of *Two Leaves and a Bud* (1951), Anand gives a hint of this early combustion behind his first novels. In writing of the pariahs and the bottom dogs rather than of the elite and the sophisticated, he had gambled into a territory that had been largely ignored till then by other Indian writers. For all their nationalistic involvements, Bankim Chandra's novels were rather romances somewhat similar to Walter Scott, with a historical or mystical angle. Tagore was chiefly interested in the upper and middle classes, and Sarat Chandra in the lower middle classes; Munshi Premchand chose his themes from the peasantry and the humble folk of Uttar Pradesh. It was Anand's aim to show to the world that there was more in the Orient than could be anecdotal from Omar Khayyam, Li Po, Tagore or Kipling. He described a waif-like Munoo in *Coolie*, and an untouchable like Bakha, an impassioned labourer like Gangu, and set them right at the centre of the design of malice and exploitation that held India in its sadistic grip. Although born in one of the higher castes, his father, Lall Chand Anand, served in the Indian Army, rising to be a *subedar*; and Mulk Raj as a child had mixed freely with the children of the sweepers attached to his father's contingent. Such associations wounding transversely caste divisions had continued into his adolescence. These early playmates and friends became, with the necessary imaginative altitude and amendment, the champions of his first few novels. About his artistic personae Anand writes,

> All these heroes, as the other men and women who had emerged in my novels and short stories, were dear to me, because they were the reflections of the real people I had known during my childhood and youth. And I was only repaying the debt of gratitude I owed them for much of the inspiration they had given me to mature into manhood, when I began to interpret their lives in my writing. They were not mere phantoms. . . . They were flesh of my flesh and blood of my blood, and obsessed me in the way in which certain human beings obsess an artist's soul. And I was doing no more than what a writer does when he seeks to interpret the truth from the realities of his life. (Dhawan, 1992)

Anand preferred the familiar to the fancied, avoiding the highways of romance and sophistication and surveying the bylanes of the outcastes and the peasants, the sepoys and the working people. It was not a laborious exercise of self-conscious proletarianism so he wrote in a brisk unselfconscious way about what he had seen first-hand in the years of his childhood, boyhood and youth. It is not necessarily that Anand, the novelist, was in restraints to the political evading, and was just the campaigner of the subjugated and the hard-up. Anand was a student of poetry, of the arts and philosophy before he turned to political accomplishment through creative writing. In fact, he had first seen his heroes as pieces of irresolute humanity and loved them before he thought of putting them into his books.

Of all his novels, *Untouchable* is the most condensed and creatively rewarding. The three 'unities' are admirably preserved—unity of time, place and action—as in a classical play, as *Untouchable* covers the events of a single day in the life of the 'low-caste' boy, Bakha, in the town of Bulashah. The eighteen-year old boy is one of the sons of Lakha, the *jemadar* or the sweeper of the town and cantonment. Bakha is a child of the twentieth century, and the collision of new influences causes commotions within him. From a Tommy he has secured a pair of old breeches, and from a sepoy a pair of old boots; he would like to look like the white foreigner and so be in the 'fasshun'. But as the day dawns, his work of latrine-cleaning also begins and his dreams shackle because he is a worker, but what is praiseworthy about him is his efficiency at work: 'Each muscle of his body, hard as rock when it came to play, seemed to shine forth like glass . . . "What a dexterous workman" the onlooker would have said. And though his job was dirty he remained comparatively clean' (*Untouchable*, p. 39). Anand describes Bakha's morning round of duties with a conscientious idiosyncrasy, bringing out both the competence with which the boy does this essential service and the coldness with which the beneficiaries receive it, as if it were a subject of no elucidation. Three rows of latrines to clean single-handed, and several times too, to bring cleanliness in the place of filth and feasible diseases of the 'babus'—such is Bakha's daily sweat which he turns into a skilful art.

Bakha's cup of aggravation and desolation is full. Anand offers three solutions to Bakha's agony of self-abasement and distress. There is Colonel Hutchinson, the Salvationist, who asks Bakha to turn into a Christian and to end his caste, by which he would not be vulnerable to the caste Hindus anymore. Next, Bakha sees Mahatma Gandhi, who addresses a public meeting which Bakha attends. Gandhiji says: 'I regard untouchability as the greatest blot on Hinduism' (*Untouchable*, p. 42). If he is to be born again, he would prefer to be born an out-caste rather than as a member of one of the so-called higher castes, thinks Bakha. Because the 'untouchable' is really the *Harijan*, the 'man of God'. It was Satanic to think that anybody was 'polluted' or could 'pollute' another. This is vastly heartening, and also bewildering for Bakha. But he comes across, before the evening wears out, a third person who is equally inspiring—this time with the poet Iqbal Nath Sarshar. He simply says that when the scavengers amend their profession, they will end their caste and a modern sanitary system—the flush—will bring about this rebellion. 'Then the sweepers can be free,' the poet concludes, 'from the stigma of untouchability and assume the dignity of status that is their right as useful members of a casteless and classless society' (*Untouchable*, p. 62). Bakha is duly overwhelmed, he feels more buoyant and hopeful in his outlook than at any time since the day dawned, and proceeds to his house to tell his father about the Mahatma and about the machine that will 'clear dung without anyone having to handle it' (*Untouchable*, p. 63).

Defending this epilogue in his Foreword to the book, E.M. Forster rightly says: 'it is the necessary climax, and it has mounted up with triple effect. Bakha returns to his father and his wretched bed, thinking now of the Mahatma, now of the Machine. His Indian day is over and the next days will be like it, but on the surface of the earth if not in the depths of the sky, a change is at hand' (Foreword,

Untouchable). Bakha is simply the archetypal 'untouchable', for he is also himself an inimitable personage and he can be called an exceptional 'untouchable'. The many things that come about him in the novel could have happened to anybody—in fact they still happen in post-Independent India in some form of the other. As a novelist addressing himself to the task of exposing social evils, Anand has been as successful as Dickens himself. In his Preface to the book, E.M. Forster wrote: '. . . the book seems to me indescribably clean . . . it has gone straight to the heart of its subject and purified it' (Foreword, *Untouchable*).

III

If *Untouchable* is the microcosm, *Coolie* is more like the macrocosm of Indian society. In this, deliberation gives place to dissemination and understanding. *Coolie* is about a cross-section of India, the observable India, that fabrication of the hideous and the holy, the inhuman and the humane, the grimy and the attractive. The general effect is panoramic and in actual life. There is no time for the reader to reflect, to judge, for the reader is constantly shifted, a new situation comes at every turn. Munoo is 'subjugated' all the time, one way or the other, by one person or another; and his fate is typical of the fate of millions whose only distinguishing badge is uncomplaining sufferance.

Like 'untouchable', 'coolie' too has been a term of derogation in India. India's surplus population has for over a century overflowed in various directions, and there are Indian 'coolies' in Africa, Myanmar, Sri Lanka, Malaysia and many other countries. While the coolie's services are welcome, he is himself hardly tolerated. Inside India too, there are those who have no property, no education, no rewarding vocation, and these drift into the commonplace trade of the 'coolie'. Anand was determined that he would pick up the 'coolie'—as in Bakha he humanized the 'untouchable'—and give him feelings, a mind, a heart, a soul, and elevate his poise as a wavering piece of flesh and blood, worthy of some tribute in solemn literature. Usually the coolie is just taken for granted, as if he were but a shadow, a cheap but quite useful machine, an uncomplaining object for abuses and indignities. But Anand would rather ask: 'Hath not a Coolie eyes? Hath not a Coolie hands, organs, dimensions, senses, affections, passions, fed with the same food, hurt with the same weapons, subject to the same diseases, healed by the same eons, cooled and warmed by the same winter and summer as anybody else is'? (*Coolie*, p. 43). The coolie too is the 'paragon of animals'! (*Coolie*, p. 44).

As a writer of fiction, Anand's notable virtues are vitality and a keen sense of actuality. He is a genuine Dickens for describing the inequities and idiosyncrasies in the current human condition with honesty as well as accuracy. The titles of his early novels—*Untouchable, Coolie, Village*—seem to emphasize the universal as against the particular; as if Bakha is every 'untouchable', Munoo is all 'coolies'. Being an accurate artist, Anand makes the individual—Bakha or Munoo—affirm his distinctiveness, without quite ceasing to be the common. There is an implied point of view; but the novels are more than the case, for it is humanity that finally triumphs. In an interview, Anand says,

> I am . . . doing some village social welfare work in order to integrate my love for the poor with actual work for them. . . . I never realized as intensely as I do now, the reasons why Tolstoy and many others write about pains of these people; I now feel that, for their sake, it may not all have been in vain. *The Old Woman and the Cow and The Road* will confirm the poetic truth that the alleviation of pain and its expiation are the only values given to our intelligentsia in the present time. (www.bolokids.com)

Anand's *Coolie* carries no specific disapproval of individuals; the condemnation is against society as a whole—a culture that breeds such discrimination and malice. In *Untouchable* the evil is secluded as caste, in *Coolie* the evil is more widespread, and appears as gluttony, self-centredness and callousness in their hundred singular forms. Yet the root of the affair is poverty; as Munoo realizes, 'all servants look alike. There must be only two kinds of people in the world: the rich and the poor' (*Coolie*, p. 21). And poverty is restrained all over India, and like a point infects all our society and renders it unsocial and ruthless. An urchin, Munoo, finds his life with his uncle and aunt loveless enough, but when he is sent to Babu Nathoo Ram's house at Sham Nagar and to Bibiji, his heart sinks: 'And, in his heart, there was a lonely song, a melancholy wail, asking, not pointedly, but in a vague, uncertain rhythm, what life in this woman's house would prove' (*Coolie*, p. 22). It actually proves to be a sort of madhouse, and people are pitiless because they cannot be happy. Only the Chota Babu is kind, for his own disposition is to be happy and give happiness. A crisis soon comes, and Munoo escapes from this penitentiary and seeks transitory shelter in a train. He is discovered lying under the bunk by a passenger, Prabha, who takes Munoo. He experiences the flutter of excitement with 'the fear of the unknown in his bowels and the stirring of hope for a better life in the new world he was entering' (*Coolie*, p. 30). In this cavernous world of the Cat Killers' Lane, tensions increase fast, there are abuses, and life endlessly enacts its trifling dramas of sadism and cruelty. Unfortunately for Munoo, his benefactor becomes bankrupt as a result of sharp practice by his partner, and has to leave Daulatpur for good. Munoo now becomes a coolie in the grain market and a porter at the station. He has seen domestic service, service in a pickle factory, service as a coolie and porter, and even disciplehood for an hour under a lecherous 'Yogi'. By accident he makes the association of an elephant-trainer in a circus, and with his help reaches Bombay. He is, however, duly warned: 'The bigger a city is, the more cruel it is to the sons of Adam. Your have to pay even for the breath that you breathe. But you are a brave lad' (*Coolie*, p. 44). Life on the pavements or in the slums, service in the Sir George White Cotton Mills, conflict with human sharks and hyaenas, the friendship of Hari and Lakshmi, the companionship of Ratan, the plunge into the Red Lights district, involvement in the 'labour trouble' and the Hindu–Muslim disturbances, Munoo experiences them all, and as he runs up Malabar Hill to escape the hectic police action, he is knocked down by a car. Its owner, Mrs. Mainwaring, decides to take Munoo with her to Simla. She is a woman of vast pretensions and no morals, and makes Munoo her rickshaw-puller and page; and worn out by work, he hastens to his grave.

Coolie is the tragedy of Munoo who moves from place to place in search of livelihood, driven by need, till he finally falls into the clutches of decease. Poverty which gives birth to abuse is the root cause of Munoo's catastrophe. Before he begins his disgraceful odyssey, Munoo is a receptive and sharp rural teenager, full of high spirits and enthusiasm for life. He is a whiz at climbing trees. He would hop on to the trunk like a monkey, climb the bigger branches on odd hours. But poverty and hunger compell Munoo to be apprenticed to life even at the age of fourteen. An innocent country boy, Munoo is far from being go-getting, being ambitious in life. His expectations are extremely modest. His only desire is to live: 'I want to know, I want to work' (*Coolie*, p. 23). From these intolerable conditions, a strike erupts and turns into a Hindu-Muslim riot. As the ill-housed, undernourished and bullied labourers like Hari are broken, both in body and mind, Munoo gives himself to a piece of self-introspection,

'Am I really ominous? . . . My father died when I was born and then my mother, and I brought misfortune to Prabha, and, it seems, I have brought misfortune to Hari now. If I am ominous, why don't I die?' (*Coolie*, p. 49). One is likely to be moved to tears by hearing this most tragic expression of Munoo. Furthermore, Munoo is the horrified witness of communal murder and senseless killings. As a rickshaw-puller, Munoo gradually grows weaker and dies at the age of sixteen. Thus, Anand dramatizes in *Coolie* the evils of poverty, exploitation and brutality that squeeze a bud of youth before it can bloom. Munoo's tragedy seems to be Anand's proclamation for transformation. Humanism could be the only response to his dilemma in the present political set-up. The novel highlights the need for re-establishment of kindness to the world lost in industrialism, capitalism and socialism. Munoo's death is a catharsis. Mother India receives Munoo to her bosom with the words: 'We belong to suffering! We belong to suffering! My love!' (*Coolie*, p. 85).

Reviewing *Coolie* on its first appearance, the *Spectator* said: 'Munoo is a universal kind of figure' (Sharma, 1977: 73). He is a sturdy hill-boy, with a taste for the joy of life which is denied to him again and again. His full-bodied health, his eagerness for life, his fundamentally innocent nature, his penchant to react to benevolence, his fear that good and evil should be so inextricably mixed up, all make him a true descendant to Bakha, who are both heirs to the sizzling disillusionment that is the only birthright for millions born as the marginalized children in India.

Although Anand's *Coolie* has received a fine deal of critical consideration from both reviewers and literary critics, it is yet to be explored in full as a social tragedy. Like Arthur Miller's Willy Loman in *Death of a Salesman*, Anand's Munoo is a catastrophic personality who inspires pity but no horror. Anand not only raises the hill boy to the rank of a hero, but also endows him with self-esteem. He does not romanticize the proletariat but renders the societal forces of catastrophe—capitalism, industrialism and communalism—as they are seen operating in the existing society. Anand's proficiency to suggest places, persons, moods, scenes, and situations is as mysterious as it is serious, and few novels of modern India can outshine its beauty and power of narration. Anand sees life sometimes as jest, sometimes as a tragedy, and sometimes the two modes fuse, and at his best his work challenges resemblance with that of the great masters for the art of narrating stories. Munoo's destiny symbolizes the tragic state of affairs of the disadvantaged and the under-privileged who in themselves are not responsible for their unmitigated agony, but who are rather the victims of cold-blooded exploitation.

The very identity of the novel is distinguishing. It is not 'The Coolie' or 'A Coolie' but *Coolie* encircling all coolies—all those marginalized ones—and their providence. What makes Coolie a potent social tragedy is the unique handling of the cruel, merciless societal forces of scarcity and mistreatment which are responsible for the tragic end. The premature death of the central character becomes all the more tragic because he is an innocent child. The narrative is restricted to an episode little more than a year, in order to stress the physical tragedy of the premature death. Anand invests Munoo with sociological significance by making him represent various phases of people's existence in definite settings in the course of the narrative, thereby organizing the action in a structurally meaningful way. If only the social and industrial system had been humane, democratic, life-enhancing and unrestricted, all might have turned out differently. Munoo had aspiration and talents. He could feel love, arouse love and loyalty in others and he could become the lover of two women. But it is his poverty that restraints him, imprisones him in the unavoidable prison of the coolie's life, and finally kills him. Nevertheless, beneath this pervasive pessimism, there is an essential under-current of optimism in that the protagonist's death poignantly establishes the rotten state of society and the consciousness of the need for its drastic reform. Munoo is not able to redeem himself because he is made to think that people like him are born to suffer. He expresses himself, 'We belong to suffering! We belong to suffering!' Anand universalizes the individual tragedy of Munoo following the anthropological dictum that the 'proper study of mankind is man', Anand presents Munoo as a victim of ridiculous systems and the inhuman cruelties of society (Verma, 2000: 33).

Even if the critics have started looking askance at Anand because of his uninnovative style of writing (Rushdiets have started disliking the trio of Raja Rao, Mulk Raj Anand and R.K. Narayan), yet his faith in tradition, in the agrarian culture of India and Gandhian values cannot be ignored. It is but for his adherence to an indigenous value system that Anand could champion the causes of the marginalized in his fiction and attempted to save these marginalized ones from the uncanny forces of double colonization. The problem of class and poverty, decadence, backwardness, ignorance and erroneous beliefs admits no easy solution. After so many years of Anand's novel (written in 1935), and 60 years after Independence, the problem with rounded boundaries and also with some relieving features still defies an unyielding and utter elucidation in India. For his realistic portrayals of the social and economic problems suffered by Indians because of the caste system and British colonial rule, Anand is considered by many critics to be one of India's best writers. The value of his novels, according to Margaret Berry, 'is the witness they offer of India's agonizing attempt to break out of massive stagnation and create a society in which men and women are free and equal' (ibid.: 34).

IV

In 1986, the Government of India heard the bereaved cry of millions of homeless, hungry and condemned children of India, and the Child Labour (Prohibition and Regulation) Act was enacted. The Act prohibits children from engaging in activities considered perilous to their health and well-being. It regulates the working conditions of children employed in non-hazardous occupations. In addition, a National Policy on Child Labour was announced in 1987. The policy envisages the National Child Labour Project (NCLP), a project-based action committee initiated to work in areas of high application of child labour. Twenty years later the bangles that women treasure, the gemstone glasses that add charm to the dining table, the finely woven carpets, the fire crackers that light the night sky on Deepawali, are still made by tiny hands of Bakhas and Munoos. The Child Labour (Prohibition and Regulation) Act has failed to smear out even a speck of the social crime witnessed in every part of the country's streets, homes, factories and shops. Indeed, according to the 2001 Census, India has 12.6 million child workers. Activists estimate the figure is more than 60 million, and they could be true.

> It was the parliament elected by a more popular suffrage in 1868 that passed, as we know, the first great Education Act. This Act introduced compulsory schooling. The principle was established once and for all that parents were not to be allowed to do as they willed with their children, if they willed either to set them to work or to let them run wild without elementary education. Freedom of contract in respect of all dealings with the labour of children was so far limited. (Green, 1900)

Meanwhile, the Union Ministry of Labour and Employment passed a notification on 11 October 2006, following a High Court order.

The notification states that service of children under 14 years as domestic workers or servants in *dhabas*, restaurants, hotels, motels, tea-shops, resorts, spas or other recreational centres is punishable with imprisonment for a term not less than three months, a fine of Rs. 10,000 which may extend to Rs. 20,000, or both. Did anything change after that? Not really. Seema, 13 years of age, from West Bengal, has been working as a domestic help in Delhi for the last two years. She has never seen her father, as he left her mother before Seema was born. She was brought here by her aunty, *mausi*, as she is popularly known. *Mausi* brings children, especially girls, with the promise of two meals a day and clothes. These children are either abandoned by their families or sent to Delhi to earn some extra money. Seema says most of the women in her village are often sick because of constant childbirths, early marriage, non-stop hard work and hazardous working conditions, due to which she chose to come here. But it was a leap from the frying pan to the fire. *Mausi* is a one-woman domestic placement agency. She brings the children from the villages, gets them a job as a domestic help, in a *dhaba*, a garage. In return, she gets a commission. The employers are happy as they have got a 'slave' without the hassle of residency agencies. It is an established truth that children who start working at a younger age attain a lower level of education, which has an understandable impact on the child's future well-being and capability to engender income. Would parents desire to send their children to work if they did not face severe economic restraint? Would parents send their children to work if they really had the prospect to choose?

There is yet another child's story to tell. Budhia, a boy from Orissa, has completed 65-km marathon from the Jagannath Temple in Puri to the CRPF campus in Bhubaneswar to establish a milestone in his early career. Though he narrowly failed to complete the run of 70-km in the obligatory time of seven hours, he still managed to make it into the *Limca Book of Records*. Budhia Singh has become well known since he participated in the Delhi Marathon in October 2007. Though by that time, he had already gained publicity in the local and national media, the Delhi Marathon helped him gain international fame. Among the thousands of people, amature runners and professional marathon runners from various countries, Budhia was at the centre of media publicity. Be it the local media, national or international, Budhia was everywhere. Obviously, it is because of his age. He was only 3 years and 9 months at that time. According to his mentor and coach Biranchi Narayan Das, the Making-of-Budhia story is fascinating and out of the ordinary. He says, once he saw this 3-year-child with a middle-aged scrap collector and got suspicious. When he enquired about the child, the man told him that he had bought him for Rs. 800. Owing to severe poverty, Budhia's mother had sold him to the scrap collector. But the destiny was with Budhia. The incredible talent of the child also attracted an international documentary filmmaker to shoot a film on the wonder-kid. A French television channel has already shot a 12-minute documentary on him. The publicity brought some twists in the tale. There were and are some controversies—Budhia's mother has accused mentor Biranchi Narayan Das of torturing, Budhia which is a matter of concern.

Perhaps the most important lesson to be gleaned from the scholastic work in this area is that child labour tends to be an occurrence related to poverty and difficult social conditions rather than an obstinate predilection of parents. In that sense, any policy oriented towards eliminating the problem must take that fact into consideration if it is to be successful. For example, improving the labour conditions of parents or compensating the families who send their children to school may be more effective ways to deal with the problem from a public policy perspective than absolute bans. 'This is strongly related to the labor market conditions of the parents. Parents who work in low-quality, poorly paid jobs, tend to be more vulnerable to poverty and thus send their children to work' (Rozensweig and Evenson, 1997). Poverty of parents is the prime cause driving children to join the labour force, although it is not the only cause. The lack of improved vision on the part of parents, their ignorance and lack of education are some other reasons they let children enter the labour market. 'The concomitant effect is that the child who is considered as a valuable asset of the nation is fore-doomed to failure and his future is stolen. Needless to add, the high incidence of working children is correlated with poverty and under-employment of parents and elder siblings' (Christiaan and Ravi, 1995). There is a tradition of the 'household farm' in which child labour is seen as a basic component of everyday life. International Labour Standards (ILS) lay down restrictions on child labour that have been internationally agreed-upon. The objective of ILS in general is to achieve a minimum standard of living across countries. A child cannot be developed in nothingness. It needs the hold up of the family and the society as a whole. Undoubtedly, parents are the principal caretakers of the child.

The development of the child depends on the development of the parents. It is this theme which needs to be focused. This can be achieved if families of the child workers are strengthened by inducting the parents into some income-generating activities which promises economic empowerment. 'It seems, for example, that permanent shocks, like divorce, have a clear impact on children's school attendance, whereas during temporary shocks, like unemployment, parents tend to protect the school time of their children whenever possible' (Parker and Skoufias, 2000).

Because many of the most exploited and endangered working children go unnoticed, their situation must be brought to the awareness of the government and the public, in an effort to activate an electorate to guard them. Innovative approach and positive interference by the government to bring about desired change in the attitude and perception of the parents and working children will help in achieving the programmed goals. 'The general aim is to help develop stable and secure families and communities. A strong emphasis should be laid on education for children and on improvements in skills and job creation for parents and adults.' (Porio et al., 1994). The guidelines should also deal with socio-economic and cultural problems of the families so they do not depend on child labour as a survival strategy. The formulation of child labour policy must emphasize on bottom-up approach in the sense that it should take into assurance the child worker who is at the bottom and is directly affected by the employer's oppression. The government should take non-governmental organizations and independent experts into confidence while formulating such a policy to combat child labour through awareness generation among parents and communities. It is a long process and hence any expenditure without proper planning cannot play a miracle in eliminating child labour overnight.

In India, the analysis of the government's child labour policy clearly reflects that children and their families are not made partners in the process of development. They have been denied participation in it because they are docile. They are voiceless because they are not voters; they are unassertive because they have no political influence. Their parents are inactive because their poverty evades them from taking any action.

There is no gainsaying the fact that child labour is the outcome of our socio-economic culture and no such problem can be solved by legislation alone. But there is a silver lining in every dark cloud, which has been depicted in literature by great thinkers like Mulk Raj Anand in pre-Independence India and by modern Indian writers as well. These writers, great thinkers, convince the society through their pen that despite the strong undercurrent of discontentment, a last ray of hope lies in the empowerment of the marginalized. If the grass-root structure is properly laid out and the child worker and his/her family are taken into confidence by the decision-making bodies, the official top-down approach can be reversed. Today the question is post the ban on child labour, will Munna, Chotu, Choti, Bahadur, Bakha and Munoo vanish from our lives? Surely, the civil society in India is also a collaborator in this structured crime against millions of children trapped in slavery. Will civil society change its ways after the ban on child labour? And post-ban, will the government and the courts of the land be able to give the hardworking little ones their lighthearted childhood? Let us look around. The answer is out there, as harsh as truth and genuineness.

REFERENCES

Anand, Mulkraj (1935), *Untouchable*, London: Penguin Classics.

——— (1936), *Coolie*, New Delhi: Oxford University Press.

Bald, Suresh Ranjan (1974), 'Politics of a Revolutionary Elite: A Study of Mulk Raj Anand's Novels', *Modern Asian Studies*, vol. 8, no. 4, pp. 473-89.

Christiaan, Grootaert and Kanbur Ravi (1995), 'Child Labour: Economic Perspective', *International Labour Review*, vol. 134 (2), p. 201.

Dhawan, R.K. (1992), *The Novels of Mulk Raj Anand*, Stosius Inc./Advent Books Division, p. 67.

Green, Thomas H. (1900), 'Lecture on Liberal Legislation and Freedom of Contract', in R.L. Nettleship (ed.), *Works of Thomas Hill Green 1836-1882*, London: Longmans, Green, and Co.

Grootaert, C. and H. Patrinos (1998), *The Policy Analysis of Child Labour*, The World Bank.

Parker, S. and E. Skoufias (2000), 'Job Loss, Change in Marital Status and the Allocation of Time Within Families', unpublished mimeo, Mexico: CIDE.

Parsons and C. Goldin (1989), 'Parental Altruism and Self-Interest: Child Labor Among Nineteenth-Century American Families', *Economic Inquiry*, vol. 27, pp. 637-59.

Porio, Emma, L. Moselina and Anthony Swift (1994), in *Urban Children in Distress*. Cristina Szanton Blank with contributors; UNICEF, International Child Development Centre, Switzerland: Gordon & Brach.

Rozensweig, M. and R. Evenson (1997), 'Fertility, Schooling and the Economic Contribution of Children in Rural India', *Econometrica*, 45, pp. 1065-79.

Sharma, K.K. (1977), *Indo-English Literature: A Collection of Critical Essays*, Vimal Prakashan.

Verma, K.D. (2000), *The Indian Imagination: Critical Essays on Indian Writing in English*, quoted from books.google.com, pp. 33, 34.

www.bolokids.com

IV. MARGINALIZATION ISSUES OF SERVICE USERS AND THE CONSUMERS

CHAPTER 16

Are We Meeting the Needs of the Most Marginalized with Service Users Involvement?

KRISTIN HEFFERNAN

INTRODUCTION

'Service user' advisory representation is required by law and/or regulation in British social, health and educational programmes. This is similar to client counsels or consumer groups in the US, which are required in some, but not all, US social service sectors. This paper seeks to contribute to our emerging understanding of 'service user' initiatives, particularly with respect to service user role identity and service user involvement. The purpose of the study was to explore 'service user' terminology and 'service user involvement' from the point of view of persons often categorized as 'service users' by social policy, health and social care providers and academics, but who may not necessarily take part in self-organized 'service user groups' of their own accord. They may, however, have belonged to other self-organized groups using health and/or social care services (i.e. support groups for overweight women, career planning group, and so on).

This research is driven by the idea that whilst there are many organized groups of individuals using health and or social care services who promote the concept of 'service user involvement' by *doing* 'service user involvement', and who are proud to identify with the term 'service user', there are still many others using services, who may remain uninvolved and perhaps even sceptical of 'service user involvement' and of having policy makers, health and social care workers and academics refer to them as 'service users'. Therefore, in order to ensure that social workers, doctors, nurses and other health and social care professionals are being representative when implementing social policy that calls for service user involvement, individuals and agencies providing services must first explore the meaning of 'service user' and 'service user involvement' for those marginalized groups that are often referred to as 'service users', but may not actually engage in 'service user involvement'.

BACKGROUND TO 'SERVICE USER INVOLVEMENT'

The term 'service user' has been adapted and applied in the provision of health and social care services in the UK as part of the New Public Management (NPM) discourse over the past two decades. NPM emphasizes public choice, claiming that it delivers improved public services and that it represents an empowerment of those it employs and those it seeks to serve (Dent and Barry, 2004). The first piece of British legislation to establish a requirement for 'user involvement' in service planning was the NHS and Community Care Act 1990, passed under a Conservative administration. The New Labour government's social policy, however, has continued the trend of placing a central role on the concept of 'user involvement' within health and social care services. Since this first act establishing the underlying credo of 'service user involvement', New Labour policy has been rife with bringing forth these principles with other legislation and policy such as Modernising Mental Health Services (1998), the National Service Framework for Mental Health (1999) and the NHS Plan (2000). Each of these places a strong emphasis on the role of service users as key stakeholders in service provision, whereby their help is needed in order to transform services in direct response to users' needs. For example, the Health and Social Care Act (2001) goes as far as placing a duty on NHS Trusts, Primary Care Trusts and Strategic Health Authorities to consult and involve patients and the public in service planning, operation and in the development of proposals for change.

While the fundamental goals of service user involvement appear to be similar in most areas of practice within health and social care professions, there is no commonly accepted definition of what constitutes 'service user involvement' and who should be involved or be considered a 'service user'. Across the nation, a great deal of variation exists in the kind of involvement being organized in these arenas. It is beyond the scope of this paper to offer an exhaustive review of social action, personal and collective identity theory, yet it is important to provide an abridged review of the basic tenets of these theories in order to better understand the process of 'service involvement'; getting individuals collectively involved, hence producing wide-scale service user involvement, hopefully leading to more choice and empowerment for those involved.

SOCIAL ACTION, IDENTITY AND 'SERVICE USER' INVOLVEMENT

In understanding the process of 'service user involvement' health and social care professionals need to understand how social movement, which facilitates social action, comes about. This includes an understanding of personal and collective identity. Personal identity being the traits and meanings attributed to actors by themselves, is self-designated. Personal identity is regarded as personally distinctive (Snow, 2001) whereas collective identity refers to a sense of 'we-ness'. It involves shared beliefs, understanding and interests constructed in interaction between and among participants and movements (Snow, 2001; Valocchi, 2001). The concept of collective identity is grounded in classic sociological constructs such as Durkheim's 'collective conscience' and Marx's 'class consciousness' (Polletta and Jasper, 2001; Snow, 2001). It is separate from personal identity (Tajfel and Turner, 1986), yet may form part of one's personal identity. The concept of collectivism puts forth the idea of something that is action oriented, and it is this action component of collective identity which suggests the possibility of collective action in line with the ideals of the 'service user' movement, but only if there is a shared identity (or collective identity) in pursuit of common interests.

For the most part, collectivism implies participatory decision-making and not hierarchical or top-down decision-making (Mullaly, 1997). Let us understand using the disability movement, as an example. This social movement was largely started and maintained by individuals experiencing a physical disability. Hence, it has been persons with disabilities who have argued that their problems are not caused by tragedy but by the failure of society to take account of their needs, arguing that illness and disability are not the same thing. Individuals with disabilities have not only been critical of the dominant perspectives on disability such as the moral model or the medical model, but have also developed their own perspective to replace them—the social model. This movement fostered concepts of equality and social justice. In fact, the civil rights movement was born out of the disability movement, in part due to the fact that many of the rights that the persons with disabilities thought they had under the existing welfare legislations, notably the Chronically Sick and Disabled Persons Act 1970, were actually being denied to them (Oliver, 1990; Barnes, 1999). The disability movement has been largely successful in changing the lives of people with disabilities and helping to change the social structures promoting the idea of disability as a personal problem. Such individuals have identified with the larger group and have acted as a collective to advocate on behalf of all disabled persons.

This is not to say that it is entirely impossible for a social movement to be successful if it is created by an outsider, in the case of 'service user involvement' the government. It has, however, been argued that collective identities come from common positions in networks and not from fixed categories like race, class, gender or, in this case, 'service user' (Polletta and Jasper, 2001). Categorizing individuals in a top-down fashion does not help to foster collective identity and subsequently social movement. The element of choice is involved in the process of adopting or accepting an identity. For the purpose of this paper, 'identity' is defined as a process through which social actors come to recognize themselves and be recognized by others as a cohesive group (Della Porta and Daini, 1999), thus emphasizing the collective nature of social movement identity.

This study explores how individuals who are largely outside the realm of 'service user involvement', having their own identity (whatever that might be), perceive the term 'service user' and the idea of 'service user involvement'. It specifically explores if the concept of 'service user involvement' has evolved beyond social policy rhetoric for those who would be targeted as 'service users' by government, social policy makers, and health and social care providers as well as academics.

METHODS

Participants and Procedures

A qualitative approach was adopted for this study with the aim of providing in-depth, conceptualized data. The main method of study was focus groups, which involved organized discussions with a select group of individuals to gain insight and knowledge of participants' personal, subjective and interactive experiences of being 'service users' and perceptions of 'service user involvement'. Key to the study was the interaction and language used during the focus groups. It was hoped that the focus groups would foster a synergistic group effect, allowing us to not only observe participants' interactions, but also accessing the substantive content of verbally expressed views, opinions, experiences and attitudes (Sarantokos, 1998). Focus groups help individuals to think about and respond to other group members' input (Yegidis and Weinbach, 2006) and, equally importantly, they also allow the researcher to observe the process through which individuals construct their own realities and/or identities, making sense of themselves as individuals and as a group. It should not be assumed that the individuals within the focus group are expressing their own definitive and individual view; the context and culture within the group influences their dialogue, hence the interaction between individuals. The questions they pose to each other and the possible re-evaluation of their statements is crucial to the research.

In this study, the focus groups were not meant to be a neutral ground to collect information. Rather, they acted as an arena for the group members to draw on discursive resources. As such, they were active, and sometimes individuals were not in agreement. This further allowed for debate over the different areas under discussion at the time, revealing the meaning of these concepts for each individual participating in the group.

Constructing the Study

Prior to beginning the study, the research plan was presented at our 'stakeholders' meetings at a British university.[1] Three stakeholders were interested in taking the project forward, two of the individuals identifying as 'service user' and one as an academic. It was decided that the best way forward was to use agencies affiliated with the stakeholders' group in order to recruit participants. The researchers put together a flyer explaining the research, which was printed and distributed to agencies affiliated with the department's stakeholder group, in the hope of opening up the study to all those who used services within the chosen agencies.

Realizing that not all individuals at the agency would have the opportunity to see the flyers, I also gained permission to network within the agencies, attending lunch programmes at the agencies to discuss the study and answer questions. Agencies and or individuals expressing an interest in the study were given an initial briefing by the researcher on the aims of the study at arranged times prior to the focus group and then again at the beginning of the focus group. This process was used for all agencies. Participants were given consent forms to sign before beginning the project, which included additional information and a guarantee of anonymity with regard to published results, but it was explained to the participants that due to the nature of focus groups, anonymity and confidentiality amongst participants within the group could not be preserved. Participation was voluntary and individuals could withdraw from the study at any time.

The focus groups were conducted within a structured framework, which enabled participants to interact and converse freely, providing in-depth information about their attitudes and perceptions, while keeping them focused on the desired topics. Each group typically lasted for around an hour and fifteen minutes. The format included an open discussion method to ensure that all participants had the opportunity to express themselves on the topics. Discussion centred around two main topics:

1. Current and historical terms used to refer to individuals who use/d health and social care services and how participants felt about these terms and/or if they identified with these terms/groups.[2]
2. 'Service user involvement'.

Recording Data

The data were recorded via pen and paper with the respondents' permission at the time of the focus group, because they did not wish to be audio-taped. Internal quality and credibility were attained by going over the recordings with the group to ensure that the interviewer understood what the participants were saying and recording the data in their own words. The data was later analysed by examining the narrative content and observed process of constructing meaning and reality of 'service user involvement'. Then it was evaluated for like themes across the different focus groups with regard to preferred terms of reference. The data was examined to identify the range of terms used to refer to individuals who used health and social care services (patients, customers, participants).

THE SAMPLE

Twenty-four individuals participated in the study; nine males and fifteen females. Participants were from three different agencies: one in South London, the second in East London, and the third in Surrey. The agencies varied with regard to the type of service offered, with one agency working with families involved in children and family social care services (n = 5), one specifically with individuals with mental health issues (n = 11), and the third with individuals with either mental health or mild learning difficulties or both (n = 8). At least seven (29 per cent) of the respondents stated that they had used more than one type of service in the past year (i.e. mental health and disability and or mental health and children and family services) with the majority stating that they use or have used mental health services in the past year (n = 20; 83 per cent). The fact that the majority of the respondents used mental health services was completely unplanned, as we were attempting to get a sample of opinions from individuals using different types of services.

TABLE 16.1: PARTICIPANT DEMOGRAPHICS (n = 24)

Agency type	Location	No. of participants	No. of groups run at the agency	Females	Males
Day Centre	Surrey	8	2	2	6
Mother and Child	South London	5	1	5	0
Community Mental Health Centre	East London	11	2	8	3

RESULTS

The research started by exploring the different terms historically used to refer to individuals that use health and social care services, such as patient and client, and slowly other terms were introduced, mainly from the participants, though when necessary the researcher too introduced new terms. This was done to help gain a better perspective on whether or not these individuals identified with these terms in the hope that this would better help me to understand individual's participation, or lack there of, in 'service user involvement' based on whether or not he/she had adapted to or identified with the concept of 'service user'. Data analysis revealed that there was no single preferred term of reference that everyone accepted; however there did appear to be some terms that were preferred over others. But this seemed to depend on the type of services received and preference was very individual.

Changing Terminology to Incorporate all 'Service Users' under One Term

Interestingly, individuals from both the Day Centre focus groups and the Mental Health Community Centre focus groups felt that the move to incorporate all individuals under one title, or more importantly to lose the focus on mental health would have more of a detrimental effect on individuals who use mental health services than on individuals using other services. The following are a few excerpts from the different focus groups demonstrating some of the feelings that were shared:

> The worst stigma of all is being a mental health service user; the government needs to do something about that. Just calling us service users isn't going to help; it means that government doesn't have to educate individuals about people like me (someone with a mental health diagnosis). . . . We're the ones who lose . . . now they (government) don't have to spend any more money to educate people about mental health issues . . . they just put us all into one big group. . . .
>
> Government is just trying to repackage the same old goods—making themselves look good . . . they should be more concerned about trying to educate people about mental health to lessen the stigma—look at the good work being done by Sainsbury's. They hire people like us (with either learning difficulties and/or mental health issues), give us visibility . . . the government should be trying to promote more programmes that make us visible . . . this is the way you alleviate stigma, not by coming up with a new term for the same old thing. . . .

These examples appear to demonstrate not so much a fear of stigma, but rather a need not to be categorized in a universal group, and as such losing the focus on mental health. The participants also seem to be aware of a need to act, educating the 'public' or promoting employment programmes and visibility, rather than a focus on rhetoric and tinkering with terminology. They also highlight negative feelings toward government and government's lack of response to the needs of those with mental health issues: '. . . by trying to lump us all together mental health issues will get pushed further down the ladder of importance, till it's like we don't exist anymore'.

These last examples seem to fall in line with those of Barnes (1999), where individuals appear to be concerned about becoming invisible with the adoption of the new language of 'service user'. During these conversations, there was a change in the tone and body language of people; their voices became higher pitched and they shifted their bodies from leaning back in their chairs to squaring off and leaning-in toward each other when they spoke. They appeared to be getting passionately involved in the focus group when this topic was being discussed. Everyone participated in this part of the discussion. Their responses seem to indicate a tension between being treated as individuals and yet not being recognized as members of a distinct group, a group—according to them, that deserves to have its image improved by the government.

Choosing a Preferred Term

Although many of the respondents settled on a preferred term of reference, most likely for the purpose of this study, this does not mean that they also identified with the term ' . . . the term (referring to the term service user) just sounds better than client or consumer, but I wouldn't let anyone call me a service user'.

There were however two exceptions. A man from the Day Centre focus group felt that he identified with the term 'participant' as he agreed with the idea of being a participant of services at the day care. 'I'm a member of the Health Centre—it's a community centre . . . I am a participant . . . I choose to participate . . . I like that term; it gives me choice. . . .'

This response also indicated that this respondent felt that it was his choice to participate in services, which as indicated in the introduction is one of the goals of the New Labour social policy encompassing 'service user involvement'. However, although this person identified with the term 'participant', he did not make the jump to the larger concept of 'service user involvement', and did not see the purpose of becoming involved. He felt it was enough to pick and choose what he wanted to do at the Day Centre and did not feel a need to be involved in planning or evaluating services on a larger scale, still demonstrating choice by choosing not to be involved. This is pertinent to the underlying understanding of the national agenda for 'service user involvement' and hence may be looked as not acceptable due to the fact that also underpinning New Labour social policy is an emphasis on people's responsibility in return for their rights. The notion of individual responsibility has become central to UK social policy as can be seen in welfare reform (Department of Social Security, 1998), health policy (Department of Health, 2003) and housing policy (King, 2006).

In addition, one woman in the Children and Family focus group identified with the term 'service user' and stated she was very much involved. This was an unexpected phenomenon as I was specifically targeting marginalized groups of individuals that use health and social care services to better understand their reality of the 'service user' and 'service user involvement discourse. The fact that we did have an individual who actively identified as a 'service user', taking part in 'service user involvement', was an added bonus, adding richness to the study. It was extremely informative to have both views to explore and further help shape our conclusions regarding service user involvement.

The Choice to be Involved

The woman from the Children and Family focus group who identified herself as a 'service user' believed that she was a part of a larger collective group of 'service users' by the language she used to explain her status as a 'service user': 'Being a service user made me what I am today and now I work with other service users to empower more people like me. I am using my experience and knowledge to help others.'

While this person explained her view, other members of the Children and Family focus group listened patiently to her explanation of why she preferred the term 'service user' and why she felt involved in the larger 'service user movement'. However, when she was done someone responded by pointing out that her experience was different than most.

Most of the individuals in the group agreed with this follow-up statement, either by shaking their heads in agreement or by one-word comments. In agreeing, someone introduced the concept of 'professional service user', which seemed to be a term that the rest of the group wanted to discuss. Members in the Children and Family focus group came to the conclusion that the person identifying as a 'service user' had had a very different experience from the rest of the group and they referred to the experience as 'unique'. In the end they all seemed to accept the idea of being able to have a 'professional service user' role, but felt that not everyone would want this role or want to be involved in evaluating services. They also appeared to reach an understanding about the limited access to this role and never being given a chance to participate.

Within this discussion it was clear that the reality was that most felt that they did not feel empowered as 'service users' to take on the role of an advocate and that they did not feel like they were treated as equals by the professionals who provided the services: 'Ya, but not everyone can get paid . . . you're in a unique position . . . no one ever asked me to participate' and 'I'm not involved with services by choice. . . . They don't listen to what I need . . . I'm just another bad mother. . . . '

It would be interesting to see if this woman would have been more apt to be involved if her experiences with service use had been more positive. Many of these women appeared frustrated at their lack of being heard or listened to by their GPs and/or psychiatrists. In the end the woman identifying with the term 'service user' stated: 'Yes I have been very lucky . . . I love what I do and I wouldn't change it.'

Involvement and Choice

The majority of the respondents, however, did not feel as if they were involved in the services by their own choice:

> When a social worker comes to your house, because a neighbour complains, and starts assessing you and your children—I would hardly say I was a consumer. Most of us involved (with social services) don't have a choice.
>
> (Family Service Group Member)

Not only were they not actively involved in the services they received, many also felt they continue to be treated poorly, while being excluded as participants in their own service plans:

> My GP doesn't pay attention to a thing I say. I used to be a size 12, now look at me (she is much bigger). I complained about weight gain due to my meds and my GP said it was just something I was going to have to live with . . . so much for involvement. Now I have high blood pressure and can barely get around . . . (due to weight gain); you call that participation?

This quote raises the possibility that participants might welcome the possibility of real action to include them and their views if action were taken to meet their requirements as expressed by themselves (e.g. pay attention to their weight when choosing medication). It was evident, however, that the 'service users' had different feelings regarding 'service user involvement', as currently reflected in social policy, from many of the discussions that took place within the different focus groups. Most of the participants in this study had yet to feel the empowering effects of 'service user involvement' and this may affect the way they feel about the terms 'service user' and 'service user involvement'. Individuals may not identify with the term 'service user' because they remain uninvolved in social policy, research, practice and training development. Many of these responses came from individuals using mental health services, and many of their negative comments about not being able to voice their needs and be heard were aimed at the medical staff. These individuals had had negative experiences with both their psychiatrists and their GPs, stating that the medical model had yet to change: 'The government might say one thing, but you try and tell that to your GP—they just think that they need to give you more meds to keep you quiet.'

These remarks suggest that although the medical staff may have adopted the term 'service user', they may still be treating the concept of 'service user involvement' as a rhetoric. Thus, these professionals have changed their language in line with social policy changes, but not their *behaviour*. Certain medical professionals are still seeing their relationship as *doctor-patient* (Bury, 1997), rather than as a more *equal sharing* or *supporting* role as envisaged by New Labour in their policy documents. If this is the case and the term 'service user' is being used synonymously with 'patient' without actually involving the 'service user' in the process of care, the term 'service user' will continue to carry with it historical emotional overtones of patriarchal practices whereby the 'service user' is seen as inferior to the doctor (Herxheimer and Goodare, 1999).

ISSUES TO BE ADDRESSED

Getting a Better Understanding of the 'Services User' Discourse

The theme of 'respect' came out in each of the focus groups as one way of empowering individuals who use health and social care services.

This was tied into both preferred terms of reference and being given a voice, not just saying that they are being given a voice via social policy. All of the respondents agreed that respect is shown when one is referred to by one's own name, clearly agreeing that being called by one's own name was the best and the most empowering way of letting people know that they are listening to them, and taking them seriously and not just paying them 'lip service'. For example, one person stated: 'It's just rude (to use the term service user). . . . Just refer to me by my name. . . . I don't go in for that kind of disrespect. . . .'

In addition, during the focus groups with the Mental Health Community Care Centre, several women voiced their feelings about using health services as something that they sometimes need to do, demonstrating that it is not necessarily a part of their identity or in some cases only one part of their identity:

> . . . being a service user is not the be all and end all of who I am. I just sometimes need to use social services. . . .

And another woman said:

> . . . you wouldn't refer to me as a coloured person, but I'm black . . . you wouldn't refer to me as a disabled person, but I'm in a wheelchair, so why call me a service user just because I may have the need to use mental health services every once in a while?

These statements demonstrate the complexity of identity and the importance for these women to distinguish their service use as something essential to their health and well-being and not necessarily a part of their identity.

Discussion

The very idea of being referred to as a 'service user' seemed foreign to most of the participants in this study. If these individuals had the opportunity to become involved their reality might be constructed differently. Becoming involved, however, is more than a government policy, it is about two-way communication and involving individuals in their care. Government can change policy, but ideological changes come slowly and it would appear as if a 'professional' or, dare one say, a 'patriarchal' belief of professional knows best, is still very much alive in health and social care practice. This is similar to the patient-doctor relationship discussed by Burry (1997).

The question remains not only how to get individuals involved and/or is there really a place for all individuals to be involved, but also how do we get professionals to understand the importance of involving the person that they are working with in the care they are receiving. Positive experiences of feeling respected and having their fears and concerns validated may have lead these individuals to a different conclusion about wanting to be involved in service provision, evaluation, research and policy development. The act of being involved could perhaps change their perception and then may be they would better be able to identify with the term 'service user'. At this point, perhaps, they have not had enough positive interaction.

One area for future research would be to focus on the professionals concerned and ask them about the changes in terminology and practice:

1. Is the use of the term *service user* merely government rhetoric or is there a real change in practice?
2. If there is a real change, how is it manifested in your own practice?
3. How do your patients, clients, service users . . . react to these changes?

If there were differences between the answers that different professionals gave to the questions above it would be interesting to see if their clients had differing reactions to the new terminology. In addition to these discussions, we can also relate back to the earlier comments made by participants in the Children and Family focus group, who also indicated that they did not feel that they were involved in the service plans or in evaluating services that they received.

CONCLUSION

At present it would appear that not all individuals that use services share a common purpose or a higher function (i.e. involvement in the development and evaluation of policy, practice and research in health and social care), which could possibly act as a catalyst to identifying with the term 'service user' and, subsequently, lead to 'service user involvement'. These views have been constructed in part through their personal experience of receiving health and/or social care services, many of which for this group have been negative.

The reality of those involved in this study is that they have not experienced being empowered as a 'service user' and continue to be marginalized by their involvement with health and social care services. This was especially evident for those individuals using Children and Family services and Mental Health services. The experience of being involved may 'empower' individuals, giving them the strength and self-esteem to become involved in the planning and implementation of social policy, research and practice via the process of 'service user involvement', as prescribed by much of the current social policy on health and social care within the United Kingdom (NHS Health and Social Care Act 1990; NHS Management Inquiry, 1984; The Patients' Charter, 1992). However, involvement for many of the participants in this study needs to start at a more primary level, mainly being listened to by the person providing services.

Discussions in all the groups revealed that these participants did not feel they had seen differences in the way they were treated by their health and/or social care service providers with the onset of new policies on 'service user involvement'. In addition, all the participants, with the exception of the woman who identified as a 'service user' and was involved in 'service user involvement', felt that changes to social policy had not changed the way they were treated by their service providers. Thus their experiences once again helped construct their reality of 'service user involvement'. It is important to note here that most of the examples were directly related to experiences with medical staff as opposed to social care staff.

In addition, researchers need to further investigate the meaning of being involved with regard to individual responsibility and empowerment as these terms may be being conflated. The idea of individuals that use health and social care services needing to be involved for the sole purpose of taking personal responsibility may undermine the actual experiences of those most marginalized. In the case of those that use health and social care services a cycle of stigmatization, oppression and further marginalization may occur, in that those using these services may already feel stigmatized and oppressed, leading to a sense of helplessness. Holding themselves accountable for their own circumstances only stands to further marginalize these individuals. The purported self-control and responsibility of marginalized people is in fact a move to treat them as culpable actors deserving of their fate if they are not going to be 'involved' (Wacquant, 2007).

STUDY LIMITATIONS

This research was limited in that it was not generalizable to the larger population of those that use health and social care services, not only due to the sampling technique, but also in that participants only represented the point of view of persons often categorized as 'service user' by social policy, health and social care providers and academics, but who do not take part in self-organized 'service user groups' as per their own accord. However, they still may have belonged to other self-organized groups using health and/or social care services. It did however gather an elaborate set of data, which brought up many interesting ideas that can help future research to explore and hypothesize about 'service user involvement' and the language we use in policy and practice.

The preceding discussion has identified some of the key concepts, strategies, and barriers that influence the effectiveness of the 'service user involvement movement', demonstrating that marginalization continues to exist in practice with regard to service user. It has also highlighted the fact that the complexity and dynamic nature of social action and forming a collective identity can provide significant challenges to the service user involvement initiative. There is a push towards including all those who use health and/or social care services to participate. As such, the language of service user should be a harbinger for service user involvement; however, if the group which the term was meant to describe does not identify with this term, then the term also has the potential to retard social action or service user involvement, because individuals (service users) will not form as a group to take social action. The meaning people attach to their experiences are not unconnected; both the experiences and the events surrounding them are essential to the construction of meanings. Thus we need to understand the meaning of 'service user' and 'service user involvement' for those that are categorized by this language. As researchers this means designing research that allows us to both observe and listen to interactions about the reality forming process.

It also is important to understand how the universal discourse of 'service user' affects the 'voice' of individuals using very specific services, especially since there is a possibility that the language of 'service user' may render particular groups of individuals with similar needs invisible. Moreover, these findings allow us to think about the implications for further research in this area. This includes conducting research on both established groups of individuals involved in promoting service user involvement and those individuals that use health and social care services, but have not been empowered to participate as service users, as well as exploring how health and social care providers interpret 'service user involvement'. Future research needs to explore the concept of paid service user involvement in organized groups of 'service users', to better understand the service user movement.

NOTES

1. Departments that teach validated social work degree courses in the United Kingdom must ensure that they involve individuals that use health and/ or social care services not only to develop and evaluate their programmes, but also in involvement with helping to carry out the programme as well. Thus, individuals that use health and social care services are active members of the programmes' stakeholder group.
2. Because we were interested in finding out what the preferred term of reference was for the participants, specific terms were introduced at the onset of each focus group: patient, consumer, service user and client were specifically introduced by the researcher. During the first focus group, the term 'participant' was introduced by someone within the focus group, thus it was introduced in subsequent groups. No other term was introduced by focus group participants.

REFERENCES

Barnes, M. (1999), 'Users as Citizens: Collective Action and the Local Governance of Welfare', *Social Policy and Administration*, vol. 33, pp. 73-90.

Bury, M. (1997), *Health and Illness in a Changing Society*, London: Routledge.

Della Porta, D. and M. Diani (1999), *Social Movements: An Introduction*, Oxford: Blackwell.

Dent, M. and J. Barry (2004), 'New Public Management and the Profession in the UK: Reconfiguring Control', in M. Dent, J. Chandler and J. Barry (eds.), *Questioning the New Public Management*, Aldershot: Ashgate Publishing Limited.

Department of Health and Social Security (1984), *NHS Management Enquiry*, London: HMSO.

Department of Health (1992), *The Patients' Charter*, London: HMSO.

——— (1997), *The New NHS: Modern and Dependable*, London: HMSO.

——— (1998), *Modernising Mental Health Services: Safe, Sound and Supportive*, London: Department of Health.

——— (1999), *A National Service Framework for Mental Health: Modern Standards and Service Models*, London: Department of Health.

——— (2003), *Choice, Responsiveness and Equity in the NHS and Social Care*, London: Department of Health.

Department of Social Security (1998), *New Ambitions for Our Country: A New Contract for Welfare*, Cm 3805, London: Stationery Office.

Herxheimer, A. and H. Goodare (1999), 'Who are You, and Who are We: Looking Through Some Key Words', *Health Expectations*, vol. 2, pp. 3-6.

King, P. (2006), 'What Do We Mean by Responsibility? The Case of UK Housing Benefit Reform', *Journal of Housing and the Built Environment*, 21, pp. 111-25.

Mullaly, R.P. (1997), *Structural Social Work: Ideology, Theory and Practice*, New York: Oxford University Press.

NHS Health and Social Care Act (1990), Office of Public Sector Information, Crown Copyright.

Oliver, M. (1990), *The Politics of Disablement*, Basingstoke: MacMillan.

Polletta, F. and J.M. Jasper (2001), 'Collective Identity and Social Movement', *Annual Review of Sociololoy*, 27, pp. 283-305.

Sarantakos, S. (1998), *Social Research*, South Yarra: MacMillan Publishers Australia.

Snow, D. (2001), 'Collective Identity and Expressive Forms', Center for the Study of Democracy (http://repositories.cdlib.org/cds/01-07).

Tajfel, H. and J.C. Turner (1986), 'The Social Identity Theory of Intergroup Behaviour', in S. Worchel and L.W. Austin (eds.), *Psychology of Intergroup Relations*, Chicago: Nelson-Hall.

Valocchi, S. (2001), 'Individual Identities, Collective Identities and Organisational Structure: The Relationship of the Political Left and Gay Liberation in the United States', *Sociological Perspectives*, 44, pp. 445-67.

Wacquant, L. (2007), *Deadly Symbiosis: Race and the Rise of Neoliberal Penality*, Cambridge, Polity Press.

Yegidis, B. and R. Weinbach (2006), *Research Methods for Social Workers*, 5th edn., London: Allyn and Bacon Publishers.

CHAPTER 17

Learning Consumerist Culture: Indian Middle Class' Experience in the Periphery

KAMLESH MOHAN

The globalization of economy coupled with the fast-paced communication revolution with its lightening speed and information flow through digital streams have impinged upon the politico-economic sovereignty and cultural specificities of the Third World countries. A number of scholars have discussed their positive and negative implications for various sectors of the economy, e.g. agriculture, trade, industry and business, within the framework of modernization from the Euro-centric perspective. But consequent sociocultural changes, anxieties and discontents have not been documented.

In this paper, I have tried to explicate the extent and nature of changes in the material culture of the Indian middle class[es] through satellite television and cable network which have become potent sources and instruments of value-formation for global entrepreneurs in finance/business, entertainment, health and religious organizations. It must be noted that material culture has a continuous and interactive relationship with cultural tradition, practices and values.

I shall argue that the persistent exposure of the illiterate as well as educated classes to colourful and seductive images of consumerist products and lifestyles through transnational flows of information and programming (primarily from USA) has brought drastic changes not only in the cultural environment but also in the mentalities, i.e. new ways of seeing and thinking. My argument is twofold. Firstly, the inverse relationship between conspicuous consumption and social development, democratic institutions, human rights, and so on has played a critical role in vitiating the perspective of various religious communities regarding composite cultural traditions and values.

Secondly, the strategic partnership between global entrepreneurs in economy and media has created a piquant situation for the teenagers and young adults in all social segments who have been forced to live in a transitional world. This world is characterized by dislocation of sensibilities, values and reference-points embedded in the ideals of Indian culture, which is known for its diversity and richness.

I have divided my discussion into four sections: Ideals of Indian culture; television and dissemination of consumerist culture and values; impact upon lifestyles, home-space, food-habits and body culture; and a conclusion.

IDEALS OF INDIAN CULTURE

A brief explication of the ideals of Indian culture is helpful for capturing its essentially different orientation, world-view and values from those of the consumerist culture. It will help us understand the tensions and dilemma(s) arising from its protracted encounter with Western modernity in its new garb.

It is not easy to generalize about Indian culture for three reasons. Firstly, it is an amalgam of diverse traditions (Hindu, Islamic, Buddhist and Jainist), religious symbols, languages and creative products of multiple ethnic imaginations. Secondly, it is constantly in-the-making, strenuously contested and reconstituted. Being dynamic and open-ended, it is best described by the Persian word *ravayaat*, i.e. flowing or constantly in motion. Indian culture, constantly engaged in the process of experimentation and self-renewal, has been redirecting its social energy throughout its evolution from ancient to modern times.[1] Thirdly, production of knowledge about Indian society and culture by Indians and others has remained burdened by the assumptions of Orientalist scholarship. For example, the Euro American academicians have articulated stereotyped understanding of caste, gender-inequalities, nationalism and communalism through such dominant paradigms as 'hierarchy' for Indian society, 'filial piety' for China and 'honour and shame' for circum-Mediterranean.[2]

The dominant ideology of Hindutva has also appropriated the homogenizing agenda of the Orientalists and thus glossed over the complexity of our cultural and ideological formations. By projecting Indian culture as monolithic and unchanging, its protagonists have distorted its original spirit and character. Despite these problems and the complex nature of Indian tradition it is possible to identify its essential ideals: (i) communitarian ideal; (ii) spiritual ethos: worldly concerns and moral values, and (iii) creativity and spirit of accommodation.

Communitarian Ideal

The most striking feature of Indian culture is the location of each individual in the network of powerful communitarian relationships such as family, kinship and caste.[3] It had positive implications for social cohesiveness, now transformed into a political asset. The patriarchal family as the reproductive unit has continued to be used as a site for the socialization of the girl-child and for the transmission of cultural values, practices and traditions of major religions. The entire complex of community networks was (is) utilized not only for schooling its members for discipline, work-culture and social and religious values but also for protecting and reinforcing the structures of land relations. The major reason underlying the communitarian orientation and practice was the country's agrarian economy. Primarily comprising huge stretches of well-irrigated plains and the advantage of ample sunshine for the greater part of the year, India has maintained an agrarian economy over the past five thousand years. The British government exploited and developed this potential with minimum financial investment and technological inputs in order to feed and expand its industrial empire. Such a policy introduced many complexities in the stratification of the peasant society.

A major characteristic of the peasant society is that it values the communitarian ideal and cultivates this orientation. Historically speaking, Indians are known for their deep loyalty to the village, family and *jati*. Another major feature of this society is its relatively peaceful and close relationship with the rhythm of cyclic seasons. A distinct emphasis upon coexistence, peace and harmony, rather than obsession with overpowering, controlling and exploiting nature, characterizes the attitude of the agricultural community. Cultivation of a friendly attitude is urgent in view of the growing awareness of depletion of environmental resources.

Spiritual Ethos

Worldly Concerns

The second important dimension of the Indian cultural heritage is its emphasis upon the realization of the ultimate spiritual ideal, i.e.

unity with the cosmos without undermining material achievements. The pervasive presence of this spiritual ethos in Indian life does not imply the negation of other aspects of life. The characterization of the Indian outlook (used synonymously for Hindu) as pessimistic and other-worldly by Western scholars is exaggerated. In fact, one of the main concepts underlying the ancient Indian civilization was the coordination of spiritual life with worldly life. For example, the Hindu religion has emphasized a balanced albeit gender-biased approach to the four ends of man, viz., *dharma*, *artha*, *kama* and *moksha*, which refer to the ideal principle or norm to which man should confirm in the course of his worldly activities. The first place is assigned to *dharma* as it is the regulating factor in the pursuit of material gain and pleasure.[4] Referring to *Rajadharma* (king's moral duty), the lawbook of Yajnavalkya states that where there is conflict between principle and policy, righteousness and material gain/advantage, *dharma* and *artha*, the former should prevail.

For *kama*, i.e. love or pleasure, control by *dharma* is obligatory. The Hindu ideal does not preach abstinence from pleasure for all or at all stages; rather it preaches, universally, the ideal of chastened love or pleasure, regulated by considerations of both morality and well-being. In more than one authoritative text, the householder's life is considered to be the greatest of the four stages of life. Hinduism does not hold up monasticism or hermetism as the desired ideal for all. The strains and trials of household management, family life and social obligations are said to discipline man and prepare him for *moksha*. The pursuit of *moksha*, i.e. liberation from the cycle of death and rebirth, is placed last as the life of retirement and spiritual endeavour is the final and ultimate aspiration of man in the Hindu scheme of values. It is evident that no aspect of life was originally considered unimportant, nothing was denied or repressed. Instead all that appears to be lower could be integrated with the higher according to Hindu philosophy. There was no distinction between the sacred and profane.

Islam, which had developed a positive interaction with Hindu culture from the thirteenth century onwards, was firmly rooted in the material world despite its dominant spiritual ethos.[5] As the 'field of action' and the farming ground for the world to come, the present world is of great importance and value to man. What the Koran emphasizes is that from the relative point of view of man, the world is as real as he himself. The affirmation of life and of physical world is peculiar to Islam.

Contemporaneous with the ongoing cultural ferment throughout India, Guru Nanak launched his crusade for the spiritual and moral purification of both Hindus and Muslims. The Sikh tradition as it evolved from the fifteenth to the seventeenth century AD, aligned religious goals with worldly concerns.[6] In the Sikh, especially the Khalsa world-view, salvation could be attained by living in the world and pursuing secular objectives such as the acquisition of political power or the accumulation of economic resources in the form of agrarian land. These secular objectives had, however, to be attained within the particular framework of beliefs and religious practices. Paramount among these beliefs was the Khalsa normative order: *Kirt karna, vand chhakna te namu japna* (to labour for one's keep, to share with others and to practice the repetition of the divine name). Obviously, Sikh religion has remained functional in its approach.

Moral Values

All major religions have concerned themselves with the generation and transmission of not merely moral values but also social values. The extent to which they have done this has varied from Islam on the on hand, where a detailed statement of not only social values but even state and social laws is incorporated in the Holy Koran itself, to Christianity where Jesus himself separated the two by the statement 'Render unto Ceaser what is Ceaser's and unto God what is God's', on the other. However, it is difficult to compartmentalize these two aspects in practice because of the scope given to interpretation in Islam and the extent of church's involvement in state affairs. The Hindu scriptures also deal with social and individual moral values. However, the position of Hinduism on this issue is as ambiguous as on any other matter owing to the wide variety of scriptures and the breadth of interpretation accepted by various authorities.

In the present situation created by globalization, it is increasingly difficult to avoid the intermeshing of individual and social values and priorities. The different functioning of a market economy requires a minimum moral infrastructure just as it requires a physical infrastructure. 'Honesty is the best policy' is not so much a moral dictum as a cost-effective method of organizing inter-human relationships whether for personal concerns or large-scale business purposes. The consequences of all-round deceit prove costly in the long run than the consequences of straight dealing.

Creativity and the Spirit of Accommodation

The great strength of Indian culture is its dynamism, creativity, and its ability to accommodate and synthesize the multiple currents and traditions. A close scrutiny of the process of its evolution shows that the resilience of the inner core has helped it to protect its fundamental values. Its openness has enabled it to respond to new currents of thought and transform them into a source of energy for new patterns of development and growth. Many voices of dissent have enriched its fabric. While Indian culture learnt important lessons from Buddhism and Jainism, it was influenced in a different way by the challenge of Islam.[7] Islam's message of egalitarianism, democracy and rights of women, though within a patriarchal framework, had been incorporated in the social vision of Hinduism in order to make it more responsive to the changing cultural ethos and popular aspirations.

It may be said that these three ideals of Indian culture ought to be regarded as ideals to be aspired for. I would not argue that Indians were always community-oriented, peaceful, spiritual and tolerant. India also passed through phases of violence, hatred and war. India also does not lack people with materialistic and individualist ambitions. However, the primacy of cultural ideals bound the people together in times of cultural upheaval, irrespective of the differences in religious faith and practice. The first cultural upheaval was caused by the British conquest and now by avaricious multinational corporates.

Indian Response to the Onslaught of Westernism/Modernity

With the coming of the West through British colonialism in India, radical departures occurred in the form of redefinition of society, polity, family and gender, rendering the eighteenth century praxis irrelevant. A drastic change in the politico-economic balance of power against Indians and blockade of channels of sociocultural communication made them insular and robbed them of creative thinking for more than a century.

I wish to focus briefly on the predicament of the nineteenth-century reformers, whose development as an intellectual community had been facilitated by the conditions created by the colonial rule but their bonding matured in the course of their social struggles.[8] It is likely to give us a clue about shifts in perspectives on Westernism/modernity in the era of liberalization.

In the nineteenth century, the British, who had underlined the weaknesses of traditional Indian social order and inferiorized its culture, epistemology and the people as a race had obliged them (Indians) to launch cultural-ideological struggles at two planes: against caste discrimination and women's oppression on the one hand and against cultural hegemonization by the colonial state on the other. While the reformers had found traditional culture inadequate to meet the challenges of Western modernity, they were not inclined to adopt the bourgeois liberal model *in toto* as the culture and intellectual engineering had caused anxiety among them about the survival of tradition itself. Thus, ambivalence and contradiction in their attitude towards tradition and modernity, which is characteristic of colonial consciousness, surfaces repeatedly in their ideological formulations throughout the nineteenth and early twentieth centuries.

It may be further added that India's encounter with Western modernity, capitalism and imperialism as well as the compelling need to articulate her complex response had fuelled the search for appropriate vocabulary and borrowing of new words such as rights, nation, secular, and so on.[9] It was reinforced by the leadership's keen sense of responsibility to communicate people's aspiration for freedom from political bondage, economic exploitation and cultural hegemony of the colonial rulers. Their dilemma was how to borrow without submitting to hierarchical relationship with the West despite the earlier experience of humiliating domination and demoralization.

However, critical temper has not been lacking. Nearer our own times, Gandhi's insightful and creative reading of Indian and Western tradition had urged him to reject the social reformers' alternative whether in terms of ideology or borrowed conceptual vocabulary. By mobilizing latent cultural resources, he had been able to turn *satyagraha* and *ahimsa* into effective strategies for social and political struggles. Thus, he had launched a 'transcultural' protest against the materialist and hyper-masculine world-view of colonial modernity.[10]

Indian attitude towards modernity had acquired more criticality, clarity and sharpness when Gandhi pulled the intellectual community out of the orbit of bourgeois values through his powerful critique of Western civilization. In his pamphlet, *Hind Swaraj* (1909), he had indicted the West for its arrogant superiority over its material achievements, barbarity and irreligiosity.[11] His cultural agenda was based on principles that seldom coincided with the ideals of Western modernity, which divided societies into traditional or modern (modernization regarded as synonymous with Westernization and secularism), and puts exclusive emphasis upon value-neutral, scientific and universalistic rationality.[12] In this world-view, modernity is gender-biased by not only continuing the gender-division of labour but also by male monopoly in public affairs, e.g. administration, politics, science and art.[13] Gandhi had rejected not only this world view but also condemned the objectification of nature and ruthless exploitation of its resources. Above all, his sensitivity to the untapped potential of India's rich cultural heritage, particularly folk-resources and relevant elements of modernity has been conceded not only by the advocates of Western modernity including feminists but also by the traditionalists.

However, the de-colonization process initiated by Gandhi has lost much of its force as his thought and practice could not fully capture India's urge for 'relevant' modernity in terms of multiple needs of its fast growing population and its national aspirations. The changing parameters of global economy and civilizing mission in the hands of corporate capitalists and the inability of India to resist multinational corporate pressures for liberalization have once again made people vulnerable to the tempting promises of Western modernity. In this context, Gidden's description of globalization as an 'enlargement of modernity from society to the world'[14] is appropriate.

It can be said that the powerful current of Western modernity, especially its ultra-consumerist orientation, is now hitting the impressionable teenagers and youth with full force owing to the deep penetration of satellite television and cable network in urban and rural areas and slums.

TELEVISION AND DISSEMINATION OF CONSUMERIST CULTURE

The preceding discussion shows that the Indian response to the challenges posed by Western modernity and civilization through the agency of British colonialism was a knotted combination of admiration and criticality, from Raja Rammohun Roy to Gandhi. In the present phase of aggressive globalization of corporate capitalism and its consumerist values spread through multiple media (specifically satellite television and cable network), the project of Western modernity has remained central as it underpins the philosophy of consumer capitalism. In other words, modernity as a grand system and the success of globalization rely upon efficient interconnections between worldwide dissemination of 'global culture', telecommunication and deregulation of markets and practice of free trade in the Third World. Thus, globalization, despite its obvious economic agenda, poses a serious threat to cultural autonomy because conditioning and fixation of human choice and value is a crucial facilitator of economic process. The era of liberalization has forced an overhauling of the existing value system with a view to uplinking the tastes of the average person, particularly the young and adolescents in middle classes, with their counterparts in the Western Europe and America. The underlying logic is that the global market economy shall create interlinkages between 'forward' and 'backward' societies.[15]

It is easy to understand the argument of the advocates of globalization in view of the fact that India's burgeoning middle class forms about one-third of the country's population, i.e. around 400 million. This chunk of population is more than what entire Europe has (excluding erstwhile Soviet Union). Its purchasing power makes India a country with a rich marketing potential. Such a possibility prompts Euro-American countries to clamour for the Indian domestic market, which they believe is largely untapped. The process of capturing it only progresses when there is a corresponding change in the value pattern of the targeted society. The target groups among Indians have to be attuned to the ethos of global culture. Even more tactical is to capture the hearts and minds of the adolescent and the young for large-scale cultural penetration.

The Euro-American nations, having tremendous techno-economic power, have appropriated the privilege to define and dictate the contents of global culture, popularly known as consumerist culture. Claiming to be based on the ideals of modernity and Western rationality, it seeks to bridge the gap between all cultures and generate a set of uniform and liberal responses as well as expectations. Using the latest communication technologies as an instrument, the Euro-American industry in collaboration with multinational business managers is transmitting words, images and symbols of consumerist culture into our world.

What is this consumerist culture? Consumerism assumes the form of a culture when its function is stretched beyond the fulfilment of basic needs of each member of society. Its salient features, based on the insights of the French scholar Jean Baudrillard,[16] may be specified as follows:

(i) In the ethos of consumerism, a successful life is equated with having every thing; not having something implies failure and loss of status. Obviously, the people living in the ethos of consumerist culture perpetually suffer from a sense of insecurity, nervous tension and an incessant craving for the latest model of products, fashions and fads. In the long run, they get addicted to the excitement of instant achievement and success and are alienated from their history, culture, and particularly folk memories.

(ii) The growing lure for consumerist culture breeds fear of solitude among teenagers and young adults who are constantly driven to eat, dress and behave like their peer group.

(iii) The target of consumerism mass culture, which requires standardization of perceptions about fun, lifestyle, behaviour patterns, and choices of products for daily use on the basis of opinion polls. Mass culture, while moulding and catering to average tastes, de-individualizes as required by the techniques for mass production and marketing.

(iv) As mass culture creates addiction for pre-fabricated experiences or emotions, majority of the people are deprived of remaining possibilities of autonomous growth and enrichment and their lives become even more boring and unfulfilled, as pointed but by Ernest van den Haag.[17]

Without getting into a detailed discussion on the perspectives of massification, I shall briefly focus upon one relevant hypothesis for visualizing the Indian situation. Peterson and Maggio have broken the mass culture argument into two parts: (i) that the forces of modernization significantly reduce cultural diversity and (ii) an increasingly homogeneous mass culture has emerged.[18] It is true that much cultural diversity of ethnic, regional and folk-type has been destroyed in the post-industrial American society. In India, a different course of development may be chartered as it is far from being an industrial society and may skip various stages in search of 'relevant' modernity.

As Indian society is not a monolith, the presence of several cultures is likely to resist the total massification of culture. The selectivity of choice, which has been empirically documented in the American case[19] shows that the development of a homogeneous culture may be uneven in such a vast country as India. However, it may be conceded that consumerism has gradually tightened its grip over India, especially the middle classes, during the past one decade. What are the long-term implications of consumerism for Indian society and its cultural values?

For a realistic assessment three specificities of the Indian situation must be kept in view. Firstly, the presence of 100 million illiterates in the age group of 15 to 35 years makes India an ideal ground for testing the power of tele-advertising in moulding the mental ethos of such a huge chunk of population. Their sense of discrimination may gradually be blunted owing to its narcotic effect over time. Secondly, the huge Indian middle class, especially the impressionable adolescents and the young men and women, are seen by the commercial interests as potential purchasing agents whose systematic conditioning would ensure long-term control. Thirdly, new communication technologies in the hands of avaricious multinational capitalists are no longer amenable to check or control either by the developed or developing countries, especially when illiteracy rules out intervention by books.[20]

Any one familiar with the media scene knows how easy it is to captivate the hearts and minds of uncritical viewers and persuade them to regard the consumerist culture as their own. Constantly exposed to the values and attitudes of a dominant culture, the illiterate and the impressionable adolescents as well as the young tend to copy the sexual behaviour and lifestyles of glamorous men and women. By watching images and advertisements of expensive clothes, cars, gadgets and luxurious houses on television, members of the lower and middle classes with limited means get frustrated by the 'hyperreal'[21] world, to use Baudrillard's phrase, that is beyond their reach. Free circulation of seductive visions of affluence, in the absence of democratization of economic resources, breeds imitative tendencies and all sorts of pathological complexes among the economically weaker sections who also happen to be illiterate.

In order to substantiate my argument regarding the role of media in the penetration of the consumerist culture, I shall draw examples from my fieldwork in the Union Territory of Chandigarh, the capital of the states of Haryana and Punjab.[22] It was revealed that constant viewing of seductive and colourful advertisements, which interspersed entertainment programmes, evoked an intense craving for new products among 57.24 per cent of the respondents and a negative response among 42.76 per cent of the respondents. The motives underlying their favourable response were varied. For 62.23 per cent respondents, desire for possessions was the primary reason; exhibitionism was the compelling motive/urge for 24.90 per cent viewers. A small percentage, i.e. 10.01 was obsessed with the desire to prove their superiority in material possessions to their peer group. It is evident that advertisers use psychological ploys to inculcate consumerist mentality among their target groups, especially children, teenagers and women. A sizeable chunk of respondents, i.e. 36.37 per cent, were critical of the media-hype about goods and services. Their resistance to commercials was information-based in the case of adult viewers in their thirties. Either strict parental control or dominant social ethos of their locality also obliged them to repress their genuine feelings and responses.

Living in a fast-spreading consumerist world, the inhabitants of Chandigarh, particularly those in their teens and twenties, have been gripped by the frenzy to collect the latest status symbols, depending upon their social class. Its affluent segment and burgeoning middle class (around 44.31 per cent) have served as the real demand base for consumer durables and personalized services.

In an emerging metropolitan city like Chandigarh, the conventional meaning of status (whether blood or culture) has been replaced by the new criteria of wealth and material possessions. In a consumerist set-up, 'social differentiation' as conceptualized by Jean Baudrillard[23] is signified by money-power and ownership of expensive consumerable durables including latest gadgetry, mobile phones, branded TV sets for each member of the family, customized cars, etc. Other objects include designer clothes, shoes and accessories with foreign labels. It is also indicated by the financial services used such as credit card, membership to swanky clubs, and so on. A new marker of status is an annual holiday in one of the Euro-American countries and frequency of visits to five-star health clubs, gyms and beauty parlours. The logic of social differentiation extends to imported brands of hard drinks, food items and objects of art such as paintings, sculptures, films, music videos, books and magazines.

Life-cycle ceremonies such as naming of babies and marriage provide occasions for adopting or improvizing new status markers.

Through the choice of venues, their decor and the other paraphernalia, for example, the band of professional dancers/singers, each social class makes its own status statement. For wealthy corporate families, expensive farm-houses-cum-marriage halls on at the outskirts of Chandigarh are coveted sites for the entire wedding extravaganza. The salaried upper middle-class families prefer to use subsidized state-owned chain of hotels or private catering establishments (depending upon the discounts offered).

It must be pointed out that social differentiation may take the form of rejection of objects of consumption by the rich elite who continue to remain the model for emulation in consumption for the lower social classes. By distancing themselves from objects used by the broad category of middle class, its upper segment continues to impose limits upon those who are likely to become their peers. They adopt new objects, which are limited in number such as authentic antiques or paintings, branded cut glass and gadgets. In short, hierarchy of social class has been transferred to the realm of objects, often used as status symbols.

That the people of Chandigarh have become strong votaries of 'conspicuous consumption' is evident from the city's vehicle-resident ratio. According to *Chandigarh Newsline* (dated 26 May 2001), the ratio of human population to vehicles in the city, despite its small size, is the highest in the country. With a population close to ten lakhs (including the fast growing migrant population), the Chandigarh Administration has roughly 5.30 lakh registered vehicles. Each family has four vehicles on an average. In the slum areas, a large number of families have six bicycles per family, of course, as a result of pure necessity. However, the penetration and grip of the consumerist culture is uneven. Its flamboyance and Western orientation is easily visible in the northern sectors of the city; its localization leading to the production of heredity in tastes and goods, is dominant in the southern sectors.

A very significant ingredient of the consumerist mindset is the overarching ambition to possess wealth. This has led is the unprecedented popularity of game shows beamed by leading TV channels. The premier quiz show *Kaun Banega Crorepati* (KBC) won instant popularity among viewers in the age-group of 40-50 years. Modelled on the BBC show *Who Wants to Be a Millionaire?*, it had evoked the longest spell of euphoria in the countless middle-class families, especially teenagers, who were coaxed to fantasize about the jackpot dangled before them from 9:00 to 10.00 p.m., three to four times a week in 2001.

The debate regarding the ethics of involving vulnerable children in the gamble of being a millionaire rages on. However, it is certain that the blockbuster game-show has assisted in giving social legitimacy to gambling for materialist riches in the name of knowledge. KBC has left an indelible mark on every games, language and pranks of school children. In the city schools, children continue to conduct their own game-shows on the pattern of KBC. Geeta Joshi, a student of Sacred Heart Convent, confided, 'We have changed everything except the name of the game. The stakes are much lower, one rupee per question'.

To cash in on the new craze, *Crorepati* general knowledge books were published and sold at handsome prices. Amitabh Bachchan's wax-image as an icon in a temple of Kolkata and the formation of fan clubs' in the south form an interesting feature of the fast spreading consumerist culture. The show's much-publicized return underlined the media-managers' keenness to encash on this popular quiz-show.

IMPACT ON LIFESTYLE: HOME-SPACE, FOOD HABITS AND BODY-CULTURE

HOME SPACE

On the basis of my empirical study, it may be averred that globalization of the electronic media, particularly TV, has played a major role in shaping a hedonist mentality and blurring the distinction between basic needs and 'conspicuous consumption'. While technology has brought the world closer, it has separated family members, especially, the senior citizens. It has brought a change in the people's sense of personal space. With every new channel in the post-satellite age, the middle-class families with less discretionary income than the rich are facing a dilemma. If one member wants to watch an India–Pakistan match, another wants to follow the love affairs and lives of celebrities or the intrigues of daily soaps, while and yet another may like to listen to MTV music, or a news programme. Such different tastes are likely to cause clash of egos and interests. Obviously, everyone wants a private niche under one roof.

Thus, the new demands created by TV as a tool of leisure and of disseminating the consumerist culture have created 'homes within homes'. The drawing room and the dining room, which used to be the core of the house, are gradually becoming showpieces or vestiges of the textbook picture of a happy family having similar tastes in food and leisure activities. The size and kind of family, whether large or small, joint, extended or nuclear, no longer matters. What matters is that the individual continues to get larger; the patriarch and the matriarch have moved to the margins as their children gravitate to the centre and grandchildren become larger than life.

The relocation of spaces is highly visible in the recently done homes. Chandigarh-based architects and interior designers, like their counterparts in Mumbai, are converting larger rooms into smaller ones. Their rich clients' complex demands constantly pressurize them to create homes within one home. It is not just beds in their rooms, they want chairs and sofas for their guests and a separate TV, music-system and multimedia computer. Their middle-aged parents, as of other people from middle and high-income groups, also showed a distinct inclination for display of their souvenirs of travels (crystal dolls, cut-glass, and so on), in India and abroad, expensive air-conditioners, carpets and such other items.

Apart from these, 'don't disturb zones' were coming up in increasing numbers as people chose to work from their homes. Driven by market-competition, young professionals prefer to communicate rather than commute. Communication within the biological family has decreased as the demand for carving isolated lives in closed quarters has grown.

Bathrooms have also been turned into extravagant and whimsical statements as these are increasingly being put on display. In the upper middle and high income homes, doors of the bathrooms are usually left ajar in order to reveal the splendour of gold-plated plumbing and shining granite tiles. Thus, an ostentatious mindset is increasingly evident in the lifestyle and homes of the rich elite as well of the upper segment of the middle classes.

Another component of home space, which has been influenced by glossy advertisement campaigns about hi-tech gadgetry, is the kitchen. As a result, architects, whether in high-rise space-starved Mumbai or more expansive Delhi or a well-designed city like Chandigarh, have been pushed to experiment with a variety of new hearths: Italian, American or traditional Indian. Why make new kitchens? One of the major reasons is the need to accommodate expensive gadgets such as food processoes and, microwaves. Second is the availability of abundant readymade materials and the need for their cold-storage. Thirdly, it is suitable for making different kinds of cuisines to suit individual tastes in the family, moulded by the media equating good life with exotic food.

Food Habits

Daily exposure to commercials about the health-giving qualities of various food items including easy-to-cook frozen vegetables and poultry, fruit juices and candies in colourful packing and images of non-stop enjoyment through their use, have influenced the attitudes of viewers cutting across age-groups, social class and rural-urban divide. It has led to a remarkable change in the composition of food and eating habits. The fast-spreading craze for buying food, spending leisure-time in fast-food joints, restaurants, pubs, night clubs and discos indicates a drastic change in the notions of 'fun' and social life.

Primarily built as a new home for refugees from West Punjab after the Partition of India, Chandigarh has become the centre for an uneasy mingling of the upbeat consumerist ethos with cultural conservatism, thus leading to the development of an interesting food culture. This new food culture consists of two distinct subcultures: (i) take home and fast food, (ii) restaurant culture. Obviously, a major factor for the social legitimacy of 'eating out' whether in a fastfood joint or a restaurant is the increasing purchasing capacity of the middle-class households, having a large number of working women. In Chandigarh, their number is roughly 90,000 out of the total of 1,75,000 households. Moderately priced food-beverage joints give a welcome relief to full-time employed women from the drudgery of time-consuming traditional Indian cooking.

The growth of so-called fastfood joints reflects the popular trend to 'grab a bite' at a place which provides exotic food such as pizzas, hot dogs, burgers, noodles, etc., at low prices. The teenaged students, shoppers in a hurry and young office-goers are tending to eat out more often. This is being done in order to satisfy their craving for change from home-cooked or hostel food and to relax in cafés and snack bars, where they can also listen to popular music, mostly Western rock. Popularity of fastfood joints can be attributed as much to the willingness to try new culinary delights as to the availability of sufficient discretionary income. No less important is the persistent craving for excitement, an ingredient of the consumerist mentality.[24]

'Restaurant culture' in Chandigarh has been promoted by excessive exposure to flashy lifestyles in films and TV serials. The hype in the media about gastronomic pleasures has played a crucial role in giving social legitimacy to this new culture. Firstly, its essentially elite quality has been regularly highlighted by stylish advertisements and exaggerated reporting on eateries. For example, a one page pull-out called 'Gourmet: A Guide to Gastronomic Pleasures' in the city edition of the *Indian Express* contains descriptions of parties and inaugural events where TV and film stars, fashion models and popular cricket idols are invited for the sake of publicity of the hosting restaurant or pub. Obviously, the message is 'drink and dine' for a successful social life. Thus, the print and the electronic media in collusion with the business entrepreneurs constantly tempt their target groups to buy leisure for full enjoyment of life.

However, the emergence of as many as 40 restaurants, big and small, as well as 22 pubs in the city requires a more satisfactory explanation. The growth of wealth in Chandigarh, with its by-product in the form of spare income, might explain the market development to some degree. An additional stimulus was provided by Chandigarh administration's not-too-hard a policy regarding prohibition over the past one decade. On the one hand, it led to the proliferation of pubs. On the other hand, many restaurants obtained service licenses.

Body-Culture

It is clear from the preceding discussion that over-consumption of food and 'eating out' has become an integral part of the lifestyle of the affluent and upper middle-class segments of Chandigarh society, as in the other big cities. The cult of physical fitness, slenderness and cosmetic beauty have acquired an urgent function for these guzzlers of food. It is not surprising that consumers' bodies and minds have become the sites of contest among entrepreneurs in the food, health and beauty business. Thus, a large number of urban elites and the rich rural magnates in Asian countries have unwittingly got trapped in this consumerist whirlpool.

TV has played a crucial role in popularizing the body culture. Fashion and health magazines and city editions of vernacular and English language dailies have sustained the campaigns for body culture through publication of colourful vignettes of models. That the media-savvy rich adults and their teen-aged sons and daughters are keenly receptive to their seductive messages is evident from the fast-growing clientele of six big health-cum-beauty parlours and twenty small ones in residential units in various sectors of Chandigarh. These big and small centres have been engaged in the lucrative business of rejuvenating the bodies of their clients over the past one decade or so. Their advertisements in local and other TV channels and city editions of national dailies appeal to emotions, dreams of eternal youth and lure of discounts for motivating viewers and readers to pay a personal visit or at least call up the health-cum-beauty parlour.

Such an effective strategy has helped them earn handsome amounts of money. For example, VLCC, established in 1985, has opened branches in a number of big cities in India and plans to extend its business to Europe. Its hudge annual turnover prompts us to draw three inferences: (i) body culture has become increasingly popular among the young and the middle-aged belonging to the salaried as well as the business classes since the 1990s; (ii) the fact that the bulk of the clientele of the health-cum-beauty parlours (70 per cent in the case of Chandigarh) is formed by female customers underlines the persistence of stereotypes regarding men and women. Physical personality continues to remain a crucial factor in the selection of potential brides in the marriage market, in addition to parents' economic status. There is a close connection between the new perception of the body as an exhibit in the consumerist society and businessmen's keen calculation of profit margin in the manufacture and dispensation of health and beauty aids including cosmetics, diet foods and exercise equipment.

In this connection, it may be noted that the globalization of media, which has facilitated the viewing of contests like Miss Universe, beauty-pageants and fashion-shows, has spread awareness about current fashions, hair-styles and European standards of being beautiful. The growing consciousness regarding brands of clothes and cosmetics has turned Chandigarh into a 'city of brands'. It has become a favourite destination for branded-products from Euro-American countries because its population consists of a large number of NRIs, well-travelled businessmen, professionals and academicians who, like the American globalizers, eloquently described by Davison and Yates, live their 'life in a bubble'.[25]

It may be pointed out that in these centres of self-indulgence, whether a food-joint or a fitness centre or a beauty parlour, the emphasis is not on genuine qualities like natural charm, taste and self-worth but on conforming to a readymade code or copying a model. Everyone, man or woman, is constantly coaxed to find his or her own personality by living up to these models. It may also be noted that body maintenance routines, exercise, fitness, dieting, use of vitamin supplements; health foods, etc., are strongly marketed within a consumer culture. These are important means to neutralize the consequences of excessive consumption of junk food and entertainment and to enable the revitalized consumer to enjoy endless rounds of sensual thrill and enjoyment.[26]

CONCLUSION

It is evident from the preceding discussion that the ideals and values of the Indian culture and those of the so-called global culture (read as consumerist culture) are based on different world-views, mental orientations, rhythms of life, perceptions of basic needs and goals. It has caused tensions between the advocates of traditional outlook, beliefs, practices, lifestyles and the votaries of ceaseless adventure, novelty, excitement, fun as well as freedom of choice in material things or 'individuation' (in Berger's words), (rather than individualism) in every moment of their lives.[27]

Obviously, crystallization of global corporate capitalism, which became the basis for the formation of the global media system, and its project of modernity have accentuated cultural turbulence. The three great ideals of Indian culture are facing a serious challenge. Firstly, the ethos of an ultra-urban industrial orientation militates against the ethos of an agricultural society—its close identification with local communities and family and kinship ties. Consumption-oriented and achievement-based view of life has disrupted the relatively peaceful character of community living. The colourful images of urban life on satellite television and media reference to legends of sexual encounters between strangers in trains, taxis and discos[28] and also by portrayals in films, magazines and novels have created a distaste for simple pleasures of life and the urge to recast their values. Secondly, externalization of modernity and its logic of technological manipulation of nature for man's continual well-being and value-neutral rationality goes against the spiritual ethos of Indian culture. The process of objectification of nature, which is the most fundamental feature of modern scientific and technological enterprise, has not been integrated into the Indian outlook and way of life. Our cultural tradition views nature as an expression of the cosmic order and not something to be objectified, controlled and exploited. As it put premium on being environment-friendly, its relevance for alternative modernity cannot be doubted. Thirdly, the ethos of Western modernity, its cognitive arrogance, scientism and universality is not comfortable with heterogeneity, plurality and differences.[29] Thus, there is an inherent clash between the homogenizing impulses of the high-consumption-oriented Western modernity and the accommodative spirit of the Indian cultural tradition.

Trapped between the ambition of grasping the glittering 'hyper-real' world of affluence and the pulls of the familiar traditional world as well as the painful awareness of their limited material resources, the middle classes have been facing a dilemma. Among its upper two segments including business elite, globetrotting professionals (academicians, engineers, doctors and bureaucrats), the craving to adopt the Western model in their professional careers is the strongest. While creating space for material status symbols and a variety of techno-objects in their personal lives, they have kept the ideological and religious affiliations, marriage customs and other traditional aspects of their daily lives more or less separate and intact. This resistance to change in the inner domain has developed into a political and ideological struggle in the Indian society. It has also been articulated by the potential aspirants to 'Davos culture', to put it in Samuel Huntington's words, and the 'faculty club culture',[30] i.e. international business culture and world intellectual culture. They, too, are experiencing tensions owing to their uneasy location in the interstices between fantasy and reality. Thus, the middle classes, who have 'demonstrative effect' on the lower social segments, are coping with a twofold dilemma: (i) intellectual and (ii) pragmatic.

Firstly, let me analyse their multifaceted predicament at the intellectual level. In this context, Mike Featherstone's argument is relevant for the resolution of this ticklish problem. In his view, the process of globalization through digital communication has facilitated the inclusion of new, emergent and unfamiliar issues and values in the ever-expanding storage capacity of global culture. It has also opened possibilities for reconstituting disciplinary boundaries and classification through increased interaction among intellectuals. Thus, the development of this 'dialogical notion' of knowledge and values is crucial for the emergence of a new world order as well as liberal and gender-sensitive social formations in South Asia. The Euro-American nations, whose paradigms/perspectives on modernity and self-view as the guardians of ecological resources, global peace and progress have been questioned, need to be more responsive towards the poorer nations.[31] The questioning mood has been intensified by the decisive shift in the balance of power in favour of South and East Asia. In view of their growing awareness regarding the relentless pursuit of militarist power and monopolization of bio-diversity and energy-resources by the US, the Western-educated elite and non-resident Indians are not too sure in their advocacy of Euro-centric notions of market freedom, peace development, human rights and global society.

For the highly educated middle-class elite, the intellectual predicament is compounded by pragmatic concerns and material interests such as luxurious lifestyles and lucrative jobs for their children as well as connections with political and business elites. Despite their critical view of the ideology underlying market fundamentalism and indiscriminate exploitation of natural resources by the developed countries, they tend to endorse the cultural power of the US, which is transmitted through many channels. These are financial subsidy, research fellowships, academic exchange schemes, grants for research projects and scholarships to individuals for studying and training in American scientific and business institutions. While their keen ambition to become beneficiaries of these schemes obliges them to mute their criticism and follow codes and practices of the Western (read it as American) funding institutions and agencies, their personal lives remain firmly anchored in the traditional social norms, practices and cultural codes. Thus, they live in a transitional mode which leads to a feeling of 'homelessness' and alienation.

Despite the dynamic presence of tradition in Indian homes, the lure of the consumerist culture has made a dent in the big cities such as Delhi, Bengaluru, Mumbai and Chennai. In Chandigarh, whose inhabitants hail from various parts of India, the spread of consumerist mentality is rather fast. It is also uneven and varied in form(s) among the rich elite, middle-class segments and slum-dwellers. Its flamboyance and Western orientation is easily visible in the northern sectors of the city; its localization leading to the production of hybridity in tastes and goods are dominant in the southern sectors. While the affluent residents have continued to regard acquisition of branded items as a routine activity, the middle classes have strained hard to camouflage their limited economic resources by proclaiming their branded status in front of their wealthy friends while scrimping on essential items of need. Thus, tension between middle-class morality and the pull of hedonistic culture of the rich elite has resulted in teenage angst, anxiety and depression. A close reading of respondents' reactions revealed that the availability of high levels of excitement in their leisure time as children has invariably made the rich boys (and girls too) insensitive, aggressive and violent when denied anything by anybody.

It must be noted that the slum children and teenagers, while working as domestic servants and helpers in the homes of the affluent and the upper middle classes, learn consumerist culture and behaviour. Spending most of their time in this ethos, they also get infected by the incessant craving for more possessions, fashions and fads because the discarded objects of daily use and status symbols are passed on to them by their well-off employers. Thus, mass culture, which requires standardization of perceptions about, lifestyles, behaviour patterns, choice of products of daily use, spreads through 'demonstrative effect'.

In short, the people of Chandigarh are fast getting addicted to 'conspicuous consumption' and high levels of excitement through various forms of entertainment provided in discos, bars and homes. It is also evident from the roaring business done by the recently opened stores for designer clothes, jewellery, fastfood outlets in modern shopping malls. It can be said that MNCs have succeeded in circulating, reinforcing and legitimizing 'consumption as a value' through class-oriented advertisement campaigns and thus in the consumption-oriented communities. These communities are developing their own cultures according to their economic standing.

However, it will be unrealistic to conclude that all segments of middle classes are lacking in critical temper, enterprise and cultural sensitivity. Being acutely conscious of the contradictions and problems arising from the implementation of economic reforms, sensitive social scientists, environmentalists and experts and professionals from various fields have consistently exposed the anti-poor, hedonistic and blatantly profit-oriented policies of the transnational companies and international agencies like World Bank, International Monetary Fund, GATT and WTO from the platform of the World Social Forum and through the peoples' movements. Their protest has been reinforced through sensitive exposition of Gandhi's sharp critique of high-consumption-oriented and exploitative industrial economies and their violent basis. Similarly, the growing appreciation of the positive Hindu view of dependence of human welfare and prosperity upon the sustenance of environmental resources has helped in forging alternative strategies of development. It may be pointed that a 'dialogic' process has been active in the making of knowledge systems and creation of a composite cultural tradition in India. As an integral part of its intellectual quest, the practice of theological disputation among competing religions had facilitated the resolution of cultural and ideological predicament flowing from encounters with different civilizations in India. In order to sustain the 'dialogic' process, development of cultural consciousness and awareness of strengths of other cultures including Western is crucial.

Indian response to market fundamentalism through the vehicles of popular culture, propagated by a variety of business enterprises (for example Adidas, McDonald, Disney, MTV, etc.), is also imaginative.

Despite no media-hype, ethnic eateries which provide pre-prepared items like pickles, *papad*, wafers and popular fastfood items such as *dosas*, *chana bhaturas* and popular north Indian curries have posed a challenge to Pizza Hut, McDonald's, Kentucky Fried Chicken and such other MNCs. They have made a niche in the US and Britain. Thus, the indigenous food boom can be described as a 'cultural emission' according to Tulasi Srinivas.[32]

Similarly, a variety of artistic Indian products such as jewellery, fabric designs, embroidered footwear and handicrafts have caught the imagination of Western designers with an eye on potential business opportunities. Like the Indian calicoes (whose import was banned under the pressure from British textile manufacturers during the late eighteenth century), these artefacts have made a powerful cultural statement, while the Western products—whether techno-objects, food and beverage items or articles of personal use—disseminate the values of a 'throw-away' society with limitless craving for novelty, excitement and adventure. Indian products on the other hand are associated with ever-renewing tradition, signifying intimate skill and creative imagination, replenished and enriched by the process of transmission from one generation to another.

It must be emphasized that the current conceptualization of globalization as linear and unilateral implantation of ideologies and values as a package with the transfer of technologies, goods, trade and financial aid under the banner of 'development' and 'modernization' must be contested. I would like to draw attention to Gandhi's critique of British imperialism's version of globalization. While rejecting its underlying value, he had chartered a different path of modernity and value formation through creative experimentation and dialogue with other civilizations without being cut-off from one's roots. In this context, his insightful observation is instructive:

> I don't want my house to be walled in on all sides and my windows to be stuffed. I want the cultures of all lands to be blown about my house as freely as possible. But I refuse to be blown off my feet by any.

NOTES

1. Kamlesh Mohan (1999), 'Surviving Through Cultural Encounters: India and Globalization', in S. Settar and P.K.V. Kaimal (eds.), *We Lived Together*, (New Delhi: Pragati Publications for Indian Council of Historical Research), p. 317.
2. Arjun Appadurai (1986), 'Theory in Anthropology: Centre and Periphery', *Comparative Studies in Society and History*, 28, 21 April 1986, p. 157.
3. My discussion of the communitarian ideal is based on David G. Mandelbaum, *Society in India* (1st printed 1972; Bombay: Asia Publishing House, 1984), pp. 33-180.
4. For a sympathetic angle on this issue see Theodre de Bary (ed.), *Sources of Indian Tradition* (1st printed 1958; Delhi: Motilal Banarsidass, 1972), pp. 211-366.
5. S. Abid Hussain, *The National Culture of India* (Bombay: Asia Pub. 1961), p. 66. Mohammed Sahib's sayings, compiled in *Hadith*, repeatedly emphasize that the present world is a preparation for the next world.
6. For a detailed discussion of this aspect of Sikhism see Upinderjit Kaur, *Sikh Religion and Economic Development* (New Delhi: National BK. Organization, 1990), pp. 70-159.
7. M. Mujeeb, *Islamic Influence upon Indian Society* (Meerut: Meenakshi Prakashan, 1972), p. 65. S.A.H. Abid, *Sufism in India* (New Delhi: Oxford University Press, 1992), pp. 81-121.
8. For an insightful discussion of the formation of the intellectual community in the nineteenth century, see K.N. Panikar, 'Culture and Ideology: Contradictions in Intellectual Transformation of Colonial Society in India', *Economic and Political Weekly*, 5 December 1989, pp. 2115-50.
9. Javed Alam, *India Living With Modernity* (New Delhi: Oxford University Press, 1999), pp. 56-7.

10. Ashish Nandy, *The Intimate Enemy: Loss and Recovery of Self under Colonialism* (New Delhi: Oxford University Press, 1983), p. 48.
11. *Hind Swaraj*, originally published in Gujarati in the *Indian Opinion* dated 11 and 18 December 1909, was issued as a booklet in January 1910. Its proscription by the Government of Bombay in March 1910 hastened Gandhi's decision to publish its English translation (with his foreword written on 20 March 1910), which was issued by International Printing Press, Phoenix.
12. Aysegul Baykan, 'Women between Fundamentalism and Modernity', in Bryan S. Turner (ed.), *Theories of Modernity and Post Modernity* (London, Newbury Park, New Delhi: Sage, 1991), p. 138.
13. Lieteke van vucht Tijesen, 'Women between Modernity and Post-modernity, in Bryan S. Turner, n. 12, p. 151. She has based her argument of 'gendtrification on L. Braun's exposition (1901: 190) whose writings are not available in English.
14. Anthony Gidden's, *The Consequences of Modernity* (Cambridge: Polity Press, 1993).
15. Sumit Kar, 'Miss World 96: Cultural Invasion of Worst Kind', *Mainstream*, 23 November 1996, p. 8.
16. Jean Baudrillard, tr. George Ritlzer, *Consumer Society: Myths and Structures* (London: Sage, 1983, 1998). His ideas regarding the making of consumer culture and its features are scattered throughout his book.
17. Ernest van den Haag, 'A Dissent From the Consensual Society', in Bernard Rosenberg and David Manning White, *Mass Culture Revisited* (New York, 1971), pp. 85-92.
18. R.A. Peterson and Paul de Maggio, 'From Region to Class: The Changing Locus of Country Music', *Social Forces*, 53, 18.
19. Edward Shils, 'Mass Society and its Culture', *Daedalus* (Spring), 1989.
20. Kamlesh Mohan, n. 1, p. 330.
21. I have borrowed this description from Jean Baudrillard, tr. Sheila Faria Glaser, *Simulcara and Simulation* (Ann Arbor: The University of Michigan Press, 1984), p. 108.
22. My discussion and analysis of the new cultural orientations in Chandigarh and the fast changing lifestyle, food habits, home-space and mentalities of its composite population are based upon my report of the one year long research-project entitled 'Globalization, Electronic Media and Cultural Invasion: Its implications for women Especially the Girl-Child', (2001). It was funded and sponsored by National Commission for Women (Ministry of Human Resource Development, New Delhi).
23. My analysis in the following paragraphs regarding the *modus operandi* of status-differention, used by the rich elite and the upper middle class is based on the concept of 'social differentiation' in Jean Baudrillard, n. 16.

24. Kamlesh Mohan, n. 22.
25. James Davison Hunter and Joshva Yates, 'In the Vanguard of Globalization: The World of American Globalizers', in Peter L. Berger and Samuel P. Huntington (eds.), *Many Globalizations: Cultural Diversity in the Contemporary World*, (New York, Delhi, Toronto: Oxford University Press, 2002), pp. 332-7.
26. Peter L. Berger 'The Cultural Dynamics of Globalization', in ibid, p. 23.
27. Ibid., p. 9.
28. Cited in Mike Featherstone, 'Globalizing Futures: Value Formation and Value of Life' Paper prepared for the Conference on Culture and Future Values, ISARC on Futures, Kyoto, Bukko University, September 2004, p. 21.
29. Kamlesh Mohan, 'Implications of Globalization and Cultural Invasion for India', in Raj Mohini Sethi (ed.), *Globalization, Culture and Women's Development* (Jaipur and New Delhi: Rawat Publications, 1999), pp. 221-2.
30. For an insightful exposition of 'Davos culture' 'Faculty Club Culture' and popular culture also called 'McWorld Culture' See Mike Featherstone, n. 25, pp. 4-5.
31. Ibid., p. 28.
32. Tulasi Srinivas, 'A Tryst with Destiny: The Indian Case of Cultural Globalization', in Peter L. Berger and Samuel P. Huntington (eds.), *Many Globalizations: Cultural Identity in Contemporary World*, Oxford: Oxford University Press, 2008.

Contributors

MALATHY A. works as an Assistant Professor in English at Indira Gandhi National Open University, New Delhi.

VIBHA ARORA is an Assistant Professor of Sociology at the Indian Institute of Technology Delhi (IIT Delhi).

SATISH DESHPANDE is Professor of Sociology, in the Department of Sociology, Delhi School of Economics, Delhi University.

KRISTIN HEFFERNAN teaches at the Brockport College, New York as an Assistant Professor.

MAREK HRUBEC is Director of the Center of Global Studies, a joint centre of the Academy of Sciences of the Czech Republic and Charles University in Prague.

JAMES M. JASPER currently teaches in the Ph.D. program in sociology at the Graduate Center of the City University of New York.

JOSE KALAPURA, is Professor of History, St. Xavier's College, Ranchi, was formerly Director of Xavier Institute of Social Research (XISR), a centre for research, development, training and action, at Ranchi.

MOKBUL ALI LASKAR is a Deputy Regional Director in Indira Gandhi Nationl Open University.

AJAY MAHURKAR is an Associate Professor in the faculty of History in Indira Gandhi National Open University, New Delhi.

KAMLESH MOHAN is Professor of Modern Indian History, Panjab University, Chandigarh.

D.C. SAH is a Professor and Director at M.P. Institute of Social Science Research, Ujjain.

NANDINI SAHU is an Associate Professor in English literature in Indira Gandhi National Open University, New Delhi.

ATLURI SATYANARAYANA is a Professor of Sociology in the Department of Psychology, Allahabad University.

ASHISH SAXENA teaches Sociology at University of Jammu and is also Director, Ambedkar Studies Centre.

SUBHASH SHARMA is an administrator. He has researched and published both in English and Hindi on environmental movements, gender, education, child labour and human rights.

DEBAL K. SINGHAROY is a Professor of Sociology, in the Faculty of Sociology, School of Social Sciences, Indira Gandhi National Open University, New Delhi.

P.S. VIVEK is a Professor of Sociology in Mumbai University. He has researched in the areas of cooperative movements, marginalized people and on the issues of Social Development.